UNESCO HANDBOOK FOR THE TEACHING
OF SOCIAL STUDIES

UNESCO Handbook for the Teaching of Social Studies

EDITED BY HOWARD D. MEHLINGER

CROOM HELM LONDON

UNESCO PARIS

© Unesco 1981

First published 1981 by the United Nations Educational, Scientific and
Cultural Organization,
7 Place de Fontenoy, 75700 Paris, France
and
Croom Helm Ltd,
2-10 St John's Road, London SW11, United Kingdom

British Library Cataloguing in Publication Data

Unesco handbook for the teaching of
    social studies
    1. Social sciences — Study and teaching
    I. Mehlinger, Howard D.   II. Unesco
    300.7'1   LB1584

ISBN 0-7099-1720-1 (Croom Helm)
ISBN 92-3-101890-6 (Unesco)

Typeset by Leaper & Gard Ltd, Bristol
Printed and bound in Great Britain
 by Billing and Sons Limited
Guildford, London, Oxford, Worcester

CONTENTS

FIGURES

TABLES

PLATES

PREFACE

As part of its programme to promote education for international understanding, peace and respect for human rights through the improvement of school curricula, teaching methods and materials, Unesco produces handbooks and guides designed to provide curriculum planners and classroom teachers with useful information and suggestions based on international expertise and experience.

The present publication was prepared for Unesco by the Social Studies Development Center of Indiana University, under the supervision of Dr Howard Mehlinger. A group of 24 co-authors selected throughout the world prepared the original draft and one hundred copies were then circulated to specialists and institutions for evaluation. The final version was prepared on the basis of their comments.

Much of the book is devoted to practical suggestions and information on ways and means of improving teaching methods and to the entire gamut of materials necessary for the effective teaching of social studies at both the primary and secondary school levels. The text encompasses a wide range of topics and issues including a survey of social studies around the world, foundations and teaching strategies of social studies, values, attitudes and skills, multi-media instructional materials, evaluation and teacher education in social studies. Unesco hopes that its publication will play a part in raising the standard of social studies teaching and that it will at the same time enlarge the contribution of this important school subject to the betterment of international understanding, co-operation and peace. It is intended essentially for primary and secondary school teachers, as well as students in teacher-training institutions of all descriptions.

Grateful acknowledgement is made to the general editor, Dr Howard Mehlinger, Director of the Social Studies Development Center, and to the co-authors and editors who helped to draft and finalise the text, as well as to all those who provided comments and suggestions. Although the final work is in every sense a co-operative effort, it should be clearly understood that any opinions and points of view expressed by the authors are their own and do not necessarily reflect those of Unesco. Furthermore, the designations employed and the presentation of material do not imply the expression of any opinion whatsoever on the part of Unesco concerning the legal status of any country, territory, city or

area or of its authorities, or concerning the delimitation of its frontiers
or boundaries.

FOREWORD

Like so many Unesco publications this book was conceived at a meeting: an 'International Meeting of Experts on the Role of Social Studies in Education for Peace and Respect for Human Rights'.* In 1976, fourteen social studies experts met for one week to consider ways that Unesco member states might better utilise social studies courses in order to implement the suggestions contained in the *Recommendation concerning Education for International Understanding, Co-operation and Peace and Education Relating to Human Rights and Fundamental Freedoms*.** While the participants had many ideas for making social studies more responsive to the need to educate children in the spirit of peace and respect for human rights, perhaps the most important and immediately practical suggestion was recommendation 102(c):

> Unesco should move ahead rapidly to prepare a sourcebook for the social studies containing information related to teaching about peace, international understanding and human rights. Included in the publication should be practical information on: values and attitudes, classroom activities, lesson strategies, data on population, industrial production, resources, employment, armaments, etc.; and lists of organisations, agencies and individuals providing services or teaching materials.

Following the East Lansing meeting, Unesco officials invited the Social Studies Development Center of Indiana University and its director, Howard Mehlinger, to assume responsibility for the preparation of a 'sourcebook on the teaching of social studies'. In May 1977 six social

---

*The meeting, organized by Unesco in collaboration with the United States National Commission for Unesco and the National Council for the Social Studies, was held on the campus of Michigan State University, East Lansing, Michigan, USA, from 23 to 29 May 1976. Experts came from Australia, Colombia, Egypt, France, Iran, Japan, Kenya, Madagascar, the Philippines, Romania, Sweden, the USSR, the United Kingdom and the USA. Stanley P. Wronski, a member of the US National Commission for Unesco and Professor of Education and Social Science at Michigan State University, was the principal conference organiser and host. The report of this meeting is reprinted as Appendix B.

**See Appendix C for a copy of the *Recommendation*.

studies specialists from five nations met in Bloomington, Indiana, USA, to plan the 'sourcebook' (later to be termed *Handbook*). This group, consisting of Rita Ana Giacalone (Argentina), Norman J. Graves (United Kingdom), Chan Lee (Republic of Korea), Talabi Aisie Lucan (Sierra Leone) and Howard D. Mehlinger and Stanley P. Wronski (USA), approved an outline for the book and nominated potential authors from every region of the planet. A majority of those who were nominated later agreed to write chapters. Some nominees were unable to undertake the assignment; a few contributed to chapters after others assumed main responsibility.

In February 1979, edited copies of nine completed chapters were mailed to approximately 100 reviewers in nearly 75 Unesco member states.* A majority of those receiving the draft manuscript responded with thoughtful, written reviews. A dozen reviewers met in Bloomington, Indiana, in April 1979 for a full day to share their reactions and advice.

In August 1979, an editorial advisory committee conferred with the editor/project director. This committee, consisting of Norman Graves (United Kingdom), Talabi Aisie Lucan (Sierra Leone), Sharada Nayak (India), and Dieter Schmidt-Sinns (Federal Republic of Germany), reviewed all of the comments and suggestions submitted by the various reviewers, thoroughly discussed each draft chapter, and recommended changes and additions to the editor. Following the meeting each chapter was substantially rewritten in keeping with the recommendations of the editorial committee. Thus, the final version of the *Handbook* represents the thoughts and suggestions of many people drawn from all parts of the world.

An Overview of the Handbook

The *Handbook* consists of eleven chapters, organised into two main sections, and three appendices. Each chapter is self-contained and stands alone. Nevertheless, the first five chapters contain common elements that distinguish them as a group from the remaining chapters that comprise Part Two.

A reader may employ one of several strategies when using this book, including reading the *Handbook* from cover to cover, selecting chapters

---

*The original plan called for ten chapters. By February 1979, nine chapters had been written and edited. A tenth chapter remained in an outline stage. Later, the tenth chapter was finished and an eleventh chapter was added upon the advice of the reviewers.

according to interest, or pursuing all of the chapters in Part One or Part Two before continuing to the other section. In general, the chapters in Part One tend to be more theoretical than those in Part Two; the latter chapters place much greater stress on practical classroom advice.

Pluralism is a hallmark of the *Handbook*. Of course, pluralism is indicated by the range of authors, who represent many parts of the world with diverse social systems and cultural backgrounds. The *Handbook* is also pluralistic in its approach to social studies; it could not be otherwise for social studies takes many forms from one country to the next. In some countries the term social studies is rarely used at all; in other cases the term is used quite differently from that of another place. To impose a single point of view about social studies would be to ignore reality and to limit the potential use of the *Handbook*.

Therefore, the *Handbook* is deliberately and proudly eclectic. For the purpose of the *Handbook* social studies refers to *courses of study at the primary and secondary levels of schooling presenting components of history, geography, economics and moral and civic education, prescribed and taught either as an integrated discipline or as separate curriculum subjects with an interdisciplinary emphasis.* The *Handbook* does not favour one approach over others; rather it seeks to clarify the differences among the approaches, to identify strengths and weaknesses of alternative approaches, and to offer suggestions for classroom practice that will improve instruction regardless of the approach preferred by the teacher.

The *Handbook* also responds to the needs and interests of a wide range of potential readers: teachers in training as well as experienced teachers, supervisors, curriculum planners, teacher educators, textbook authors and editors, officials in ministries of education, examination boards and school administrators. The book contains ideas for primary school teachers and for secondary school teachers, for those seeking theoretical challenges and those who want suggestions for classroom practice. The *Handbook* can be used as a textbook for the pre-service or in-service education of teachers; it is also a library volume to be consulted periodically by those seeking advice on social studies instruction.

The focus is mainly on *how* to teach social studies rather than *what* should be taught. The content of social studies courses varies too much from one country to another to be represented adequately in a single book, but teaching methods and practices do not recognise national boundaries. Examples of social studies content are contained in lesson illustrations, but the emphasis throughout is on classroom practice.

The *Handbook* will appear initially in English and French. However, the book can and should be translated into other languages in order to make it available to the greatest number of educators possible. Some may wish to translate the entire volume; others may prefer to produce a condensed version, selecting those chapters or sections of greatest use to their teachers; a few may be interested in the sample lessons only. In the initial version, Appendix A, 'A Guide to Selected Resources for Teaching about Social Studies', is limited to sources in English. Editions printed in other languages should replace this 'guide' with one that refers to sources available in the language of that version of the *Handbook*.

Acknowledgements

A book of this kind requires the assistance and co-operation of many people and organisations. Unfortunately, only those who made the most important contributions can be mentioned here. Others who cannot be listed must take satisfaction in knowing that their contribution is known to the editor and appreciated.

First and foremost are the 24 authors who provided the eleven chapters that comprise the book. These authors, each an expert on some aspect of social studies, willingly offered their knowledge while adhering to a general outline established by others. Some of the chapters have multiple authors, requiring close collaboration between the principal author and contributing authors, who were often widely separated from one another.

A number of people who are not listed as authors contributed importantly by serving as special advisers or by providing lesson illustrations. Special notice should be given to Jerry Brown and Beresford Jones for their contributions to Chapter 3; to Harry Hutson for his lesson suggestions that appear in Chapter 6; to Philip Smith and Judith Berling for donations to Chapter 8; and to Victor Smith for his help with Chapter 10.

Lynn A. Fontana deserves special credit for compiling the 'Guide to Selected Resources for Teaching about Social Studies' and her research assistance throughout the project. Anne Beversdorf contributed importantly to several chapters as an editorial assistant.

Several individuals and organisations provided photographs and illustrations. These include the United Nations, UNICEF, Science Research Associates, Jiro Nagai, Absorn Meesing, Talabi Aisie Lucan,

Foreword

David Dufty and Ikon.

Those experts who set the guidelines for this volume and the editorial advisory committee deserve special consideration. (Their names were listed earlier.) More than 75 people reviewed all or portions of this volume at one time or another. I am grateful for their many ideas, most of which have found their way into the chapter revisions. A special debt is due to colleagues in the Social Studies Development Center and the Social Studies Education Department of Indiana University who offered advice on several occasions.

Four additional people deserve recognition. James Becker, a friend and colleague in the Social Studies Development Center and an authority on global studies, was a source of counsel throughout the project. Stanley P. Wronski, who organised the East Lansing meeting that gave birth to the *Handbook*, has contributed variously to this book. My secretary, Eve Russell, assumed responsibility for much of the project's administrative detail and typed all of the early drafts of the manuscript. Carolee Mehlinger skilfully typed the final draft.

To all of these people — and others who could not be mentioned — I am deeply grateful.

Howard D. Mehlinger
Director, Social Studies Development Center
Indiana University

PART ONE:

PLANNING A SOCIAL STUDIES PROGRAMME

INTRODUCTION

The first section of the *Handbook* is designed to be helpful to those who have now (or may have in the future) responsibility for planning social studies curricula, whether as part of a national programme or at the level of an individual school. A persistent theme throughout the chapters concerns the nature of social studies and how it is like or different from other school subjects in the humanities and social sciences. The authors discuss social studies goals, sources of social studies knowledge and the processes one might follow in introducing social studies into the school curriculum.

Each author has his or her own perspective; taken together they provide a balanced introduction to the challenges facing social studies educators everywhere.

Chapter 1, 'Social Studies around the World', is an introduction to various approaches and practices that appear, under the label social studies, world-wide. The reader will quickly learn that social studies comes in many shapes and sizes. Despite what appears to be an endless variety, the author provides ways of sorting out the differences to uncover some persistent issues and questions that confront social studies educators in all countries.

Chapter 2, 'Foundations for the Social Studies', presents some factors that influence social studies in every nation. The author is particularly interested in how the academic disciplines serve as sources of knowledge for social studies and he offers suggestions for how to use them more appropriately.

Chapter 3, 'Social Studies as an Integrated Subject', addresses one of the central dilemmas of social studies: how is social studies different from the academic disciplines? How can a social studies educator use the academic disciplines as sources of information while teaching a social studies course with its own integrity? This chapter offers concrete suggestions for planning a social studies programme that integrates knowledge from many fields.

In Chapter 4, 'The Study of Social Studies as a Means of Educating Children in a Spirit of Peace and Mutual Understanding among Peoples', the author reminds readers that all of the debate about the nature of social studies and advice regarding which teaching methods are best are pointless unless social studies is directed by a clear sense of social purpose. She identifies one of the central purposes of social studies and describes programmes addressed to that purpose.

And in Chapter 5, 'Planning Social Studies Instruction', the author points out that whatever one's purposes are, social studies programmes must be carefully planned if they are to be effective. He defines key terms used in curriculum planning, providing a model of the curriculum development process and concludes with two case studies of social studies curriculum planning.

1 SOCIAL STUDIES AROUND THE WORLD

Stanley P. Wronski

The Nature of the Social Studies

Consider the following two excerpts describing social studies instuctional activities. The first concerns a project conducted in a primary school in Nigeria.

> The pupils in the Fifth Form (approximately 12 years old) were confronted with a problem of what to do about the increasing accumulation of garbage near their school. They discussed the problem in class with their teacher and decided to solve it by building a mud incinerator in which they could burn the garbage and other debris. They wanted their school environment to be both healthful and pleasant. With the guidance and active help of the teacher the incinerator was built. Not only did it beautify the school grounds, but the ashes from the incinerator were used to fertilise the school garden.[1]

The second excerpt is more complex and deals with the rationale for internationalising education in Sweden:

> Certain segments in many subjects treat problems that require international comparisons in order that they assume proper proportions and that pupils be presented with a global perspective on those problems. (Examples: population problems, utilisation of resources, energy supplies, environmental pollution, social security, industry and commerce, economic growth, equality of the sexes.)
>
> ... Contrasting, for example, the concept of the so-called threat of over-population with that of over-consumption provides a new and better perspective on these issues ... Using this method, it should be possible to make pupils more clearly aware of their place in the world and their share of responsibility for what happens in it.[2]

These excerpts exhibit a way of thinking about social studies we shall call an 'integrated approach'. While it represents one way of considering social studies instruction, it is not the only way — nor probably the prevalent approach.

If one were to ask most ministry of education officials to describe their social studies programmes, they would likely respond by identifying history and geography as the core — and sometimes the only — subjects subsumed under the social studies. In some countries social studies may also include civics (or political education), economics (or political economy), anthropology, sociology and psychology, or some variation of these courses. And in still other countries the term social studies is not used at all, although courses of the kind listed above are vital parts of the school curriculum.

Between the ends of this continuum of social studies perspectives — from separate subjects at one end and integrated social studies at the other — lie other views, including two that may be termed inter-disciplinary and multidisciplinary approaches. As their titles imply, interdisciplinary and multidisciplinary approaches reject loyalty to any single discipline. An interdisciplinary approach deliberately links two or more separate subject areas; for example, politics and economics may join to form political economy or sociology and anthropology combine to form social anthropology. The new subject is a merger of major portions of two distinct disciplines. The term multidisciplinary approach is often used to describe efforts to take advantage of concepts, methods of enquiry and conceptual schemes from many disciplines, bringing them into a combination deemed useful to the course designer. The position that interdisciplinary and multidisciplinary approaches occupy on the continuum between the 'separate subjects approach' and 'social studies as an integrated subject' depends largely upon how they are used. In some cases the instructor seeks to stress the disciplinary source of the knowledge he is using; the result is a course that is similar in purpose and design to a single subject approach. In other cases little regard is shown towards preserving the academic source of the concepts and the focus is their use to solve problems or illuminate issues. Used in this way the interdisciplinary or multidisciplinary approaches shade into an integrated approach to social studies. Figure 1.1 depicts these relationships.

Important Features of an Integrated Approach to Social Studies

From the Nigerian and Swedish examples, one can identify certain characteristics associated with an integrated approach.

(1) The social studies student is confronted with one or more

Figure 1.1: Approaches to the Organisation of the Social Studies Curriculum

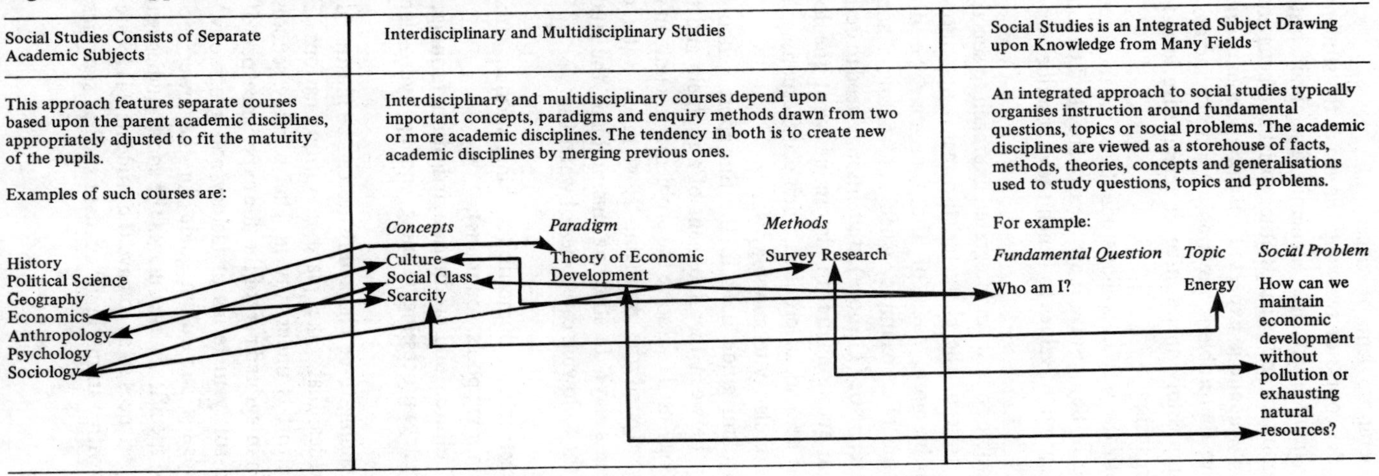

Social Studies Consists of Separate Academic Subjects	Interdisciplinary and Multidisciplinary Studies	Social Studies is an Integrated Subject Drawing upon Knowledge from Many Fields
This approach features separate courses based upon the parent academic disciplines, appropriately adjusted to fit the maturity of the pupils. Examples of such courses are:	Interdisciplinary and multidisciplinary courses depend upon important concepts, paradigms and enquiry methods drawn from two or more academic disciplines. The tendency in both is to create new academic disciplines by merging previous ones.	An integrated approach to social studies typically organises instruction around fundamental questions, topics or social problems. The academic disciplines are viewed as a storehouse of facts, methods, theories, concepts and generalisations used to study questions, topics and problems. For example:

History
Political Science
Geography
Economics
Anthropology
Psychology
Sociology

Concepts
Culture
Social Class
Scarcity

Paradigm
Theory of Economic Development

Methods
Survey Research

Fundamental Question
Who am I?

Topic
Energy

Social Problem
How can we maintain economic development without pollution or exhausting natural resources?

societal problems or issues.

(2) In the course of resolving the issue, the student must make use of more than one academic discipline: history, geography, economics and perhaps other social and behavioural sciences.

(3) The student is expected to employ some form of enquiry to solve the problem, preferably a rational and analytical approach but possibly an intuitive or imaginative leap to an unforeseen conclusion.

(4) Both the way in which students define the issue and the way in which they resolve it are inextricably tied to some kind of value or system of values to which they subscribe.

It is possible to have an integrated approach to social studies without having all four of the characteristics mentioned above present at all times. Furthermore, each of the four may be divided into sub-characteristics. For example, when confronting a social problem or issue (characteristic (1) above), students may need to define the problem, construct a questionnaire to determine what the local community perceives to be a social problem, elicit class responses, identify testable hypotheses or clarify terminology.

A curriculum guide used in the Singapore schools illustrates the relationship between the statement of a problem and the clarification of terminology used to resolve the problem.[3] In a unit on water resources, a class investigated the problem, 'How much water does the whole world use in a day?' In studying this problem, the students saw slides suggesting the following categories of water use:

(1) infrastructure: domestic (cooking, washing, etc.) and aesthetic (swimming pools, fountains);

(2) agriculture: food production, irrigation, farming;

(3) industry: processing, refining, cooling, hydro-electric power.

The remaining three characteristics can be illustrated by citing class-room activities that take place in various nations. For example, a concerted effort is under way in Thai primary schools to view social studies as an integrated part of the 'life experience' part of the curriculum rather than solely in terms of history and geography[4] (characteristic (2)). In Japan a curriculum guide for the lower secondary schools (ages 13-15) specifically encourages the social studies teacher to provide learning experiences so as to have the students '(a) locate and familiarise themselves with various kinds of data such as statistics, chronological tables, yearbooks, newspapers, etc., (b) further the habit of thinking things out, (c) learn the ways of looking into and handling various data and (d) cultivate the ability to make effective use and objective evaluation of the data'[5] (characteristic (3)). And in Thailand it would be unusual to resolve a problem without considering the relationship of the solution to Buddhist values (characteristic (4)).

Those who favour social studies as an integrated approach see at least four advantages this approach offers over social studies as merely school courses based upon the academic disciplines.

(1) An integrated approach to social studies can avoid the arbitrary distinctions that divide academic disciplines in colleges and universities, distinctions that are of little significance to students in primary and secondary schools.

(2) Because social problems and issues have many dimensions, they are rarely the property of a single academic discipline. An integrated approach enables students to understand the complexity of social problems.

(3) The purpose of school courses in social studies should be to prepare youth broadly for adult citizen roles in the society. An integrated approach provides the general education that is required better than courses featuring the specialised knowledge associated with the individual social science fields.

(4) An integrated approach to social studies encourages greater flexibility, imagination and creativity on the part of teachers, many of whom are trained in more than one academic discipline.

Social Studies as School Courses in the Academic Disciplines

The most prevalent world-wide view of the social studies sees the field consisting of separate subjects. Although the term social studies may be used generically to encompass the field, the actual curriculum usually consists of separate subjects related closely to parent academic disciplines.

Proponents of a separate subject approach to social studies cite the following advantages of this perspective.

(1) Separate school subjects based upon the academic disciplines are much easier to define and delimit.

(2) School subjects based upon academic disciplines are inclined to be rigorous and intellectually demanding. When social studies is taught as an integrated subject, there is a tendency for

instruction to become superficial and subjective.

(3) Students find it easier to learn the material presented in separate subjects. What they learn will be more useful to them as they continue their education.

(4) Because there is a solid base of scholarship underlying each of the academic disciplines, it is easier to maintain academic integrity when school courses are based upon this scholarship.

Social studies programmes based upon separate school courses linked to academic disciplines can be found on all continents. An examination of other representative curricula, syllabuses and courses of study reveals that the most prevalent separate subjects taught under the category of social studies are history and geography. But it would be a mistake to assume that history and geography courses are not influenced by other disciplines. Within individual classrooms, teachers can and frequently do introduce multidisciplinary information and viewpoints. For example, it is difficult to deal adequately with the history of any nation without introducing some basic geographic factors that have influenced historical development. The social studies curriculum in Egypt aptly illustrates this in the primary grades; in the higher grades, separate subjects prevail.

Interdisciplinary and Multidisciplinary Approaches to Social Studies

While the practice is not widespread, curriculum planners are giving increased attention to interdisciplinary and multidisciplinary approaches in devising social studies curricula. In the Philippines, the University of the Philippines and the National Science Development Board funded a textbook-writing project which, according to its author-director, attempted 'to gear curriculum development in social studies to national developmental goals as well as to foster understanding about the peoples and cultures of other nations'.[6]

What is the Social Studies?

For the present, there is no generally accepted answer to the question, 'What is the social studies?' Opinions about what social studies *is* or *should be* vary from country to country; even within a single nation experts are divided on this question. In the absence of agreement, those who are responsible for developing social studies programmes should listen to the arguments made by proponents of various points of view, study the alternatives and devise what seems most appropriate for their own country and cultural milieu.

While experts cannot agree on what social studies *is*, there is more agreement about what it is *not*. Here are three widely shared assumptions regarding the boundaries of social studies.

(1) Those who believe that social studies should focus on 'problems' do not include purely individual problems or problems that are peculiar to a given individual. The study of prescriptions for the medical treatment of an individual would not typically be conceived as a social studies problem. But the study of whether medical prescriptions should be issued under a state-controlled or privately conducted practice would be a proper area of investigation in the social studies.

(2) Social studies is not concerned with the natural or physical world except as these relate to humankind. The study of the nucleus of an atom is within the domain of the physical sciences. The proper use and control of nuclear energy is a legitimate topic for the social studies.

(3) Social studies is not synonymous with indoctrination nor with the uncritical acceptance of beliefs. All societies have some fundamental values and beliefs which they convey and reinforce through their social institutions, including the schools. But to ascribe to the social studies programme the major responsibility for such enculturation is to assign it a burden which must be shared by all social institutions — including the family, the political system, the economy and institutions catering to the human spirit. The social studies curriculum and the social studies teacher have a primary obligation to teach, not to preach.

The Purpose of Social Studies

Three kinds of responses are often given in reply to the question, 'Why is it necessary for pupils to study social studies?' These are:

(1) social studies can help youth address their own individual needs;
(2) students need to acquire academic, social scientific knowledge;
(3) society requires adults who know their rights and responsibilities as citizens.

These categories frequently overlap. For example, one might argue that, as a result of social studies instruction, students may meet some of their individual needs *and* become better acquainted with the social sciences *in order* to become better citizens. No nation puts exclusive emphasis on only one of these three purposes, and there is variety in the relative emphasis assigned to each.

Individual Needs

The list of individual needs the social studies might address is extensive. Some authorities stress 'survival skills'; these tend to emphasise how to cope successfully within the economic system. Such skills may include finding a job, becoming a thrifty buyer and planning for retirement. Other specialists stress interpersonal skills — how to get along better with other people. Still others emphasise the importance of understanding one's own feelings and emotions, of learning how to handle stress, of choosing proper life goals and of achieving success.

An American seventh-grade social studies textbook illustrates how textbooks can emphasise individual needs.[7]

Book title: *Sources of Identity*
Behavioural theme: The individual: Who am I? Where do I belong in my society?
Conceptual scheme: An individual's identity is affected by the ways he learns to satisfy his basic needs.
Sample objective: Each student will develop in his ability to empathise with other people, observing their behaviour as evidence of their concepts and values, and to make such observations from different perspectives.

From the book title and the permeating characteristics of this textbook, it is apparent that a relatively heavy emphasis is attached to the purpose of individual self-realisation and self-fulfilment. Frequently accompanying such a social studies programme is a related series of learning experiences identified as values-clarification strategies that help students understand the values that prompt their behaviour. (See Chapter 8 for a further treatment of values in social studies teaching.)

Academic Subject-matter

Many educators believe that students require fundamental knowledge of the kind provided by academic disciplines. Most would agree that adults in every country should know the history of their own country and some world history as well, that they should understand the operation of their political and economic systems and that they should be acquainted with key geographic features of the world. Any dispute is mainly over how much emphasis to give this purpose as compared to the others and how to organise courses so that all purposes are served equally well.

As pointed out earlier, many educators believe that information from history, geography and other social sciences can be conveyed best via separate school courses that are related to the parent academic disciplines. Proponents of integrated social studies believe that other purposes of social studies — individual needs of students and citizenship education — tend to be overlooked by teachers of academic subjects.

The Federal Republic of Germany is one nation that has struggled over the purposes social studies should serve and its best organisation. At the secondary school level, despite some attempts 'to integrate history and social studies and form new courses', the dominant view reinforces 'preserving the role of history as a separate subject in the schools'.[8] Similarly, in Australia, a State Project Officer for Social Studies stated emphatically: 'Geography and history are the traditional and established disciplines within the social science offerings throughout Australia. Social studies ... is seen as something new and has not as yet established itself as a Public Examination Board level subject.'[9]

Citizen Education

Every country employs a wide range of social institutions to induct new members into its society, to transmit the cultural heritage to the young and to develop in its people a feeling of national pride. The major means for accomplishing these goals is through its educational institutions, both formal and non-formal. Within the schools, the major responsibility falls upon the social studies programme.

Ministries of education, professional educational organisations and leading political figures have issued statements assigning to the schools in general and to social studies in particular the goal of 'promoting citizen education'. For example, the first objective listed in the course of study for social studies issued by the Ministry of Education in Japan is: 'To guide the children to deepen their grasp of social life and enable them to cultivate the foundation of citizenship to live as members of a democratic nation and society'.[10]

The National Council for the Social Studies, a professional association of social studies teachers in the United States, recently reaffirmed its commitment to citizenship education. Its Board of Directors instructed its Executive Director 'to take such steps as are deemed necessary to ... continue efforts to define social studies education in terms of the central citizenship education thrust and to represent this orientation in his role'.[11]

In Greece, the school system today continues to reflect the concerns for citizen education first expressed by Plato in the *Republic*. On the other side of the planet, a philosopher of this century, Dr Sun Yat Sen, asserted that schools should focus on the 'three principles of the people — nationalism, democracy, and livelihood'. And in Africa, Julius Nyerere, commenting on the importance of citizenship education for the United Republic of Tanzania, wrote:

> The education provided by Tanzania for the students of Tanzania must serve the purposes of Tanzania. It must encourage the growth of the socialist values we aspire to. It must encourage the development of a proud, independent, and free citizenry which relies upon itself for its own development, and which knows the advantages and the problems of cooperation. It must ensure that the educated know themselves to be an integral part of the nation and recognise the responsibility to give greater service the greater the opportunities they have had.[12]

Education for citizenship is not the exclusive property of social studies. Other subjects — literature, art, music, science and even sports — contribute. But social studies has a special role. From their social studies courses students learn of their nation's past, its heroes and their deeds; they learn how the government is organised and the roles they are expected to play as citizens; and they learn the ideology which binds citizens together and gives meaning and purpose to their national identity.

There is no single style or content to citizenship education. Each country has a different idea of what citizenship entails. But each depends, in part at least, on social studies to provide the instruction youth require to fulfil their roles as responsible members of the society.

Citizen Education for Global Understanding. One citizenship education concern shared by social studies educators everywhere is how to prepare youth to live in an increasingly globally interconnected world. As seen from outer space, the Earth may appear as a fragile spaceship whose passengers live in a delicately balanced environment. An assault upon that ecological balance by one segment affects the entire human community. The interrelatedness of humankind may be a pious platitude to some, but it is an overpowering fact of life to all.

Global interrelatedness has begun to influence the social studies curriculum. In many countries, the traditional way of organising social studies was according to the 'expanding environment' — children were first introduced to their immediate environment (the home, school and neighbourhood); they then learned about ever-expanding geographic areas until finally by grades six or seven they were permitted to study regions far removed from their own homes and neighbourhoods. Unfortunately, such a neat progression does not correspond with the real experiences of children. Given almost instantaneous global communications, more and more young children receive messages from all parts of the world. The orderly progression implied by the 'expanding environment' is now irrevocably altered.

Citizenship education for global understanding seeks to develop in the learner not only a planetary perspective but also the survival skills needed to ensure the continued existence of the human species. High on the priority list of such skills are competencies in decision-making that people require when confronted with such global problems as:

— How can we achieve a world population growth that will provide the optimum quality of life?
— To what extent can we permit individuals or groups of individuals to pollute the environment so as to cause harm to others?
— What kind of world order should we strive to achieve?

While no one assumes that students now in social studies classes are prepared to comprehend fully, let alone solve, these problems, they illustrate problems that must be resolved by someone, sometime, in some manner. The decision-makers will be fallible human beings who are now, or will be, students in the world's schools. Incremental but significant steps are now being taken in some social studies classrooms to develop the basic skills to cope with such issues. The citizenship education purpose of social studies requires attention to such problems.

The Teaching of Social Studies

Social studies is a multi-faceted mosaic, a patchwork quilt, a collage of forms, structures and colours. Social studies is not a precise field with widely accepted content, goals, methods and procedures. Although a secondary school course in physics or algebra is much the same from one country to the next, no such consensus exists for social studies.

What form an integrated approach to social studies will assume in one nation is likely to be quite different from another. Nor do countries that favour a separate-subject approach to social studies offer identical courses. Even courses with the same title (for example, world history) vary widely among nations.

Social Studies 'Snapshots'

If there is variety in definition and in social studies purposes, there is no less variety in the methods of social studies instruction. Part Two of this *Sourcebook* deals primarily with teaching methods, using examples drawn from many countries. Here it is enough merely to give a brief glimpse at the variety that exists. Each 'snapshot' of instructional activity is accompanied by commentary indicating how it depicts one example of the nature or purpose of social studies.

Denmark. In secondary school, the students not only learn about social democracy but also practise it by deciding collectively on class projects. Many of these projects involve activities outside the school building and are intended to promote community solidarity. For example, a model village is used by the students to learn trades and gain practical business experience.

Both individual and societal needs are met through such a learning situation. By becoming productive members of society, the students experience one aspect of self-fulfilment. While providing for individual needs, the state is also promoting its own societal goals of maintaining a reasonably stable and viable economy.

Egypt. Primary school children participate in a role-playing exercise to depict the urgent problem of population growth. With low-cost building materials and old clothing, they construct the outlines of a bus and overcrowd its interior.

'We have a problem,' they observe.
'Yes, we have a shortage of buses and they are always overcrowded.'
'One reason for this is our increasing population.'
'How can we reduce population?'

Even at the elementary level, it is possible for children to experience an enquiry process in the social studies. Although it is unlikely that sophisticated solutions will emerge at this grade level, children can become involved in some of the fundamental procedures in solving

Plate 1: A Secondary School in Japan

Children in a lower secondary school study geography in Hiroshima.

social problems. Clarifying and defining the problem is one such procedure. Formulating hypotheses or speculating about possible solutions is another. And throughout the enquiry process, all problem-solvers, young or old, need to gather and assess factual data.

China. In one of the Chinese textbooks, there is a map of the United States with the major cities identified. They include New York, Washington, Los Angeles – and Little Rock, Arkansas. Little Rock is included because that is the city where army troops were used in 1957 to enforce a court order to desegregate the public schools, permitting black children to enrol in previously all-white schools.

Like many illustrations, this one can elicit various interpretations, depending on one's perspective. From a positive point of view, it can illustrate the fact that all societies are attempting to cope with the problem of minority groups in their midst. Sometimes the minority groups are accommodated peacefully, at other times conflict occurs. It demonstrates that social studies deals with real and significant issues. The fact that such issues are also controversial is not a deterrent to

Plate 2: Schoolchildren in Oman

Children are listening carefully to the teacher in a school in Oman.

Plate 3: Schoolchildren in Somalia

Despite severe hardships caused by drought in the Sahel, children find a way to attend school.

including them in the curriculum.

Poland. Students celebrated the one-thousandth anniversary of the Polish nation by presenting a pageant in the school assembly room. They further studied their school's immediate past by collecting memorabilia such as old class photographs, textbooks and slate boards from their parents and others.

The affective dimensions of the social studies are especially well illustrated in this instance. In addition to learning names, dates and places, students also acquired attitudes, feelings and values. Whether these affective outcomes are 'caught' rather than 'taught' is a moot pedagogical issue. The important point is that social studies deals with the heart as well as the mind.

Thailand. A Thai history textbook containing information about Western civilisation contains no reference to events of the past ten to fifteen years. The teacher explained that the main function of history is to deal with the past and not with the present or very recent events.

This view of social studies stresses the learning of subject-matter. It parallels the academician's argument that we cannot really understand the present until 'the dust has settled'. In such a classroom, history is not seen as having immediate utilitarian value. It is a separate subject having its own integrity and validity. Its benefit to students is its capacity to develop in them a long-range, balanced perspective that is not attainable through the study of contemporary-oriented social sciences.

Predominant and Emerging Modes of Teaching

The most common approach to classroom instruction is *read-recall-recite*: (1) *read* from a textbook (or listen to the teacher), (2) *recall* the information and (3) *recite* either orally or in writing. This ubiquitous approach is used to some degree by almost all social studies teachers whatever their nationality, however they may conceive of social studies and regardless of the course goals. This approach encourages short-term retention of factual information and frequently thwarts creative thought. Yet it remains a favourite teaching method.

Nevertheless, social studies teachers increasingly plan their instruction so as to encourage student learning beyond mere recall of information. An illustration of how higher cognitive processes may be incorporated into social studies programmes is contained in a curriculum guide prepared for teachers of 12-14-year-old students in the Netherlands. In a project on energy, the following objectives are identified.[13]

— To discover main trends in energy use after 1945.
— To discover the relation between energy use and life-style.
— To develop the ability to analyse statistical figures.
Among the learning activities for students are the following:
— Analyse pie charts of production and consumption of energy since 1945. Comparing charts of 1950 with those of the present, show (a) the shift from coal to oil as a major source of energy since 1945; and (b) the growing imbalance between supply and demand within

given countries.
– Cite specific examples of luxurious and wasteful goods requiring much energy. For example, how much energy is required for the use of (a) aeroplanes; (b) fertilisers and (c) household appliances?

The abilities to analyse, hypothesise and synthesise are examples of the higher cognitive processes that can be nurtured by social studies instruction. Lessons directed at promoting higher levels of thinking can change the image of social studies as a 'soft' subject in the curriculum.

The Affective Dimensions

Social studies is concerned with more than the intellectual development of youth. Individuals also have feelings, sympathies and attitudes. Many social studies programmes deal with the constant values, attitudes and beliefs that motivate and control people's behaviour. Consider these statements from various philosophical sources:

Buddhism: Hurt not others with that which pains yourself.
Christianity: All things whatsoever ye would that men should do to you, do ye even so to them; for this is the law of the prophets.
Confucianism: Is there any one maxim which ought to be acted upon throughout one's whole life? Surely the maxim of loving-kindness is such. Do not unto others what you would not they should do unto you.
Judaism: What is hurtful to yourself, do not to your fellow man. That is the whole of the Torah and the remainder is but commentary. Go learn it.
Hinduism: That is the sum of duty: do naught to others which if done to thee would cause thee pain.
Islam: No one of you is a believer until he loves for his brother what he loves for himself.
Taoism: Regard your neighbour's loss as your loss.

These beliefs, while stated differently, share a common principle – respect other people and treat them fairly. Teachers cannot ignore instruction about values. No teacher would consider his teaching successful if his students were able to recite verbatim the laws of the land concerning thievery and then steal from their schoolmates. Honesty is one of those substantive values promoted by teachers in all countries.

Procedural as well as substantive values are also supported by social studies. For example, when analysing the reasons for a given historical event, students should be taught to value such processes as the use of evidence rather than unsupported opinions and the use of logic rather than illogic. The relative emphasis placed upon substantive versus procedural values varies from one society to another, but few educators take the position that the social studies can be value-free. As social studies increasingly addresses itself to the crucial issues facing human-kind, it inextricably assumes normative, or value-laden, dimensions.

Summary

One's perspective on the world-wide character of social studies depends upon the lenses used in viewing it. Definitions of the *nature* of social studies range from one favouring a separate-subject approach (history, geography, civics, etc.) to an integrated approach in which subject-matter distinctions are either blurred or indistinguishable. The *purpose* of social studies may be (a) to meet individual needs, (b) to acquire knowledge of subject-matter, (c) to become a better citizen — or, more likely, some combination of the three. The *teaching* of social studies, enjoying the greatest variation, ranges from a didactic and expository presentation of factual data to an open-ended and enquiry-oriented search for understanding. All of the above are taking place in a world that is becoming inexorably more interrelated. Within this increasingly interrelated world setting, no other school subject seems so dynamic, so amenable to improvements and so capable of borrowing from the experience of other countries.

Notes

1. From an interview with the teacher, Joshua Akinola, whose class con-ducted the project in the District Council School, Ile-Ogbo Town, Ibadan Province, Oyo State, Nigeria.

2. Inger Andersson and Lars Sundgren, *The Internationalizing of Education in Sweden* (Swedish International Development Authority, Stockholm, 1976), p. 11.

3. Soo Tian Goh, 'Teaching about the United Nations through a Study of Water' in the *Final Report* of the Triangular Fellowship Programme Seventeenth Seminar, Unesco Educational Liaison to ECOSOC (United Nations, New York, 1977), p. 103.

4. Asborn Meesing, 'Social Studies in Thailand' in Howard D. Mehlinger and Jan L. Tucker (eds.), *Teaching Social Studies in Other Nations*, Bulletin 60 (National Council for the Social Studies, Washington, DC, 1979), p. 39.

5. *Revised Course of Study for Lower Secondary Schools in Japan* (Japanese

National Commission for UNESCO, Tokyo, 1969), p. 56.

6. Leonardo de la Cruz, 'Philippine Social Studies: State of the Art' in Background Paper for Unesco-sponsored meeting on The Role of the Social Studies in Education for Peace and Respect for Human Rights, held at Michigan State University, East Lansing, Michigan, USA, 1976, pp. 6-7 (unpublished).

7. Paul Brandwein *et al.*, *Principles and Practices in the Teaching of the Social Sciences: Concepts and Values* (Harcourt Brace Jovanovich, New York, 1973).

8. Annette Kuhn, 'Social Studies in the Federal Republic of Germany' in Mehlinger and Tucker (eds.), *Teaching Social Studies*, p. 27.

9. Rodney Kuchel, 'Position Statement on Social Science Teaching in Australia', in Background Paper for Unesco-sponsored meeting on The Role of the Social Studies in Education for Peace and Respect for Human Rights, held at Migchigan State University, East Lansing, Michigan, USA, 1976, p. 2 (unpublished).

10. *Course of Study for Elementary School in Japan*, Notification No. 268 of Ministry of Education, Science and Culture (Printing Bureau, Tokyo, 1976), p. 31.

11. National Council for the Social Studies, Minutes of Board of Directors, May 1975 (unpublished).

12. Julius K. Nyerere, *Freedom and Socialism* (Oxford University Press, Dar-es-Salaam, Tanzania, 1968), p. 290.

13. Paul Van Dellen, 'Outline of a Project about Energy' in the *Final Report* of the Triangular Fellowship Programme Seventeenth Seminar, p. 47.

2 FOUNDATIONS FOR THE SOCIAL STUDIES

Denis Lawton

All societies are similar in some respects and different in others. Some social scientists like Clyde Kluckholn[1] have stressed the similarities; others like Ruth Benedict[2] have been more interested in the differences.

Chapter 1 drew attention to some of the similarities and differences in social studies. By exploring the foundations of the social studies, this chapter will seek to explain why some of these similarities and differences occur. From one perspective social studies foundations are the same in nearly all societies. For example, the discipline of history is a major source of knowledge for school history instruction in every country. Yet, history instruction is not the same from one country to another. How can this be?

Adult hopes and expectations for their children and for their society shape the school's mission in each country. While the scientific study of man and society is a phenomenon transcending national boundaries, the state of academic knowledge is not identical in all countries. This chapter will make clear how these conditions influence curriculum decision-making. It will focus in particular on the contributions of academic disciplines to social studies instruction in schools.

Three Factors that Influence the Social Studies Curriculum

Three main approaches to education have been described as child-centred, society-centred and subject-centred. Nevertheless, many modern curriculum theorists now reject a commitment to any one of these three approaches. They prefer a holistic view that seeks to reconcile the needs of the individual child, the needs of society and the need to pay some regard to the structure of knowledge.

In Chapter 1 social studies purposes were discussed in terms of 'individual needs', 'academic subject-matter' and 'citizen education'. These purposes should not be treated atomistically; they must be brought into balance and appropriately integrated. A good social studies curriculum is one which *helps young individuals to develop into fully human adults by relating them to their society by means of appropriate knowledge and experience selected from the social sciences*

36

and other disciplines. The task of planning a social studies curriculum is primarily one of selecting content appropriate to this general aim. The results will surely vary from one time to the next and from country to country because assumptions about individual needs and society needs vary and because people think differently about which academic knowledge is of greatest worth. Despite these differences integration among the three purposes is necessary in every country.

Because it is impossible for children to experience everything and to learn everything in their culture, someone or some group must decide on a list of priorities: perhaps what everyone should learn, what can be included in optional courses, what can be reasonably left out altogether. Who ultimately makes these choices differs from one society to another. In some societies curriculum decision-making is determined largely by one central agency; in others the decisions are shared among various groups: curriculum planners, teachers, inspectors or advisers, test constructors, ministry officials, school officials, parents and even text-book publishers. Whoever makes or influences the decisions, the decisions should be determined through a process of rational planning.

Figure 2.1: Influence Factors on Curriculum Decision-making in Social Studies

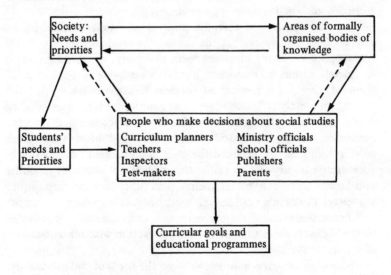

_____ direct influence

_ _ _ _ _ _ _ _ _ possible influence

Figure 2.1 indicates the factors that influence curriculum choices and their impact on curriculum decision-makers. Whatever differences there may be among societies and curriculum decisions, the diagram appears to be appropriate in all settings.

Contrasting Contexts for the Curriculum Model

In the United Kingdom the social studies curriculum, or indeed the curriculum as a whole, is somewhat different from that in a society such as the United Republic of Tanzania. The United Kingdom is an industrial society with a background of elitist education and a curriculum based on subjects that are planned very largely by the teachers themselves. By contrast, the United Republic of Tanzania with its rural economy aspires to an egalitarian system of education where the curriculum is based on what is useful. Here the curriculum model shown in Figure 2.1 operates in each case. Between the United Kingdom and the United Republic of Tanzania one can find some overlap both in the content of the curriculum and in what ought to be taught, but there will be many interesting differences as well. The comparison is made more complicated by the fact that both societies are changing. The curriculum model indicated in Figure 2.1 is not a static one. It makes clear that changes in any of its components may alter the ultimate curricular goals and education programmes.

It should be stressed that the position of 'student needs' in the diagram does not imply that the needs of individual children should be subordinated to the supposed needs of society. A curriculum that is completely dominated by societal needs is a weak one from a theoretical point of view for a number of reasons: it assumes falsely that the curriculum merely reflects society, that education has no responsibility to improve society and that all children will react identically to the curriculum. On the other hand, those child-centred theorists who think only in terms of 'the needs of the child' are also guilty of gross over-simplification: they fail to realise that a child can attain his potential as a human being only by interacting with other human beings within a society. Children's educational needs include exposure to various social experiences and the opportunity to acquire the kind of knowledge that will enable them to benefit from interaction with other members of society.

There is no natural opposition between the needs of children and the needs of society; they are complementary. But we can translate children's needs into a curriculum only by following a cultural analysis of a particular society. We must ask questions about the kind of society in which the child lives, before we can deal with individual needs in any meaningful way. When considering the needs of society, we tend to think of industry and manpower needs and possibly the society's need for well informed citizens; but modern societies also need individuals who think for themselves. On this latter point, the distinction between individual needs and societal needs becomes meaningless.

Societies differ in how *basic needs* will be interpreted. Children everywhere should study science in order to understand their physical environment, but children in a rural developing country may need to concentrate on the kind of science useful in an agricultural society, whereas children in a developed country may need science more appropriate to an industrial economy. Few would object to these differences so long as all of the children concerned were studying 'real' science. Similarly children everywhere need to possess the kind of knowledge that will help them to understand how their society works. But the actual social studies content will be different in, for example, the United Kingdom and the United Republic of Tanzania. In some countries a higher priority may be given to the development of national identity; in others national identity is already well established. In all cases it may be appropriate to help children move beyond solely a national identity.

Cultural Analysis. One aspect of curriculum planning relies on 'cultural analysis', that is a systematic process of examining a particular society in its social and historical context. Curriculum decision-makers should examine such aspects of the society's culture as language, technology, knowledge, values and beliefs in order to make judgements about what should be transmitted to the next generation. Cultural analysis should take into account not only changing manpower needs but also more fundamental questions about what binds a society together. In some societies it will also be necessary to examine carefully ethnic, religious or other minority differences before coming to final conclusions about a common curriculum for everyone.

Having made some basic decisions about what should be selected from the culture for transmission to the next generation, it is then necessary to organise this knowledge. Here again societies will differ in their approach to this stage of curriculum planning. The disciplines from which social studies is derived are not identical in all countries. In addition to this lack of agreement, educationists also differ about the importance that should be given to disciplines or subjects as a basis for syllabus construction. Some theorists believe that students can best understand society if their study is organised under such subject headings as history, economics and sociology. Other curriculum planners prefer to use an integrated approach to social studies, organising the syllabus around problems or issues, drawing upon relevant aspects of the various disciplines to help students understand the issues or problems selected. Whatever approach is adopted, social studies teachers must be familiar with the methodology and the subject-matter of the academic disciplines and other subjects that have a close bearing on 'understanding society'. A main purpose of this chapter is to identify the most relevant disciplines and to indicate those areas within the various disciplines that are most likely to be useful to the teaching and learning of social studies, keeping in mind that the disciplines and boundaries between them may vary from country to country.

Contributions of Academic Disciplines to Social Studies

There is no intention in the material that follows to reify the academic disciplines or to indicate that they are the sole sources of knowledge for social studies. Moreover, considerable multidisciplinary and interdisciplinary work takes place that can be employed usefully for social studies. What is recognised is that social studies depends heavily upon the products of scholarship. Traditionally, much scholarship has been organised according to certain academic disciplines that find expression through formally organised university and college departments, journals and associations. Social studies specialists need to be familiar with the resources offered by the various academic disciplines in order to construct strong social studies programmes in schools. Several of the most important of these disciplines and their relevance to social studies are discussed below.

Sociology

Human behaviour follows certain observable patterns, even if these patterns vary from one society to another. Sociology is a discipline that recognises, describes and analyses patterns or regularities in social behaviour.

In the quest for regularities sociologists encounter many scientific difficulties. Although behaviour patterns can be discerned, human relationships are highly complex. The large number of variables makes it difficult to isolate the motivating forces operating on any particular individual in any one set of circumstances, and controlled experiments in sociology are much more difficult than in the natural sciences.

Sociologists are also divided regarding the role of values in social science. Some argue that sociology can and must undertake descriptive, explanatory and predictive functions in a neutral manner; others doubt or deny the possibility of neutrality, on the grounds that the selection of evidence or topics for enquiry is itself a reflection of values.

The second group of theorists say that sociology should face up to this problem and accept the difficulty. A more extreme position asserts that sociology is not concerned merely with the neutral study of society but with the active promotion of change. To the advocates of this position sociology should promote those values deemed useful to the society.

While recognising these difficulties and controversies, sociologists attempt to use, adapt and invent scientific methods for the study of human society. In practice, sociologists have to operate within some kind of theory, collecting data in order to test their theories. It is not possible within a brief treatment to describe all of the procedures they employ, but in general, sociologists accept the hypothetico-deductive model of the natural or physical scientist. They begin with a theory, collect data and confirm or reject their hypotheses.

While the approach to investigation is identical between natural scientists and sociologists, the subject-matter, the data and the procedures used to gather data vary enormously. The subject-matter of sociology might be divided into the following five categories: problem-solving research, study of particular institutions, local studies, studies of institutions within localities and theory testing.

Since sociologists have few opportunities to conduct controlled experiments, they must seek data of various kinds to test their hypotheses. The data may already be available in the form of official statistics, historical documents, contemporary records and so on. In all cases the sociologist must judge the quality of the data before using them to test a hypothesis or to establish generalisations. If these kinds of ready-made data are not available, sociologists must produce their own. The most common methods for generating data are observations systematically recorded, case studies, questionnaires or interviews, and surveys.

Sociology and the Curriculum. Even the most ambitious school cannot expect to teach sociology thoroughly. Some selection is necessary. For example, most pupils will not need to study sociological theory. But there is a wide range of concepts and models that might be introduced in schools — even at the primary age. Quite young children can be taught such terms as norms and values, beliefs, social institutions, organisations, groups, role, family, community, etc. For example, knowledge of a concept such as 'community' has clear benefits. Students can profit from distinguishing the kind of human relationships experienced in a 'community' from those typical of 'association' — that is face-to-face contacts as compared with impersonal, anonymous relations in larger-scale industrial societies. An understanding of 'community' can help students in industrialised and developing societies understand many of the problems of living in large, urban groups and what might be done to overcome some of these problems.

It is also possible to teach sociology as a mode of enquiry. Students can be allowed to conduct small-scale enquiries and develop skills of data collection and hypothesis testing. Teachers should always bear in mind, however, that the purpose of using sociological materials and methods is to inform the young person about his own society and the human relationships within it. It would be out of place for sociology to be studied as a discipline for its own sake, apart from the most mature students in secondary schools.

Anthropology

In some countries, anthropology is regarded as part of sociology and may be taught within the same department; in other countries, anthropology is treated as a completely separate discipline and only social anthropology is related to sociology in any way. There is, however, a good deal of overlap between much of social anthropology and sociology, even if the origins of the two disciplines are distinct.

Anthropology may be defined as the study of the social and cultural systems of total, usually small-scale, societies and social organisations. Anthropology emerged during the nineteenth century from the attempts of historians to discern general types of society in human history. In most cases their efforts at 'armchair theorising' were valuable but limited. They gradually gave way to a more scientific anthropology rooted in systematic field observation.

Early social anthropology was a reaction against nineteenth-century amateurs — missionaries, administrators, etc. — who saw preindustrial cultures as immoral, irrational or at a very early stage in social evolution. The reaction against these prescientific studies took the form of *functionalism*, a view that has tended to dominate anthropology ever since. For example, Malinowski, in his study of the Trobriand Islanders, rejected the evolutionary view of primitive peoples.[3] Instead, he studied the whole way of life of a people and their response to the problem of survival and living together harmoniously as a community in a particular environment. The social life and technology of a primitive people began to be understood as a system of interrelated situations: every aspect of life could be seen as 'functional' in the sense that it played a useful part in conjunction with all other aspects of life in permitting the culture to survive and the society to work smoothly. Malinowski argued that the magical practices of the Trobriand Islanders were functional in that they relieved anxiety, enabling people to carry on with food production under very difficult conditions. There practices were 'irrational' only from an untrained, outside observer's point of view.

One disadvantage of functionalism has been that it assumes a static, unchanging society to be 'normal'. Change is seen as a dangerous, abnormal phenomenon threatening the stability of the society. Yet, as researchers have produced more studies of primitive societies, it has become clear that some, possibly all, primitive communities do change, even when left untouched by Western influences. The rate of change may be slow, but change is certainly not abnormal. This realisation produced a shift in perspective, away from studies that were devoted only to the present time towards studies that were historical as well as contemporary. One result of the development of these studies has been a blurring of the distinction between social anthropology and sociology. It may still be true that anthropologists tend to study society as a whole while sociologists study particular aspects of complex modern societies, but this may not apply in particular cases. Anthropological methods have been used to great advantage in industrial societies and many sociological techniques are similar to anthropological methods.

Culture. Perhaps the most useful concept derived from anthropology and now used throughout the social sciences is that of culture. According to Tylor, 'Culture refers to that part of the sum total of human action and its products which is socially, rather than genetically, transmitted.'[4] More recent definitions place the emphasis on learning through socialisation, accumulated knowledge and artifacts, and shared understandings. Other social scientists define culture as a set of rules that includes objects that are symbolic and evaluative. Sociologists tend to see culture as ideational, whereas anthropologists see the whole of their subject-matter as culture, with custom as their main focus of interest.

Some of the best-known anthropologists, such as Malinowski and Benedict, were cultural relativists. They argued that one could understand a culture only on its own terms. They studied a culture for its own sake and were cautious about drawing comparisons between one way of life and another. On the other hand, some anthropologists have been particularly interested in comparisons; they seek similarities and even cultural universals.[5]

Another difficulty in the cultural-relativist position is that some anthropologists and sociologists refuse to make any kind of moral judgement about a society. At first this was a healthy reaction against the naïve moralising of missionaries and colonial administrators, but the difficulty of taking this doctrine to an extreme has been pointed out by Ginsberg,[6] who showed what happens if one applies cultural relativism to modern societies, such as Nazi Germany. Is it really possible to reconcile the extermination of the Jews as being 'functional' or part of Nazi culture that should be respected in its own right? Culture can develop in many ways that are anti-humanistic. Some kind of moral rules should be applied to all societies. What must be discouraged in the young is the tendency to apply merely local rules to other societies when they ought to be trying to work out universal moral rules. (See Chapter 8 for a further discussion of this point.)

Anthropological Method. The basic anthropological method is field-work. Theories and concepts can be developed and validated only by empirical research. Anthropologists usually act as participant observers in the societies they study. Devoting as much as six months or more living in the society under investigation, an anthropologist tries to observe as much as possible of the whole way of life. Some of this may be meaningless or misleading even to a trained observer. By learning the language, by asking for explanations of what he sees and by systematic interviewing of informants, the anthropologist seeks to arrive at valid conclusions. Information must be cross-checked for accuracy and reliability and also related to other information. The process is time-consuming and subject to error and misinterpretation. Many reports and books written by anthropologists have distorted evidence, over-generalised conclusions or shaped data to fit preconceived theory.

Anthropology and the Curriculum. The concept of culture is a very useful one for study in any school curriculum. The general aim ought to be to help young people understand that all important differences in human behaviour can be seen as differences in learned patterns of behaviour, rather than differences in biological make-up. For example, the Aborigine or Bushmen's way of life is different from others because of cultural reasons. A Western European baby, reared among the Aborigines, would become an Aborigine in all important respects. Some school curricula now include a detailed study of one society, such as the Netsilik Eskimos or the Bushman, in order to illustrate the essential needs of man and the common elements in society. It can be demonstrated, for example, that all societies have some kind of kinship system, some method of utilising and distributing resources (an economic system), a form of decision-making (a political system) and a system of beliefs. The emphasis on *man* is one of the ideas behind the social studies programme entitled *Man: A Course of Study* (MACOS), an American social studies programme designed for use with eleven-year-old pupils and whose ideas derive from the work of Jerome Bruner. Basic questions are asked about 'What is human about human beings?' and 'How did they get that way?' Eskimo society provides the focus of instruction.

It is important that decision-makers be prepared to encounter criticisms if they recommend such courses as MACOS. Even in supposedly sophisticated societies parents may object to the study of other cultures on the grounds that such instruction may undermine beliefs in one's own society. In recent years MACOS has been attacked because it attempts to be ethically neutral and morally relativistic in its treatment of other cultures. Few parents wish their children to become ethically neutral. Curriculum planners, as well as teachers, have to be able to reassure parents and other members of the public that it is possible to understand other cultures without either losing respect for one's own or abandoning one's capacity for moral judgement.

There are other dangers to be avoided in using anthropological material. School courses can become superficial and narrow, concentrating on only trivial differences in behaviour in other societies. Such studies ignore the basic anthropological precept that a society should be seen as a whole and that to describe isolated bits of it is misleading. Students should also learn there is a difference between collecting facts about other societies and developing an understanding of another culture. Some educationists doubt the wisdom of attempting to develop anthropological understanding with pupils who have not yet attained maturity in their own society. Teachers must also be cautious about the risks of introducing misunderstandings about so-called 'primitive peoples', leading to greater expressions of chauvinism on the part of the students. However, by studying different types of society and by a consideration of social change, pupils can benefit from properly conducted anthropological studies: first, by perceiving human behaviour in much broader terms; second, by deriving some comparative perspective by which to evaluate their own society or certain aspects of their own society; and third, by developing the ability to understand their own society as a whole as a result of looking at small-scale societies holistically. Properly used, anthropological materials can help overcome racial intolerance and exaggerated kinds of nationalism.

Political Studies

Political education is neglected in most education systems, although according to most definitions of social studies, some understanding of political ideas is indispensable. There is, however, much confusion about the nature of politics both within the same country and between countries. In some there is an emphasis on political philosophy; in others there has been an effort to treat political studies as a social science.

Two kinds of questions are addressed by traditional political philosophy: first, questions about how and why men devised systems of government; second, ethical questions about the authority of government, the moral basis of that authority and obedience to it. Political science, on the other hand, has been described by Lasswell[7] as a study of 'who gets what, when and how'. This view has tended to take politics away from an exclusive concern with government and elections to much wider aspects of the politics of everyday life. When we state our support for a person or an institution, when we make demands or state preferences, we are acting politically by Lasswell's definition. According to Lasswell, politics is concerned with conflicts and their resolution.

The term 'political science' is not widely used in many European countries. When it exists, it often denotes a field of research by someone whose training was probably in history or law. In France, political science covers ground which in the United Kingdom and the United States of America is referred to as political sociology. The overlap between politics and other social sciences is often considerable; no attempt will be made here to define the boundaries.

There are other perspectives about the nature of politics. For some theorists, including many Marxists, politics is essentially about conflict: power enables groups and individuals who possess it to keep their domination over others and to exploit others; groups and individuals with less power oppose their domination, object to being exploited and try to resist and overthrow those with power. The opposing interpretation understands politics as an attempt to establish order and justice in society. Power may be used to protect the general welfare and the common good from particular groups of people and particular individuals from the stronger. While these two views are often seen as completely opposed to one another, both can be seen to operate in different kinds of situations.

Whereas the traditional political philosophy approach is closely related to other forms of philosophical understanding, political scientists tend to see their methods as being similar to, and possibly derived from, the social sciences. In some countries the overlap between political science, political sociology and sociology is very great. Empirical methods of collecting and analysing data have become increasingly common. Reports of committees and the proceedings of official hearings, official records and other documents, personal papers and memoirs, sample surveys and depth interviews are just a few of the data sources used by political scientists. There has also been a tendency to use field study methods in order to find out why individuals behave in the ways they do. However important these empirical methods become, the historical and philosophical traditions remain important.

In writing for an Australian audience, G.S. Harman[8] divided political science concerns into six categories. These categories might be accepted by many political scientists in other countries as well: the individual, political parties and pressure groups, parliaments, cabinets and public bureaucracies, comparative political systems, the study of the international political system and relations between nations, and political ideologies and doctrines.

Politics in the Curriculum. Most societies recognise the need to teach the young something about the government of their own and other countries, but in practice there are many difficulties associated with this intention.[9] In those countries where 'civics' or 'government' is compulsory, the courses are often unpopular with students and much criticised by political scientists. Civics is compulsory in many states of the United States and in Sweden, for example; in both countries the subject tends to have low academic status and is disliked by students. In recent years some reformers have sought to change civics from a study of how the government works in terms of its written constitution towards the study of politics and the impact of political decisions on society.

One proposal for improving instruction in politics has been offered by Professor Bernard Crick and his colleagues who have put forward the ideas of 'political literacy'.[10] Crick argues for a conceptual approach to the subject of politics on the grounds of Toulmin's view that 'each of us thinks his own thoughts; our concepts we share with our fellow men'. While this is true of any field of learning, it is especially true in politics. Compared with some programmes that have sought to teach students technical concepts advanced by the academic disciplines, Crick has sought to help students make better use of political concepts that are part of ordinary language.

Crick begins with two basic concepts, *government* and *people*, which he links by a third important concept, *relationships*. This very simple model then gives rise to a rather more complicated model that relates the three main concepts to twelve subsidiary concepts. These fifteen concepts can be used as a conceptual framework within which teachers may devise their own syllabuses. The concepts do not presuppose any particular sequence of teaching; in fact, Crick recommends that it is often better to start with immediate issues of interest to the students. Thus a possible teaching plan for a practising teacher might be to start with some immediate political issues, preferably of direct concern to the students themselves; then ground these issues in recent history; and finally draw from the discussion of the issues concepts and principles that are of more general use.

A conceptual approach alone, however, will not ensure a politically educated person. As well as understanding about the relationship between individuals and government, young people must also acquire appropriate attitudes. In another paper Crick has suggested that the following values should be recognised as indispensable for politically educated people: freedom, toleration, fairness, respect for truth and respect for reasoning.[11] While the fifteen-concept model and the values specified above could be applied in all societies which desire a politically educated population, the actual content in terms of political issues would vary from one country to another, and indeed from time to time in the same country. The advantage of this model is that it is flexible enough to permit teachers or groups of teachers to use their own teaching materials within an acceptable public framework.

Economics

As with sociology, the growth of economics as a discipline was directly linked with the development of modern industrial capitalism and reactions against it. At first, unrestricted competition was praised and justified in Adam Smith's classic *Wealth of Nations*,[12] where it was argued that with minimum government interference the economic actions of individuals would automatically work out to the best advantage of society as a whole. This view was soon challenged by the writings of

Karl Marx and others who followed in that tradition of economics.[13] But even within the capitalist tradition, by the twentieth century doubts were being expressed about unrestricted economic freedom of individuals. By the 1920s J.M. Keynes and others were in the process of revolutionising capitalistic economics.[14]

The central idea of economics is the concept of scarcity, the notion of the existence of unlimited wants but limited resources. Even the youngest students can readily appreciate this idea. From scarcity can be derived the idea of production as an activity converting resources into goods and services for which consumers pay money. Linked to production is the notion of specialisation and the division of labour. A historical approach may be the best method for tackling these ideas; in fact, most would now agree that economics without an understanding of economic history is a rather arid activity.

Economics and the Curriculum. Considerable work on the teaching of economics in schools has been done in the United States. For example, G.L. Bach[15] has suggested that economics should provide students with four simple things: a rough overview of how the economic system works; an awareness of some of the major economic problems of the day; a rough understanding of a few major economic institutions and the fundamental concepts and relationships needed to understand the issues faced by people in their daily lives; and some experience in applying these concepts and relationships to a few typical economic problems.

Students should also have an opportunity to consider economic systems of other societies. All economies have the same problem — how to make the best use of resources to satisfy economic needs. It is important to examine how each system attempts to solve this problem. Perhaps every student should study one socialist-type economy, one mixed economy and one small-scale economy as well as the way in which the capitalist system, as originally envisaged, has gradually changed. There are available materials suitable for such study, even on an international basis.

Some believe that economics is too difficult to be taught in schools and that it is better to leave it for university study. Some university teachers of economics have stated that they prefer to teach students who have *not* studied economics at school, because they may have picked up incorrect or over-simplified economic knowledge. This reactionary view is fortunately disappearing, but it may be useful to state the counter arguments anyway.

It is important for all adult members of society to have at least a basic understanding of economic affairs. To limit the study of economics to only those who attend higher education colleges and universities perpetuates an undesirable and dangerous form of elitism. The schools need a curriculum that will permit all students to understand economics. Such a curriculum will, of necessity, be less complex than the kind of courses pursued by university students, but simplification is possible without distorting the truth. Fortunately, the basic ideas of economics are very simple. If appropriate materials and teaching methods are used, there is no greater reason to fear over-simplification in economics than in physics or chemistry.

Psychology

Psychology is concerned with the study of behaviour in humans and animals. Other disciplines such as sociology, anthropology and politics may also be behavioural in this sense, but they have a different focus and emphasis. Morgan and King[16] have suggested that 'psychology is a kind of meeting ground for the natural sciences such as physics, biology and physiology and the social sciences such as sociology, economics and political science'.

One might argue that psychology can be left out of the curriculum as a separate subject because much of its content will be included elsewhere. On the other hand, psychology is an especially useful subject because it brings together so many other disciplines. In some countries aspects of psychology are a part of the science curriculum; in other countries psychology is treated primarily as a social science.

What Kind of Psychology should be Taught? Psychology is a 'scientific' field since it systematically collects and tests data for the purpose of understanding and predicting behaviour. Its roots as a discipline extend to the philosophical psychology of the seventeenth and eighteenth centuries, particularly associated with Hobbes, Berkeley and Mill. Although psychologists such as Freud relied heavily on introspection and speculation, the modern tendency has been for scientific experimentation to be the main area of interest. Subdivisions within psychology are very common in university departments. One popular distinction is that between general psychology and social psychology, although it is difficult to see exactly where the boundary should be.[17]

Physiological psychology which has traditionally been concerned with the study of animal behaviour and their learning processes is closely linked to the physical sciences. The work of Pavlov in the USSR and that of Skinner in the United States have developed within that tradition, although they now have very different stances. In addition there is a good deal of work on the innate behaviour of animals, for example that of Lorenz[18] and Tinbergen.[19] Human, experimental psychology in most parts of the world has been concerned primarily with problems of human perception, memory and thinking.

Psychology and the Curriculum. There are good arguments for including some aspects of general and social psychology in an integrated social studies curriculum. There is less support among teachers and psychologists for offering psychology as a separate school subject. Many feel that while all pupils should have a basic understanding of human behaviour related to society and its political and economic structure, the separate study of psychology involves too much advanced work for it to be appropriate for specialised study below the age of about sixteen.

Important psychological concepts can be introduced into various social studies courses or other parts of the curriculum such as biology. In addition it is possible to devote time to helping young people understand their own feelings under crisis situations such as divorce or the death of a parent. Other feelings such as jealousy, selfishness and greed may also be handled in instructional materials, perhaps under the heading moral education. In such situations the intention is not to teach psychology as a subject or as a discipline, but to increase students' capacity to cope with difficult situations and to come to terms with their own emotions. There are risks in using psychology in this way. It is essential that teachers have a good general knowledge of psychology and be trained in the use of relevant instructional materials and counselling techniques. Amateur psychological analysis in the classroom can be extremely dangerous.

History

In most countries history has held a position in the traditional curriculum as a subject in its own right, apart from social studies. It is not the intention of this section to discuss the nature and philosophy of history in any depth or to discuss the problems of teaching history as a separate subject. Rather, our intention is to examine the relationship between history and the social sciences and to make suggestions about teaching history within social studies.

The Relation between History and Social Science. Although there are distinctive ideas and procedures that can be described as 'historical', many historical arguments are not so much concerned with matters of evidence as with non-historical questions about human motivation. Therefore, the overlap between history and the other social sciences, particularly psychology and sociology, is so great that some degree of convergence is desirable.

Many historians wish to keep history distinct from social science. They argue that history deals with the uniqueness of individual events, whereas sociology is concerned with generalisations. While not completely untrue, it is an over-simplified view that can mask a number of difficulties. Historians also indulge in generalisations, but their generalisations may be different from sociological generalisations. Moreover, there is a difference between generalising at the level of 'labelling', for instance using terms such as 'feudalism' or 'revolution', and the kind of generalising speculation promoted by historians such as Arnold Toynbee, who are sometimes described as meta-historians.

Another distinction sometimes drawn between history and sociology relates to the question of aims. It is said that sociology collects facts to explain laws, but history exploits laws to explain facts. This simple distinction stereotypes both history and sociology. Both empirical studies that are theory-oriented and theory that is empirically verifiable are needed.

History and the Curriculum. All pupils should have the right to acquire historical perspective. Unfortunately in most countries conventional history taught in schools is insufficient. Two kinds of history instruction may be distinguished: history for its own sake that may be appropriate for older students and history that is essential for an understanding of social studies and social change. In both cases the problem of selection exists. Teachers cannot include the whole of history, so on what basis do they decide what to include and what to ignore? Teachers, whether they are specialist historians or general social studies teachers, need to find a balance between covering vast amounts of material at a very general level and focusing in detail on unique events. Inevitably, history requires a certain amount of narrative and chronology. But good history teaching depends also upon logical analysis.

In the past many history teachers have erred in two ways. First, they have not fully appreciated that learning history requires understanding generalisations and abstract concepts to a greater degree than most other subjects. Second, teachers have assumed that students understand concepts and laws based on the social sciences when in reality these must be learned by the pupils. The close relationship between history and the social sciences may buttress the argument that social studies should be taught through an integrated approach rather than allow each subject to develop in its own way.

The task of the history teacher is to 'recreate a past which is significant and intelligible'.[20] A historian is not merely a chronicler of events; he must also structure and interpret the past. Just as historians need to do this for ordinary people, history teachers have to perform this task for their pupils, or better still, teach them to do it for themselves.

Apart from those older students who may specialise in history and study history 'for its own sake', there are good arguments for encouraging the development of contemporary history and world history in schools. In most cases the kind of history that will provide adequate background for political, economic and sociological understanding will be recent and contemporary history. The arguments in favour of world history are also strong. In the past, history has tended to intensify rather than to diminish a narrow nationalistic outlook. For example, many European children gain the impression from their historical studies that America hardly existed until Europeans arrived there. Nationalistic history may undermine the kind of sociological and anthropological understandings of human beings discussed earlier in this chapter. Some kind of world history should be included for all students.

Geography

In some countries at both school and university levels, geography is an important discipline in its own right. In other societies geography is but one aspect of social studies. In still others it *is* social studies, incorporating many aspects of politics, economics and social life as well as some elementary aspects of anthropology. It may be useful, however, to define geography in order to identify its unique concepts and principles and to decide what elements should form part of the curriculum for every student.

In recent years geographers have attempted to identify geography's main interests and traditions. Such an analysis typically results in at least three kinds of overlapping approaches.

(1) *Physical geography* is often referred to in the United States as earth science. This is concerned with the spatial distribution and functioning of natural phenomena on the earth's surface. It includes the study of land forms, weather, climate and biogeography, the

study of spatial relationships between living forms other than man and man himself.

(2) *Human or cultural geography*. This is concerned with the relation between man and his environment. This approach includes economic geography (the study of man's economic activities from a spatial point of view); political geography (how the political activities of man affect the landscape, etc.); urban geography (the study of the forms and functions of towns, etc.); historical geography (how the geographical changes of the past may affect the geography of present times).

Some geographers prefer to speak of human geography as an entity in its own right. This involves the study of people, their way of life in various parts of the world, and how they interact with their environment.

(3) *Regional geography or areal studies*, the comprehensive study of a single area.

Certain major concepts have become important within these divisions of geography. For example, a cultural perspective focuses attention on man and on his economic, social and political activities. The Earth is seen as composed of '*cultural* regions' rather than solely '*natural* regions'. In this respect geography has much in common with anthropology which, as we have seen, emphasises the concept of culture. The concept of region is a second major idea in geography. This concept helps geographers examine likenesses and differences on the Earth's surface. A region must have some internal consistency and homogeneity that distinguishes it from other regions. The distinctive character of a region may lie in its landscape, in its mode of life, or in the functional unity of several combined characteristics. A third important concept is *areal association*. This suggests that phenomena within an area exist together in association. The symbiotic relationships among the various elements are the result of many processes and events, including human and climatic ones. Geographers attempt to discover the nature of relationships and to determine the spatial correlations of locations and phenomena within an area. This approach clearly has links with biology and ecology. Other important geographical concepts include *spatial interaction*, *location* and *change*, all of which have clear links with the other social sciences.

Geography and the Curriculum. A recent development within geography of special relevance to social studies is the idea that geography at the school level should show much greater concern for social issues. In some countries recent textbooks have concentrated on world problems or on the problems of living in cities. One such book is *Geography of the British Isles.*[21] This book emphasises the need for children to understand and apply basic geographical principles and concepts, and to develop skills of learning. Such learning skills include the observation, recording and interpretation of data collected from a wide range of first-hand and second-hand sources. This new approach involves not only more active learning by the pupils; it also stresses the need for geography to be relevant to students' lives.

An emphasis upon the students' own experience need not prevent students from looking at other regions as part of their geographical education. Indeed, it is essential for students to apply the skills and principles they have acquired to societies other than their own. Without such comparative material they would miss a deeper understanding of their own society as well as neglect important aspects of international understanding. The use of geography to promote international understanding can be served whether geography exists as a separate school subject or in situations where the skills and concepts of geography are integrated into a more general social studies curriculum.

The Curriculum as a Set of Rights

Thus far, this chapter has focused on the task of planning social studies curricula by drawing upon the academic disciplines and by linking instruction to social needs and personal concerns of youth. It would be easy to move from that position to accepting the social studies curriculum as a package of knowledge selected by one generation for transmission to the next. To see the curriculum in this way would be a grave error. This view has been criticised by Freire[22] as the 'banking concept' of education.

It is far more satisfactory to understand the curriculum as a *set of rights*. In most societies education is compulsory for a stipulated number of years. This means that for a certain period children are deprived of their liberty. Unless it is clear that in return for this loss of liberty there are corresponding advantages, then it can be argued that children are being treated unjustly. An attempt must be made to justify their loss of freedom. When schooling is justified in this way, the curriculum becomes a set of rights of access to certain kinds of knowledge and educational experiences. A science curriculum is defended and perceived differently from this point of view. Children must have right of access to scientific knowledge, not because they might use such knowledge to get a good job, but because they live in a world that is dominated by science and technology. Unless they have a basic understanding of science and mathematics, they will be incapable of benefiting from some of the advantages of science and they will be unable to participate in some aspects of decision-making that involve scientific problems. For example, it makes little sense to talk of pollution and conservation as political issues in a society if the populace as a whole has no knowledge of the scientific principles involved.

The world is not only scientific in its orientation, but it is increasingly 'social scientific'. Thus young people need to acquire accurate knowledge of certain aspects of their own society if they are to participate effectively within it. By this argument, all children have a right to certain kinds of political, social and economic knowledge.

To see the curriculum as a set of student rights not only provides a more honest means of motivating children; it is also likely to generate better criteria for selecting appropriate knowledge. There is a constant danger that knowledge will be inserted into the curriculum 'for its own sake'. This is avoided if social science knowledge is selected not because it exists but because it is deemed important for the access rights it affords all children.

If we apply this formula for curriculum planning to a variety of countries, it is apparent that some basic rights of access to knowledge fit all nations, although the detailed content in terms of subject-matter will vary considerably from one country to another. For example, all children have the right to know how their own society has developed historically. They also need to know something about the political, economic and social structure of their society: they can only participate in, and possibly change, their society if they have a good understanding of how it works at the moment. And all children have a right to knowledge of world society and international relations, together with recent historical developments at that level.

Conclusion

All societies are different, and some of the differences must be valued and preserved. It is, however, very easy to exaggerate the differences and ignore the values and perceptions they share. Countries may wish to select different kinds of knowledge for social studies teaching, and they may wish to organise the curriculum differently. But all live in a universe where the laws of science operate; similarly, the basic principles of social science and social philosophy must be — to some extent — universal. It is a useful exercise to see the extent of this universality. A practical outcome might then be an improved understanding by young people of those in societies very different from their own.

Notes

1. Clyde Kluckhohn, *Culture and Behaviour: Collected Essays*, ed. Richard Kluckhohn (Free Press of Glencoe, New York, 1962).

2. Ruth Benedict, *Patterns of Culture* (Routledge, London, 1935).

3. Bronislaw K. Malinowski, *Argonauts of the Western Pacific: Studies in Economics and Political Science* (Routledge and Kegan Paul, London, 1964).

4. E.B. Tylor, *Primitive Culture* (John Murray, London, 1871).

5. 'Ethical universals are the product of universal human nature which is based upon a common biology, psychology and generalized situation.' Kluckhohn, *Culture and Behaviour*.

6. M. Ginsberg, *Essays in Sociology and Social Philosophy* (Penguin, Harmondsworth, 1968), p. 384.

7. Harold D. Lasswell, *Politics: Who Gets What, When, How?* (McGraw-Hill, New York and London, 1936).

8. G.S. Harman, 'Political Science' in David G. Dufty (ed.), *Teaching about Society: Problems and Possibilities* (Rigby, Kent Town, Australia, n.d.).

9. See the recent report *Civic Education in Five Unesco Member States* (Unesco, Paris, 1979).

10. Bernard Crick, 'The Introducing of Politics' in Derek Heater (ed.), *The Teaching of Politics* (Methuen Educational Press, London, 1969), pp. 1-21.

11. A much fuller discussion of these ideas can be found in the Working Papers produced by the Programme for Political Education associated with the Hansard Society, London, and in Bernard Crick and Derek Heater (eds.), *Essays on Political Education* (Ringmer Falmer Press, London, 1977).

12. Adam Smith, *An Enquiry into the Nature and Causes of the Wealth of Nations* (Everymans Library, Dent, London; Dutton, New York, 1910).

13. Karl Marx, *Capital (Das Kapital)*, 3 volumes (Lawrence and Wishart, London, 1970-2).

14. John Maynard Keynes, *The General Theory of Employment, Interest and Money* (Macmillan, London, 1936).

15. G.L. Bach, 'What Economics Should We Teach?' in Edwin Fenton (ed.), *Teaching the New Social Studies in Secondary Schools: an Inductive Approach* (Holt, Rinehart and Winston, New York and London, 1966), pp. 333-9.

16. C.T. Morgan and R.A. King, *Introduction to Psychology* (5th edn., MacGraw-Hill, New York, 1975).

17. Z. Barbu, 'Social Psychology' in Norman MacKenzie (ed.), *A Guide to the Social Sciences* (Weidenfeld and Nicolson, London, 1966), pp. 151-83.

18. Konrad Lorenz, *King Solomon's Ring: New Light on Animal Ways (Er redete mit dem Vieh, den Vögelm und den Fischen)* (Methuen, London, 1952).

19. N. Tinbergen, *A Study of Instinct* (Clarendon Press, Oxford, 1951).

20. D. Thompson, 'Colligation and History Teaching' in H. Burston and D. Thompson (eds.), *Studies in the Nature and Teaching of History* (Routledge

and Kegan Paul, London, 1967), pp. 85-106.

21. Norman Graves and John Talbot White, *Geography of the British Isles* (Heinemann Educational Press, London, 1971).

22. P. Freire, *Pedagogy of the Oppressed* (Penguin, Harmondsworth, 1971).

3 SOCIAL STUDIES AS AN INTEGRATED SUBJECT

Talabi Aisie Lucan

Introduction

Social studies has no widely accepted content or method of investigation. What is called social studies in one country may be quite different from social studies in another. Differences in content and approach often vary widely even among schools within the same country. What social studies teachers within a nation and across nations have in common, and what distinguishes them from those who do not teach social studies, is a sense of shared purpose. *All social studies teachers attempt to help young people learn about themselves, about other human beings and about society and culture so as to enable them to develop to their maximum human potential while functioning effectively as members of society.* What precisely a person must learn to achieve this result is unclear and the answers vary from one society to the next and among individuals within a society. Nor do people agree upon the meaning of such terms as 'maximum human potential' or 'function effectively as a member of society'. It is partly because these terms are interpreted differently that social studies assumes different forms.

Nevertheless, despite variations in social studies patterns, those who share the purpose stated above can be distinguished from those who do not. For example, two teachers may teach courses with identical labels, for example, a secondary school course in world geography, but their courses can serve wholly different purposes. One geography teacher may believe that the purpose for teaching geography is to help pupils gain some understanding of the discipline of geography and some information about geographic features of the Earth. The other geography teacher believes that the purpose for teaching geography is to equip students with information and ways of thinking that will enable them to understand important social problems. The first defends the teaching of geography for its intrinsic merits; the latter justifies the study of geography on extrinsic grounds.

In Chapter 2, Lawton wrote, 'A good social studies curriculum is one which *helps young individuals to develop into fully human adults by relating them to their society by means of appropriate knowledge and experience selected from the social sciences and other disciplines.*'

59

Lawton emphasises the instrumental use of knowledge for social studies. A social studies teacher uses information from history and the social sciences *in order* to satisfy individual needs and the interests of society. There are those who do not accept this point of view. They believe history, geography, economics and other social science courses should be taught for their own inherent worth, perhaps as part of a liberal education. They assert that one should know the history and geography of a community, region, nation and the world primarily because possessing such knowledge is one of the attributes of an educated person. Such knowledge may or may not make one a better citizen or a more complete person. Indeed, they fear that to force such courses into serving instrumental goals — however worthy they may appear to be — can lead to bias, distortion, propaganda and erosion of academic rigour. This is a defensible point of view; it is not a social studies point of view.

Social Studies Purposes can be Achieved by Organising Courses according to Academic Subjects or by an Integrated Approach

Those who adopt a social studies perspective towards the purpose of school instruction do not organise their courses identically even when their purposes are similar. Let us assume that a teacher wishes students to gain some understanding of the horrors of war and become committed to finding peaceful alternatives to international conflicts. These objectives can be served by a course in world history. Following a study of World War One, students might explore the costs of that war, ways the hostilities might have been prevented, how the war was settled and whether the settlement laid the grounds for World War Two. This teacher is using a specific war as a springboard for teaching students about the tragedy of war generally and why wars must be avoided. Another teacher, with the same objectives in mind, might organise a two-to-three-week unit on the question: 'World War Three: Can it be Prevented?' During the unit students might study such topics as the nature of warfare in the twentieth century, the psychology of war prevention and nuclear deterrence, the economics of armaments races and international conflict resulting from competition in ideology and trade. Throughout their study students would use information from a variety of disciplines. The first teacher is teaching social studies by means of an academic subject; the second is pursuing social studies as an integrated subject. The purpose of social studies can be achieved by either approach.

A course in history or geography can be taught from a social studies perspective or from a non-social studies perspective. What matters most is what purposes the teacher has in mind. One cannot conclude from a mere list of courses whether social studies is being practised or not. It is necessary to observe instruction and talk to the teacher to learn the purposes of the course, what knowledge is selected, and how — or even if — it is applied to current situations.

Among the advocates of social studies are those who view efforts to promote social studies within traditional course labels as needlessly burdensome. They argue that this requires that the teacher balance two competing criteria: to represent the discipline validly and to employ the content of the discipline for instrumental purposes. While social studies *can* be taught within courses labelled as history, geography, civics, economics, psychology, sociology, anthropology and political science, critics of this approach insist that a better social studies programme can be provided if social studies is approached as a subject of its own, through an integrated approach drawing upon knowledge from many fields. This chapter discusses some of the advantages of the integrated approach, alternative ways of achieving integration of the academic disciplines and some suggestions for organising courses and lessons in an integrated manner.

Some Arguments on Behalf of an Integrated Approach to the Social Studies

There are at least three reasons for favouring an integrated approach to social studies. It is sound psychologically and philosophically, and it responds to the changing nature of scientific study.

Psychological Justification

Children, especially of elementary school age, do not naturally observe the world through the perspectives of the academic disciplines. The academic disciplines are cultural artifacts with their own language and ways of thinking that must be imposed on the naïve learner. On the other hand, a child

> sees the world as one unit and naturally asks questions which cut across artificial subject divisions. An integrated approach to learning in the social studies attempts to follow the child's natural ways of learning, viewing the world as a whole, the teacher's role being to provide experiences and to assist the inquiry process by suggesting

further lines which might be followed.[1]

Moreoever, successful instruction in any field requires paying close attention to the stages of cognitive development of children. Academic disciplines depend upon abstract symbols. These symbols are difficult for young children to grasp. As a result, in order to teach history in the elementary grades, it is often necessary to reduce history to story-telling, thereby distorting history as an academic discipline and destroying whatever advantages the discipline has to offer. An integrated approach to social studies can avoid this problem and design instruction that is consonant with children's stages of mental growth.

Philosophical Justification

Instruction, especially when it is compulsory, must be justified according to the contribution it will make to the individual and to society. People who are forced to undergo instruction must be assured that the result will be somehow good for them. Furthermore, to ensure that public funds are employed for educational uses rather than for other social needs, the public – through its leaders – must be satisfied that the society will somehow gain more by such expenditure for education than for any other purpose.

An integrated approach to social studies is more likely to maintain focus on the instrumental purpose of instruction – both to enhance the individual and to promote social goals – than is social studies instruction that depends on the validity of separate academic subjects.

Justification according to Nature of Scientific Knowledge

Focusing strictly upon the traditional academic disciplines poses the risk that important advances in scientific knowledge will be overlooked. Not only are the boundaries between the traditional academic disciplines being bridged by new disciplines such as social anthropology, political behaviour, economic history and cultural geography, but also important new fields such as population studies, environmental studies and global studies draw content from various traditional disciplines. Scholars from both the natural sciences and the social sciences have found it necessary to combine their knowledge and methods to make progress in these areas. Social studies cannot afford to be cut off from these promising lines of intellectual activity, because the research of such scholars lies near the core of the social studies.

Alternative Ways of Achieving Integration of the Academic Disciplines

Teachers may find the arguments supporting the merits of an integrated approach to social studies compelling but be puzzled about how such an integrated approach is possible. On what basis does one draw data, concepts, methods and perspectives from separate fields and combine them into a new subject called social studies?

Undoubtedly, there are many ways such a task can be carried out. For our purposes three will be discussed. We shall call these: integration while preserving discipline identification; integration through social science concepts and generalisations; and integration through unification.

Integration while Preserving Discipline Identification

This approach seeks to retain the advantages separate academic subjects afford while weaving them into a pattern that satisfies the particular purposes of the curriculum developer. Usually there is no desire on the part of the developer to connect the disciplines in any formal way, except through the focus of a particular course of study. Nor is there any particular effort to break down any of the component academic disciplines so that they are called upon to function in unfamiliar ways.

A study of Sierre Leone provides an illustration. Whether it is a unit within a course, a complete course or the entire social studies curriculum, a study of Sierre Leone depends upon contributions from various academic disciplines. However, the purpose of instruction is not to teach the academic disciplines *per se*, but to teach about Sierre Leone, using the academic disciplines as sources of knowledge where appropriate. (See Figure 3.1.)

Figure 3.1: Relationship of Academic Disciplines to a Study of Sierra Leone

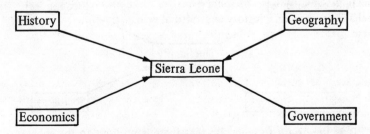

This approach also characterises Lawrence Senesh's notion of an 'orchestrated' social studies curriculum. According to Senesh, his elementary school textbooks were designed to represent the nature of the academic disciplines at each grade level. Nevertheless, as the curriculum developer, he combined them appropriately for his purposes and decided the role each academic discipline would play. As in an orchestra, sometimes political science has a 'solo' with other disciplines playing supporting parts. On other occasions, other disciplines have solo opportunities. But as with any good orchestra, what is important is how the parts fit together to make a pleasing result.

Senesh described how this scheme works when introducing first-grade children (6 years old) to the concepts of family:

> The children discover (1) that the family is a decision-making body (political science), (2) that the family is a producing, distributing and consuming group (economics), (3) that the family has different members with different roles to play which they fulfill according to a certain pattern (sociology), and (4) that one family differs from another, since each family is guided by different ideas and customs (social anthropology).[2]

Although such a theme may be selected to present to young children the structure of knowledge of the various social sciences, the children will not be expected to recognise the differences between the disciplines. The common denominator, 'The Family', will always be kept in focus and materials will not be constructed haphazardly. The analytical tools of the different disciplines are used to perform within the 'orchestra'. (See Figure 3.2.)

Figure 3.2: Contributions of the Academic Disciplines to a Study of the Family

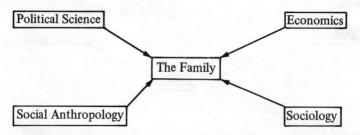

It is important to recognise that there is no limit to the spheres of knowledge that might serve as the bases for such an approach to an integrated social studies. For example, a Unesco-associated school in

Turkey reported that the following fields were used to prepare instruction about Turkey.[3]

(1) Religion – Islam in Turkey
(2) German – old Turkish folk tales
(3) English – Ataturk and modern Turkey; Turkish food
(4) Latin – lecture and slides on Hellenism in the Near East
(5) French – influence of French on nineteenth-century Turkey
(6) History – history of Turkey
(7) Geography – geography of Turkey
(8) Natural sciences – flora of the Near East
(9) Philosophy – Ionic philosophy
(10) Music – Muslim prayer calls and Turkish folk songs
(11) Art education – Turkish carpets, miniature paintings

Many teachers contributed to the unit on Turkey (which was not limited to the social studies classroom). Teachers representing various school subjects joined efforts to provide their students with a comprehensive view of Turkish society and culture.

Integration through Social Science Concepts and Generalisations

A second approach is to draw freely upon concepts and generalisations represented by the various academic disciplines without regard for maintaining each discipline's identity. In this case the curriculum developer wishes to use the social sciences in the design of integrated social studies courses but has no desire to maintain the 'structure of knowledge' represented by each of the academic disciplines, as was the desire of Lawrence Senesh mentioned earlier. The result of the integration is a new course, wholly unlike the parent academic disciplines but drawing upon concepts, generalisations and data that owe their origins to the academic disciplines.

Figure 3.3 indicates the process by which concepts, generalisations and data from the academic disciplines are filtered and organised until they become a patterned sequence of discrete social studies courses and units of study in schools.

The Taba School Studies Project chose eleven key concepts from the various social science disciplines and a number of related generalisations, and used topics of the traditional expanding environment programme to develop the key ideas of that programme. The eleven organising concepts are: *'causality, conflict, co-operation, cultural change, differences, interdependencies, modification, power, societal*

Figure 3.3: A Model of Social Studies Integration through Social Science Concepts and Generalisations

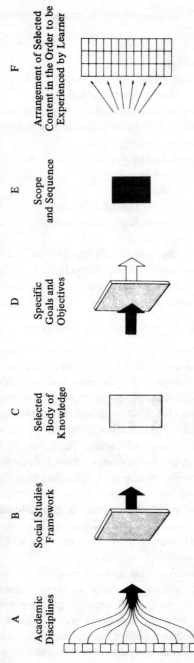

A	B	C	D	E	F
Academic Disciplines	Social Studies Framework	Selected Body of Knowledge	Specific Goals and Objectives	Scope and Sequence	Arrangement of Selected Content in the Order to be Experienced by Learner

A. *Academic Disciplines*. The academic disciplines serve as the principal source of concepts, data and generalisations. Other sources of knowledge can also be used. This knowledge is shown as interrelated but not unified. B. *Social Studies Framework*. The social studies framework consists of the formal and informal guidelines that affect what will be taught in each nation. Formal rules include statutes and regulations governing education. Informal guidelines include the interests of youth and the needs of society. Taken together these serve as a filter for what will be taught in schools. C. *Selected Body of Knowledge*. This represents the body of social studies knowledge deemed appropriate and important for youth to acquire. D. *Specific Goals and Objectives*. This filter represents the particular priorities of individual school officials or teachers. In other countries, there is less choice at this level and this filter may not be needed. E. *Scope and Sequence*. This is the result of the process by which concepts, data and generalisation have been organised into a structured curriculum. F. *Order of Content for the Learner*. This is the way in which the learner will actually experience the content during his tenure in school.

Source: This diagram is based upon an idea that appeared in Unesco, *Population Education: a Contemporary Concern*, Educational studies and documents, No. 28 (Unesco, Paris, 1978), p. 53.

control, tradition, and values.[4] Related generalisations appropriate to the age level were used to develop units ranging from such traditional topics as 'the family' in the first year to 'the world' in the final year.

The Social Studies Center at the University of the Philippines advocates a conceptual approach to social studies for the purpose of selecting and organising curriculum content. The Philippine social studies programme places emphasis upon concepts and generalisations for the development of organising themes which, taken together, comprise the organising framework for social studies in that country. However, this does not mean eliminating facts. According to Dr Leticia S. Constantino,

> Facts serve as building blocks for the formation of concepts and generalisations . . . It is simply impossible for the human mind to contend with the explosion of knowledge. So if the aimless memorisation of isolated facts is to be minimised, the fundamental ideas or concepts and generalisations of each major branch of knowledge need to be identified; and learning should be geared to conceptual structure.[5]

In the Philippines the scope of the social studies curriculum is determined by the concepts and generalisations selected to constitute the conceptual framework, whilst the social studies sequence is provided by the spiral development of the concepts and generalisations. Skills and values, as integral parts of the conceptual framework, are treated in the same spiral fashion. The basic concepts are divided into sub-concepts and the generalisations into sub-ideas expressed in terms suitable to the ability of pupils at each grade level.

Integration through Unification

Ideally, the most complete form of integration would be total unification, leading to the emergence of an entirely new discipline. Such a discipline would be constructed on the shoulders of the existing ones, but it would also employ concepts and perspectives not currently used by any of the existing disciplines. Thus, social studies would no longer be forced to create practical instructional applications based upon borrowings from other fields; it would become a new discipline with its own scientific methods, procedures, conceptual frameworks and knowledge.

Alfred Kuhn is a leader in the effort to create a unified social science. He has 'discovered concepts and relationships that exist in one or more of the social sciences (usually under different guises) and generalised them across his unified body of social sciences'.[6] Another proponent of the unified approach, Kenneth Boulding, employs systems analysis to present an overall view of the world and society, using concepts and relationships that are new to the social sciences rather than being drawn from them. He believes, however, that if we look closely at the various social sciences, it becomes clear that they are all studying the same thing and all are operating at the same systems level.

> The economist, the political scientist, the anthropologist, the sociologist and the social psychologist, even the historian and the human geographer are all really studying the same thing which is the sociosphere, that is, the billions of human beings on the earth, all their inputs, interactions, organisations, communications and trans-actions.[7]

These scholars believe that there are concepts and principles that underlie all of the social sciences, providing a foundation for learning about individual disciplines.

The concept of a unified approach appeals to many social studies educators. Some have called for social studies to become a separate academic discipline and to break its dependence upon the traditional disciplines as the primary sources of knowledge. It may be true that future social studies programmes will rest upon a new, unified theory of knowledge, but for the present, less ambitious approaches to an integrated approach to social studies are more probable.

An Example of an Integrated Approach to Social Studies: the Case of Sierra Leone

The Sierra Leone Social Studies Programme, initiated by the author, depends mainly upon integration through the use of social science concepts and generalisations. Social studies is not treated as a separate discipline; nor is any effort made to preserve the integrity of each academic discipline. Rather the curriculum is organised around concepts that facilitate the integration of the various disciplines. These concepts are *Adaptation, Communication, Similarities and Differences, Interdependence, Co-operation, Change, Growth and Development* and *Cause and Effect*. The eight concepts are presented at each grade level in an increasingly sophisticated way appropriate to the cognitive development of children. The programme also employs the notion of an 'expanding environment'. Thus, at the first grade, children learn about

Plate 4: Social Studies Classroom in Freetown, Sierra Leone

The pupils are studying a lesson from the integrated social studies programme established in Sierra Leone.

their most immediate environment, school and home. In the second grade, they study their community, and so on until they learn about the world at grade seven.

A glance at the organisation of the first-level course in social studies, intended for five-year-old and six-year-old children, will help the reader understand more about the programme in Sierra Leone. The entire year is divided into three major units and four sub-units within each of the major units. Four concepts are presented during the first year. They are *adaptation*, treated in Unit One, because it helps students adapt to the unfamiliar school environment; *change* and *similarities and differences*, designed to help link home and school; and *interdependence*, which focuses on the interdependent roles and functions to be discovered within one's own family.

The opening unit of the first-level course clearly has a strong socialisation purpose. The intention is to help students make an easy transition to school, including learning how to get along with the teacher and the peer group.

Some Suggestions for Organising Courses, Units and Lessons in an Integrated Way

There are at least three main ways that teachers typically organise social studies courses, units and lessons when they wish to employ an integrated approach. These are by *topics or themes*, by *fundamental questions*, or by *problems*.

Topics or Themes

Focusing instruction on topics or themes may be the most common approach. Even teachers who organise their courses according to academic disciplines frequently find it useful to plan lessons or units around topics. Secondary school teachers often base history instruction on such topics as the Greek city-states, the Roman Empire, feudalism, the French Revolution and World War Two. Civics teachers plan lessons around such themes as the origins of government, constitutionalism and administration of justice. In the elementary school grades, national heroes, holidays and important historical events are used to focus instruction.

Sometimes entire courses are based upon topics such as those noted above. More frequently, such topics serve as the bases for units or lessons within courses. In planning integrated units or lessons based upon topics teachers typically draw upon whatever information is relevant and available, regardless of the academic discipline, while using a wide variety of instructional media. Although the unit or lesson will ordinarily include concepts and generalisations from various academic disciplines, the focus remains the *topic*, not the academic disciplines from which information was taken.

Fundamental Questions

Fundamental questions can also serve as the basis for organising social studies instruction. Fundamental questions are those that persist over time and perplex people world-wide. Examples of such questions are: who am I? Why am I here? Why are there such differences among people? Why do nations go to war against each other? Why are some people objects of discrimination? These and other fundamental questions cannot be answered simply and with finality, but many social studies specialists believe that a primary purpose of social studies is to help students reflect on such questions.

In 1976, Houghton Mifflin Publishing Company produced an entire social studies textbook series for kindergarten to grade six (five years old to twelve years old) around the question, 'Who am I?' The developers of the textbook series believed that there were at least four dimensions of human identity that should guide social studies instruction. Teachers should help students understand themselves as *individuals*, as *members of groups*, as *human beings* and as *inhabitants of Earth*.

Each textbook in the series and each unit and lesson within a book attempts to enhance this understanding. Students are helped to acquire facts, concepts and generalisations about individuals, groups, human beings and Earth; to develop skills in acquiring, processing and reporting information; and to explore values relating to self, to other people, to the national environment and to uncertainties in the human condition.

Throughout the series the authors have borrowed perspectives, approaches, ideas and methods from various social science disciplines, from the natural sciences and from the humanities. They are blended together so as to be indistinguishable in the final result. But the focus throughout the entire series remains on the fundamental question, 'Who am I?'

Problems

Some social studies teachers organise their instruction around socially significant problems. They believe that one of the main objectives of social studies is to help students understand the social problems of their own time. By focusing on such problems, students must draw concepts, ideas and perspectives from many disciplines. Students may also find themselves cast in the role of a policy-maker, deciding what should be done to alleviate the problem.

Examples of social problems that are sometimes used for organising instruction are: the threat of nuclear warfare, population explosion, environmental pollution, world hunger, violations of human rights and the growing gap between rich and poor nations. While students cannot resolve the problems, they should understand them, learn about efforts to find solutions and lend their support to the most effective and equitable approaches.

In selecting which problems to treat in class, teachers might be guided by three rules.

Rule 1: *The problem must seem real to the student.* Many problems that are important to adults are of little interest to youth. Teachers cannot assume that a particular problem that seems important to adults will be perceived that way by youth. This requires that teachers strive to make each problem real by approaching it in such a way that students can sense its impact on their own lives. One teacher, confronted by students who had never experienced the effects of racial discrimination, began the unit by quietly establishing discriminatory rules in the classroom. Blue-eyed children were given privileges not available to brown-eyed children. The brown-eyed children were first puzzled, then angry. They could not understand why they were being treated unfairly and, when they were told it was because their eyes were brown, they found the explanation to be unreasonable and unfair. Later, the teacher reversed the pattern of discrimination and favoured the brown-eyed children. In the process the teacher caused her students to think seriously about the consequences of racial prejudice because they had felt the effects for a short time on their own lives.

Rule 2: *The problem must be capable of analysis in class.* Some important problems do not lend themselves to class discussion and analysis. Certain subjects may be taboo in particular schools or communities. In other cases students will not have access to reliable information. Devoting attention to problems that cannot be handled adequately can lead to misinformation and negative consequences.

Rule 3: *The problem should be socially significant.* Some problems that are 'real' to students do not deserve serious attention in class.

For example, a particular student may be excessively shy and have trouble making friends. This is of great importance to this individual, but it is not an appropriate topic for social studies. On the other hand, the problem of alienation as a phenomenon of modernisation and urban life is an appropriate topic for discussion. 'Whom should I marry and what should be my lifetime occupation? ' are major personal questions facing people, but the teacher must find a broader base for analysis before these can be considered as part of social studies.

Example: Organising an Activity around a Problem: Population Game

The activity that follows is part of an instructional unit on population. The unit's purpose is to inform students about the facts of population growth in the world today, to teach them about factors that encourage and retard population growth, and to help them consider the implications that follow when a nation elects to adopt a national policy towards population. Beyond these substantive goals the unit seeks to help students understand the consequences of their behaviour on themselves and others. By providing students with knowledge about demographic processes and relationships and by helping them examine the implications of existing trends, the unit points to options that are open, their consequences and the relative advantages and disadvantages of these. Students are encouraged to consider their own values and to make choices that reflect their values, evaluating carefully the likely consequences of their choices.

The activity is a simulation game that assumes the students have some knowledge about the influences upon family size in rural villages. The simulation places the learners in the role of population policy planners. By requiring them to work systematically towards the development of a population programme, the simulation teaches a decision-making process while requiring participants to confront the hard choices necessary to forming a viable population policy.

Simulation Exercise[8]

Overview

This exercise consists of four steps. Each is part of a process for systematically planning a population programme to slow population growth in a less developed country.

Role and Assignment

You are a population expert. You are part of a team helping the government. Your job is to help plan a population programme for villages. The goal is to reduce family size from an average of 5-6 children to an average of 2-3 children.

Step 1: Clarifying the Problem: Time: 5 minutes
         Individual Activity

         State in your own words what the government wants you to do.

         Problem:_____

         _____

         _____

         _____

Step 2: Identifying forces for and against Change: Time: 5 minutes
Phase 1: Individual Activity

Directions: Your goal is to reduce average family size.

         Think about life in a rural village. What things encourage people to want small families? What things discourage small families? On a sheet of paper, make two columns. In one column, list as many things as you can that *encourage* small families. In the other column, list as many things as you can that *discourage* small families.

Phase 2: Generating a Common List: Time: 5-10 minutes
         Group Activity

Directions:

         A. Form a team of two to five experts. Each expert should share his answers to these two questions:

            (1) What things *encourage* small families in a rural village?

            (2) What things *discourage* small families in a rural

village?

B. Prepare a master list of factors that encourage or discourage small families. Column A should contain a list of factors that *encourage* small families. Column B should contain a list of factors that *discourage* small families.

Step 3: Overcoming Obstacles to Change: Time: 5-10 minutes
Group Activity

Directions:

1. Assemble the deck of cards (see page 76).

2. Use this deck for ideas about how to encourage people to have small families.

3. As a team, try to think of one or more activities that might take advantage of each factor listed in Column A. Write these down on a separate sheet of paper.

4. As a team, try to think of one or more activities that might overcome or cancel out each factor listed in Column B. List each activity for overcoming restraints to a small family on a separate sheet of paper.

Step 4: Activity Selection and Programme
Generation: Time: 5-10 minutes
Group Activity

Directions:

A programme is a group of activities selected and organised to achieve a goal. The activities in a programme should work to support one another.

Activities in a programme should be effective by themselves or in combination with other activities. They should not be unreasonably expensive or difficult to carry out and they should be appropriate to the culture.

1. You are now to construct a population programme you would recommend to the government to use in its rural areas.

2. Look at the activities you listed in Step 3. Select those activities you would recommend to the government. Each activity selected *must* be

accepted to *each* member of your group. All
members must agree.

Idea Cards

Do people realise the government's position and the reason behind it?	Posters can convey messages.	Teams can travel through countryside educating and helping people.	People can be paid to undergo sterilisation.
People can be forced to limit their family size.	Attempts can be made to increase career opportunities for women.	Children can be educated about about rapid population growth and its implications.	Some people are more influential in communities.
? ? ?	Fear, suspicion and rumour can undermine efforts to help people.	Many people who want to limit their family size don't know how to do this.	Do people understand how their lives are affected by population changes?
Radio can inform and educate people.	Face-to-face contact is the most effective form of communication.	Lack of knowledge can discourage active behaviour.	The easier it is to obtain services, the more people are likely to take advantage of them.

Conclusion

The integrated approach to social studies may demand more of teachers
than instruction based upon a single discipline. In 1967 the University
of Monash in Australia established a curriculum development project
that drew upon many social science disciplines in the design of a new
social studies programme. After some years of work, the developers
concluded that 'teaching an integrated subject in a coordinated project
has been a stimulating experience',[9] but they admitted that

    teaching units which draw upon several social science disciplines places a considerable responsibility on the teacher. He must ensure that pupils' educational experiences are organised so that they have opportunities to develop a balanced and comprehensive understanding of whatever it is that they are studying and to employ the concepts and techniques of the several social sciences authentically and competently.

An obstacle to encouraging an integrated approach to social studies is that the pre-service training of most teachers does not prepare them adequately for such a task. Typically, primary school teachers gain only a superficial knowledge of the social sciences from their pre-service education; secondary teachers are often prepared in a single discipline, especially history and geography. Neither feels comfortable approaching social studies in an integrated way, although elementary teachers usually show the least resistance.

Whatever obstacles must be overcome, acceptance for teaching social studies in an integrated way, especially in the elementary schools, is growing world-wide. Social studies specialists should consider how this idea might be successfully implemented in their countries.

Notes

1. T.A. Lucan (ed.), *New Programme in Social Studies*, Teachers Guide and Syllabus, Primary One (Social Studies Curriculum Unit, Institute of Education, University of Sierra Leone, Freetown, 1978), p. 2.

2. Irving Morrissett and William Stevens (eds.), *Social Science in the Schools: a Search for Rationale* (Holt, Rinehart and Winston, Inc., New York, 1971), pp. 25-6.

3. *International Understanding at School: Unesco Associated School Project*, No. 32 (Unesco, Paris, 1976), pp. 26-7.

4. Norman E. Wallen, Mary C. Durkin, Jack R. Fraenkel, Anthony J. McNaughton and Enoch I. Swain, *The Taba Curriculum Development Project in Social Studies Final Report* (Addison-Wesley Publishing Company, Menlo Park, California, 1969), pp. 20-3.

5. This idea was expressed by Dr Constantino during a discussion with district supervisors who were participants in a special training programme conducted by the Social Studies Center at Banguio City, Philippines, in 1979.

6. Alfred Kuhn, 'Synthesis of the Social Sciences in the Curriculum' in Morrissett and Stevens, *Social Science in the Schools*, pp. 137-8.

7. Kenneth Boulding, 'What Can We Know and Teach about Social Systems?' in ibid., p. 151.

8. This simulation activity was developed by Dr Jerry Brown of the Agency for Instructional Television, Bloomington, Indiana, for inclusion in this chapter.

9. F.J. Hunt *et al.*, *Social Science and the School Curriculum: a Report on the Monash Project* (Angus and Robertson, Cremorne, New South Wales, 1971), Introduction.

4 THE STUDY OF SOCIAL STUDIES AS A MEANS OF EDUCATING CHILDREN IN A SPIRIT OF PEACE AND MUTUAL UNDERSTANDING AMONG PEOPLES

Zoya A. Malkova

Introduction

The Earth and its inhabitants have been compared to a space ship travelling through time. If it were possible to compute the sum of all past events and plot the direction of spaceship Earth, we would conclude it has been progressive. On the whole mankind has advanced through the ages. The necessary conditions for happiness are available to more people than before and the opportunities for individuals to use their abilities and to live to their full human potential are greater than in earlier times.

Yet the line of development has been uneven. Digressions, difficulties and historic conflicts have sometimes retarded progress. War, launched by a few greedy people with insane ideas about world domination, racial purity and the inferiority of other people, has been the worst enemy of human progress.

Wars are a horrible scourge for mankind, producing suffering, destruction and immense loss of life. It has been estimated that, over the period of 5,500 years, war has erupted in the world 14,500 times, causing the death of some 4 billion people. Each war consumes productive forces, destroys culture and art and sets humanity back many years by retarding its onward march. Moreover, the destructive power of war is increasing steadily. World War One (1914-18) involved dozens of countries and cost some 20 million human lives. World War Two, which was unleashed by Fascism, caused inestimable damage. Thousands of industrial towns were razed to the ground and priceless cultural monuments, schools, theatres and museums were consumed by flames. In the western areas of the Soviet Union, for example, the war completely destroyed industrial enterprises and educational and cultural institutions. Many of the major cities of Poland, Germany and the United Kingdom were bombed into ruins. Atomic bombs reduced the Japanese cities of Hiroshima and Nagasaki to ashes. Indeed, the effects of the atomic bombs are still felt by leukemia victims alive today. All in all, 60 million people may have perished during the six-year-long conflagration.

The close of World War Two did not bring an end to militarism. Nations continue to accumulate weapons and to fan military tension. United Nations experts have calculated that world military expenditure is currently $400 billion per year, or more than $1 billion per day. In the world as a whole, some 25 million men are in uniform, training for destruction, not construction. Contemporary weapons, with their enormous destructive power, have brought the world to the brink of catastrophe. According to United Nations figures, the power of modern weapons, based upon the latest advances in science and technology, are equivalent to that of 1,300,000 atomic bombs of the type dropped on Hiroshima.

War Prevention is of Paramount Importance

The prevention of new wars is mankind's number one task. The fulfilment of that task should be the goal of all peace-loving forces, of all thinking people who feel a responsibility towards future generations.

Some countries have made the consolidation of peace an official policy of the state. For example, the Soviet Union's first act following the Revolution of 1917 was the adoption of a 'Decree on Peace' signed by Lenin. Since then, all of the actions of the USSR have been directed by a policy of peace. The Constitution (Fundamental Law) of the USSR declares that 'the USSR steadfastly pursues a Leninist policy of peace and stands for strengthening the security of nations and broad international cooperation' (Article 28). It defines propaganda for war, violence, racism or chauvinism as a crime against the people. A further example is the Constitution of the German Democratic Republic that states that 'the German Democratic Republic strives for a system of collective security in Europe and a stable order of peace in the world. It commits itself to universal disarmament' (Article 6, para. 3).

Those nations which have made the search for peace an official policy have not been satisfied with merely asserting such a principle. They have also developed national programmes in support of peace, disarmament and international co-operation. In particular, the Soviet Union, which suffered enormous material and human losses in the struggle against Fascism from 1941 to 1945, consistently pursues a programme encompassing the reduction of strategic armaments, a halt to tests of nuclear weapons, the prohibition of the creation of new types of systems of weapons of mass destruction, the implementation of a just and lasting Middle East settlement and other peaceful acts.

A goal of Soviet foreign policy is to preserve peace against all threats of new wars. This officially sanctioned policy regarding the consolidation of peace governs the activities of all institutions and public organisations and shapes the school curricula for Soviet youth.

The United Nations and Unesco Promote Peace

The United Nations and Unesco, international organisations to which the overwhelming majority of the world's countries belong, play an important role in the consolidation of peace. The 'Declaration on the Strengthening of International Security' and many other documents adopted by the United Nations, discussions concerning a treaty prohibiting the use of force in international relations, the preparation of a world disarmament conference and similar actions are important parts of the effort to strengthen world peace.

In their activities to exclude war from human life, the United Nations and Unesco have devoted special attention to the education of young people in a spirit of peace and international understanding. The 'Universal Declaration of Human Rights' adopted by the United Nations states that education 'shall promote understanding, tolerance and friendship among all nations, racial or religious groups, and shall further the activities of the United Nations for the maintenance of peace'. Unesco repeatedly underscored the need to educate children and young people in a spirit of peace. For example, as a result of persistent efforts by peace-loving forces, at its eighteenth session in 1974 the General Conference of Unesco adopted a special 'Recommendation concerning Education for International Understanding, Co-operation and Peace and Education relating to Human Rights and Fundamental Freedoms', which describes in detail the role of educational institutions and all aspects of upbringing in consolidating world peace. The Recommendation states that education

> should bring every person to understand and assume his or her responsibilities for the maintenance of peace. It should contribute to international understanding and strengthening of world peace and to the activities in the struggle against colonialism and neocolonialism in all their forms and manifestations, and against all forms of racialism, fascism, and apartheid as well as other ideologies which breed national and racial hatred.

This document formulated the fundamental principles of education, whose aim should be to prepare people who are capable of renouncing war for aggressive expansionist or hegemonic purposes and committed to removing violence, repression and threat of attack from human existence. The principles in question include the development of a feeling of international solidarity and co-operation and the cultivation in children of respect for all peoples, their cultures, traditions and so on.

Associated Schools Project

As one part of its effort to give substance to its concern, Unesco established the Associated Schools Project. At the present time, there are over 1,300 Associated Schools in 74 Unesco member states. The main goal of the Project is to assist schools in developing new and effective teaching methods, techniques and materials with a view to furthering education for international understanding; and to facilitate the exchange of experiences gained in member states taking part in the Project. Associated Schools focus their activities on four main themes: world problems and the role of the United Nations system in solving them; human rights; other countries and cultures; and man and his environment.

Specific programmes vary from school to school and from nation to nation. In Poland, for example, more than forty Associated Schools make children broadly familiar with other countries both near (for example the USSR, the German Democratic Republic, Czechoslovakia, Yugoslavia) and far (for example India, Japan, the United States). Each year pupils from the Associated Schools in Poland spend their summer holidays in camps with youth from other countries. In these camps they begin or continue foreign language studies while becoming acquainted with the culture and customs of other nations.

The Schools have a Responsibility to Promote a Spirit of Peace

Everyone is familiar with the saying, 'A teacher holds in his hands the key to the future.' Those who quote it emphasise the important role played by general education schools and their staffs in educating young people. After all, it is a fact that schools have an opportunity to reach children and adolescents at an age when they are most susceptible to socialising influences. The future of every country, and of mankind as a whole, depends to a large degree on the views, attitudes, values and standards of behaviour that schools instil in young people who will someday replace the current generation of adults. By providing pupils with a system of knowledge about the world and about the past and present of the human species, by developing the cognitive ability of children and adolescents and by integrating them into social activity and work along with adults, the school shapes the most important element of a human personality: a scientific world-view.

An individual's outlook on the world is a complex phenomenon encompassing the system of opinions, beliefs and ideals that determine his conduct and attitude towards life. Specialists usually distinguish between two levels of human consciousness: scientific, or theoretical, consciousness; and ordinary, or everyday, consciousness, which is the product of an individual's life experience and personal observations. At the level of ordinary consciousness, individuals perceive and evaluate the world in a relatively superficial fashion, taking as a point of departure their own direct needs, with little or no attempt to probe into the essence or the interrelationships of phenomena. Ordinary consciousness is limited and is, as a rule, the source from which spring superstitions, prejudices and erroneous judgements. More often than not it is at the level of ordinary consciousness that specious ideas about other peoples arise, prompting nationalistic prejudices based upon mistaken stereotyped views of other people.

The school's task is to move pupils beyond the limits of ordinary consciousness, developing their scientific consciousness to a level that more deeply and fully reflects objective reality. Scientific consciousness requires the progressing of direct sensory experience, the analysis and statement of general conclusions from the data, and the identification of essential relationships and laws. At the level of scientific consciousness, human beings employ concepts and formulate conclusions and theoretical judgements. Scientific consciousness makes it possible for pupils to acquire an objective picture of the world in evolution, the interrelationship between times and peoples, the causes of war and the conditions for the preservation of world peace.

But while the acquisition of knowledge is basic for a world-view, it does not ensure formation of such a view. A world-view that guides an individual's conduct requires the transformation of knowledge into convictions, unshakeable opinions, attitudes and ideals. Such a transformation is possible only when the individual is motivated to take action in accordance with the concepts already mastered, to behave according to inner conviction and to take an individual position concerning the issue at hand. The education of an internationalist requires that people not only be provided with all the requisite concepts and knowledge, but also that their personal experience be organised, because personal experience is the driving force for emotions and volition and it motivates conduct. The ability of a person to translate principles into action is an indicator of the degree to which his world-view has been completely formed.

Research has shown that the process of forming a world-view is complex and multi-faceted, and varies according to age. In children of early school age, views and attitudes are still unstable and depend largely on the circumstances in which pupils find themselves. A qualitative jump in the formation of views about the world occurs in children about the ages of twelve or thirteen. At this time they not only have larger stores of knowledge, but this knowledge is of a more genuine nature. They are able to use abstract concepts and are capable of elucidating causal relationships and of explaining the inner essence of phenomena. Their views, ideas and attitudes, being more stable, now largely determine their actions and conduct.

Social Studies has a Responsibility to Promote a Spirit of Peace

In fostering internationalism — that is, educating people with a broad outlook and an international view of the world free from nationalistic views and sentiments — the contribution of all school subjects (mathematics, biology, literature, foreign languages and others) is important. But the most important school subject of all is the social studies. History, social science and geography inform pupils about the development of mankind, about its present and its past, about what has befallen various countries and peoples and about their mutual relations and ties. The content of these and other social studies courses has a direct influence on the formation of pupils' scientific world outlook, on their views of the world and on their attitudes to people in their own country and elsewhere.

Careful planning, suitable instructional materials, proper organisation and appropriate teaching methods are all necessary for social studies to achieve its considerable potential for educating children in a spirit of peace and mutual understanding. But the effort will be fruitless unless education for peace and mutual understanding is accepted as a primary goal of the social studies, because this will affect the objectives specified in the syllabuses and influence the teacher's choices of instructional material and the approach to instruction.

Education for peace and mutual understanding is a principal social studies goal in socialist countries. For example, the history syllabus for general education schools in Poland states one of the main goals of history teaching to be: 'Education in a spirit of respect for other peoples and for their cultural achievements; education in a spirit of humanism, tolerance and rapprochement between peoples.' The law known as the 'Fundamentals of Legislation of the USSR and the Union Republics Concerning Public Education' which governs activities of educational establishments declares that one of the main tasks of schools is to promote internationalism. The history syllabus for Soviet schools states that history teaching must lead to the formation of internationalist qualities in pupils. One purpose for teaching history and civics in schools in Czechoslovakia is to establish a feeling of respect for other peoples and to shape an internationalist person. And in the German Democratic Republic, one purpose of social studies is stated as follows: 'Teaching must be aimed at educating pupils in a spirit of respect and friendship for other peoples. Students must understand that all forms of aggression and racial hatred or racial discrimination are inimical to humanity and constitute a crime against it.' Enormous harm is done to the spirit of peace and mutual understanding whenever social studies, directly or indirectly, is used to kindle nationalism and revanchism or to promote a desire to revise state boundaries.

As indicated in Chapter 1, social studies is not the same in all countries. History, social science, law as it relates to individual citizens, sociology, geography and anthropology are some of many school subjects included in the social studies. Despite the great variety of social studies subjects in nearly every country, the most important are history, social science and geography. It is important for the education of children in a spirit of peace that these subjects provide the basic concepts which help them understand the problems of the modern world and determine their own role and responsibility in the effort to prevent war. Instructional material for these courses must present pupils with a scientific explanation of the causes of war, telling them how wars arise and by what factors they are engendered. A world history course must explain to students one of the most fundamental ideas in this field, namely that the causes of war do not reside in the aggressive nature of human beings or in the ill-will of individuals. Wars are a consequence of social relationships based on exploitation. That is how things were in antiquity and in the Middle Ages, and that is how they are in the modern era.

The Role of Textbooks

Textbooks used to teach ancient, modern and contemporary history in schools in Bulgaria, the German Democratic Republic, Hungary, the USSR and other countries contain a large body of material illustrating the inter-connection between wars of expansion and acts of aggression on the one hand, and the exploitative essence of social relations on the other.

By means of an extensive selection of factual material, *Modern History*, a textbook used in the USSR, explains that World War One was provoked by the desire of the ruling classes to redivide the world and to seize territory belonging to others. Because of the selfish aims of an exploitative minority avid for self-enrichment, humanity suffered enormous losses; irreplaceable material and cultural resources were destroyed in the flames of war.

In the German Democratic Republic, Hungary, Czechoslovakia, the USSR and other countries, history textbooks devote considerable space to a section entitled 'The Causes, Nature and Results of the Second World War'. That war caused particular suffering to the peoples of Europe. Many who experienced World War Two, the bloodiest in the history of mankind, are still alive. They can remember its horrors and tribulations. In order to prevent a new and more horrible world war, the younger generation must be given science-based objective answers concerning the causes of World War Two. They should also learn how freedom-loving people joined in an anti-Fascist alliance in the struggle to liberate themselves from the Fascist aggressor.

But social studies should not be restricted solely to explaining the causes of war. Social studies courses must also help youth learn effective means for stamping out war for all time. For this to occur it is important that pupils master one of the basic concepts of historical science: the role of the masses as the real makers of history and the meaning of the individual in history. While they do not overlook the activities of prominent personalities, history textbooks used in socialist countries concentrate on the role of the masses. It is the people who create material and spiritual culture and it is the people who, by their actions, create history and advance human civilisation. Taking as examples the revolutionary movements of the working masses in seventeenth-century England the French Revolution and the American War of Independence in the eighteenth century, social studies teachers point to those actions by the masses that had a substantial influence on the course of history and are the determining factor in consolidating new, more progressive social relations. Textbooks in socialist countries explain that the social transformation carried out by the masses, the foundation for which was laid in Russia in 1917 by the Great October Socialist Revolution, eliminate exploitative classes and the social forces that have an interest in unleashing war.

An understanding of the masses' leading role in history enables youth to believe in the possibility of putting an end to war. It gives meaning to their participation in the peace movement, in protest campaigns against the arms race and in other acts aimed at strengthening peace. History curricula in socialist countries include provision for special lessons on 'The popular peace movement' in which teachers describe ways in which the broad masses of all countries are struggling for lasting peace on our planet.

The entire social studies curriculum must help pupils understand that human progress is incompatible with acts of violence, aggression or oppression of other peoples and that wars cause untold suffering. The history, political science and geography textbooks used in schools in Bulgaria, Czechoslovakia, the German Democratic Republic, Hungary, Poland, Romania, the USSR, Yugoslavia and other countries tell of the incalculable losses suffered by people of those countries during World War Two. Textbooks are not the only source of information for Soviet schoolchildren. In a country that lost 20 million lives, every family lost a relative in the war. The echo of World War Two is still heard, and people still mourn their dead.

Students are Not Limited to Information Contained in Textbooks

Many Soviet schools organise 'follow-up units' or 'hero identification groups'. These groups of pupils record stories and recollections of those living in their region who served in the war, collect documents and photographs of those sad times, and organise school museums honouring the armed forces and workers. For example, in order to create a memorial museum, pupils at the village school in Tsipya (Tatar Republic) worked for several years to collect material about members of the armed forces from their own village who perished in the war against Fascism. They visited families, wrote biographies of the heroes and collected letters sent from the front as well as various other documents. Among the exhibits are 'Memorial Books'. These albums, compiled by the schoolchildren after extensive research, contain photographs and descriptions of the lives of those who died in the war. On Victory Day, widely and solemnly celebrated in the Soviet Union, all of the inhabitants of the village gather in the school courtyard. The 'Memorial Books' are carried reverently out of the museum and the entire population proceeds to the war memorial for a solemn and sorrowful meeting.

Pupils in Polish schools also maintain the memory of those who fell in the war against Fascism. One Victory Day, pupils from the Y. Korchak

School in Klucze planted oak trees in memory of those who had given their lives for freedom and peace.

Use of Primary Sources. In Soviet schools, the portions of textbooks devoted to World War Two and to the destruction that it brought are supplemented by talks by members of the older generation who bore the brunt of all the horrors of that War and the difficulties of the post-war years when the country had to restore its shattered economy. The teachers also use literary works illustrating the suffering and destruction caused by Fascism. War memoirs are a particularly valuable source of material. Soviet pupils take an enormous interest in *Malaya Zemlya* (*Little Land*) and *Vozrozhdenie* (*Renaissance*), two books by Leonid Brezhnev, in which the President of the Presidium, who experienced all the trials of war, vividly and impressively describes the sacrifices and heroism of Soviet citizens as they conquered Fascism and repaired the destruction caused by war.

Films. During class time teachers show documentary films that graphically portray the suffering caused by World War Two. In this respect, the series of films entitled 'Velikaya Otechestvennaya Voina' ('The Great Patriotic War'), including accounts of Fascist atrocities, is of immense educational value. These striking films have also been shown in other countries, including the United States (where they have appeared under the title *The Unknown War*.

Contemporary Material. The inhuman nature of a policy of usurpation and aggression must also be illustrated through the use of contemporary material. The human suffering and massive destruction caused by recent warfare in South-East Asia and elsewhere should be brought home to children's hearts and minds, so that they realise that a policy of aggression, violence and oppression is contrary to mankind's aspirations, causes material damage, misery and loss of life, and must be eliminated for all time.

By citing concrete facts and figures prepared by United Nations agencies, a teacher is able to demonstrate the negative impact of the arms race on human progress. The arms race monopolises resources that could be used to make life better for human beings. For example, one fighter plane costs as much as nine schools, and one tank as much as 36 three-room apartments. The sum required to build one nuclear submarine could pay the costs of educating 16 million children for one year. By halting the arms race, nations could release funds now spent on armaments (more than $1 billion per day) to build kindergartens and schools in such short supply in Asia, Africa and Latin America (where one-third of all children die before the age of five and half the children of school age do not attend school), to provide housing (more than 1 billion people, or one-third of the World's population, live in substandard conditions) and to raise living standards generally.

What is more, the unremitting arms race and the development of increasingly sophisticated weapons of destruction bring our planet ever closer to the brink of disaster. Schoolchildren must be told that man has already accumulated sufficient arms to destroy 35 times over the planet on which he lives.

Despite the risks of war mentioned earlier, the present generation is growing up in relatively peaceful circumstances. Fortunately the majority of the world's children have thus far escaped the horrors of war. That makes it all the more imperative to instil in them, through the use of various teaching aids, the ideas that the planet must be preserved from war and that peace is necessary for progress and happiness. Films, slides and a selection of documents and facts confirming the need to strengthen peace must occupy an important place in the social studies.

Questionnaires. In studying the theme, 'The Movement of People for Peace', the pupils at one Soviet school drew up a questionnaire, entitled 'Why we need peace', and conducted a survey among their fellow pupils, teachers, parents and other inhabitants of their area. Not one of those approached refused to fill in the questionnaire. The collected evidence of people's feelings and thoughts on this question was very encouraging, for all of the respondents agreed that people need peace as much as they need air, food and water. Without peace there can be no life.

The importance of consolidating world peace requires that the social studies teach pupils that the peaceful coexistence of countries with differing social systems, the exclusion for international politics of recourse to violence and the complete elimination of all vestiges of the colonial system and of inequality between nations would decrease the likelihood of wars and aggression. For this reason, the social studies curricula for schools in socialist countries devote special attention to the above goals.

In order for people to apply consistently the principles of peaceful coexistence, they must first overcome feelings of hostility, distrust and prejudice with regard to other nations. Social studies must provide young people with extensive and objective knowledge of the history and contemporary situation of the nations of the world.

Limitations Caused by Inadequate Textbooks and Some Efforts underway to Improve Textbooks

Schoolchildren receive their basic information and ideas about other peoples from history, geography and social science textbooks. Unfortunately, it is still common for textbooks to give only limited information about other nations. The phenomenon of 'Eurocentrism', which causes textbooks to ignore the peoples of Asia and Africa, remains a problem. In some countries world history is not compulsory for all students. In such nations only the initial grades include material on other countries, and then often about only exotic aspects of everyday life, rituals and clothing. Providing children and adolescents with limited information devoid of scientific perspectives leaves them with distorted, stereotyped ideas about other peoples. Still greater harm is done by textbooks that provide biased information about other people in order to promote ideas of superiority, hegemonism, racism and revanchism. In some textbooks one can find maps calling for a revision of established frontiers.

All school textbooks, and particularly those relating to the social studies, must serve the cause of peace by providing pupils with education in a spirit of mutual understanding and respect and by promoting internationalist qualities. Unesco, which attaches enormous importance to textbooks as the form of literature most widely available to young people, has stated in one of its recommendations that 'Member states should promote appropriate measures to ensure that educational aids, especially textbooks, are free from elements liable to give rise to misunderstanding, mistrust, racialist reactions, contempt or hatred with regard to other groups or peoples.' Unesco has also stated that a particularly fruitful means of action to that end is the establishment of bilateral or multilateral committees to study and revise the content of social studies textbooks. Committees of this kind have already been formed and have commenced work in a number of countries. For example, specialists from Poland and the Federal Republic of Germany, working together for several years, have prepared recommendations for the revision of history textbooks. A committee comprising representatives of the Soviet Union and Finland is doing valuable work and has been responsible for introducing a number of corrections in textbook descriptions of the history and current situation of each of those countries.

USSR-United States Textbook Study Project. The USSR and the United States have also established a joint textbook project involving experts from both countries. Following an exchange of history and geography textbooks, experts in the two countries analysed those sections of textbooks that treat respectively the USSR and the United States. They shared the results of their reviews and drew attention to errors and inaccuracies. At a 1979 meeting of the two delegations, they discussed summary reports of the textbook reviews submitted by the leaders of the Soviet and United States groups. They also heard the views of eminent historians on a number of historical problems that are not yet given altogether correct treatment in textbooks. For example, Soviet members of the textbook committee drew attention to United States textbooks' distorted interpretation of the Great October Socialist Revolution, which was the turning-point in the history of Russia. United States specialists pointed to a number of inaccuracies found in Soviet textbooks concerning the description of the regional development of the United States. Despite their differing methodological approaches to the presentation of history and to political opinions, the common concern of the Soviet and United States specialists for the education of young people in a spirit of mutual understanding and trust has enabled them to devise recommendations for the improvement of textbooks and to identify further ways of implementing these recommendations.

Social Studies has a Responsibility to Promote Respect and Understanding for Other People

Educating children in a spirit of internationalism begins by fostering respect and understanding for neighbouring people. Soviet schools have acquired a vast fund of experience in the international education of children, for the USSR is a country which counts among its inhabitants more than 150 different peoples and nationalities. Providing instruction in one's own language is a fundamental principle of the Soviet educational system. In all 15 national republics, each of which is sovereign and has its own ministry of education, schoolchildren study the history of their own people. They are also given a course on the history of the USSR which describes how the USSR came into being and each people's contribution to achievements in science, culture and production. Students learn of the Russian, Ukrainian, Kazak, Georgian, Byelorussian and other peoples' common struggle against

Tsarism on behalf of socialism. Textbooks emphasise the friendship between the Soviet peoples and their unity in laying the foundations of socialism, defending it against Fascism and encouraging the progress of society towards Communism.

An integral part of classroom lessons, various holidays and festivals help pupils learn about their contemporaries from the other republics. Schools frequently hold festivals on the theme 'The Fifteen Republics are Fifteen Sisters.' For these occasions, each class prepares material relating to a republic of its choice. The pupils learn national songs and dances, make national costumes and write reports on the achievements of workers in the republic concerned. The festivals are very colourful occasions and give a great emotional impetus to international education.

Tourist trips, excursions, joint republic summer camps and joint labour brigades all help to promote friendship among adolescents of differing nationalities and are widespread in the Soviet Union.

Textbooks Contribute to Teaching Respect and Understanding of Other People

Soviet schoolchildren are given extensive, science-based information about the peoples of other countries. The intensive history course (which lasts six years and is compulsory for all children) includes ancient history (class 5), history of the Middle Ages (class 6), history of the USSR and recent and contemporary world history (classes 7-10). Textbooks describe the history and current situation of peoples of all continents – Asia, Africa, the Americas, Australia and Europe.

Extensive information about foreign countries and peoples is also given in the history and the geography textbooks used in Bulgaria, Cuba, Czechoslovakia, the German Democratic Republic, Hungary, Mongolia, Poland, Romania and Yugoslavia. The geography and history programme for schools in the German Democratic Republic states that

> Pupils must be made to understand that imperialism is an enemy of the peoples of the world which hinders their progress towards final liberation. Their education must foster respect for the economic and cultural achievements of the peoples of Asia and Africa.

The instructional material is scientifically consistent and is designed to equip pupils with the basic concepts and the scientific world outlook that constitute a firm basis for internationalistic opinions, attitudes and conduct.

The idea of the struggle of the masses for progress and freedom against despotism and social inequality is the *leitmotif* of the material on foreign countries. Textbooks emphasise the heroism of the French masses during their struggle against absolutism, the selflessness of the people of the Netherlands in their protracted rebellion against Spanish domination and the attachment to freedom and the self-denial of the American people when it won independence in the eighteenth century. Considerable space is given to World War Two and to a treatment of each nation's role in that struggle.

Plate 5: Ninth Grade Class in USSR

Soviet secondary school students at PS 45 in Moscow study about people in other countries.

If they are to impart respect for the peoples of other countries, social studies courses must also demonstrate to pupils that every people contributes in some way, however small it may be, to expanding the sum of man's achievements in science, technology and culture. School textbooks in socialist countries contain special sections describing the culture and the technical and scientific achievements of various countries. The history curriculum of Soviet schools provides for the study of culture and science in Western Europe from the fifteenth to the seventeenth centuries (the work of Michelangelo, Raphael and

Leonardo da Vinci, and discoveries of Copernicus, Bruno and Galileo); literature and art throughout the world from the seventeenth to the nineteenth centuries; the culture of Asia and Africa; and other topics.

Textbooks do not ignore present events in helping students gain respect for other people. History and geography textbooks in the German Democratic Republic, for example, make great efforts to familiarise pupils with the current struggle for independence from colonialism and neo-colonialism by the peoples of Asian and African countries. School programmes in the German Democratic Republic stipulate that 'Pupils must be taught to respect the economic and cultural achievements of the peoples of Asia and Africa and their desire to combat the forces of imperialism, hindering the progress of the masses towards final liberation.'

School Museums can Contribute to Promoting Mutual Respect and Understanding

It is not only from textbooks that schoolchildren learn of the French Resistance, the Yugoslav partisans, the Polish peoples' army, the activities of the United Kingdom and United States forces in Europe during 1944-5; almost every Soviet school has a Museum of Military Prowess. Here pupils work as historical researchers. Their motto is 'No one and nothing is forgotten.' Over the years, they collect information and seek out survivors of various conflicts and record their recollections. They recreate in detail the history of military detachments, the exploits of heroes and instances marking the solidarity of people of differing nationalities. In a school in Moscow, for example, the museum is dedicated to the exploits of the Normandy-Niemen Regiment, in which French pilots fought side by side with their Soviet counterparts. Schools in the German Democratic Republic, Poland, Bulgaria and elsewhere have museums dedicated to the exploits of Soviet soldiers who gave their lives to free the peoples of Europe.

Such school museums are not merely an excellent means of activating the learning progress by turning the pupils themselves into researchers. Active investigations also help transform knowledge into convictions, form a life-long internationalist world outlook and promote awareness that freedom and independence are age-old aspirations of all peoples. All people have a highly developed sense of their own dignity and pride; all people deserve respect.

Other Approaches to Teaching a Spirit of Mutual Understanding

Schoolchildren in the USSR receive a great deal of information about newly independent countries from their studies of current events. School history rooms contain large world maps. Each week, pupils take turns presenting reports on international events. Study of the topic 'The World Map' is supplemented by reading works by African poets, by talks by people who have visited Asia or Africa and by photographs and slides.

Some schools follow the practice of compiling an 'oral newspaper' on the subject 'The Struggle and Victory of the Peoples of Asia and Africa'. All pupils take part in this activity by preparing statements, drawings and photographs and by searching for fresh material. Quite often, visitors from Africa who are studying nearby help present the journal. Quiz games like 'Do You Know Africa?' or 'Do You Know India?' are very popular in schools. Pupils study a range of material about the history, geography, economics and cultures of the countries in question and then compete to see who can give the best, most complete answers to questions. Winners receive prizes of books and postcards relating to countries dealt with in the quiz.

When teaching respect for other peoples, it is helpful to familiarise schoolchildren with those people's national heroes and outstanding personalities. Books in the series 'The Lives of Remarkable People' are very popular among Soviet schoolchildren. They recount in a lively and interesting manner the lives of Thomas More, William Shakespeare, Robespierre, Marie Curie, Abraham Lincoln, Thomas A. Edison and many others.

Teachers in Hungary, Poland and other countries evoke student interest in their lessons by arranging 'Collectors' Days'. On these days the pupils bring to their history or civics lessons the stamps or matchbox labels they have collected. These artifacts provide a wealth of material for discussion of other countries' cultural and scientific achievements. The owners of the collections are transformed from solitary specialists into interesting story-tellers who can help the whole class.

In order to increase their pupils' familiarity with people of foreign countries, Soviet teachers often employ the device of 'classroom trips'. For example, pupils in Voronezh (USSR) made such a 'trip' to France. They were divided into groups, each of which made an imaginary visit to a French city. Using encyclopaedias, questionnaires and actual travel accounts, the groups made detailed studies of the cities – their industries, their historical sites and monuments and their educational institutions – and prepared reports illustrated with photographs. During their 'trips' they wrote letters to French schoolchildren who had sent them brochures, tourist maps and other materials providing more detailed information.

Also of interest are the festivals held in many schools on such themes as 'The Music of Our Friends in Africa', 'Contemporary United States Poets', 'The World of French Painters' and 'Drawings by Japanese Children'. For example, schoolchildren in the small city of Kaluga spent much time preparing for a festival of 'The Songs of the Peoples of the World'. They found recordings of some of the songs; others were sent to them by friends in the German Democratic Republic, Hungary, Poland and Finland. The children learned to sing them in the respective national languages and made appropriate national costumes, all of which culminated in a colourful and striking festival they shall remember the rest of their lives.

Social Studies has a Responsibility to Promote a Commitment to International Solidarity

The development of internationalist sentiments and attitudes is closely linked to promoting pupils' understanding of the international solidarity of the working peoples of the world and of their common struggle for peace and security on earth. In socialist countries, the development of international solidarity begins in the primary school. For example, when studying their mother tongue, children in Czechoslovakia memorise a poem about May Day. Their teacher describes to them how that day is dedicated to the brotherly solidarity of working people. They read stories about the lives and friendship of children in various countries and learn children's songs from the German Democratic Republic, Poland, Bulgaria and elsewhere. One song sung by Soviet boys and girls is very popular among children of many other countries. It goes:

The sun is a circle in the sky
In the drawing by the boy,
A drawing done on a paper
Where he wrote in the corner,
'Let there always be a sun!
Let there always be a sky!
Let there always be Mummy!
Let there always be I!'

More complex material for older children supplements and expands the concept of solidarity. In the study of history, the instructional material points to instances in which peoples of varying nationalities joined forces and offered each other solidarity and assistance. For example, history textbooks used in schools in socialist countries give detailed descriptions of the campaign by working people of many countries to support the Soviet Republic in the period 1918-20. Textbooks also describe the international solidarity of people of many lands during the Civil War in Spain, when, in 1936, international brigades comprising French, United States, Soviet, German and British citizens joined Spaniards in their struggle against Fascism. Further, they discuss how nations with different political systems joined in an alliance against Hitler during World War Two.

The present-day world offers an abundance of material that can be used to help schoolchildren understand the importance of human solidarity. Scientific and cultural ties between countries are growing, and the volume of international trade is expanding. Socialist countries are undertaking joint construction projects within the framework of the Council for Mutual Economic Assistance (CMEA). For example, many countries helped to build the 'Friendship' oil pipeline. Workers involved in the project came from the German Democratic Republic, Czechoslovakia, Bulgaria and other countries. In the German Democratic Republic, schools near the construction site took the opportunity to give their pupils a concrete example of international solidarity. They arranged meetings with construction workers; senior pupils actually participated in building the pipeline. Soviet schoolchildren gathered scrap metal for use in making pipes for this project, with each pupil collecting a number of kilograms of metal equal to his age. For schoolchildren, such practical participation in international construction work makes the concept of solidarity tangible and accessible.

By promoting internationalist sentiment and encouraging interest in events in other countries, schools everywhere can inspire their pupils to help those who are in need and to fight against aggression, oppression, racism and discrimination. The credo by which pupils should be guided in studying the contemporary international situation is 'One man's misfortune is the misfortune of all.'

Schools in socialist countries plan activities that help their students recognise their responsibilities to others. For example, schoolchildren in the German Democratic Republic collected funds to assist children in South-East Asia suffering from the consequences of aggression. When they heard of the difficulty of obtaining school supplies in some African countries, pupils in Hungary collected thousands of exercise books, pens and pencils for the benefit of their African counterparts.

Funds collected by Soviet schoolchildren were used to send hundreds of parcels of medical supplies to Romania and Yugoslavia when those countries were hit by earthquakes. Examples of this kind are innumerable.

Human solidarity and co-operation are particularly important in the modern age, when mankind is confronted by such complex global problems as environmental pollution, the depletion of natural energy resources and of raw materials and demographic problems. Despite their complexity, these problems can be solved — a fact that should be emphasised in social studies textbooks — but their resolution will require the joint efforts of people of all countries. In Soviet schools, teachers direct their pupils' attention to common efforts of socialist countries to preserve nature and to joint research by scientists from various countries on ways of conquering space and utilising the world's oceans.

Programmes to Promote Solidarity on Behalf of Peace

But the most important global problem is that of preserving world peace and halting the arms race. As noted earlier, history textbooks in socialist countries contain information about ways to avert wars, about the main principles of peaceful coexistence and about procedures for developing international solidarity in the struggle for peace and against aggression and armed coercion. Textbooks describe the popular campaign for peace and show the various forms it can take, including collecting signatures against nuclear weapons testing and holding international conferences, colloquia or meetings to protest against acts of aggression. But more than books is involved; schoolchildren also take an active part in the peace movement. They hold meetings to protest aggression — meetings to which they come with placards, slogans and photographs they have made denouncing violence, injustice and racism. Such events are particularly frequent during the week designated as 'The Week of the Accusations of Youth Against Imperialism'. To give another example, schoolchildren in the German Democratic Republic form musical groups that perform before various audiences; in song and verse they expose aggressors and urge support for the fight for peace.

Many schools have set up special 'Peace and Friendship Rooms'. In School No. 175 in Moscow, the Peace and Friendship Room has several sections. One section, entitled 'They Have Won Independence,' describes the national liberation movement's struggles and successes against colonialism; the section entitled 'Peace is Fighting, Peace is Winning' contains many documents and photographs bearing witness to various forms of the peace movement; the section entitled 'Your Friends Abroad' displays collections of documents about child and youth organisations abroad, letters and gifts received from the pupils' contemporaries in other countries and works of student art devoted to the struggle of the masses for peace. Exhibits in the Peace and Friendship Room are extensively used in lessons and are constantly supplemented by work completed in the social science course.

Considerable attention is given to studying activities of the United Nations and Unesco in their capacity as international organisations responsible for preserving world peace and strengthening the links between nations. Not content with mere academic study of such activities, schools in Yugoslavia and Hungary organise 'mini-United Nations', where pupils are brought into contact with the work of these influential international organs through practical activities.

Successful Social Studies Instruction must Engage Students in the Learning Process

Teaching social studies for the purpose of promoting peace and understanding among peoples requires more than appropriate course content; it also necessitates the careful combination of various instructional methods directed as stimulating pupils' consciousness and emotions. It is important to make wide use of methods that elicit thought and cognitive activity from pupils. Especially valuable are discussions concerning current problems relating to the preservation of peace, as well as colloquia and various types of dramatised activity such as the holding of mini-United Nations.

Activities carried out independently of the teacher are also important in the educational process. A widespread instructional device used by teachers and described earlier in this chapter is a 'classroom trip', an imaginary expedition by pupils to a foreign country. Together with the teacher, pupils decide on a route for their 'expedition'. They devise a work plan and assign responsibilities. In one Moscow school, pupils conducted a month-long 'expedition' to Czechoslovakia. They studied the natural phenomena along the expeditionary route as well as the history of the sites they 'visited'. They read Czech literature, began the study of the Czech language, sampled Czech culture and corresponded with pupils from schools along their 'route'. By the month's end, they had collected an enormous amount of material and had drafted interesting reports. The following summer, those who had participated in the 'expedition' made a real trip to Czechoslovakia and, following the route they had chosen earlier, met people whom they had known previously only from a distance.

Whatever the students' ages, internationalist education requires methods that appeal to emotions. Seeing films or slides, studying photographs, learning the songs, dances or customs of other peoples, meeting with people who have visited the countries concerned and holding discussions with visitors from foreign countries: all engage pupils' attention and help implant internationalist ideas deep in their hearts and minds.

But intellectual understanding and emotional commitment are not sufficient. Man is also a creature of action. Action promotes the character development of those helping others. It is only through action that the habits of a true internationalist can be formed. Lenin observed that internationalism is not a matter of phrases, of expressions of solidarity or of resolutions, but one of deeds. Therefore, socialist schools believe it necessary to organise a wide range of activities for adolescent pupils in order to strengthen their internationalist sentiments and aspirations by practical activity. Examples of such activities have been described previously in this chapter.

Soviet schools use a number of devices to make activity in the service of peace and solidarity among peoples more constructive and systematic. Often, they establish a 'peace and friendship purse' scheme: during the course of a year, classes in the school fill a 'purse' or money box by undertaking various kinds of activity (working on building sites in order to earn money for the peace fund, planting memorial trees in a 'friendship avenue' or preparing gifts for foreign children).

The 'International Friendship Clubs' found in schools of all socialist countries offer splendid opportunities for organising practial activities. The International Friendship Club in a school in the city of Orel has its own charter, motto and rules. The charter states: 'An internationalist is a friend to the children of all countries, reveres the memory of those who have given their lives in the struggle to liberate mankind, and contributes to the struggle for peace.' The club has several sections: a section devoted to peoples of the USSR, the foreign countries section, a reading group, a publications group and a translators' group. It carries out a wide range of activities complementing history, geography and social studies lessons. Such clubs reinforce classroom instruction.

Conclusion

People need peace. Leonid Brezhnev has said that mankind has had enough of sitting on mountains of weapons. It wants a stable, lasting peace that will allow it to enjoy happiness and progress. But peace cannot be achieved without cultivating respect and mutual understanding for other people. A major goal of the social studies is to promote a spirit of peace and mutual understanding for other people.

5 PLANNING SOCIAL STUDIES INSTRUCTION

David Dufty (case study: John Cleverley)

Social studies teachers should think broadly and deeply about the purposes of education and the contributions their courses offer to the development of young people. Teachers who rarely think about the meaning of their work may become mere technicians; on the other hand, those who cannot convert their purposes into instructional practice may be ineffective dreamers.

This chapter opens with a discussion of goals, because we must consider why we are teaching before we know what to teach. It moves on to procedures, while stressing the relationship between goals and procedures. Then the discussion expands to include the entire curriculum planning process. This process is represented by a model that is later tested in two concluding and contrasting case studies.

Social Studies Goals and Objectives

Goals and objectives give meaning to human activity and help us avoid some of the frustration and waste of resources that accompany confused and non-purposeful behaviour.

The Interdependence of Goals and Objectives

Goals, or aims, are broad, general statements that communicate long-range purposes or intentions. They represent their author's values, or educational philosophy, because they express what is considered worth teaching. Some examples of goal statements are: 'Social studies should prepare students to become responsible and active citizens in their communities' and 'Social studies should promote respect and appreciation of other cultures.'

Objectives are more precise statements of purpose. They may be seen as sub-goals because they indicate what should be taught if the goals are to be achieved. Objectives can be placed on a continuum from broad educational objectives to specific instructional objectives. Instructional objectives often accompany particular classroom activities and are useful in assessing whether instruction has been effective. An example of an instructional objective for a particular lesson is: 'As a result of this lesson, students should be able to explain how a preferential voting system works and to fill in a sample ballot paper.' A specific objective of this type may seem trivial by itself, but it becomes important when understood as one component of a total instructional programme of citizenship education. Thus, goals and objectives go together and support one another. Goals set the overall direction of a programme; objectives mark the steps in the process of achieving each goal.

Goals can be vague and platitudinous; they can also be powerful, permeating ideals. Objectives can be trivial and overly concerned with factual knowledge; they can also provide structure to otherwise confused and unsatisfying units and lessons.

Establishing National and International Goals

Countries with centralised education systems often prepare explicit statements of national education goals. In such countries teachers are expected to use these goals when planning their instruction. In systems where educational decisions are decentralised, greater emphasis is placed on having teachers prepare their own goal statements consistent with generally recognised needs and priorities. Linking stated goals to classroom instruction is no less important when goals are determined locally.

In a centralised education system, an approved syllabus typically prescribes course content and sometimes the teaching methods. Approved textbooks establish further constraints on content and methodology. None the less, most teachers have some degrees of freedom to plan their teaching programmes and to make final choices on specific objectives, content examples, methods of teaching and evaluation procedures.

In some countries, an official state philosophy affects educational goals. For example, the philosophy of Pancasila is paramount in Indonesia. This philosophy consists of five principles:

(1) belief in One Supreme God;
(2) just and civilised humanity;
(3) united Indonesia;
(4) democracy, guided with tactful wisdom through deliberation and representation;
(5) social justice to all people.

While each principle is reflected in every aspect of the educational system, social studies is assigned a special role in implementing this philosophy.

Many countries do not have stated philosophies such as that in Indonesia. In very pluralistic societies, with many minority groups, it may be difficult for educators to determine the goals and priorities shared by most in the society. In the face of such pluralism, governments may be reluctant to state national educational goals.

Educators in Unesco member states may seek educational goals by referring to the ideals contained in such documents as the Universal Declaration of Human Rights, the Declaration of the Rights of the Child and the United Nations Charter. Ideals such as maintaining peace, developing friendly relations among nations, working together to wipe out poverty, disease and ignorance from the world, and promoting respect for human rights and basic freedoms can inspire social studies programmes in all Unesco member countries whatever their systems of government. Drawing attention to shared international aspirations can help students feel that they belong to humankind, that common interests exist not only in their families, peer groups, communities and nations, but among all human beings who must work together to solve common problems. This viewpoint, an essential prerequisite for the survival and well-being of the human species, is worth encouraging in schools.

It is important to have idealistic teachers who feel that their work is contributing to international and national goals, but it is not sufficient merely to advocate an ideal. Teachers must learn to interrelate goals, objectives, methods and evaluation procedures in particular situations, in order to develop consistency between the highest goal and the most detailed classroom task. The case studies described later in the chapter should help clarify this process for teachers.

Kinds of Objectives

Typically teachers think first about knowledge objectives when they begin to plan instruction. While there are many kinds of knowledge objectives, Bloom and his associates have developed a taxonomy of the cognitive domain that helps curriculum planners consider a variety of knowledge outcomes.[1] There are other kinds of legitimate objectives for classroom instruction. Some of these are concerned with feelings and attitudes; others with skills.

A very general goal can be broken down into different kinds of objectives. The goal 'promote international understanding', for example, might include the following objectives:

(1) learning and recalling knowledge about other countries
(2) inquiring into problems relating to other countries
(3) appreciating cultural aspects of other countries
(4) developing skill in relating to people of other countries

Because some educators have separated knowledge (cognitive) objectives and attitudinal (affective) objectives and appear sometimes to give greater priority to one over the other, it is necessary to emphasise that thinking, feeling and doing cannot be rigidly separated but overlap or flow together. George Brown uses the term 'confluent education' to emphasise this process. (See Figure 5.1.)

Figure 5.1: The Relationship among Thinking, Feeling, and Doing

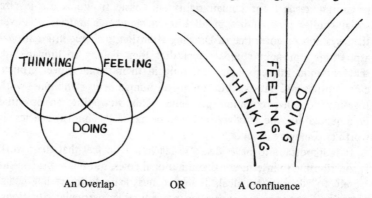

An Overlap   OR   A Confluence

Brown argues that 'whenever one learns intellectually there is an inseparable accompanying emotional dimension. The relationship between intellect and affect is indestructibly symbiotic.'[2] For example, most of the great thinkers and scientists of the world were 'passionately interested' in their subject and their knowledge and passion supplied the energy for their long hours of work. In learning about Cortez in Mexican schools, students' cognitive understanding will be coupled automatically with an emotional response to the Spaniards' destruction of Aztec culture. In almost any endeavour students will acquire both knowledge and feeling about the topic of study.

Any generalised list, such as Bloom's, must be applied to a specific course and ultimately to a specific classroom. For example the Asian Social Studies course used in schools in the State of New South Wales in Australia[3] includes the following affective goals:

(1) awareness of the existence of peoples and civilisations other than one's own;

(2) alertness to, and interest in, current events and social trends in Asia and the world;

(3) a sense of challenge, adventure and enjoyment of life: the development of a lifelong interest in exploring the environment and discovering more about persons and societies in Australia, Asia and the rest of the world;

(4) interest in, and appreciation of, the religions and philosophies of Asia and recognition that there are other value systems and aesthetic standards besides one's own;

(5) interest in, and appreciation of, aspects of the arts in Asia, including music, drama, dance, painting, pottery, handcrafts, architecture, etc.;

(6) a feeling of strong human bonds with peoples of other lands and a sense of neighbourhood of Australia with Asia and of the interdependence of all the world's peoples.

Each teacher should strive to state objectives in the least ambiguous, most achievable way possible. For example, affective objectives in a unit on Indonesia might include:

(1) *becoming aware* of the existence of the unique music of the gamelan orchestra;

(2) *responding* to this unique music, perhaps leading on to genuine enjoyment of the music and even a lifetime interest in the music.

However, one may not necessarily achieve both these objectives. There may be 'awareness' by all but some students may like the music, some may be indifferent, others may dislike the music. The affective domain involves a region of privacy that the school should not necessarily invade, let alone attempt to control.

Good instruction requires a clear sense of direction. Such direction begins with goals. Unless teachers and students know where they want to go, they are likely to wander aimlessly and instruction will prove ineffective because of absence of purpose. Progress towards the achievement of goals is retarded without clear statements of instructional objectives. Each lesson should contribute somehow to course goals. The best way to ensure that this occurs is for teachers to specify lesson objectives that are consistent with and contribute to the unit and course goals. Paying attention to the variety of available objectives and to levels of sophistication among objectives within each domain can help teachers plan instruction so that important dimensions are not slighted.

Plate 6: Australian Student Teachers

Australian student teachers at Darling Downs College of Advanced Education, Queensland, learn to appreciate and perform Indonesian music while their parents and friends gain an initial awareness of Indonesian music.

Clarifying Instructional Procedures

Planning not only involves stating objectives; it also requires choosing methods or procedures to achieve objectives. Because the term 'methods' is used broadly, we shall clarify some basic procedural terms in social studies education to facilitate communication. In the absence of definitions that are recognised in all nations, some stipulated definitions may serve as a useful starting-point for discussion.

Four terms are particularly important. These are *strategy, method, techniques* and *devices.*

Strategy is defined as a combination of methods, techniques and devices used in a particular unit or course to achieve predetermined goals. Strategy refers to the overall plan used by a teacher to guide instruction during a period of time. As an analogue from games, strategy allows changes in procedure to occur as new developments arise in the sequence of teaching and learning events.

Method refers to a particular style of instruction. A teacher using the 'discovery method' or 'the inductive method' will sequence instruction differently from a teacher using an 'expository method' or a 'rule/example method'. Teachers proceeding 'inductively' provide students with evidence in one form or another, while encouraging them to reach their own conclusions based upon the evidence. 'Rule/example' instruction begins with the teacher presenting the 'rule' principle, generalisation or conclusion and then providing examples and illustrations to support the rule. Few teachers use one method exclusively. Good teachers select the method that seems best for the circumstances and is within their general strategy.

Technique refers to specific instructional procedures employed in teaching and learning. Such techniques are many and varied. Checklists can help teachers vary techniques according to the needs and personalities of both students and teachers. Students themselves can participate in choosing techniques for studying a particular topic.

Fraenkel[4] has classified techniques into those concerned with intake of information, with organising data, with demonstrating what has been learned, and creative expression.

Device refers to ideas or objects used to illustrate points in a lesson or to facilitate a teaching strategy. Devices are the tools used for teaching. Technique is the process that employs the tools. The device may be a non-physical one, as in the use of a particular story, poem or historical example, or it may be an actual physical prop such as a map or a display board.

It is important to distinguish between the device and the technique of using the device. Some teachers use filmstrips or pictures purely for narrative purposes. More imaginative teachers will use them for motivation, data gathering, creativity and assessment. Both sets of teachers are using the same device but employing different techniques. In poor countries few manufactured physical devices may be available, but a good teacher can use those available in many ways. Physical devices may be augmented by illustrations from the folklore and literature of the culture and other non-physical devices in order to enrich instruction.

In order to bring these terms into relationship with one another, suppose there is a teacher who is planning a classroom activity on China. The principal lesson *objective* is: 'Students will speculate about factors prompting the cultural revolution in China.' The teacher expects to present data in various forms, asking students to generate hypotheses on the basis of the data (*method*). One piece of evidence is a quotation (*device*) from Mao Tse-tung that will be projected on to a screen (*device*) in order to focus student attention and promote discussion (*technique*). The teacher has planned a series of lessons using various *devices*, *techniques* and *methods* as part of a general *strategy* to encourage greater interest in contemporary China and more knowledge about the world in general (*goal*).

Other Useful Terms. Some other terms that frequently arise in discussions of social studies are *curriculum process* (or curriculum development), *syllabus*, *programme*, *unit*, *instruction*, *lessons* (or activities) and *evaluation*.

The *curriculum process* represents the entire scope of activity that begins with the statement of goals, carries through the selection of content and extends through the actual instruction and the evaluation of the results. Some educators see the process as concerning not only intentional learning (that which is consciously planned) but also the unintended learning (sometimes referred to as the 'hidden curriculum') communicated by everything that occurs in the school. In this chapter we are focusing exclusively on the planned curriculum that typically takes the form of specific courses.

A *syllabus* is a specific document, commonly drawn up by authorised governmental committees, which provides details about prescribed or recommended content, usually in a particular subject area, to be taught by teachers within the system. Some systems have replaced syllabuses with *curriculum guides* that suggest content, techniques and resources rather than prescribe them. Curriculum guides typically place somewhat greater responsibility on the teachers.

A *programme* refers to a detailed plan for teaching a course of study over a period such as a term or a year. A programme is based upon a syllabus, where one exists, or serves in the absence of a syllabus, where syllabuses are not used. Programmes may be developed by teacher committees or by teachers acting alone.

A *unit* is part of a programme, but it has an identity of its own. A typical unit focuses upon a specific topic or theme and requires two or more weeks of study. Unit plans commonly include reference to goals and objectives, content, methods and resources.

Instruction refers to putting plans into practice. An integral part of the curriculum process is what takes place when teachers actually confront pupils with what they are to learn. Better planning usually leads to better instruction. Many teachers devise plans to guide their instruction through a lesson.

Evaluation is an assessment of one or more phases of the curriculum process. Students can be evaluated prior to, during and after instruction. The programme and the instructor are also legitimate objects of evaluation. (See Chapter 10 for more details about evaluation.)

A *lesson* (activity) is a single, planned segment of instruction that occurs during a specified portion of time. A typical secondary school social studies lesson would occur in a single class period. In some cases, a lesson might extend over two days or more. Part of a unit, a lesson usually aims to satisfy one or more instructional objectives that comprise a portion of a unit plan.

Improving Learning and Instruction

Is instruction simply a matter of defining objectives and choosing procedures suggested in textbooks? Do people teach best by instinct or are there expert opinions and research evidence to suggest that some instructional procedures may be better than others? Educational research, like all social research, has many limitations. But, despite these limitations, some conclusions are worth noting.

After reviewing many studies, a United States report[5] concluded that students learn best when teachers give clear directions, show enthusiasm, focus attention on particular tasks and expect task-directed behaviour on the part of students, encourage students to reflect on topics rather than merely dispense information through lectures, praise students for good work, encourage frequent pupil-to-pupil interaction, give adequate opportunity for students to learn the material and provide multiple levels of questions. On the negative side, teacher criticism has been shown to have an adverse effect on student learning.

When teachers' directions are confusing, incomplete or too complex, students have trouble focusing on what they are to learn.[6] 'Advance organisers', i.e. providing a simple introduction to the lesson and what must be learned, have been shown to help direct pupils' study and to contribute to mastering the material.[7]

There is, however, a reaction to an over-emphasis on predetermining everything that happens in the learning situation. While good teachers should strive to achieve their objectives, there are risks in treating learning as if it were a closed system, one in which teachers fail when they are unable to achieve all of their objectives. Unplanned developments can arise during a lesson that contribute to positive, unanticipated consequences. For example, the Humanities Project in England, a social studies project involving students in discussing controversial issues, found to the staff's surprise and delight that use of its materials contributed to improving students' reading performance. This unplanned-for effect may have resulted from the high interest value of the materials.[8] Flexibility and open-mindedness, as well as good forward planning, are desirable in teachers.

Studies of thinking in the classroom show a direct correlation between how a teacher expresses questions and the level of thinking by students; many helpful methods are available to guide teachers in this important task of stimulating thinking.[9] The way teachers respond to answers is also important. Cognitive achievement, attitudes to learning and social skills are improved in classrooms where teachers accept, build upon, clarify, extend, restate or summarise the students' ideas.[10]

One seemingly obvious research conclusion is that if teachers give children a chance to respond to questions by waiting longer, say three to five seconds, there is an increase in student-to-student response and interaction and in the creativeness and speculativeness of the response.[11] Unfortunately, research also indicates that teachers do far too much talking and seldom give students a chance to give adequate responses.

Modelling, or matching behaviour to that of significant others, is an important way that children learn new behaviour.[12] Presumably such teacher qualities as love of history, a vital interest in world affairs or a concern about racism can rub off on some students.

Good teaching is efficient, economical and suited to the

circumstances. Good teaching fits the personality and capacity of the teacher. Today, educators recognise the possibility of developing different models of teaching to fit different teachers as well as different learners. Some teachers and students may work very well in group discussion situations; others may function better with a more individualised learning programme. Many will benefit from a mixture of both.

Putting it All Together

Curriculum design and implementation is a complex human activity. A model that indicates the interrelations among various aspects of the curriculum process can contribute to its understanding.

The following model (Figure 5.2) extends the one found in Chapter 2. Whereas the earlier model was designed to show the factors that influence curriculum decisions (i.e. the selection of educational goals), this model shows what occurs after these judgements are made. And whereas the previous model focused on factors influencing curriculum decision-makers, this model adopts the perspective of the decision-makers themselves.

The model has the following features.

(1) It indicates that the curriculum process is a complex, interactive human activity that may begin with some situational analysis and reflection but is transformed into an all-at-once process requiring ongoing change as new social developments occur and feedback becomes available on one's efforts.

(2) It puts people and their decisions in the forefront, thus stressing the rights and responsibilities of everyone involved, including the students themselves.

(3) It treats instruction as an integral part of a total curriculum process rather than as something quite different from curriculum. Therefore, it stresses the ideas that curriculum is a practical art,[13] involving building as well as designing, politics as well as philosophy, doing as well as thinking and valuing, conflict and compromise as well as co-operation.

(4) It notes that evaluation is not something to be applied only at the end of the curriculum process but a process that is conducted throughout the curriculum process.

Figure 5.2: A Model of the Curriculum Process

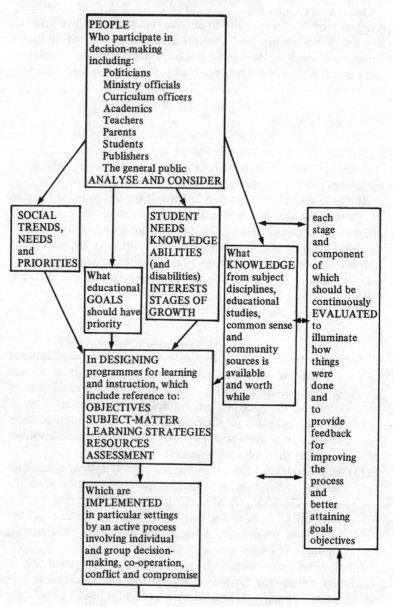

Applying the Model in Particular Settings

Following are two case studies that illustrate the curriculum process at work in real settings. One case study is about efforts to change the curriculum, especially the social studies, in Papua New Guinea. The second treats curriculum development in Australia. The countries are quite different; the general process is much the same. Both serve as applications of the model represented by Figure 5.2.

Case Study 1: Planning a Community Life Course for Elementary Schools in a Developing Country: Papua New Guinea[14]

Analysing the Situation and Involving People. Papua New Guinea has a population of 2.5 million people who live predominantly in rural areas where as many as 700 different languages are spoken. It is a developing country making use of substantial overseas finance to maintain its national budget. At the same time, it has rich national resources and economic potential.

With the coming of independence in 1975 it became a multi-party democracy, and its present leaders are attempting to modernise it without the racking of revolution, entrenched corruption and the crippling outlay of massive defence expenditure. As a former colony it inherited many of its social institutions from the United Kingdom and Australia, including the English language which is the medium of instruction in the national school system, comprising government and mission schools that cater to about 60 per cent of the school-age population.

The nation also inherited a hybrid Australian-New Zealand education system whose output of educated youth was once absorbed easily into the economy. However, many vacancies are now filled and the country, for the first time, faces serious unemployment among high school graduates. Also the wastage rate through the system is high. Semi-educated and unemployed young people, alienated from the village and traditional society, drift to the townships where they compound social problems.

In recent years there has been a flurry of curriculum development activity designed to keep pace with sound educational practice and, just as important, to make the existing system more responsive to community needs. Much of this curriculum activity has been inaugurated by the Papua New Guinea Ministry of Education's Curriculum Unit with its mixed expatriate and local teams under national direction. This Unit has sought to produce syllabuses suited to local conditions.

They have also produced innovative programmes such as the secondary social science course, the first concept-based social science curriculum in the Pacific. The Unit has benefited from the excitement that comes from designing new curricula and the vigour that stems from involving teachers in this process.

Setting Goals. In 1976 the Curriculum Unit began work on a new social studies syllabus for the primary schools, now called community schools. The demand for a new syllabus was both a response to fresh educational thinking about the social studies and an attempt to produce material more relevant to perceived social needs. Thus, the change in the subject was part of a newly articulated set of goals for the community schools whose major aim was to have a school system guided by the government's Eight Point Plan, setting forth the priorities for the nation.

In undertaking reform, the Ministry devoted particular attention to two ideas: schools for rural development and the need for self-reliance. The change of name to community school was to emphasise that education should be related to the community and its activities in order to give students training that would be useful in whatever community they lived and worked. Self-reliance was directed towards strengthening the nation's capacity to support itself. This did not imply that the local community would become the only theme of the curriculum offered in the school, but the local community should become the base from which to lead children outwards to the national and world scene.

Some in the Ministry would probably have liked to relate the activities in these schools even more closely to the local situation than appeared possible. However, they would have met strong parental objection. Parents must pay some costs of their children's education and many parents regard schooling as a form of private investment that will bring a cash return in the future when their children enter the economy. Why waste time on local, practical activities in school, some argue, when the school's job is to prepare their offspring for the white-collar ranks?

The community school syllabuses cover English, Expressive Arts, Health, Mathematics, Physical Education, Science and Community Life; there is also an 'Agreed Syllabus' for Christian education. However, it is understood that only a core of subjects — English, Health, Mathematics and Science — need be common to all schools. The other courses can reflect whatever the community members, through provincial government and school boards of management, wish to have included subject to national approval.

The above statements indicate ways Papua New Guinean schools have attempted to accommodate national goals. They have tried to retain quality as it is typically measured in Western schooling; at the same time they have sought to relate the curriculum to the local situation.

It is necessary to make an important point here: national goals do not themselves determine definite strategies. Papua New Guinea had the choice of many curricular paths to follow in implementing national aims. The path it adopted was based on a complex set of values representing traditional and current pressures.

Designing the Community Life Syllabus. The Community Life Syllabus will replace existing social science syllabuses in grades one to six. Its stated aim is to prepare community school-leavers for the life they will live in a rural community. Therefore, it is more community specific than other elements of the curriculum.

The topics for each grade are organised under five main themes:

(1) individuals;
(2) groups;
(3) environment;
(4) agriculture;
(5) events.

These themes have been developed further in syllabus expansions across the six grades. It is intended that the material should be adapted to local condititons and situations; special provision has been made for this. This syllabus is also designed to permit some instruction in the vernacular language in the first years. Lessons can be introduced in ways that will take account of individual differences among children.

One major problem facing Papua New Guinean teachers in the community schools is how best to translate the syllabus into satisfactory classroom instructional programmes. Because of the hurried nature of the expansion of schools since World War Two, not all teachers have received a full secondary education and teacher training. Many schools are in isolated parts of the country where library and other facilities are minimal or non-existent, and the arrival of supplies from head-quarters is unpredictable. Teachers may be from districts that speak a different language and have quite different customs to those found locally. Visits by specialist staff are infrequent and teachers are thrown back very much on their own resources; the chance to attend in-service training is restricted and time available must be shared among other subjects.

Keeping these considerations in mind, the Ministry decided to introduce teachers' guides in Community Life, prepared under the editorial supervision of Dr J. Cleverley of the University of Sydney and Mr R. Hunter of Mt. Gravatt College of Advanced Education, Brisbane. These handbooks are designed to help teachers prepare their day-to-day lessons and to provide additional resources to support the new subject. Under the co-ordination of staff of the Curriculum Unit of the Ministry, work groups of teachers, teachers' college lecturers, inspectors and university staff were established to collect and organise data. The guides were designed to be published by the Curriculum Unit itself, in a low-cost format, printed on the Ministry's press.

While the basic lesson outlines were carefully planned in regard to goals, attitudes, materials, pupil activity, illustrations and follow-up points, the final shape has an integrated form. The language is direct and purposeful, pupil activities are clearly outlined and further ideas and resources indicated. The contents are illustrated and stories, games and other activities are included. The work has a uniquely Papua New Guinean flavour. The compilers believe that the handbooks should be interesting to read and attractive to the eye so that teachers will be encouraged to use them. It is not intended that the teachers should follow them slavishly, but that sections of them, or individual pages, be drawn upon when necessary. (See Figure 5.3.)

Implementing and Evaluating. Specimen pages and a rationale were circulated for comment during National Inservice Week. The intention was to give a range of people an opportunity to express their opinions before the handbook was actually printed. It is anticipated that a picture kit, pupil materials and radio broadcasts will be developed as well.

A further factor has given impetus to the project. Since the beginning of 1978, certain provinces in Papua New Guinea have received authority to extend their control over schooling. They can determine the opening and staffing of primary schools, high schools and vocational centres, and can produce their own teaching materials and textbooks subject to national approval. Under these circumstances, it is in the interest of national and provincial governments that well planned and executed

Figure 5.3: A Page from the Draft Teachers' Guide for the Papua New Guinea Community Life Syllabus for Grade One*

Agriculture

[garden story]

Get a story teller (a visitor to the school)
to tell the class a story about a garden.
This could be in the vernacular or in English.
Make sure that you listen to the story first
so that you know that it is suitable. It should
not be too long.

Let the children sit around the story teller and
ask questions afterwards. They could hear the
story in the house of the story teller or invite
him or her to the school. If the story has a name
print it on the blackboard. Let the children repeat
it.

Afterwards split the class into groups and
let one child tell the others a part of the story.
The teacher and the class should listen carefully
to the story teller.

* Reprinted by permission of the Papua New Guinea Ministry of Education.

materials be at hand.

The Community Life teachers' guides and materials should be useful. Provinces will be free to employ these materials or modify them to suit their educational context. Their usefulness will be determined in part by the market-place; if administrators and teachers find that the project suits local needs, it should have heavy adoption. If, on the other hand, they are willing and able to produce competing materials, these would themselves represent a form of project evaluation.

The project also provides the opportunity for individual teachers, field supervisors and teachers' college staff to respond to the materials. Lastly, the comparatively low print run and the ease with which the format can be changed will allow early and reasonably economic revision. Current evaluation is thus of a formative variety aimed at constant improvement of present syllabuses and resources.

Commentary. This case study illustrates the curriculum process model by showing the number of people who were involved in the curriculum process. It indicates how social needs and priorities, as well as the needs of children in a changing society, were taken into account when designing the school courses. Knowledge was drawn not only from academic sources but from community members who knew the history, customs and arts of the region. Designs and objectives are important but the curriculum process is also a practical art that is carried on in unique social settings and may involve initiatives and decisions which the designers never envisaged.

Case Study 2: Planning Social Studies Courses in a Pluralistic, 'Post-industrial' Society: Australia

This case study is aimed not so much at applying the model to describe established courses but in using the model in the creative process of designing new courses to meet the needs of today's, and hopefully tomorrow's, students. Examples will be drawn particularly from New South Wales in Australia.

Analysing the Situation and Involving People. Human settlement in Australia began some 40,000 years ago with the coming of the first Aboriginal people, not in 1788 with the coming of the British. The British brought both convicts and free settlers to the new country who farmed and grazed the land which they appropriated from the Aboriginal people. The British also established capital cities on the coast where the majority of the population clustered, and commerce and industry expanded. Decision-making in commerce, industry, government and education tended to be centred in these capital cities, including the federal capital established inland in Canberra.

The British established a dual system of state and private schools, providing an ongoing tradition of independence and pluralism. This freedom was somewhat tempered, however, by a system of public examinations strongly influenced by the universities.

In more recent years, people have challenged the centralisation of government, education and curriculum development. Educational regions have been formed, public examinations abolished at junior levels and parents given some reason to become more interested in schools. Teachers have been encouraged to become active in school-based curriculum development and open and alternative schools have become more common. At the time of writing, however, there is a conservative reaction against such trends and a demand by many people for a return to 'basics' and a reintroduction of public examinations.

Even this reaction, however, reflects a greater public interest in education and in planning for the future.

The curriculum process notes the importance of permitting many voices to be heard in the curriculum process, including students themselves. Students face a different world from that which their parents and teachers encountered when they left school and student viewpoints must be heard. The many other groups also taking an active interest in curriculum development include parents' associations, trade unions, employers' associations, law societies, consumer organisations, migrant associations, environmental groups and, very important, Aboriginal associations.

Australia's population consists of many ethnic groups with varied cultural backgrounds. There are about one hundred different languages and dialects spoken within Australia. As a result of the post-war migration program, over 20 per cent of Australia's current population was born overseas and over half of these people arrived from countries with very different languages and cultures.

Migrant Services and Programs (Australian Government Printing Service, Canberra, 1978), p. 3.

Australia can no longer be perceived as a homogeneous, British-descended, colonial outpost, but rather as a pluralistic, polyethnic society set in the Asia-Pacific region. Such a reorientation has important implications for the curriculum. Of even greater significance is the high level of inflation and unemployment Australia is experiencing together with many other 'post-industrial' nations.

The current economic situation particularly affects youth leaving school, some of whom face a prospect of certain unemployment. A recent, major report has criticised the narrow academic nature of much of our education and called for technical and lifelong education.[15]

What Knowledge? What knowledge do young (and older) people need in such changing circumstances?

The Australian Council for Educational Research undertook a major study in 1975 to try to answer the question: 'Is there a body of learning about society and about living in society that can be considered to be not merely desirable but essential?' A sample population of teacher educators, curriculum consultants, academic social scientists, school teachers, trade unions, employers and politicians was asked to fill in a questionnaire probing this basic question.

Figure 5.4 shows the framework that was developed as a result of this investigation.[16] The strongest public support was for knowledge relating to inquiry and decision-making skills, personal development and skills of social interaction. Informational and conceptual knowledge generally received less support, especially knowledge dealing with specific subject-matter. The exceptions were items thought to have a direct relevance to everyday living in society. Of course, there may be a gap between ideals and practice since traditional subjects and specific subject-matter are very much a part of the social studies in Australia.

Goals for Tomorrow. The setting of goals involves a process of dreaming, of imagining possible futures and not just the stating of behavioural objectives. The concept of Australia as a 'Multicultural Society' is one of these dreams. In a sense, Australia is already a multicultural society but in another sense this remains an ideal. If a multicultural society is defined as 'a society where separate groups co-exist harmoniously, secure in their distinctive biological, religious, linguistic or social customs, equal in their accessibility to natural resources, civil rights and political power and sharing particular values with the rest of society',[17] then Australia has not yet achieved its goal.

Another important goal is that of helping young people adjust to rapid technological change: encouraging them to be flexible in their thinking and in their aspirations, for many people may have to change jobs several times during their lifetime.

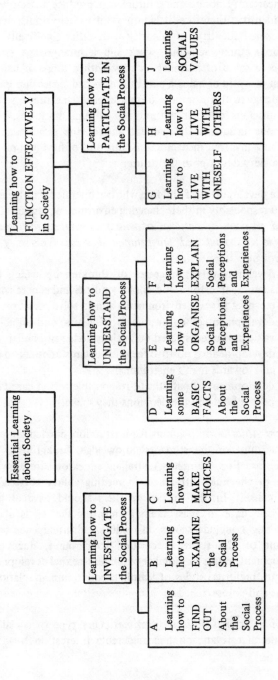

Figure 5.4: A Framework for the Formulation of Key Items of Social Learning

Uncertainty about one's future can produce insecurity as to one's own identity; therefore, it is important to help youth develop a sense of personal identity, of identity with other significant social groups including ethnic, religious, work and leisure groups, and, finally, to balance a sense of national identity with a sense of belonging to the human race and of being a part of life aboard 'spaceship Earth'.

Related to this is a sense of past, present and future so that students are conscious of their natural and cultural heritages, of how these traditions influence the present and of the creative possibilities of becoming involved in decision-making and of having some influence on how society develops in the future.

The development of children who can operate flexibly, autonomously and responsibly in their changing environment requires the *formation and creation of patterns of thinking, valuing, feeling and acting in personal, social and environmental areas.* This may be achieved through:

development of processes of thinking by which children can acquire, transform and apply concepts and generalizations to give meaning to their environments and to solve social problems:

development of an awareness of values, and an ability to make value judgements based on both evidence and belief;

development of positive feelings towards oneself and other people, and towards man's environment;

development of patterns of responsible action based on the values people hold and the decisions they make.[18]

Student Abilities. In planning for instruction, curriculum planners must take account of the students' knowledge, background, abilities and disabilities. For example, Australian educators are slowly becoming aware of the huge differences in reading ability between and within their classes. In the future, teachers should have at hand varying diagnostic data to assist them in meeting the needs of their pupils. These might include scores on reading and intelligence tests that take account of the student's cultural background, stages of cognitive development, stages of moral development, sexual development, identity strength, preferred styles of learning, skill in human relations and other factors still unresearched.

Designing Living Skills Programmes. One type of social studies pro-gramme that is attracting considerable interest in New South Wales and other states is the Life Skills or Living Skills programme, seen by many as very important for young people as they attempt to cope with contemporary society. These courses are part of a core of personal and social education that each student should acquire in addition to other existing social subjects.

While traditional subjects are usually designed by centralised syllabus committees, most Living Skills courses have been prepared as exercises in school-based curriculum development, sometimes with the assistance of curriculum consultants and sometimes supported by grants from a national body, called the Schools Commission, which encourages innovatory programmes.[19]

While they are not linked to a single discipline, such as geography or history, Living Skills courses draw upon relevant academic disciplines; and they also depend upon a number of other knowledge sources as suggested in Figure 5.5.

Figure 5.5: People Contributing to Living Skills Programmes

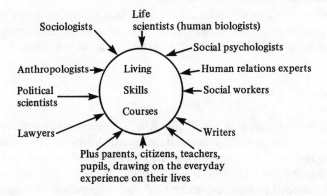

In addition to the more socially oriented topics illustrated above, many courses deal with such topics as health and sex education. In the latter case parents are consulted before courses are taught.

Implementing and Evaluating. The success of such programmes depends very greatly on close co-operation with other members of the staff and also on gaining the support of the parents and the local community. For example, at Henry Kendall High School, Gosford, New South Wales, the process began by circulating a draft outline to all members of staff.[20] Following their comments, a more detailed syllabus was developed. This was presented for comments to the Parents and Friends Association, who received it favourably.

The Programme was taught by those staff who were genuinely interested in the ideas. Efforts were made through discussions and surveys to ensure student participation in the programme. Teachers invited people from the community to speak to the classes and gathered information on such topics as current job opportunities. The local press, radio and television gave the programme favourable coverage. Living Skills teachers taught in-service courses for teachers from other schools in order to share their ideas and stimulate further interest. The course was evaluated by the staff and by external assessors. The programme's success depends not so much on the factual knowledge possessed by pupils at the end of the course but on their knowing how to seek answers to problems when a critical situation arises in life. While this is a difficult assessment problem, Henry Kendall's students leave with a valuable dossier of resource materials for later reference as well as considerable experience in such practical exercises as filling in job applications and maintaining budgets.

Of course, new courses create conflicts within schools when existing interests are threatened; handling such conflicts and seeking compromises are part of the practical skills needed in curriculum implementation.

Conclusion

Planning for social studies instruction is a complex human activity encompassing many diverse elements, from the establishment of national goals designed by politicians to the daily activities of the youngest child in the classroom. Those who are engaged in this activity should be aware of the total process and understand their responsibility for and contribution to this significant social activity.

The curriculum process model, shown on page 112, is intended to clarify this complex process and indicate the various roles people perform in the activity. The model also serves as a reminder that the education is a part of the social system and that every social studies programme must be related to the special character of its society and time.

Terminology, models and research can provide the reader with only a superficial understanding of the curriculum process. The best way to learn how to plan successfully for social studies instruction is to become involved in this theoretical and practical art.

Notes

1. B.S. Bloom *et al.*, *Taxonomy of Educational Objectives, Handbook I: Cognitive Domain* (David McKay, New York, 1956). A taxonomy of affective objectives followed later. D.R. Krathwohl *et al.*, *Taxonomy of Educational Objectives, Handbook II: Affective Domain* (David McKay, New York, 1964). Others have developed objectives that take advantage of Bloom's work but serve as variations on it. See for example, H. Taba, *Curriculum Development: Theory and Practice* (Harcourt Brace and World, New York, 1962).

2. G.A. Brown, *Human Teaching for Human Learning: an Introduction to Confluent Education* (The Viking Press, New York, 1972), p. 11.

3. Sydney, Board of Secondary School Studies, 1967.

4. Jack Fraenkel, *Helping Students Think and Value* (Prentice-Hall, Englewood Cliffs, NJ, 1973).

5. 'The Use of Direct Observation to Study Teaching' in R. Travers (ed.), *Second Handbook of Research on Teaching* (Rand McNally, Chicago, 1973) and as reported in T.L. Good *et al.*, *Teachers Make a Difference* (Holt, Rinehart and Winston, New York, 1975), pp. 58-9.

6. J. Kounin, *Discipline and Group Management in the Classrooms* (Holt, Rinehart and Winston, New York, 1970) and G. Dalis, 'Effect of Precise Objectives upon Student Achievement in Health Education', *Journal of Education*, vol. 39 (1970), pp. 20-3.

7. D.P. Ausubel, *The Psychology of Meaningful Verbal Learning* (Crune and Stratton, New York, 1963).

8. D. Hamingsen, *Towards Judgment* (Centre for Applied Research in Education, Norwich, England, 1973).

9. See materials developed by the Taba Social Studies Curriculum Project and published by Addison-Wesley Publishing Company, and handbooks to the *Man: a Course of Study Program*, published by the Education Development Center.

10. Ned Flanders, 'Teacher Effectiveness' in R. Ebel (ed.), *Encyclopaedia of Educational Research*, 4th edn. (Macmillan, Toronto, 1970).

11. M. Rowe, 'Wait-time and Rewards as Instructional Variable. Their Influence on Language, Logic and Fate Control: Part One. Wait-Time', *Journal of Research in Science Teaching*, vol. 11, no. 2 (1974), pp. 81-94.

12. A Bandura, 'The Role of Initiation in Personality Development', *Journal of Nursery Education*, vol. 18, no. 3 (April 1963), pp. 207-15.

13. J.J. Schwab, 'The Practical: a Language for Curriculum', *School Review*, vol. 78, no. 1 (November 1969), pp. 1-24.

14. For further information on Papua New Guinea, see J. Cleverley and C. Wescombe, *Papua New Guinea: Guide to Sources in Education* (Sydney University Press, Sydney, 1979).

15. *Report of the National Inquiry into Education and Training* (Government Printer, Canberra, 1979).

16. K. Piper, *Essential Learning about Society* (ACER, Hawthorn, Victoria, 1977).

17. 'Education for a Multicultural Australia: Rationale and Framework', paper prepared by M. Skilbeck (Curriculum Development Centre, Canberra, 1978).

18. From the *Social Studies Guidelines for N.S.W. Primary Schools* (Department of Education, Sydney, 1975), p. 7.

19. See G. Andrews (ed.), *School Based Decision Making Some N.S.W. Case Studies* (Schools Commission, Sydney, 1979).

20. *Living Skills Syllabus and Notes on Implementation* (Henry Kendall High School, Gosford, NSW, 1976).

PART TWO:

IMPLEMENTING A SOCIAL STUDIES PROGRAMME

INTRODUCTION

Whereas Part One was directed primarily at those who are responsible for planning social studies programmes, Part Two is aimed at those who must put social studies programmes into practice: classroom teachers and teacher educators. Part One emphasised goals, purposes and general approaches to social studies. This section focuses on teaching practices, guides to instruction and classroom activities.

Chapter 6, 'Concepts, Generalisations and Social Studies', discusses concepts and generalisations — what they are and how they can be taught most effectively at all levels of schooling. Whether one organises instruction around academic subjects or uses an integrated approach to social studies, teaching concepts and generalisations is a major responsibility of all social studies instructors.

Chapter 7, 'Essential Skills in Social Studies', provides a set of categories for thinking about essential skills in social studies and offers suggestions for teaching them effectively in both elementary and secondary schools. Sample classroom activities accompany each major skill category.

In Chapter 8, 'Values, Moral Education and Social Studies', the authors confront one of the most difficult dilemmas facing social studies teachers: should values be taught in social studies? If so, which values? And how can values be taught properly without contributing to ethical relativism on the one hand or engaging in indoctrination on the other? After providing a general discussion of values, the authors concentrate specifically on moral education and its role in the social studies curriculum.

Chapter 9, 'Multi-media Instructional Materials and Social Studies', is filled with specific information about the use of a wide variety of media that enhance social studies instruction. Along with ideas for how to take greater advantage of commercial media, the authors provide suggestions for ways in which teachers can produce their own inexpensive instructional materials.

Chapter 10, 'Evaluation in Social Studies', contains suggestions for diagnostic, formative and summative evaluation. The author offers guidelines on test selection, test preparation and interpretation of test results. The chapter deals with both student and programme evaluation.

Chapter 11, 'Teacher Education in Social Studies', discusses pre-service and in-service teacher education world-wide. Following a discussion of some general problems affecting teacher education in many countries, the authors present case studies describing efforts to introduce or improve social studies in selected nations.

6 CONCEPTS, GENERALISATIONS AND SOCIAL STUDIES

Howard D. Mehlinger

Introduction

Imagine that you are listening to your radio. As you turn the dial, you hear an excited voice:

'Kempes brings the ball down and there's a light touch to Passarella. But look out, here comes Bonhof in there. He takes the ball away, and he's sending the long ball down the right side. Müller takes it on the run and bears down toward the goal. Here comes Bertoni and — Come on now! What a horrible foul! Müller's on the ground rolling around in pain. Bertoni's not happy either, especially since he's being shown the yellow card.

'The stands are full for this friendly match between Argentina and West Germany. — Bonhof'll take the direct kick, and — wow! — what a shot! It hit the far post and bounced out. What a kick! Now, we can see why only Bonhof takes those direct kicks for the West German side. Score still one-all.

'The ball's being lined up by the goalie and out it goes. It's a long high one. Kempes is on it and with a cunning heelpass sends it down the right side to Ardiles — and he's going to take on the fullback right down the centre. Hello, there's a whistle on the play. You won't believe this but the ref is calling a penalty. Russman obstructed Ardiles. The crowd's not happy about that one, especially Russman. Look at him gesticulate, but it won't work. The Argentines'll get the penalty. The Argentines are going wild. Kempes gets ready and — there it is! But Meier got a finger on it. Kempes can't believe it. He's distraught!'

Every soccer fan will recognise the description at once. Others, unfamiliar with soccer, will learn little from the narrative except that it is a description of some kind of contest between Argentina and the Federal Republic of Germany.

Why do some gain more from the narrative than others? It is because soccer fans understand 'soccer language'. Terms such as 'take the direct hit', 'score one-all', 'cunning heelpass' and 'whistle on the play' convey meaning. Listening to a radio, soccer fans can imagine the action as it is taking place on the field, although their only connection to the match is the announcer's voice. Those who do not know the terms and their various relationships might as well be listening to a foreign language broadcast.

While few social studies teachers believe it necessary or important to teach their pupils about soccer, all help students acquire other terms (*concepts*) and statements (*generalisations*) enabling them to derive greater meaning from their experience. Consider the following quotation on a topic that lies much closer to the mission of social studies:

> Justice is the first virtue of social institutions, as truth is of systems of thought. A theory however elegant and economical must be rejected or revised if it is untrue; likewise laws and institutions no matter how efficient and well-arranged must be reformed or abolished if they are unjust. Each person possesses an inviolability founded on justice that even the welfare of society as a whole cannot override. For this reason justice denies that the loss of freedom for some is made right by a greater good shared by others. It does not allow that the sacrifices imposed on a few are outweighed by the larger sum of advantages enjoyed by many. Therefore in a just society the liberties of equal citizenship are taken as settled; the rights secured by justice are not subject to political bargaining or to the calculus of social interests. The only thing that permits us to acquiesce in an erroneous theory is the lack of a better one; analogously, an injustice is tolerable only when it is necessary to avoid an even greater injustice. Being first virtues of human activities, truth and justice are uncompromising.[1]

This simple, elegant passage is full of meaning to those who know the concepts and have the knowledge to grasp the generalisations. To naïve pupils the passage would be as puzzling as the hypothetical radio broadcast to those unfamiliar with soccer. Yet, *concepts* such as 'justice' and *generalisations* such as 'Justice is the first virtue of social institutions' comprise a major portion of the content of a social studies programme.

A principal task of social studies teachers is to enrich their pupils' store of concepts and generalisations about society and human affairs. Just as a soccer fan speaks confidently about 'heelpasses' and 'direct kicks', so social studies students should be able to comment appropriately on 'social revolution', 'economic growth' and 'alienation'. And while soccer fans can offer generalisations that evaluate the performance of teams and predict the outcome of the World Cup, social studies students should be able to state generalisations about election results and demographic trends.

Pupils should improve their use of familiar concepts and acquire new ones. They should learn to evaluate generalisations constructed by others and develop their own. This chapter will suggest some ways in which social studies concepts and generalisations can be taught successfully.

Nature of Concepts and Generalisations

Before examining how best to teach concepts and generalisations, we should first establish what these terms mean. This will not be as easy as it may appear.

Definition of a Concept

A concept is a term used to group objects, events and processes which share essential characteristics. A concept is a category that makes a general case from many special instances. The term 'mountains' is a concept; the Alps Mountains are a particular instance of the concept mountain.

Some concepts are rather easily defined; others are not. 'Triangle' is an example of a concept whose 'essential characteristics' are readily described. A triangle is a three-sided plane figure, the sum of whose angles equals $180°$. All and only those figures that satisfy this definition can be correctly called triangles. On the basis of this definition, it is rather easy to distinguish triangles from squares, rectangles, circles and cones.

Other concepts defy easy definition. In such cases it is necessary to identify the various ways the concept can be used. To *know a concept* of this type means an ability to understand its various uses and to be able to use it appropriately in relevant circumstances. 'Love' is such a concept. What are the essential attributes of love, i.e. its defining characteristics? A man may claim to love his wife, his son, his brother, his job, his automobile, his country, his dog and classical music. Love has a somewhat different meaning in each case. All imply a positive, affectionate attitude towards an object, but the nature and degree of feelings are quite different. No single definition of love is likely to be sufficient; having a complete concept of love requires knowing the variety of ways in which the concept can be properly used.

Concepts can be taught and their use judged. Concepts cannot be true or false but they are used correctly or incorrectly. Women, wives, mothers and widows are all concepts. Given a population representing men and women of all ages, it is possible to group people according to these four concepts. For example, all men can be excluded because they lack one essential attribute of each of the four concepts. A person who is confused and uses the term 'mother' to refer to the male head of a family is wrong. Infant girls are likely to fit only the concept women. A particular adult woman could conceivably fit all four categories.

Some of the four concepts are easily defined. A woman cannot be a widow without first being married. The concept 'mother', on the other hand, cannot be defined so readily. Must a mother be married? Must a mother bear children or can a woman be a mother to the children borne by another? Does one cease to be a mother when children leave home or if children die? Can one be a mother to adults? The term mother is used in so many ways that no single definition adequately captures its essential characteristics.

People may use the same term while holding the concept at various levels of meaning. These levels of meaning are affected by age, experience, training and culture. A girl, playing with her dolls, may be acting out the role of 'mother', but her understanding of the concept will grow significantly when she matures and has actual children of her own. A person whose mother died at an early age or whose mother deserted him will hold a somewhat different conception of mother from one whose experience with a mother was happier. A doctor or another specialist who has been trained to work with mothers understands the process of being a mother differently from one who lacks such training. And different cultures place different expectations on the role of mother. To a degree everyone has a personal understanding of the concepts they share with others.

There are two sources of concepts in language. Some concepts are part of the culture and are passed on from one generation to another. These 'ordinary' concepts are part of the culture that must be learned by every person who is to participate adequately in it. Mother, father, child, brother, sister, family: these are concepts that a child learns early in life as part of learning the language. Confusions occur, but they are quickly corrected; and children learn to use the concept appropriately. Soon, when a friend introduces an adult as 'my mother' or 'my uncle', the child understands the relationship between the friend and the adult.

Some concepts are 'invented'.[2] The reason concepts are invented may be to draw attention to a phenomena that may have passed unnoticed before or to define a process more precisely. In order to invent a concept, it is not necessary to coin a new term. Often, a familiar word will do; it merely requires a new and more technical definition. Sometimes, the new meaning is close to the more general meaning. In other cases it is not, as for example, when the term 'love' is employed in tennis. 'Love' is part of the scoring system of tennis. When the score is 30-love, it means that one person has scored two points and the other none. Clearly, this is a very special, technical meaning of the term. Those who wish to play tennis can easily master it, but knowing the ordinary uses of the term love is of little help in learning its technical use in tennis. 'Culture' is another common, ordinary term that takes on many different meanings. When people say, 'He is a cultured person', they usually mean something different from the anthropologist who cannot imagine anyone lacking a culture. The anthropologist uses the term 'culture' quite differently from the biologist who is experimenting with 'cultures' in his laboratory. The anthropological use of the term 'culture' is at least related to its more popular use; the use of culture in biology requires an entirely new use of the term.

Sometimes, entirely new terms are invented. The 'Peter Principle' is one of these. This 'principle' was invented by Lawrence Peters and named after him. It is: 'In a hierarchy every employee tends to rise to his level of incompetence.'[3] While it is intended to be more humorous than serious, even humorous concepts have their uses.

Definition of Generalisation[4]

Generalisations are Statements Indicating Relationships between Two or More Concepts. A generalisation is a sentence, whereas a concept is a term. Some sentences are *not* generalisations. The sentence 'John Smith married Beverly Jones' is a factual statement; it is not a generalisation because it fails to show a relationship between concepts; on the other hand, the statement 'Men marry women' is a generalisation. It describes a general situation, one in which 'John and Mary' may be cited as particular examples.

Generalisations can take many forms. They appear as descriptions, principles, explanations, interpretations, rules, hypotheses, evaluations and predictions. The following are all forms of generalisations:

'War is hell!' (description)
'War begins in the minds and hearts of men.' (explanation)
'Future wars will employ nuclear weapons.' (prediction)

'Any nation capable of waging war will fight when it feels its vital interests are threatened.' (principle)

'There are no winners in modern warfare; only losers.' (evaluation)

Generalisations cannot be understood fully unless their constituent concepts are understood. The sentence 'War begins in the minds and hearts of men' requires the reader to understand the concepts of 'war', 'minds', 'hearts' and 'men' as well as the relational concept 'begins'. Moreover, the understanding of key concepts cannot be at a superficial level. Clearly, if the meaning of 'heart' from the sentence above is understood literally — i.e. an organ that pumps blood in animals — as opposed to its poetic meaning — i.e. the source of human motivation and desire — the sentence is nonsensical. A child might be required to memorise the sentence and repeat it upon demand with little, if any, understanding of its meaning. On the other hand, a teacher who believes the sentence to be true, who accepts the responsibility implied by its truth and who opposes war, may conclude that helping children understand that sentence and resisting its implications is a high priority for social studies instruction.

Limitations on Concepts and Generalisations

For scientific purposes, concepts can be judged as 'good' or 'bad', depending upon how useful they are. Concepts are useful to the extent that they discriminate among phenomena and provide categories that draw attention to important relationships. While it has a place in literature, the concept 'elves' is a useless concept for the purposes of science. People can hold the concept, agree on its essential characteristics and communicate about 'elves', but the term contributes little to a scientific understanding of society in the past, present or future. Concepts may be used long after the reality they are intended to represent has changed. 'Capitalism' and 'free enterprise' are two terms used frequently to refer to the United States economic system when in fact the economic system of the United States today is vastly different from the one these terms were intended to describe. Sometimes people have a concept but struggle to find the terms to represent it adequately. No one disputes that the countries that are heavily industrialised share characteristics that separate them from nations lacking an industrial base, but the terms 'developing nation' and 'developed nation' distort the meaning of the differences and gloss over enormous differences among the 'developing nations' and among the 'developed ones'.

Sometimes people use the same term but assign it a different meaning. A current example is the concept 'imperialism'. Lenin referred to imperialism as the highest stage of capitalism, a stage in which the exploitation of one class by another was transformed into the exploitation of weak nations by economically powerful countries. Therefore, Marxists use imperialism as a scientific concept indicating a certain pattern of social relationships. Non-Marxists typically think of imperialism differently, equating it with hegemonism, an effort by one nation-state to exert political control over another. Arguments between Marxists and non-Marxists sometimes arise because of their inability to agree upon definitions of such concepts as imperialism, an inability rooted in different philosophies and world-views.

Concepts cannot be judged true or false; they are either relatively useful or relatively useless. The ultimate test is whether a person can use the concept effectively to derive greater meaning from experience.

Generalisations, on the other hand, can be judged as true or false. A main task of scholars is to generate statements about human behaviour and society and then test them for their validity and reliability. In science, generalisations are usually treated as being *tentatively* true or *probably* true, because beliefs accepted at one time on the basis of evidence then available often prove to be false or only partially true at a future time when more evidence is uncovered. It is also possible to offer generalisations when methods of offering final proof are lacking. Thus, scientists may offer different, even conflicting, interpretations on the origins of the universe, knowing that their capacity to provide absolute proof for one version over the others will likely never exist. This means that while teachers seek to impart generalisations about human behaviour and society based upon current knowledge, they must also convey certain attitudes of caution and scepticism that encourage students to continue to test generalisations against reality.

Relationships between Concepts and Generalisations, and Data, Facts and Theories[5]

Concepts and generalisations should also be considered in terms of their relationships to *data, facts* and *theories. Data are bits of inform-ation.* By themselves they may provide little meaning until they are put into some structure.

Factual Statements are Sentences about Data. They refer to unique events, people, objects, processes and so on. For example, 'the United States imported over 40 per cent of the petroleum it consumed in

1978' is a factual statement based upon data regarding oil use and imports into the United States. Similar statements employing different percentages could be made about Japan and many countries of Western Europe. Other nations, for example Saudi Arabia, Iran, Nigeria, Kuwait and Venezuela exported oil rather than imported it in 1978. Therefore, it is possible to place nations into two categories on the basis of their relationship to oil: those that import oil in varying amounts and those that export oil.

Drawing upon factual statements about oil production, trade and use, we have created two concepts — 'oil importing nations' and 'oil exporting nations'. Whether the concepts are useful or not depends upon whether they help interpret current social experience. For example, do the concepts 'oil importing nations' and 'oil exporting nations' draw attention to certain features of foreign policy? Has the dependence of some nations on foreign sources of oil led to new alliances, commercial treaties or threats of aggression among countries?

The statement 'As oil importing nations increase their dependence on foreign oil sources, they will seek ever closer cultural, commercial and diplomatic ties with oil exporting nations' is a generalisation employing the two concepts 'oil importing nations' and 'oil exporting nations'. Other generalisations could be generated using the two concepts and various factual statements about those nations which produce oil and those which are large oil consumers.

A Theory is a Systematically Organised Structure of Knowledge Containing Facts, Concepts and Generalisations Joined Together so as to Offer Widely Applicable Explanations and Predictions. An example of a theory is Isaac Newton's law of gravitation: 'Every particle of matter in the universe attracts every other particle with a force inversely as the square of the distance between them and directly proportional to the product of their masses.' Newton's theory accounted mathematically for action of the moon and planets, the tides and the motion of objects on the Earth.

In the nineteenth century Charles Darwin in his *Origin of Species* offered a theory accounting for the evolution of man himself. He called this process 'natural selection' and defined it as follows:

As many more individuals of each species are born than can possibly survive, and as, consequently, there is a frequently recurring struggle for existence, it follows that any being, if it vary however slightly in any manner profitable to itself, under the complex and sometimes varying conditions of life, will have a better chance of surviving, and thus be naturally selected. From the strong principles of inheritance, any selected variety will tend to propagate its new and modified form.[6]

The social sciences have not been able to match the physical sciences in the strength and number of theories that are capable of explaining and predicting reliably a wide range of phenomena. Nevertheless, theory development and testing remain a central mission of social science.

Guidelines for Instruction in Concepts and Generalistions

Why should Social Studies be Concerned with Concepts and Generalisations?

Whether the social studies programme is based upon the academic disciplines or whether it is conceptually organised through an integrated approach to social studies is not the most important issue. Either approach has the capacity to provide a sound education. What is critically important is whether the instruction provides students with greater insights into their experiences. Has their capacity to reflect more carefully and profoundly upon their own personal experience, their society and the world been enhanced as a result of instruction in social studies? Or has their ability to reason about society remained at a level largely undifferentiated from that of people who lack formal education?

Reasoning requires a capacity to think abstractly. Human beings, alone among animals, have the ability to reflect on the present, learn from the past and plan for the future. Helping students to increase their capacity to reason and to think reflectively is the principal challenge facing social studies teachers everywhere.

People think and draw meaning from their experience by using concepts and generalisations. They are the building blocks for thought. Concepts enable individuals to interpret experience by linking unique events to others. Generalisations permit people to describe and explain their experiences, judge their significance and predict their future impact. According to David Ausubel,

Anyone who pauses long enough to give the problem serious thought cannot escape the conclusion that man lives in a world of concepts rather than a world of objects, events and situations ... Reality, figuratively speaking, is experienced through a conceptual or a categorical filter.[7]

Social studies instruction should be largely instruction in concepts and generalisations. The study of history, geography and civics may become mere rote memorisation of factual details unless students are encouraged to think conceptually about what they are studying.

Emphasis upon concepts and generalisations facilitates 'transfer of learning', a particular concern of education. A task of schools everywhere is to design instruction so that what is learned in the classroom is of maximum value to the learner later when he faces new and unforeseen situations. Specific information about the facts of a particular economic crisis are ultimately of less importance than general knowledge about the causes of inflation and depression in the economy. Understanding the 'law of supply and demand' is more useful than remembering the price of automobiles in 1930.

Moreover, information about details is remembered longer if it is retained as part of a structure. Discrete facts learned in isolation have a short life. Linking facts to general structures (i.e. concepts and generalisations) facilitates recall.

Specific data and factual statements are important. Unless concepts and generalisations can account for real phenomena, they are worthless. But it is necessary to establish priorities. And the first priority is to help students increase their knowledge of concepts and generalisations.

Suggestions for Teaching Concepts

Concept learning is acquiring the capacity to make discriminations among objects and events, to categorise objects and events that share essential attributes and to use the categories as a basis for generalisations. Concept learning can occur at lower and higher levels of cognition.[8] Lower-level concept learning requires the capacity to make discriminations, to be able to identify instances from non-instances of the concept. Higher-level concept learning is using a concept in combination with other concepts to construct generalisations.

Very young children learn many concepts indirectly, almost incidentally, as part of their everyday experience, rather than from formal instruction. Their conceptions of 'tall', 'old', 'hot' and 'danger' may be acquired in this way. No formal definitions of the concepts are possessed or needed; children are able to communicate their thoughts satisfactorily to their peers and adults at their level of concept understanding.

Later, as they mature and become more verbally adept — about the age they begin school — formal instruction assumes greater importance for imparting concepts, but it does not replace informal processes. Now, children are taught concepts someone else believes they should acquire. The meanings of concepts are conveyed verbally; the pupils are expected to manipulate the verbal symbols so that the concepts become part of their own conceptual repertoire.[9]

Very young children have difficulty manipulating new concepts presented in verbal form alone. Young students can learn concepts more fully if they can also manipulate concrete objects that represent the concepts. For example, students may be unable to grasp the meaning of an assembly line from merely a verbal description. But if they are taken to a factory in order to observe an assembly line in operation or if a simple assembly line involving task specialisation is established in the classroom, they can understand the concept quite well. A skilled teacher designs instruction for concepts so as to fit the knowledge, experience and cognitive development of the learners. While both seven-year-old and seventeen-year-old children can profit equally from instruction focused on concepts, teachers must approach instruction quite differently in the two cases.

Much social studies instruction, especially at the upper grades, depends upon helping students conceptualise things they will never experience directly, for example feudalism. A major task for teachers is to help students understand such concepts without their being able to experience the phenomenon. Teachers must also be sensitive to the fact that students may acquire a capacity to use a term without much understanding of the concept. For example, when children are asked what they like best about their country, they may respond 'our system of government' or the 'freedom we have'. Students may have learned these are 'good answers' — i.e. approved by the teacher — but have only the most superficial understanding of their meaning.

Distinction between Instruction in 'Ordinary' Concepts and 'Scientific' Concepts.[10] Some concepts are part of the ordinary language of society. Social studies teachers should help students understand the meaning of these concepts and how to use them more effectively. Politics is such a concept. People often say: (1) 'He likes to play politics'; (2) 'I think there was too much politics in that decision'; (3) 'It sounds like more politics to me'; (4) 'I plan to enter politics upon graduation from the university.' Each of these statements conveys a somewhat different meaning of politics; the meanings may overlap at certain points but they are not alike. For example, the fourth speaker is discussing politics as a career; presumably the person expects to find work in government or perhaps compete for an elective office. The other three statements may or may not deal with government; it is impossible to tell. When using ordinary concepts, it may be difficult to construct a single definition that will account for all instances of the concept's use. In helping students acquire greater control over an ordinary concept, it may be better to 'map' its use in a wide variety of circumstances, to indicate how other terms are used with the concept being studied and how new situations and terms can change the meaning and use of the concept.

At other times, social studies teachers want to teach students new terms or assign new meanings to familiar terms. History and the social sciences are filled with concepts and associated generalisations that have the capacity to help young people draw greater meaning from their experience, to 'see' things that would otherwise pass unnoticed.

'Role' is an example of an ordinary concept that can be assigned scientific meaning. As used by sociologists, roles are guides to behaviour. Knowing one's role informs people how to act. The role of a child is different from the role of a parent. The role of student varies from that of teacher. In most cases the role of a man differs from the role of a woman. Teaching students the scientific meaning of the concept role draws attention to aspects of their society; it helps them understand better their behaviour and that of others.

'Ethnocentrism', a preference for the customs and practices of one's own group and a belief that one's group is better than other groups, is an important concept for students to acquire. Understanding the concept of ethnocentrism helps to explain variations in cultural patterns and how tensions arise between groups of people. Understanding ethnocentrism as a human tendency affecting all cultures is a prelude to taking steps to overcome the most dangerous forms of ethnocentrism while contributing to cosmopolitanism.

When teaching students an entirely new term or teaching a technical or scientific use of a familiar one, the teacher should:

(1) determine if students possess the appropriate subordinate concepts and knowledge required to use the new concept;
(2) define the concept clearly in order that students can use the rule to discriminate among instances and non-instances of the concept;
(3) present positive examples of the concept as well as negative

examples; explain clearly why the examples either satisfy or fail to satisfy the definition of the concept; avoid introducing extraneous information that is unnecessary to understanding the concept;

(4) ask students to apply the concept to new instances to determine if they can use the concept correctly: some students may be able to repeat the definition of the concept but be unable to use the concept to discriminate among new examples appropriately.

(5) require students to link the new concept with other concepts previously acquired to form generalisations.

Suggestings for Teaching Generalisations

Generalisations are not usually difficult for students if they know the concepts and have the knowledge base required to appreciate the relationships presented by the generalisation. If these conditions do not exist, the students may merely memorise the generalisation, repeat it verbatim when asked to do so by their teacher but fail to integrate it into their own structure of knowledge. Therefore, the first step in teaching generalisations is to make certain that the generalisations to be taught fall within the students' experience and background.

Teachers should conduct instruction about generalisations at two levels. The first is to teach pupils to make judgements about the generalisations contained in their textbooks or presented by other sources. The second is helping pupils to acquire the capacity to formulate their own testable generalisations.

Generalisations are statements about reality. They may appear as conclusions based upon an examination of data (inferences); they may be estimates about the state of affairs (hypotheses); they may be intended as rules that govern human behaviour or society (principles); they may be predictions about the future (speculation); they may be interpretations or explanations of events. Whatever their form, they are all potentially testable. The first principle for teaching generalisations is to seek the factual basis for the generalisation, to ask: 'What is the evidence for this statement?'

Teaching students to seek evidence and to make sound judgements about the validity and reliability of available evidence should be a main goal for social studies teachers. Lessons on how to make choices among conflicting points of evidence, to judge the reliability of witnesses and to test the validity of documents should be part of every social studies programme. Moreover, students need to learn how to create their own evidence in order to support or to disconfirm generalisations. Social scientists conduct experiments and undertake studies in order to generate evidence aimed at supporting or discrediting hypotheses. Students can gain direct experience in how such studies are done by completing small-scale studies of their own, in their own classroom, school or community.

Students should be taught also to construct their own generalisations. They require instruction in how to frame proper statements that are warranted, given the existing evidence, that can be tested and that reflect the tentativeness of social science statements. Learning the difference between correlational and causal statements, recognising the logical traps inherent in generalising from specific cases to general conclusions and appreciating the distinction between 'tendency statements' and conclusions that imply no exceptions are part of what students must achieve when formulating their own generalisations.

The Concept of Justice: Sample Instructional Materials

Justice is a concept worth knowing — and worth teaching in social studies. The meaning of this concept has been debated by the most learned philosophers and the most ordinary people throughout the ages. And the debate goes on. People everywhere expect to be treated with justice; governments exist to dispense it. People seem never to get too much of it; yet they are not agreed on what it is.

The concept of justice can effectively illustrate some aspects of teaching social studies concepts and generalisations because the concept has both 'ordinary' and 'scientific' meanings, because people's understanding of the concept changes and increases with education and experience and because it can be taught with a variety of techniques and devices.

Ordinary and Scientific Meaning of Justice. Justice is an example of a concept that is used in both 'ordinary' and 'scientific' ways. Through social studies instruction pupils should know both uses of the concept and their relationships.

People without formal education use justice and its cognate forms in everyday speech and are able to convey meaning. For example, they say: (1) 'He got his just reward.' (2) 'Justice was served.' (3) 'You are not being just.' (4) 'There is no justice.' (5) 'Justice was meted out.' All of these uses of the term justice convey slightly different meanings.

For example, when a person says, 'There is no justice,' he may mean something like, 'Life is not fair.' He is probably not commenting on the availability of a governmental system to dispense justice. He may hold the opinion that those who do the hardest, most dangerous physical labour often receive less compensation for their efforts than do better-educated, white-collar workers who toil in clean, secure surroundings. This is a quite different meaning from one using justice in the sense of a 'just sentence' imposed by a judge on a convicted criminal. Much more could be written about the 'ordinary' use of the concept justice, but this should be sufficient to make the point.

From time to time individuals or societies as a whole impose 'scientific' definitions on justice or one of its aspects. Thus, when people in ancient times wrote that punishment should be according to 'an eye for an eye, a tooth for a tooth', they were establishing a concept of criminal justice. Execution of convicted murderers, practised in some countries, is a modern-day application of this principle.

Societies have also puzzled over the problem of just distribution of those things the society values – its material wealth, power, prestige and so on. John Rawls has provided a recent 'scientific' definition of distributive justice; his view will be discussed below.

The task for social studies teachers is to make certain that students know justice in both ordinary and scientific senses. Ordinary uses of the concept are necessary to facilitate regular communication; scientific uses can encourage fresh ways of thinking about justice and draw attention to aspects of society previously ignored.

Intellectual Growth in the Use of Justice. Justice is an example of a concept that can be understood at a simple level by young children; it is also a concept whose meaning expands and changes through experience and education. Young children may lack the capacity to understand complex features of justice, its application through law, and so on. But they both understand and regularly employ elements of justice in their everyday lives.

Older youth can deal with more sophisticated aspects of justice. They can explore the multiple ways that justice is used in ordinary language and they can understand and apply technical uses of the concept. Their stage of mental growth also permits them to use the term when considering situations far removed from their own personal experience.

Use of Multiple Techniques and Devices. This concept also serves as a convenient illustration for a book on social studies teaching because the concept justice can be taught in many different ways, using a wide range of instructional devices. Textbook presentations are but one – and sometimes the least effective – way to teach the concept of justice. Since children experience justice (or injustice) regularly, they can draw upon their own experience to learn the concept. The concept is routinely the subject of children's literature and the public media. Imaginative teachers will have no trouble locating source materials to support instruction on justice.

Teaching about Justice in Elementary Schools

It may not be useful to impose a scientific meaning of justice on very young children. More attention should be devoted to helping them understand how the term justice is used in ordinary discourse. Teachers may also learn that using the term justice itself, too early, can also be an obstacle to learning. While justice is typically in ordinary use among older youth and adults, it is less frequently employed by children. It is often better to begin with terms children use that convey elements of justice, linking their terms to the concept justice, rather than rush too quickly to impose an unfamiliar term requiring abstract reasoning processes.

While most young children do not regularly use the term justice in their discourse, none the less they are developing a concept of justice that is expressed through other terms. In some cultures, the term 'fair' holds meaning that represents some of the meanings contained by the concept justice. In the United States children use the term 'fair' in their play. When someone violates the rules of a game, they say, 'That's not fair!' When a teacher appears to favour one student over another, they are quick to recognise that the teacher is acting 'unfairly'.

Teachers can help students reflect on the concept of fairness in order that they will know it more fully, thereby contributing ultimately to the development of a sense of justice. Students can learn that 'playing fair' in a game means playing according to the rules; that a 'fair trial' is one in which the evidence is presented according to established procedures before an impartial jury; and that being 'treated fairly' is being given your due.

Example 1: Hypothetical Situations. To help students think about what is fair, a teacher might present them with a series of hypothetical situations such as those indicated below. These situations might be presented on individual cards. Students could be asked to select one card at a time and respond to the questions: Do you think this situation is fair? Why do you think so?[11] Pupils' responses should serve as opportunities to encourage class discussion and to explore the meaning of the concept fair.

1. Oleg is the fastest runner in his class. Recently, so that he will no longer win every race, the teacher has started to make Oleg run a further distance than his classmates.

   IS THIS FAIR?

2. Carlos and Maria are identical twins. However, they are not treated the same by their parents. When they are at home, Carlos is free to play with his friends while Maria is expected to help her mother with household chores.

   IS THIS FAIR?

3. Absorn and Thanalai are students in the same school. Absorn makes good grades, but she does not have to study hard. Thanalai works hard but still makes poor grades.

   IS THIS FAIR?

4. Henry would like to be a doctor, but his parents are poor and cannot afford to send him to college. Henry's father has told Henry that he must be content to be a farmer as he and his grandfather are.

   IS THIS FAIR?

5. Anna is a pretty, pleasant girl who is liked by all of her classmates. Because she also likes Anna more than the other students, the teacher gives Anna many privileges that she does not give the others.

   IS THIS FAIR?

6. The coach has picked only the fastest and strongest boys from the school to play a soccer match with players from another school.

   IS THIS FAIR?

7. Nadia and Yuri are students in the same class. Yuri has more trouble learning mathematics than does Nadia so the teacher has been giving more time and assistance to Yuri than to Nadia. IS THIS FAIR?

From these and similar anecdotes students may learn that deciding what is fair is not always easy. Sometimes, being fair means treating everyone exactly alike. In other cases, treating people alike, when different treatment seems justified, may be unfair.

In general, being fair usually means giving all equal rights. When unequal treatment of a few is tolerated, such inequality must be identified as being somehow to the long-range benefit of all. For example, it would seem unfair to prevent some students from playing soccer on the school playground because they are not so skilled as others. On the other hand, in preparing for inter-school competition when only a few students can compete, it would seem unfair *not* to favour the most skilled players in choosing the members of the team.

Example 2: Folk Tales. Children are usually fascinated by fanciful folk tales involving animals or people. Folk tales can contribute to helping children understand the concept of justice. Following are two tales that can be used to help young students think about fairness. Children could be asked to read each folk tale, decide if the outcome seemed fair and offer reasons why the result seemed fair.

The Onion and the Rose[12] (Korea)

Now in the days long ago when good King Chung Jong ruled Korea there was a very wise, but somewhat tricky judge named Im Bang who held court in Suwon city.

Now it happened that Im Bang had been away from Suwon for several weeks on a mission for the king. When he returned the first villager who came to see him wept and cried that his daughter was going to be killed by the royal swordsman.

'You must be mistaken,' Im Bang said kindly. 'I know your daughter. Since she was a child I have never seen a better behaved little girl. I am sure she would do nothing to cause the king to have her killed.'

'It is not my daughter,' the old man said, weeping so hard the judge could scarcely hear his words. 'It is Wol Mai.'

'You mean that rich old woman who causes us so much trouble?' Im Bang asked. 'She is worse than a dragon. What has she done now?'

'For years this wicked creature has been cheating everyone,' the old man said. 'Each time she is caught she manages to put the blame on someone else. When she cheated on her taxes, she blamed her chief clerk and he was put to death in her place. When she was caught giving short measure in her store, she blamed a servant and he was whipped in her place. And so on and on many times others paid for her crimes and sins. Why, even as a child, the servant's children were punished when Wol Mai was naughty. Someone else has always taken the blame for her.'

'I know,' Im Bang said. 'But she is so clever no one has been able to catch her until lately. I found proof and sent it to the king in Seoul. He has ordered her to be placed in prison for the rest of her life.'

'Oh, but that is the trouble, Judge Im Bang,' the old man said. 'Lately our house has fallen on sad days. To keep from starving, we sent my daughter to work as a servant in Wol Mai's house. Yesterday, the old dragon got word from a spy that the king had ordered her put in prison for the rest of her life. So she ordered my daughter to exchange garments with her and go in her place to prison. You know that women in prison wear heavy veils to hide their shame. So none would know of the exchange.'

'Your daughter should have refused,' the judge said.

'Wol Mai threatened to have me thrown in prison if my daughter did not take her place. She claimed she would tell the police I stole some gold from her. To save me, my daughter agreed to go to prison in Wol Mai's place.'

'So?' Im Bang said. 'What do you want me to do?'

'Please stop Wol Mai from forcing my daughter to exchange clothes with her.'

'I cannot do that,' Im Bang said thoughtfully. 'Wol Mai has been blaming her servants for her crimes so long that it has become a custom in Suwon. You do not want me to change an old custom, do you?'

'But, honorable Im Bang!' the old man said. 'I . . .'

'Let me hear no more! What is to be, will be. Go home and do not trouble me again.'

Within an hour the whole town knew that Im Bang had refused to save the poor girl. Then those who had loved the old judge now hated him. They thought that he had taken Wol Mai's gold to save her from prison and sent the little maid in her place.

And so on the next day the young girl, wearing the rich robes of

Wol Mai and with a heavy veil over her face, was led to the prison gate. With her came the old woman wearing the servant girl's clothing. She, too, wore a heavy veil.

Im Bang, as the judge, met them at the prison gate. 'Are you Wol Mai?' he asked the little maid.

'Yes, she is,' the old woman said quickly before the girl could speak.

'You have no family, Wol Mai,' Im Bang said to the girl. 'Who will look after your home and your fortune while you spend the rest of your life in prison?'

'I will do it for her,' the old woman said eagerly.

'No,' Im Bang said. 'For fifty years Wol Mai has been blaming others for what she did and they have always taken her punishment for her. This has happened so long that it has become a custom. I will not change an old custom. Jailer, take this servant woman and put her in prison in Wol Mai's place!'

The prison guards grabbed Wol Mai who was in the servant's clothing.

'Wait!' the old woman cried. 'I am really Wol Mai. She is the servant. Jail her!'

'Impossible,' Im Bang said. 'Servants do not wear such rich clothing.'

He turned to the large crowd of people gathered around them.

'Have any of you good people ever seen a servant so richly dressed?'

'No! Oh, no, honorable Im Bang!' they cried, delighted at the way things were turning out.

'Neither have I,' said the old judge. 'Throw this servant in the darkest cell and never let her out.'

And when they led her away and Im Bang could no longer hear the old dragon's shouts of rage, the judge turned to the little maid who wore the rich clothes of Wol Mai.

'And as for you, Wol Mai,' he said. 'I charge you to change your ways of the past. Go home and use your great wealth to help your fellow men and women of Suwon.'

And as it happened, she did just that.

Partnership[13] (*Burma*)

An otter and a jackal lived near a river, and after a while they decided to form a partnership. They agreed that they would pool all the food each was able to gather, and that they would share it equally at the end of the day.

On the first day of their partnership, the otter caught some shrimps and the jackal picked some bananas. The food was shared equally, and the partners were satisfied.

On the second day, the jackal gathered some bamboo shoots, but the otter had an off-day and could find nothing. Faithful to the agreement, the jackal shared the bamboo shoots with the otter.

On the third day, the jackal had no luck at all, but the otter went fishing and succeeded in catching a small carp. Now, as the otter was greedy, he announced, 'I will cut the fish into four parts. I will take the head and the belly, and you can take the rest.'

'Be fair,' replied the jackal. 'I shared the bamboo shoots equally with you yesterday.'

'And I am sharing the fish equally with you, also,' argued the otter. 'You will get two pieces and I will get two pieces.'

'But you intend to take the tastier parts,' protested the jackal.

'Remember, it is I who caught the carp,' boasted the otter. And they argued for a long time, getting nowhere, until they agreed to ask the rabbit to help them settle their disagreement.

The wise rabbit listened patiently to the arguments presented by each other. Then, taking a sharp stone, he cut the fish right down the center from head to tail in two equal parts. 'Now both of you shall have a piece of the fat belly,' he explained, 'and both of you shall have a piece of the tasteless tail.'

The otter and the jackal went away quite satisfied, and they lived together in happy partnership for many days.

Teaching about Justice in Secondary Schools

Unlike elementary school pupils, secondary school students can be expected to have some understanding of the term justice. They also have a capacity to imagine a greater array of examples of justice and injustice, and they can deal with ordinary and scientific meanings of the term.

To help students grow in their use of the ordinary meaning of the term justice, teachers should help students reflect on the various ways in which justice is used in daily language. Five typical uses were cited earlier.

(1) He got his just reward.
(2) Justice was served.
(3) You are not being just.

(4) There is no justice.
(5) Justice was meted out.

Teachers might begin by asking students to think of cases in which each of these statements are used properly and instances when they are improperly employed. For example, take the sentence: 'He got his just reward.' Would it be appropriate to use this statement to apply to a criminal who was recently given a harsh sentence by a judge? Would it be appropriate to apply to one who was guilty of a crime, avoided arrest, but later met with an accident? Would it apply to someone who worked hard all his life and then came into an inheritance that made him a wealthy man? If so, what do these situations have in common? What instances can be imagined in which the sentence would not apply?

Another technique is to link the term justice with terms often used in connection with it: duty, right, privilege, obligation, equality, rationality, impartiality, liberty, toleration. For example, to what extent and in what situations is our notion of justice conditioned by our understanding of equality and impartiality? Does justice always imply *equal* treatment, *impartial* treatment? Students should also explore terms that rarely seem to correlate positively with justice, terms such as 'arbitrariness' and 'favouritism'. Why is arbitrary punishment frequently considered unjust when the results may be the same as that produced by non-arbitrary punishment? Why do we ordinarily consider granting favoured treatment to some people but not to others unjust treatment? Is favoured treatment ever just?

These kinds of explorations and discussions can strengthen a student's understanding of the ordinary use of justice. But students should also learn 'scientific' or technical uses of the concept.

A 'Scientific' Conception of Justice. One scientific or technical conception of justice is the theme of a book entitled *Theory of Justice* by John Rawls. According to Rawls, justice can be conceived as follows: 'All social primary goods — liberty and opportunity, income and wealth, and the bases of self-respect — are to be distributed equally unless an unequal distribution of any or all of these goods is to the advantage of the least favored.'[14] While this chapter does not provide an opportunity to explore the justifications for Rawls' position or all of its implications, it is not necessary for the reader to agree with Rawls in order for the illustration to be useful. Whether one agrees with Rawls or not, consider what the implications are for instruction.

First of all, Rawls is referring in particular to that aspect of justice known as 'distributive justice'. Distributive justice is concerned with the manner and the degree to which a society's values are shared. Are material goods, offices, power and prestige open and available to all? If not, why not?

Rawls believes that justice requires that the things the society treasures should be available to all on an equal basis unless it can be demonstrated that those who have less are somehow better off because the values are unequally distributed.

Let's imagine an extreme situation. An army is about to enter a battle. Among the members of the military unit are men with great differences in experience, talent, intelligence and courage. There is on the one hand the most recent recruit and on the other hand the most experienced officer. The question is: should the leadership of the army be open and available to all on a totally equal basis or should leadership be vested in the most experienced, talented and courageous? Which procedure for vesting leadership would best serve the typical soldier? If victory and the opportunity to survive the battle are greater by choosing the most talented leader, the most recent recruit would appear to be served best by an unequal distribution of power, even if this results in his missing an opportunity to share command.

For a teacher of secondary school students seeking to teach students Rawls' conception of justice, the task is first making certain that students *understand* the concept; the next task is to teach them to apply it correctly. A teacher might begin the application process by using social situations familiar to the students. The instructions to students might be as follows.

(1) Identify situations in which all people are treated the same. Example: people are given the same pay for the same work. Is this just? What if one person is single and has no dependants while another is married and must support six children on the identical salary? Is this just? Would it be more just to give the person with dependants a somewhat greater salary than the single person for the same work?

(2) Identify situations in which people are treated differently. Are the following situations just?

    (a) In order to enter medical school, students must take an examination. Only those receiving the highest scores are admitted.

    (b) Men in a particular country are expected to serve two years in the army following graduation from school. Women do not have to serve in the army.

(c) Salary in a particular firm is based mainly upon length of service and experience. Employees with twenty years' service receive more than twice the salary of those who are just beginning, although they do not perform twice as much work.

Teachers should be concerned first that the students understand Rawls' conception of justice, can apply the principle correctly and can justify their choices on the basis of the principle. Later, the teacher can ask students to evaluate the Rawls' conception. Does it serve as a useful guide to just choices? Is the student satisfied that distributive justice is rendered when Rawls' terms are met?

Applying the Conception to a Fresh Situation. One reason for organising instruction around concepts and generalisations is to facilitate transfer of learning. Thus, one task of teachers is to ensure that transfer can occur in situations outside the classroom.

A typical opportunity to test transfer of learning is by assessing whether students can apply what they have learned in class to something that has arisen in the community or reaches them via the media. The following excerpt is an example of commentary on the state of the world economy that appeared in a periodical. Figure 6.1, 'Big Fish Need Little Fish', expresses an opinion about the world economy and how resources and influence are distributed.

The first step in teaching this lesson is to make certain that students understand the drawings and the statements that accompany them. Next the teacher might ask the following questions.

(1) Given what you know about the state of the world economy, do either of the drawings or any of the statements seem flawed?

(2) What is the attitude of the cartoonist and author? Are there other points of view not represented here? What is the view of those favouring a 'new international economic order'?

(3) Does the international economic system described in Figure 6.1 work to the equal benefit of all? Is it just?

(4) If the situation appears unjust, what would be required to make it just according to Rawls' formulation of justice?

Figure 6.1: Big Fish Need Little Fish

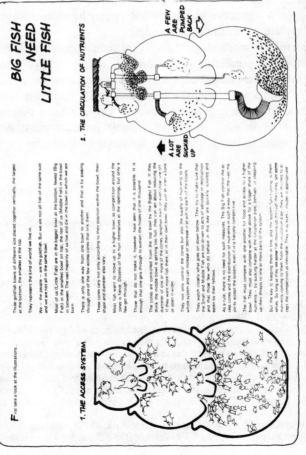

Source: The cartoon appeared in 'A Fishy Tale: Big Fish Need Little Fish', *Ideas and Action*, Bulletin 117, no. 5 (1977), pp. 14-15. *Ideas and Action* credits a publication entitled *The Poverty Makers* published in July 1977 by the Commission on the Churches' Participation in Development for the diagram.

Conclusion

Jerome Bruner once wrote: 'Any idea or problem or body of knowledge can be presented in a form simple enough so that any particular learner can understand it in a recognisable form.'[15] This oft-quoted statement is largely true. However, merely repeating knowledge learned in a rote manner does not constitute understanding. To achieve understanding, i.e. to make the learning meaningful, requires that new knowledge be presented in such a way that pupils can link it to knowledge already under their control. And while it may be possible to teach any idea or problem or body of knowledge so that even the most naïve learner can understand it, teachers must decide whether the task will require more effort than it is worth. Certain ideas that can be learned only very slowly by the young can be understood quickly by older students with a more sophisticated fund of knowledge.

A carefully planned social studies programme provides for teaching concepts and generalisations from primary school through secondary school. Students should increase their understanding and use of ordinary concepts and acquire scientific concepts based upon the academic disciplines. They must learn to evaluate generalisations prepared by others and to develop their own testable generalisations. A social studies programme that achieves this will surely be successful.

Notes

1. John Rawls, *A Theory of Justice* (Harvard University Press, Cambridge, Massachusetts, 19), pp. 3-4.
2. In one sense, of course, *all* concepts are invented. They are, after all, products of the culture and had to be created sometime in the past. For example, there was no concept of the automobile in 1500. However, once a concept has been termed and passes into the ordinary language of the culture, there is no need to re-invent it for each new generation; it is merely passed on.
3. Lawrence J. Peter and Raymond Hull, *The Peter Principle* (William Morrow, New York, 1969), p. 7.
4. Following a discussion of concepts, the reader should be suspicious of efforts to impose definitions on concepts such as generalisations. Generalisation, like concept itself, enjoys popular use and has multiple meanings that might be explored at length were there space to do this. However, in order to get on with the task, the author has stipulated or 'invented' a definition of generalisation.
5. This section is based heavily on Peter Martorella *et al.*, *Concept Learning: Designs for Instruction* (Intext Educational Publishers, Scranton, Pennsylvania, 1972).
6. Charles Darwin, *Origin of Species* (New York, 1872), vol. I, p. 3.
7. David P. Ausubel, *Educational Psychology: a Cognitive View* (Holt,

Rinehart and Winston, New York, 1968), p. 505.

8. Robert W. Gagne, *The Conditions of Learning* (Holt, Rinehart and Winston, New York, 1965), pp. 126-39.

9. David P. Ausubel, 'Meaningful Reception Learning and the Acquistion of Concepts' in Herbert J. Klausmeier and Chester W. Harris (eds.), *Analyses of Concept Learning* (Academic Press, New York, 1966), p. 164.

10. This section drew significantly on the ideas contained in Robert P. Aumaugher, 'A Philosophical Analysis of the Concept of Concept and its Application to the Social Studies', unpublished doctoral dissertation, Michigan State University, East Lansing, Michigan, 1978.

11. Ideas for this lesson and the next are based upon lessons found in Harry Hutson, *Human Rights in a Global Age* (Social Studies Development Center, Bloomington, Indiana, 1977).

12. J.G. Edmonds (ed.), *Trickster Tales* (J.B. Lippincott, Philadelphia, 1966), pp. 138-43.

13. Maung Htin Aung and Helen G. Trager (ed.), *A Kingdom Lost for a Drop of Honey* (Parents Magazine Press, 1968), pp. 39-41.

14. Rawls, *Theory of Justice,* p. 303.

15. Jerome Bruner, *Toward a Theory of Instruction* (W.W. Norton, New York, 1966), p. 44.

7   ESSENTIAL SKILLS IN SOCIAL STUDIES

John J. Patrick with Alan Backler, Sae-gu Chung and
Raji Jaiman

Social studies education should be measured by what learners can do
with what they know. It should be designed to help learners use
knowledge for significant and laudable purposes. Although the definition
of a 'significant and laudable purpose' may vary from one society to
another and from group to group within a society, in every case the
accomplished student will be able to use acquired information and ideas
to achieve goals. Students who accumulate facts and skills as ends in
themselves are less well educated than those who are able to use
knowledge as a means to understand their world.

Those teachers who emphasise doing, as well as knowing, are teaching
essential skills. This chapter examines the meaning of essential skills in
the social studies and discusses how these skills may be taught to
students of different ages. First, essential skills are defined as consisting
of three categories: (1) skills in studying and learning; (2) skills in
enquiry and decision-making; and (3) skills in responsible group participation and civic activity. The remainder of the chapter examines each
of these categories and offers examples of ways to teach each skill
category.

Introduction to Essential Skills

A *skill* is the ability to perform repeatedly an activity with competence.
The criterion for competent performance may vary from group to group.
An *essential skill* is a skill which must be mastered before a student is
able to perform related, higher-level activities satisfactorily. Essential
skills are basic and primary foundations for higher-level learning.

What are Essential Social Studies Skills?

Essential skills in the social studies are the tools of learning, thinking
and acting that are basic for competent living in one's social world.
They are necessary for acquiring and applying knowledge. Essential
skills must be acquired before one can think systematically and
effectively about social reality or perform certain social roles adroitly.[1]

158

The three categories of essential skills include competence in studying and learning, competence in enquiry and decision-making and competence in responsible group participation and civic activity.

Competence in Studying and Learning. A student competent in studying and learning is able to use a book's index to find information, use a definition to classify information, understand information presented in a graph, ask questions of a consultant and interpret information gained from direct observation of an event. Skills in studying and learning enable one to find, comprehend, organise and interpret information. They are prerequisites to acquiring knowledge and putting it to practical use, and are necessary for conducting sophisticated enquiries or solving significant social problems.[2] These skills are the means to independent and advanced learning in the social studies or in any other academic field. Without these skills, continued learning becomes difficult or impossible; academic achievement and the capacity to perform important social roles suffer.

Competence in Enquiry and Decision-making. This competence is demonstrated by the ability to formulate and test hypotheses about social reality. John Dewey referred to this competence as 'reflective thinking', which,

> in distinction from other operations to which we apply the name of thought, involves (1) a state of doubt, hesitation, perplexity, mental difficulty, in which thinking originates and (2) an act of searching, hunting, inquiring, to find material that will resolve the doubt, settle and dispose of the perplexity.[3]

According to Dewey, the essence of reflective thinking is formulating and testing hypotheses and considering the implications of warranted hypotheses. He wrote, 'Active, persistent, and careful consideration of any belief or supposed form of knowledge in the light of grounds that support it, and the further consequences to which it tends, constitutes reflective thought.'[4]

Skills in enquiry and decision-making involve the highest levels of thinking.[5] In order to conduct social research, make defensible policy decisions, construct and justify hypotheses or marshal evidence to support or reject beliefs about one's social world, one must have mastered enquiry and decision-making skills. These are the skills that enable students to make warranted descriptive, explanatory and evaluative statements about social reality.[6]

Competence in Responsible Group Participation and Civic Activity.
Responsible group participation and civic activity mean the ability to
demonstrate skills in leading a meeting, advocating opinions as a group
member, making rules for a group and organising resources needed to
complete a community service project. Group members must have these
skills in order to co-operate for a group purpose. Bargaining and compromise are necessary for groups to meet common goals responsibly.
These group participation skills also enable one person to represent a
group effectively when dealing with outsiders.[7]

Since effective group participation requires applying skills used in
studying, learning and enquiring, the final test of the effectiveness of
social studies education is the student's ability to participate effectively
in a group. Students who can only recall and recite information upon
command are not as fully educated as those who can use knowledge to
solve both academic and practical problems. Students who can only
study, learn, enquire and solve problems when alone are less educated
than students who can also work as group members.

Skills in group participation are prerequisite to responsible citizenship
in the modern world. Important individual and social goals are
unattainable unless people are able to relate to one another. Family
and work groups, community service groups and recreational groups
are only a few of the groups in which people hold membership. In
addition, groups the world over are becoming increasingly interdependent. Group participation skills are basic to the survival and
fruitful development of individuals in today's world.[8]

Distinguishing Characteristics of Well-designed Plans for Teaching Essential Skills

The following discussion can serve as a frame of reference for educators
interested in teaching essential skills effectively. These five ideas can
guide selection of instructional objectives, sequencing of lessons and
teaching procedures. They can also direct the evaluation of curricula
and teaching plans.

*Skills Selected for Curricular Emphasis should Help People become
Effective Contributors to the Groups in which they Live.* All people,
regardless of cultural differences, have basic needs stemming from their
common humanity. They must acquire essential knowledge and skills
to meet these basic needs if they are to survive. Beyond survival, they

need to acquire skills essential to self-fulfilment — skills essential to achieving their potential as human beings. In addition, certain essential skills are conditions for perpetuating and improving any cultural heritage.

Skills essential in differing environments may vary, but in all societies essential skills relate to competence in learning, thinking, enquiring, decision-making and acting responsibly and effectively as a group member. Curriculum developers should justify selection and sequencing of essential skills by their relationship to human needs for survival, self-fulfilment and responsible membership in a particular society.[9]

Skill-learning Experiences in School should be Connected to Students' Out-of-school Experiences. Learning becomes more attractive when students realise that their school experiences are linked to life outside school. Students should view essential skills as tools helping them to deal more effectively with their world. The consequence is likely to be students who acquire more knowledge and remember it longer.[10]

Lessons should connect students' experiences with other people in the community.[11] Alternatively, students should be exposed to novel situations and encouraged to use skills to generalise from familiar events to those outside their immediate experience. As students progress from lower to higher levels of a curriculum, their ability to comprehend and enquire about experiences outside their immediate environment should be increased.[12]

Skill-learning Experiences should be Integrated Vertically and Horizontally within the Curriculum. Early skill-learning experiences must be connected with subsequent experiences. This means skills learned within a particular course and skills learned as a student progresses from lower to higher grade levels must be sequenced so that each skill builds upon those that preceded it.[13] One such skill sequence would include asking first-level students to look at a simple map of the classroom and identify classroom furniture as shown on the map; second-level students could look up the address of a food market and use a community map to identify the market's location; third-level students could use a map to give clear directions from one point on the map to another. The skills in this example are integrated vertically in the curriculum.[14]

In order to integrate skills vertically, the teacher must identify which skills are more appropriately taught at each age level. Studies have shown, for example, that children are not capable of sophisticated hypothetical or deductive thinking before reaching early adolescence.[15]

Vertical integration also requires increasing standards of proficiency at each successive grade level. Although students in both lower and higher grades should be able to locate and interpret information, higher-level students should demonstrate greater proficiency. While very young children may be able to read a simple bar graph about world population trends, older students should know how to construct their own bar graphs.

Horizontal integration has occurred when skills taught and used in one subject can be related to skills taught and used in different subject areas at the same level. An eight-year-old child who is asked to find the shortest distance between two points on a map of Bombay, India, must demonstrate skills relevant to both social studies and mathematics. Social studies teachers must think carefully about how essential social studies kills may be related to learning in mathematics, science and language courses at the same level.[16]

Vertical and horizontal integration of skill-learning experiences forges links between teaching units. Every teaching unit should present students with both knowledge and skills to be mastered. By drawing attention to connections between material in one unit and material presented in previous units, teachers help students build upon knowledge and practise skills. This compounds the effectiveness of each learning experience, helps students find their own connections between specific learning experiences, reinforces prior learning and encourages students to new achievements.[17]

Skills should be Learned through Continual Practice and Application. Skills are not learned in a single lesson. Continual practice is necessary for skill mastery and practice should be designed systematically to improve performance. It is helpful for teachers to acknowledge successful skill performance and analyse and correct inadequate student performance of skill activities. Indicating correct responses reinforces learning and helps guide students in the direction specified by instructional objectives. Indication of incorrect responses is a guide to students of deficiencies that must be corrected before the skill can be mastered.[18]

To demonstrate mastery of a specific instructional unit, students should be able to apply the skills learned to successful completion of a new task. For example, students wishing to demonstrate mastery of interpreting bar graphs should be able to interpret bar graphs they have not seen before.[19]

Skill-learning Experiences should be Designed to Promote Transfer of Learning. Transfer of skill learning means that competencies learned in one lesson can be applied to the mastery of other lessons. Teaching units should be designed so that competencies learned in one unit can be applied to mastering other units and to situations encountered outside school. Teaching units requiring continual practice and the application of many skills to diverse tasks are likely to produce students able to transfer their learning to other situations. Teaching programmes with skill-learning experiences carefully integrated vertically and horizontally will help teach students to transfer their learning.[20] A fifth-level teacher who links graph-making skills in social studies and mathematics (horizontal integration) will encourage learning transfer. The teacher of sixteen-year-old students who stresses the connections between students' previously learned hypothesis-testing skills and their present learning activity (vertical integration) will facilitate learning transfer.[21]

Clearly, the curriculum which effectively teaches essential skills must be planned with care. The well designed plan will (1) highlight skills necessary for effective group membership; (2) connect school-based skill-learning experiences with out-of-school experiences; (3) integrate skill-learning experiences vertically and horizontally within the overall curriculum; (4) provide continual practice and application of skill learning; and (5) encourage the transfer of learning from one experience to another. These characteristics of a well designed curriculum are a guide to teaching strategies and sample units presented in the remainder of this chapter. The remaining pages suggest ways of teaching each of the three categories of essential skills.

Teaching Skills in Studying and Learning

Skills in studying and learning should be a part of the entire curriculum programme. One purpose of education is to help students become self-reliant in learning what they want to learn. During their school years, students have teachers to guide their learning; but this teacher-guide will not always be available. Students should acquire skills for independent studying and learning. This means students should develop skills pertaining to finding, comprehending, organising, interpreting and evaluating information. Interpreting maps, tables, graphs and charts; reading newspapers and magazines effectively; distinguishing fact from fiction and facts from opinions; building a social studies vocabulary; classifying information; summarising information; asking clear questions in an interview; identifying examples of fallacious reasoning; and learning to arrange events in chronological order are all specific skills students should be expected to master. Most of these skills can be taught simply and effectively to children in the first six years of school. As students move to higher grade levels, their sophistication and performance levels should increase.

Studying and learning skills must be taught systematically, beginning with lower performance levels and continuing to higher levels. Therefore, teachers must carefully examine skills prerequisite to each particular learning experience and identify and teach these prerequisites in the appropriate order.[22] In a map-study programme, the teacher must be sure the students know the difference between mercator and equal-area projection maps before asking students to compare and interpret information from these two map types.

The following section contains examples of how to teach particular studying and learning skills. They should suggest to the teacher ways in which other specific studying and learning skills might be taught and offer inspiration to developing and utilising other relevant teaching strategies.

Developing Skills for Studying and Learning from Textbooks

Textbooks are an important medium of social studies instruction throughout the world. They are designed to communicate information by means of printed words, numbers, pictures, diagrams, graphs, charts and maps. They are a useful tool for teaching students of any age how to acquire and use information from books.

There are five categories of skills necessary for acquiring and using information from books. Each of these categories suggests many classroom activities for helping students accomplish the teacher's skill objectives. Although the examples presented here refer to textbooks, these skills should be transferable to other prepared sources of information such as newspapers, magazines and encyclopedias.

Finding Information. Students should be able to locate facts and concepts within a reading assignment. They should also learn to use the study aids that are part of most textbooks. Specific skill-building activities include locating information by using the text's index and using headings within chapters to find details about a person, place or event.

Literal Comprehension of Information. Students should have a literal understanding of data presented in maps, graphs, tables, charts, diagrams and — above all — in prose passages. This includes such skills as identifying the main idea, recognising contrasting points of view and knowing the literal meanings of words. Students should practise reading paragraphs or sets of paragraphs to identify the main idea. Their comprehension should be tested by having each student write a sentence identifying the most important point, or by offering students a choice of several ideas from which they must identify the main point presented in their reading. Other activities to build literal-comprehension skills include identifying details which support or contradict a main idea or an opinion and identifying data which support or contradict contrasting opinions in a reading assignment.

Organising Information. This skill category is based on the ability to classify information. Children begin to develop these skills when they group items that are alike and then identify the group with a label (category). Very young children might be asked to classify pictures of tools according to their use. Older students could be asked to sort information to demonstrate examples and non-examples of ideas or defined concepts. For a concept such as 'interdependence', students could first be given written or pictorial examples of situations demonstrating 'interdependence'. Then students could be asked to sort new material as examples or non-examples of the concept 'interdependence'.

There are other ways to organise information. One is to identify steps involved in a process, such as listing the steps in the food distribution chain. Another way is to organise events in chronological order.

Interpreting Information. When students can identify the implications of information provided in a paragraph, graph, chart and illustration and speculate about the connotations of information, they are making inferences. Students must be skilled in making inferences in order to interpret information.

Students develop interpretive skills when they use data to make factual statements or to support or reject opinions. They are using skills in interpreting information when they suggest different meanings that might be implied by a picture.

Evaluating Information. Evaluating information requires critical reading and thinking. It involves detecting flaws in reasoning and analysing an argument to see if it is consistent with facts. Evaluating information means making judgements about the validity of information.

Children begin to develop evaluation skills when making judgements to determine if a drawing accurately represents an event or place. Older students develop these skills when they make judgements about the accuracy of information presented in a graph, chart or paragraph.

Developing Skills in Using Graphs

Graphs are widely used to display information. They can be found in newspapers, magazines, commercial reports, political campaign literature and textbooks. Since a graph makes minimal use of words, it can be understood by people from many cultures and language areas. Knowing how to construct and interpret graphs is a basic part of a good education.

Graphs can be identified by type: there are pictorial graphs, bar graphs, circle (or 'pie') graphs and line graphs. Pictorial graphs usually depict a sequence of events; bar graphs are best used to compare discrete bits of information; line graphs are used to show continual changes; and circle graphs are best for showing the relationship of parts to the whole. Students should be taught how to read all types of graphs.

Graph reading is another skill which can be learned only through practice. Teachers can guide this practice by teaching students to identify the various components of a graph. Students should use the heading to identify the subject presented by the graph. They should learn to find and understand the key to the graph's symbols and they should be able to construct a graph from raw data. By reading and interpreting many graphs students will develop their graph-reading skills. The sample teaching exercises which follow provide practice in reading different types of graphs.

Sample Teaching Activity I. This exercise is designed to develop skills in literal comprehension of information in a line graph and can be used to develop interpretive skills. The first four questions exercise the students' ability to comprehend the graph literally. The fifth question requires students to make an inference which goes beyond the data to develop a justifiable answer.

(1) Did the population of the world increase or decrease between 1800 and 1850? (increase)
(2) During which fifty-year period was the total growth in numbers of people greatest? (1900-1950)

(3) Which fifty-year period experienced the least growth in total numbers of people? (1750-1800)

(4) Which fifty-year period experienced the greatest rate of population growth? (1900-1950)

(5) If the trend in population growth for the period 1900-1950 continues between 1950 and 2000, what is a reasonable estimate of the total world population in the year 2000?

Figure 7.1: World Population, 1750-1950

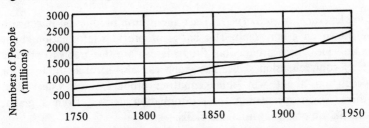

Source: The data for this exercise are from J.D. Durand, 'The Modern Expansion of World Population', *Proceedings of the American Philosophical Society*, vol. 3, no. 3 (22 June 1967), as reported in *The World Population Situation in 1970*, UN Department of Economic and Social Affairs, Population Studies No. 49, p. 4.

Sample Teaching Activity II. This exercise provides practice in literal comprehension of information found in circle graphs.

Figure 7.2: Major Corn Producers among the Nations of the World for 1978

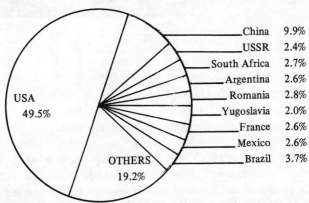

Source: *Statistical Abstracts of the United States* (US Department of Commerce, Bureau of the Census, Washington, DC, 1979), p. 907.

(1) Which country produced the most corn in 1978? (United States)
(2) What was Romania's share of corn production in 1978? (2.8%)
(3) What percentage of the corn crop, as shown in this graph, was produced by a Western European nation? (2.6%)
(4) If other Western European nations produced corn, where, in this graph, might this information be found? (Corn production of other Western European countries might be included in the 'Others' category included in this graph.)

Sample Teaching Activity III. Data about crop production might also be shown on a bar graph. This bar graph provides information about world-wide wheat production. Students can use this graph to practise literal comprehension skills. The graph can also serve as the basis for speculation about why some countries produce more wheat than others. When speculating from information derived from a graph, students are practising inference skills.

Figure 7.3: Major Wheat Producers among the Nations of the World for 1978

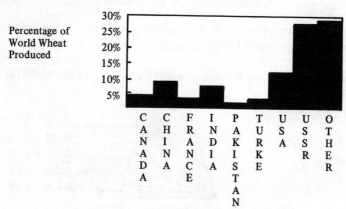

Source: *Statistical Abstracts of the United States*, p. 906.

Many other activities will help develop students' skills in reading graphs. Teachers could show students examples of graphs with flaws in data presentation. Students could practise critical reading skills by identifying the flaws in the graphs' construction. These flaws could include lack of clear labelling, lack of a key to symbols and unclear or ambiguous identification of information. Students should also be required to construct their own graphs. Intermediate- and higher-level students will increase their proficiency in skills of organising and interpreting information with practice in graph construction.

Developing Skills in Using Maps

Map-reading skills, like skills in graph-reading, can be taught at progressive levels of complexity from the lowest to the highest grades. By demonstrating methods of reading different kinds of maps, teachers can prepare students for interpreting and constructing original maps. Students should be able to apply the teacher's demonstration on map-reading to interpreting maps with which they are unfamiliar.

A map is a graphic representation of information in which the location of facts relative to one another is preserved. Information related to most social issues is usually portrayed on one of three kinds of maps: (1) the dot map; (2) the area value (choropleth) map; and (3) the isoline map.

The Dot Map. On this kind of map, dots are used to represent the information under consideration. Each dot is assigned a value. The dots are placed so as to reflect the location of the facts portrayed. The dot map below shows the arrangement of world population. Each dot on the map stands for one million people. The dots are placed to reflect where people actually live.

Figure 7.4: World Population Distribution in 1979

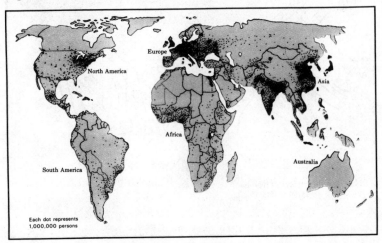

The Area-Value Map. On an area-value (chorpleth) map, shading is often used to show differences in value among the facts portrayed. In the area-value map shown below, different intensities of shading are used to represent different levels of gross national produce *per capita* for the countries of the world.

Figure 7.5: Rich Nations and Poor Nations

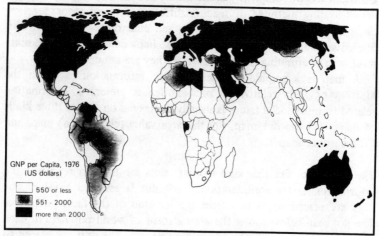

Figure 7.6: Air Pollution in the United States, 1970

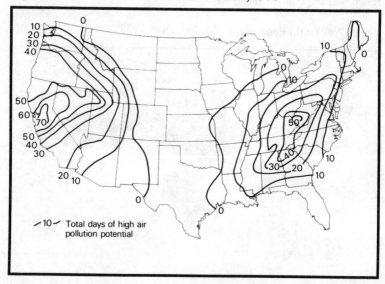

The Isoline Map. 'Iso' means 'equal'. Isolines are lines which connect all locations on the map at which the facts under consideration reach a particular value. In the isoline map which appears above, each numbered line on the map joins places with the same air pollution potential (as measured by the total number of days on which the possibility of high levels of air pollution were forecast). Places between each pair of lines on the map have pollution potentials between the values of those lines.

The discussion which follows refers almost exclusively to dot maps. This is because dot maps are relatively easy to use, even by very young schoolchildren. The techniques described for examining dot maps, however, are equally appropriate when examining area value and isoline maps.

Where Things Happen. Knowing where facts occur often provides important insights into an issue. As an illustration, look at the example of Dr John Snow, an English physician working in the early nineteenth century.[23] Dr Snow spent several years studying the spread of cholera in London. He believed that somehow cholera entered a water supply and that the water carried the disease to its victims. He tested his belief by examining information about cholera deaths in the Soho district of London in 1848.

On a street map of Soho he located every cholera death that occurred in 1848 by marking each victim's home with a dot. The map also showed the location of pumps from which people got their water.

The completed map revealed that a large number of the victims lived close to the pump on Broad Street. At Dr Snow's request the handle of the pump was removed, making it impossible to draw water. The number of new cholera cases in Soho then declined almost to zero. This confirmed the doctor's belief about the role played by drinking-water in the spread of cholera.

This case study indicates that Dr Snow gained useful insights about the spread of cholera by using a graphic portrayal of information in which the location of relevant facts with respect to one another was preserved — that is to say, by using a map to show where cholera deaths occurred. He discovered a concentration of deaths around a particular pump. The doctor then inferred that this clustering indicated a relationship between the water from the pump and cholera deaths. The decision to dismantle the pump was based on Dr Snow's analysis.

Students, too, can gain insights into a wide variety of issues by carefully examining relevant maps. The cholera case study suggests that three questions are involved in examining a map: (1) What is the map about? (2) What does the map say? (3) What does the map mean?

Figure 7.7: Cholera Deaths in Soho, 1848

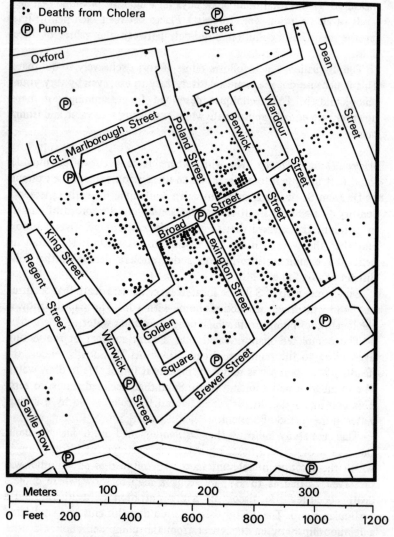

What is the Map about? The first step in examining a map is determining what the map is about. Map users should always inspect the map title, check the map scale and review the map legend when first looking at a map.

By inspecting the *map title*, the user can quickly determine the map's subject, the area for which information was collected and the year of the information. In the cholera case study the map used was entitled 'Cholera Deaths in Soho, 1848'. The title indicates that the map contains information about cholera deaths, that the information is for Soho and that the year of the information is 1848.

The *map scale* should also be checked when determining a map's subject. All maps represent features of the Earth's surface shown much smaller than they are in reality. The map scale is the relationship between map distance and real distance. By checking the scale, the map user can estimate how detailed the information on the map is. *Small-scale* maps (in which short map distances are used for long real distances) can show a large area, but with little detail. *Large-scale* maps (in which long map distances are used for short real distances) can show only a small area, but with much greater detail. In the cholera case study, the map scale was large enough so that individual pumps and victims' homes could be plotted. The map shown below, a small-scale map of the whole London area, is not suited for plotting individual cholera deaths in Soho.

Sometimes the scale is written on the map. For example, 'One inch equals 400 miles' means that one inch on the map represents 400 miles on the Earth. 'One centimetre equals 200 kilometres' means that one centimetre on the map represents 200 kilometres on the Earth. On another map, the scale might read '1:24,000'. This means that one unit of map distance equals 24,000 units of real distance, regardless of the unit of measurement — inches and miles, or centimetres and kilometres.

The scale can also be shown in graphic form, subdivided for easy measurement. For example, Dr Snow's map contains a graphic scale showing that one inch on the map stands for about 300 feet on the Earth. (Or one centimetre stands for about 25 metres.) By knowing the map scale, the map user can readily measure distances. Dr Snow's map showed that most cholera deaths in Soho occurred within about 400 feet (120 metres) of the pump on Broad Street.

Finally, the *map legend* should be reviewed when determining what a map is about. The symbols contained in the legend stand for both natural and human features. Familiarity with the symbols used on a particular map simplifies the task of characterising what is shown on the map. For example, knowing that the symbols on Dr Snow's map refer to water pumps and cholera deaths makes describing the information on the map easier.

Figure 7.8: London and Soho

What does the Map Say? The second step in examining a map is determining what the map says. This requires looking carefully at the particular way in which facts are arranged over the *entire map*. The map facts may be displayed in clustered, even or random arrangements. When facts are clustered, they are located close together; when even, they are uniformly spread; and when random, no particular pattern is apparent. In the cholera case study, for example, the map showed that cholera deaths in Soho were 'clustered' around the water pump on Broad Street. (Figure 7.9 points out the differences among clustered, even and random arrangements of facts.)

The existence of an even or clustered arrangement of facts suggests that there is an explanation for why those facts are located where they are. Random arrangements, on the other hand, are likely to have occurred by chance.

Figure 7.9: Clustered, Even and Random Arrangements

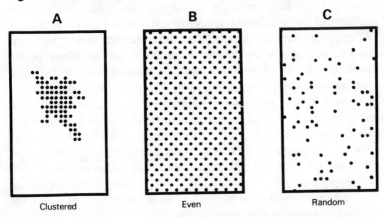

A   B   C

Clustered   Even   Random

What does the Map Mean? Once the arrangement of facts on a map has been described, the map user's final step in examining it is to determine what it means. This involves suggesting and testing hypotheses to explain why the facts portrayed on the map are arranged as they are. In the cholera case study, the map showed that cholera deaths in Soho were clustered. Dr Snow hypothesised that this arrangement was somehow related to the water supply.

Comparing the arrangements of two or more types of information on one map or comparing maps showing arrangements of different information is a technique often used to test a locational hypothesis. By comparing the arrangements of pumps and victims' homes, Dr Snow was able to establish that a relationship actually existed between water supply and cholera deaths. The results of closing the Broad Street pump proved that the relationship was causal in nature.

To conclude this section, a short activity is outlined that uses all of the map skills described.

Sample Teaching Activity IV. In this activity, students are presented with a map such as the world population map shown on page 169.[24] First, the teacher should ask students, *'What is the map about?'* In this example, the title indicates that it shows world population distribution for 1979. No specific scale is indicated, but it is clearly a small-scale map. The legend indicates that each dot represents one million people.

Students are then asked, *'What does the map say?'* Obviously, people are not evenly arranged over the Earth. The map suggests that most of the world's population is concentrated in a few areas — East

Asia, South Asia, South-East Asia, Europe and east-central North America. Many large areas are almost completely uninhabited. This suggests that the world's population is more clustered than random.

Finally, students are asked, *'What does the map mean?'* Since the clustered arrangement on the map suggests that people are not located where they are by chance, students can be encouraged to speculate freely about possible explanations of world population distribution.

Some may be tempted to hypothesise that human population concentrations only exist in certain natural environments. They might hypothesise, for example, that desert areas – which are characterised by very hot summers, very little rainfall, scattered vegetation cover and poor soils – would not support large population concentrations. This hypothesis can be tested by comparing the world population map to a map showing the location of desert areas. Students could use the following map to make such a comparison.

Figure 7.10: World Natural Environment Regions

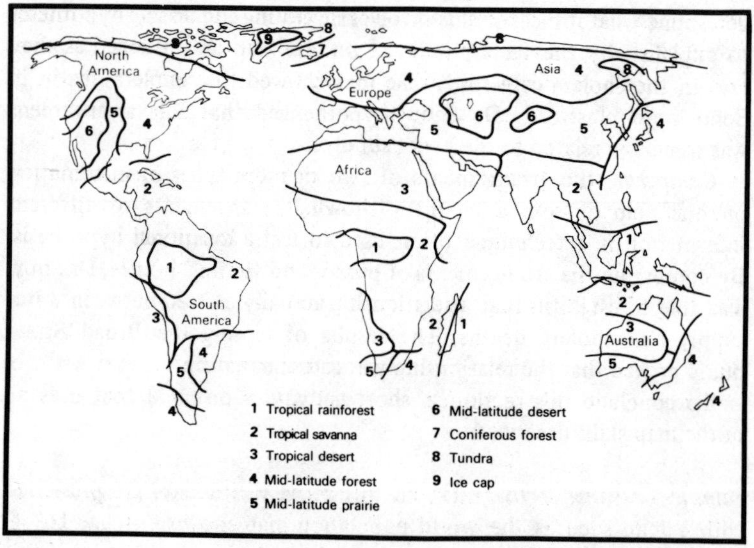
North America
Europe
Asia
Africa
South America
Australia
1 Tropical rainforest
2 Tropical savanna
3 Tropical desert
4 Mid-latitude forest
5 Mid-latitude prairie
6 Mid-latitude desert
7 Coniferous forest
8 Tundra
9 Ice cap

The locations of desert environments (regions three and six) and areas with few people are generally similar. It is true that several areas outside the desert environments also have few people. But for the most part, very dry environments have few people. Look, for example, at the interior of Australia, at the interior of North Africa and at Central Asia. All have desert environments and few people.

There are, however, several desert areas that are exceptions to this relationship. For example, much of southern California has a desert environment and yet contains a large population concentration. Population concentrations also exist in parts of North Africa and South-West Asia, despite their desert environment.

In this case, the comparison procedure did not completely support the student hypothesis. This should stimulate the students to examine the exceptions carefully, in an effort to develop further hypotheses to explain world population distribution.

Concluding Commentary about Teaching Skills in Studying and Learning

The preceding examples represent only a fraction of the vast array of study and learning skills that should be taught in school. The main purpose for teaching these skills is to encourage students to think and learn independently. Students can be required to practise skills in finding, comprehending, organising, interpreting and evaluating information. They can be assigned tasks that require them to practise these skills as they read and think about their textbooks. Reading and thinking about graphs and maps are especially important examples of activities designed to foster various skills in working with information.

These study and learning skills are applicable to many experiences outside school which people encounter as youngsters and adults. Furthermore, these skills are prerequisite to acquiring skills in enquiry and decision-making.

Teaching Skills in Enquiry and Decision-making

Skills in enquiry and decision-making require the highest levels of thinking. They require students to formulate and test hypotheses and to make judgements.

Skills in enquiry and decision-making greatly enhance a student's ability to think and learn. When students personally experience the process of searching for knowledge, they are acting to the fullest as independent thinkers and learners.

Skills in enquiry and decision-making should be acquired through guided discovery learning. Guided discovery learning occurs when students find their own answers to problems designed by their teacher to meet specific objectives.

Studies in thinking patterns have indicated that most adolescents have the capacity to acquire skills in enquiry and decision-making.

Many youngsters begin to manifest higher-level thinking capacities during the ages between eleven and thirteen. These children are at the threshold of effectively handling abstractions, reasoning from premises, theorising and making warranted decisions about facts and values. Fifteen-year-olds show potential to acquire and use higher-level thinking skills consistently and competently.[25]

A Strategy for Teaching Enquiry Skills

Skills that are basic to enquiry include recognising a problem, developing hypotheses, exploring implications of hypotheses, supporting hypotheses with evidence and drawing conclusions.[26] These skills can be taught systematically, as part of a step-by-step strategy.

Skill in Recognising a Problem. Skill in recognising a problem is the ability to point out the problem's critical issues. To help students develop this skill, teachers should encourage them to identify and select the problems they consider important. Teachers can generate student interest by presenting discrepancies between student opinions and actual, conflicting data; by showing curiosity-producing pictures and other thought-provoking materials; and by reading aloud selected current news stories. But developing an appetite for enquiry among students is not always easy. Because of students' varying interests, it can be difficult to create provocative problems that involve all class members. Furthermore, problems must be difficult enough to challenge students without being too difficult for them to understand.

Skill in Developing Hypotheses. Skill in developing hypotheses is the ability to formulate tentative statements or propositions which can be tested by further enquiry. Hypotheses are preliminary conclusions that are testable by collecting evidence to support or reject them. To help students develop this skill, teachers should provide them with repeated practice in identifying and writing testable hypotheses about issues the class is studying. As students first learn to develop hypotheses, teachers should be supportive and offer minimal criticism. Students should be encouraged to express ideas freely and creatively. But teachers should help students stay within the criteria for testable hypotheses about the problem being studied.

Skill in Exploring. Skill in exploration is the ability to examine a hypothesis and determine potential sources for evidence to support or reject it. Students must be able to make logical inferences to identify the types of evidence that would exist should the hypothesis be valid. This requires students to construct 'if-then' statements, such as '*If* synthetic fertiliser is found to increase agricultural production, *then* farmers will switch from organic fertiliser to the synthetic type.' Teachers should provide many opportunities for students to identify and construct 'if-then' statements and should guide them in inferring what kinds of evidence could validate these statements.

Skill in Using Evidence to Support Hypotheses. This skill includes the ability to identify evidence relevant to a hypothesis and find empirical data for support and proof of the hypothesis. Data are information about either people or things. Statistics about the distribution of income in a country are data that could help test hypotheses about the extent of poverty in that country.

To develop skills in using evidence to support hypotheses, students should engage in information-selecting processes. Social studies textbooks and supplementary materials, first-hand reports from observers of the situation and physical evidence left by people or events related to the situation are all sources of information for students to use in testing hypotheses. Interviewing, systematic observation and sample surveys all provide fresh data for testing hypotheses, but teachers should protect students from research activities that are too complex or esoteric for their skills or for the time and purposes available.

Skill in Drawing Conclusions. The skill of drawing conclusions is sometimes called the skill of 'generalising'. It is the ability to rearrange evidence in such a way that it becomes relevant to the hypotheses being tested. It requires the same kind of mental skills used in formulating a hypothesis. To develop this kind of skill, students must search for relationships among the evidence and the hypotheses. These relationships should then be synthesised into statements that support or reject the initial hypothesis. If the evidence is not sufficient to validate the hypothesis, students should return to the original problem, develop a different hypothesis and test the new one. This process of repetition is the way most problems are solved.

Sample Teaching Activity V. This enquiry activity is designed to teach the following objective: the student will be able to use evidence to support the generalisation that ancient civilisations originated *only* in places where there was a surplus of basic resources.

The teacher should open the unit by using a map to identify the sources of four ancient civilisations. These would include the Nile River, the Indus River, the Hwang Ho River and the Tigris-Euphrates rivers. Next, the teacher should distribute to the class four brief packets of data about the four ancient river civilisations. These packets should include bits of evidence about the climate, natural resources and ways of satisfying basic human needs in these four cultures. While examining the packets, students should search for evidence that shows how the four river cultures were alike and how they were different.

After looking over the limited evidence available in the data packets, students should formulate hypotheses about why ancient peoples settled in these four locations rather than in other nearby areas and what existed in these locations to support the development of a complex culture. Students should explore their hypotheses and seek additional evidence to test their hypotheses. Textbooks, encyclopaedias, library resources and museums may be used to find additional evidence. After several days of finding and using evidence from various sources, students should be ready to draw conclusions. They should be able to decide whether their original hypotheses are warranted or not. If not, they should alter their hypotheses to fit all the evidence they have collected.

The Decision Tree Strategy

Decision-making is choosing from two or more alternatives. Students can be taught to make reasoned, rather than haphazard, decisions. Reasoned decisions are based on valid evidence and lead to consequences that are consistent with the decision-maker's values.

A person without skills in studying, learning and enquiry is handicapped in making reasoned decisions. However, these skills alone cannot yield sound decisions, because they have to do only with facts and factual judgements. In contrast, personal and group decisions also involve value judgements.

There are six steps, each involving distinct skills, that are part of any reasoned decision-making strategy. The first is recognising an occasion for making a decision. The second step is identifying alternative courses of action, or choices. The third step is predicting the various consequences that might result from each of the alternatives. The fourth is assigning positive or negative values to the various potential consequences. The fifth is assessing the values that pertain to the decision-making situation and thinking about which values are more or less important. And finally, one chooses an alternative that seems likely to lead to an outcome most consistent with one's preferred value or values.

These decision-making skills can be taught with a 'decision tree' strategy, which is represented in the chart below. This decision tree is a chart of the basic steps in making personal or group decisions.[27]

Figure 7.11: The Decision Tree

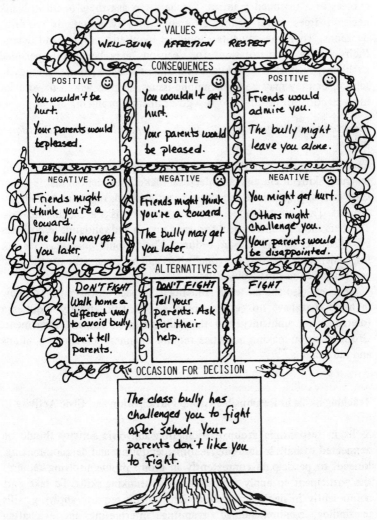

VALUES
WELL-BEING AFFECTION RESPECT

CONSEQUENCES

POSITIVE ☺
You wouldn't be hurt.
Your parents would be pleased.

POSITIVE ☺
You wouldn't get hurt.
Your parents would be pleased.

POSITIVE ☺
Friends would admire you.
The bully might leave you alone.

NEGATIVE ☹
Friends might think you're a coward.
The bully may get you later.

NEGATIVE ☹
Friends might think you're a coward.
The bully may get you later.

NEGATIVE ☹
You might get hurt.
Others might challenge you.
Your parents would be disappointed.

ALTERNATIVES

DON'T FIGHT
Walk home a different way to avoid bully.
Don't tell parents.

DON'T FIGHT
Tell your parents. Ask for their help.

FIGHT

OCCASION FOR DECISION

The class bully has challenged you to fight after school. Your parents don't like you to fight.

In this decision tree chart, the 'occasion' for a decision is a personal problem — how to cope with the class bully. This particular episode was designed for use with ten- to twelve-year-olds. However, the decision tree strategy can also be applied to cases that are appropriate for older students.

By using the decision tree, students can be helped to practise making choices in a reasoned manner. Teachers can ask them to fill in blank decision trees about many different kinds of situations requiring decisions. Then the students should be required to report and defend their choices. The occasions for decisions may be various personal problems, such as how to budget money or select a course of study in school, or they may be about public issues, such as whom to vote for in an election, or how to resolve a governmental problem.

Classroom Conditions and Attitudes that Support Enquiry and Decision-making

Certain classroom conditions and attitudes are necessary for effectively teaching skills in enquiry and decision-making. Students must feel that they can raise questions and explore various kinds of evidence to derive answers. They must also feel that they can take risks in seeking answers. Teachers should build respect for using reason and validating hypotheses by scientific canons and procedures. They should encourage respect for evidence as the basis for conclusions and encourage the practice and acceptance of scientific objectivity.

Teachers also should teach students to respect various points of view in areas that have no certain answers. Scientific enquiry requires a tolerance for ambiguity and the willingness to suspend judgement. Group decision-making activities require openness to various opinions and judgements.[28]

Teaching Skills in Responsible Group Participation and Civic Activity

Skills in responsible group participation and civic activity should be connected to skills in studying, learning, enquiring and decision-making. Indeed, to participate competently in group problem-solving requires the participant to apply various kinds of thinking skills. To take part competently in significant civic action projects requires applying skills in finding, comprehending, organising, interpreting and evaluating information.

One ultimate goal of social studies instruction is to provide students with the ability to apply knowledge and thinking skills to projects with social significance. This requires the development of group participation skills such as the abilities to lead, organise, bargain, compromise and manage group meetings and activities lawfully, co-operatively and effectively.

In all societies and countries of the world and at every level within those societies and countries, some kind of group decision-making takes place. However, many people are not skilled in the arts of group discussion and decision-making. Because effective procedures and principles of conducting a meeting are not followed, many meetings end in frustration. There may be endless argument without producing decisions. There may be a lack of leadership and co-operation.

Group participation skills can be taught effectively at all levels of education. In the earliest years, the emphasis might be on interaction in committees and on role-playing. Older students can be introduced gradually to civic action learning experiences outside the classroom.

The discussion that follows emphasises three kinds of learning experiences that develop group participation skills. These are (1) small-group, or committee, problem-solving; (2) role-playing; and (3) participating in civic action projects.

Small-group Problem-solving

Group participation skills may be learned through orderly classroom discussion of standard teaching programmes. As teachers present material on social studies topics, they can also teach and reinforce group behaviour skills. Reinforcement of these skills occurs when teachers remind students to respect the rights of others in the group, to speak when called upon, and to co-operate with others to reach the group's learning goals.

Small-group activities that are led alternately by different students can also build group participation skills. Dividing the class into several groups of five or six students with each group being given responsibility for completing an assignment requires individuals in each group to co-operate. Students can work on real or hypothetical problems in small groups. The teacher can provide information relevant to the problem in data packets or fact sheets.

Small-group discussion assignments should involve systematic application of knowledge and thinking skills to solving problems or making decisions to resolve an issue. Group members can practise skills in deliberation and human interaction in order to achieve a group goal co-operatively.

Each group should select a chairperson who is responsible for managing meetings. Another person should be designated recorder, to keep a record of the group's decisions and significant viewpoints. At the conclusion of the problem-solving activity, a member of each group should report and justify the group's problem solution or issue resolution to other students.[29]

Teachers may find the 'decision tree', discussed previously an aid to teaching group decision-making. Students working in small groups can use their own copies of the decision tree to structure and chart deliberations in making a group decision.[30] The boxes in the decision tree should be filled in as the group tries to make decisions about an assigned issue.

Social group decisions, such as where to go for a day of relaxation and fun, could also be studied. Should the group attend a concert at the neighbourhood centre? Or should the group attend the football match at the city stadium? If group members do not have time or money to do both, what should be done? Students can be given data about resources and values of group members to help them decide.

Teachers can assign students who are working in small groups to make decisions about a public issue, such as whether community government officials should vote to approve construction of a new civic centre or of an addition to a crowded high school in one section of the town. Since the community does not have enough money to build both facilities, a choice must be made. What should be done? Teachers may distribute fact sheets with relevant financial data and various arguments about the public issue to help students make a reasoned judgement.

Through small-group problem-solving and decision-making activities, students can learn from experience about the give and take of group decision-making. They may also learn the value of orderly procedures, division of tasks and co-operation in reaching a group goal.

Role-playing

Role-playing is a structured activity permitting students to take the part of a person in an imaginary situation and to act the part in as realistic a manner as possible. A role-play is like a drama except that a drama has a prepared script and each actor learns the lines provided by the writer. In a role play the situation is given, but it is the responsibility of each actor to supply the dialogue and the action. Typically a role-play situation is one that is sufficiently familiar to the players that they can be expected to imagine how people might act in such situations.

Girls who act the role of mother while they play with dolls, or boys who role play warriors when they play with toy weapons are engaged in simple role-play experiences. Role-plays can be used by teachers to give students practice in group participation skills.

Teachers often initiate a role-playing exercise by presenting a brief description of a human relations situation. Each student selects a role or is assigned one by the teacher. Role cards, containing specific characteristics of each role, are distributed to the appropriate students. Some students may be assigned to observe the role play and to evaluate the performance.

At the conclusion of the role play, the teacher should lead students in a discussion of what happened, why it happened, alternatives to what happened and the significance of the human behaviour they observed. They should also evaluate the skill with which different roles were played and make suggestions about how to improve performance of the group participation skill that was illustrated by the situation. The teacher should conclude the role-play activity with a summary of the main points learned from the activity.

Role-playing is very effective in developing skills in group leadership, interviewing, selling, bargaining, compromising and decision-making. Through performing and observing role-play activities, students can increase their skills in diagnosing interpersonal situations, in behaving effectively in interpersonal situations and in resolving interpersonal problems.[31]

Teachers can also organise role-play activities that simulate institutions of government. For example, students might simulate a session of the Security Council or the General Assembly of the United Nations. Students could take on the roles of representatives of various member states and United Nations officials. After studying issues before the United Nations and the positions being taken by various member states, students could provide realistic portrayals of a typical session. Such an exercise can increase their skills, enhance their interest in the United Nations and inform them of important world issues.

Civic Action Projects

Civic action projects develop participation skills through action outside the classroom. The projects may be carried out in the school community or in the larger community outside the school. Civic action projects require applying knowledge and thinking skills developed through other kinds of learning to projects that can benefit the community. The emphasis should be on learning how to use knowledge and skills to contribute to the community. Learning to define, describe, explain and evaluate political realities should not be an end in itself. Rather, students should be taught to apply their knowledge and skills to participation in civic life.

Fred Newmann, a noted American civics education theorist and curriculum developer from the University of Wisconsin, has proposed an extensive reform of social studies curricula to focus on teaching knowledge and skills for community action.[32] He believes that instruction should interlace knowledge and skill-learning in the classroom with practical applications in the community outside the classroom. These community applications involve exploratory research about social processes that can be used later to improve public services. They also include volunteer service activities, such as performing duties in a day-care centre or in a home for the elderly, managing a campaign to remove litter from the streets, or conducting a tutoring service to help uneducated people learn to read and write. The focus of participatory learning in the community is on social action projects in which participants try to improve the policies and practices of community institutions.

Through experience in the community, students use knowledge and skills to cope with ongoing public problems. These practical experiences also extend their knowledge and skills far beyond what can be learned in the classroom.

Sample Teaching Activity VI. This civic action project uses the school community and is appropriate for beginning to middle-level students. The aim of the project is for students to improve the appearance of the school premises. The project combines the use of knowledge, thinking skills and small-group participation skills for civic action in the school community.

The teacher may begin by asking students whether the school premises are clean enough or whether they need some improvement. Students are likely to suggest needed improvements. The teacher should encourage students to ask, 'What can we do to improve the appearance of the school premises?' Students will suggest various ways of bringing about improvement.

Although students will have their own opinions about specific problems, the teacher can help them formulate ideas by pointing out broad areas. For example, the teacher can ask what the students think about the condition of the bulletin boards. Students may point out that some material on the boards is old and out of date. Discussion about the condition of the floor may reveal that after each rain the entrance to the school building becomes muddy. It may be that some window panes are broken and door hinges are noisy. Walls may have pencil or crayon marks. The washbasins may be clogged. The garbage cans may be surrounded with papers that were thoughtlessly scattered. The grounds outside the school may be covered with litter. Discussion of these issues can lead students to prepare a list that represents the larger problem of disorder on the school grounds.

At the suggestion of the teacher, small groups of students can then investigate and gather facts about each item on the list. Fact-gathering will confirm or deny the importance of each item as part of the overall problem. Then students and the teacher should hold a problem-solving session. Students should offer their ideas for solving these school problems. They may suggest that the front entrance requires a bigger floor mat to encourage children to wipe their shoes, particularly after rain. They may suggest oiling the door hinges, painting some areas of the walls with waterproof paints and providing larger garbage cans at appropriate places. Each suggested solution should be discussed in order to arrive at a consensus and students should develop a list of possible remedial actions. At this point, students might try to generalise from this problem and solution to similar neighbourhood problems. They can also suggest solutions to problems facing the entire community.

After discussing the problem, students should act to solve it. They can develop an active campaign to prevent littering. They can prepare and place signs near the rest room washbasins requesting students not to drop paper, food items, gum or other debris in the washbasins. Similar action can apply to community problems outside the school.

Civic action projects are becoming common in schools around the world. Here are some examples of projects from four different countries:

(1) The Manila City schools in the Philippines stress civic action projects. These projects have included cleaning and beautifying the school and its grounds. Other projects have involved clean-up and beautification campaigns in the centre of Manila and in various outlying neighbourhoods. Students have planted decorative hedges and trees around the city.[36]

(2) In Thailand, students have worked in rural community development projects.

(3) In India, students have undertaken social work projects such

Plate 7.2: Schoolchildren in the United Republic of Tanzania

Children happily participate in a village construction project as a part of the
school instruction programme which gives them a sense of community
participation.

as designing a playground or spreading information about health care to outlying villages.

(4) In Poland, students helped to rebuild the Chateau Royale in Warsaw as a school civic action project.[37]

Conditions that Encourage Learning of Group Participation Skills

Group participation and civic action projects should enable students to apply knowledge and thinking skills to significant experiences. Activities must be designed to help students understand that knowledge and thinking skills are most valuable when they contribute to improving the quality of life.

Group participation and civic action projects require active learning in which students face realistic and practical problems, issues and decisions. They should challenge students intellectually, practically and collectively to address problems relevant to life outside the classroom.

Teachers must establish a supportive learning environment that encourages students to contribute ideas. In this way students can learn to respect the efforts and contributions of all students, from the most to the least able. Teachers must work to prevent any student from feeling threatened by or left out of group projects.

Summary and Conclusions

Essential skills should be a basic part of the social studies curriculum at every level. By acquiring essential skills, students become active in the search for knowledge rather than passive recipients of facts. Essential skills provide the power to think and learn independently. They allow students to apply knowledge to solving academic and practical problems. There are three main categories of essential skills in the social studies: (1) skills in studying and learning; (2) skills in enquiry and decision-making; and (3) skills in responsible group participation and civic action.

Curriculum developers and teachers should design teaching programmes that relate skill-learning experiences to each other. Students at lower levels in school should learn basic skills as prerequisites for the higher-level thinking and learning required in enquiry and decision-making. As students move from lower to higher levels in the curriculum, they should be required to perform skills at higher levels of proficiency. As they progress through school, students should be faced with gradually more complex and sophisticated skill-learning tasks.

Skills should be practised again and again. One test of skill-learning is an application activity that requires students to use one or more skills to complete a novel task.

Skills should be applied to the solution of academic problems in the classroom and to practical problems outside the classroom. By learning to apply skills in the classroom, students develop the ability to transfer learning to other situations. This also demonstrates the meaning and relevance of skill-learning to students.

Finally, knowledge and thinking skills learned individually should also be applied to learning in groups. Through group learning experiences, students can practise using thinking skills and can develop skills in human relationships and group governance.

Teachers who emphasise essential skill development do more than transmit factual information. Rather, they participate in teaching students skills for seeking and using knowledge in order to think for themselves. Freedom begins with the opportunity and capability to make reasoned choices and to think and learn independently. Freedom with social responsibility requires citizens to possess the desire and ability to use skills to benefit individuals as members of society.

Notes:

1. John Jarolimek, 'The Psychology of Skill Development' in Helen McCracken Carpenter (ed.), *Skill Development in Social Studies* (National Council for the Social Studies, Washington DC, 1963), pp. 17-34.

2. Harry Maddox, *How to Study* (Fawcett, Greenwich, Connecticut, 1963), pp. 11-22.

3. John Dewey, *How We Think* (D.C. Heath, Boston, 1933), p. 12.

4. Ibid., p. 9.

5. Robert M. Gagné, *The Conditions of Learning* (Holt, Rinehart and Winston, 1977), pp. 25-49.

6. Lee H. Ehman, Howard D. Mehlinger, and John J. Patrick, *Toward Effective Instruction in Secondary Social Studies* (Houghton Mifflin, Boston, 1974), pp. 120-5.

7. Joseph A. Olmstead, *Small-Group Instruction* (Human Resources Research Organization, Alexandria, Virginia, 1974), pp. 1-10.

8. Murry R. Nelson and H. Wells Singleton, 'Small Group Decision-making for Social Action' in Dana Kurfman (ed.), *Developing Decision-Making Skills* (National Council for the Social Studies, Washington, DC, 1977), p. 141.

9. Abraham Maslow, *The Farther Reaches of Human Nature* (Viking Press, New York, 1971), pp. 41-56.

10. S. Schribner and M. Cole, 'Cognitive Consequences of Formal and Informal Education', *Science*, vol. 182, no. 4112 (9 November 1973), pp. 553-9.

11. Richard C. Remy, Richard C. Snyder and Lee F. Anderson, 'Citizenship

Education in Elementary School', *Theory Into Practice*, vol. 15, no. 1 (February 1976), pp. 31-6.

12. John J. Patrick and Richard C. Remy, *Essential Learning Skills in the Education of Citizens* (Agency for Instructional Television, Bloomington, Indiana, 1977), p. 3.

13. Dorothy McClure Fraser and Eunice Johns, 'Developing a Program for the Effective Learning of Skills' in Carpenter (ed.), *Skill Development*, pp. 296-327.

14. Lee F. Anderson, 'A Guide to Thinking about Social Studies in Elementary School', *Newsletter* (African Social Studies Programme, Nairobi, Kenya), vol. 17 (December 1978), p. 17.

15. David P. Ausubel, *Educational Psychology: a Cognitive View* (Holt, Rinehart and Winston, New York, 1968), pp. 175-224.

16. Fraser and Johns, 'Developing a Program', pp. 306-8.

17. Ehman, *et al.*, *Toward Effective Instruction*, pp. 173-5.

18. Jarolimek, 'The Psychology of Skill Development', p. 23.

19. Ehman, *et al.*, *Toward Effective Instruction*, pp. 295-8.

20. Henry C. Ellis, *The Transfer of Learning* (Macmillan, New York, 1965).

21. Fraser and Johns, 'Developing a Program', p. 298.

22. Robert M. Gagné and Leslie J. Briggs, *Principles of Instructional Design* (Holt, Rinehart and Winston, New York, 1974), pp. 99-119.

23. This is adapted from a lesson appearing in Alan Backler and Stuart Lazarus, *World Geography* (Science Research Associates, Chicago, 1980), pp. 39-41.

24. This is adapted from Backler and Lazarus, *World Geography*, pp. 130-4.

25. Jean Piaget, *Six Psychological Studies* (Random House, New York, 1968).

26. Byron G. Massialas and C. Benjamin Cox, *Inquiry in Social Studies* (McGraw Hill, New York, 1966), pp. 114-21.

27. This example is based upon a similar exercise found in Roger LaRaus and Richard C. Remy, *Citizenship Decision-Making* (Addison-Wesley, Reading, Massachusetts, 1978), p. 126.

28. Barry K. Beyer, *Inquiry in the Social Studies Classroom* (Merrill, Columbus, Ohio, 1971), pp. 18-20.

29. Olmstead, *Small-Group Instruction*, pp. 58-64, 79-102.

30. LaRaus and Remy, *Citizenship Decision-Making*.

31. Ibid., pp. 65-9, 102-7.

32. Fred M. Newmann, *Education for Citizen Action* (McCutchan Publishing Corporation, Berkeley, California, 1975), p. 41.

33. Unesco Associated Schools Project, *International Understanding at School*, Circular 29 (1975), pp. 34-5.

34. Adelaide Kernochan, 'The Evolution of Educational Practises in UNESCO Associated Schools', *International Understanding at School*, Circular 25 (1973), pp. 32-4.

8 VALUES, MORAL EDUCATION AND SOCIAL STUDIES

H.C. Ganguli, G.P. Mehrotra and Howard D. Mehlinger

We are what we value. We try to live according to our values; we judge institutions, situations and other people by the degree to which they measure up to our values; we expect others to admire and respect us on the basis of our values. To be human is to possess values.

Values are an inextricable part of the social studies. Whatever the students' age, whatever the course title, whatever the country: social studies instructors teach values. It cannot be otherwise.

Values are embedded in the subject-matter of social studies. Take history, for example. Values influence the choice of topics and how they will be treated. Historical figures appear as heroes in the books of one country and as villains in those of another. Who is a 'great man' or a 'great woman' in history is in part a question of values.

Teachers communicate values by the way they teach. Do they act in an authoritarian manner or do they encourage students to challenge their textbooks and their teacher's judgements? Classroom rules, the structure and organisation of the school and the system of rewards: all contribute to the formation of student values.

Social studies is not the only place where children acquire values. Other school subjects, the school's extra-curricular programme and other social institutions – especially the family, religious institutions and peer groups – contribute as much as or more than social studies. But social studies has unique opportunities for values instruction which teachers should not ignore.

If there are opportunities for values instruction in social studies, there are also dilemmas. Are there universal values which are constant across time and place to which all people subscribe, or are all values relative to the period and the culture? Is the job of the social studies teacher to impose certain values or is it to help students to develop their own value systems? If it is the former, which values should be taught – those of the local community or more cosmopolitan values – and how can these values be transmitted most efficiently? If it is the latter, how do teachers defend their educational stance when students choose values different from others, especially their parents, or select values which seem inhumane? At what age should students be

192

encouraged to begin exercising critical judgement concerning the value of things and deciding what is right or wrong regarding certain actions in various circumstances? These are dilemmas that trouble social studies teachers everywhere.

Values

A value is a principle, a standard or a quality that is considered worthwhile or desirable. Values help us to decide whether certain objects are good or bad, right or wrong, desirable or worthless, important or insignificant. The objects can be ideas, decisions, persons, statements, actions or things. The statement 'War is evil' is a value judgement. Behind the statement lies a principle which guides this belief. Apartheid has been condemned by Unesco. This is so because the practice of apartheid violates a principle (a value) that is important to it. From a psychological point of view, the purpose of values is, negatively, the control of dangerous or destructive impulses in the individual and, positively, the harnessing of one's constructive energies, the clarification of purpose and meaning of life, the setting of goals of behaviour and adaptation to complex cultural conditions.

Value can also be used as a verb. A person who *values* something assigns merit to it. The sentence 'I value your friendship' means that your friendship is treasured by me. The reason a person is desired as a friend may be a result of the values they exhibit — for example integrity, intelligence, a sense of humour, humility.

Valuing something is different from *evaluating* something. To value a person, an object or idea is to *assign* it worth. To evaluate a person, an object or idea is to *assess* its worth according to some standard. Teachers may both value students and evaluate students, but the process is not identical.

To value something is also not the same as reacting emotionally to it. One may value telling the truth but find that telling the truth to be painful in a particular situation. A person may enjoy a fine meal without placing a particular value one way or another on food. And a diabetic may value insulin but gain no pleasure from taking it. When we speak of a person's values, ordinarily we are not referring to all of the things he enjoys or all of his preferences; rather we are commenting on the abstract ideals, principles and standards that guide his behaviour.[1]

Distinguishing Factual Statements from Value Statements. A value statement is not the same as a factual statement, although they are often confused. 'The temperature today is 25 degrees Celsius' is a factual statement. While the statement involves an assessment, anyone with a thermometer can check its accuracy. Furthermore, there is general agreement about what 25 degrees Celsius means. The statement 'It is better to live in a hot climate than a cold climate' is a value statement. It cannot be settled by facts alone. A value claim requires some supporting reasons. Perhaps a person prefers to live in a hot climate because the cost of shelter and clothing is less than in colder climes. One may then agree or disagree with the factual claim embedded in the value claim. Yet, even if it can be established that clothing and shelter are indeed less expensive in hot climates, this is unlikely to end the argument. People may now disagree on the relative worth of the advantage of paying less for shelter and clothing compared to the advantage of living in cooler regions that enjoy changing seasons. Therefore, while factual information is required to understand value claims, such information is unlikely to resolve most disagreements.

Although value statements cannot be proven in the same way as factual statements, value statements are subject to analysis and evaluation. Thus, value statements are not all of equal worth. They can be judged according to whether they are rational and defensible. At least two tests can be applied. (1) Is the judgement based upon known facts about the situation? (2) Is the judgement consistent with other value principles held by the speaker? If the judgement is based upon incorrect information or insufficient information, it can be criticised because the speaker fails to know all of the relevant facts. If the speaker is inconsistent across value principles, he is caught in a logical contradiction. Perhaps, if he learns the facts or if the contradiction is made known to him, he will change his judgement.

For example, suppose someone asserts that he favours capital punishment for convicted murderers on the grounds that this will deter such crimes. Assume that it was found that in fact capital punishment did *not* deter crime. The person should either change his judgement or find new grounds. Suppose the same person indicates that his judgement rests upon the value principle that life is sacred and since it is sacred, no one has the right to deprive another of living. We might then ask, 'On what grounds does the state have the right to terminate the murderer's life?' The speaker is caught in a logical contradiction: he wishes to deprive one person of his right to life because that person caused the death of another. There *is* a value principle at work — i.e. 'an eye for an eye, a tooth for a tooth' — but it is not the principle that was articulated.

This is not the place to discuss the procedures one can follow in evaluating value judgements. It is enough here merely to note that:

(1) factual statements are not identical to value statements;
(2) the merits of value statements can be evaluated.

Why is Something Valuable? In general something can be judged valuable for intrinsic or extrinsic reasons. An object is judged intrisically valuable because it is worth while for its own sake, or its own terms, without reference to anything else. A beautiful sunset may be treasured by observers for its own intrinsic value. The observers may or may not be able to agree explicitly on the criteria they are using; they may or may not agree that it is the finest sunset they have ever seen; yet they are likely to agree that it is valuable for no other reason than it is there to be observed.

An object may also be valued because of its actual or potential relationship to other values. For example, freedom of speech may be valued because it is seen as instrumental to or necessary for other values prized by people — for example the value of self-government. On other occasions, especially during wartime, the same people may accept censorship and curbs on free speech because of fear that the security of the nation itself is threatened — and the security of the state is deemed of greater importance than short-term restrictions on freedom of expression.

An object may also be valued because it is seen as an exemplification or a part of a larger value. We may value honesty when dealing with other people because treating people honestly is our way of exhibiting our most important value principle: we shall treat people in the same way we wish to be treated. Telling the truth, charging a fair price for our labour and so on are ways in which we exhibit our commitment to the first principle. On the other hand, sometimes we may find it necessary to tell a lie so as not to hurt a person we love. In such a situation we may be living in accord with our major principle while violating one of our minor principles. In such situations we find it necessary *to do evil in order to do good.*

Kinds of Values

There are many kinds of values. Putting values into categories can help bring order to thinking about values and can also help teachers decide which values deserve the greatest attention in social studies classrooms. Two categories of values will be discussed here, although there are many other ways to structure values.[2]

Classification of Values according to the Relationship between the Subscriber and the Beneficiary. One way to organise values is according to the relationship between the person holding the values and the group towards which they are directed. For example, two broad groups of values might be imagined: values directed towards oneself and values directed towards others.

Among the 'self-oriented values' are those relating to success, comfort, privacy and independence. A person motivated primarily by values linked to personal success is likely to behave differently from someone who does not believe such a value to be very important. People who value the companionship of friends are likely to behave differently from those who cherish privacy above all other values.

People also adhere to 'other-oriented values'. These may be of two general kinds: 'in-group' or parochial values and mankind-oriented values. The 'in-group' values are directed towards groups with which the person feels a close association. These may include a family, a profession, a political party, a religious group and a nation. Typically, people hold membership in many groups simultaneously. A person may feel loyalty to family, profession, ethnic group, religious group and nation silultaneously – or loyalty to one may put him into conflict with loyalty to another. People also hold values that are generalised across all mankind. Aesthetic values are typically not limited to a particular group; a beautiful painting or a musical composition can be appreciated regardless of nationality. One may also exhibit tolerance and respect to all human beings regardless of race, creed or nationality.

Self-oriented values may conflict with one another; self-oriented values can also come into conflict with 'other-oriented' values, for example when one's drive for personal success weakens family ties or causes harm to others. Nations vary according to the encouragement they give to the development of self-oriented values as compared to other oriented-values. In some nations devotion to individual success is encouraged; in other countries commitment to such a value is considered a character weakness and should be resisted.

Classification of Values according to the Nature of the Benefits. Another way of structuring values is according to the benefits expected. Thus values might be organised as follows:

	Category of Value	Sample Values
(1)	Material and physical	health, comfort, safety
(2)	Economic	productivity, efficiency
(3)	Moral	honesty, fairness
(4)	Social	charitableness, courtesy
(5)	Political	freedom, justice
(6)	Aesthetic	beauty, symmetry
(7)	Religious (spiritual)	piety, clearness of conscience
(8)	Intellectual	intelligence, clarity
(9)	Professional	professional recognition and success
(10)	Sentimental	love, acceptance

Using these categories school officials might decide to accept greater responsibility for the cultivation of some values than for others. For example, teachers could decide that they have principal responsibility for 'intellectual values'. that they share responsibility with other groups for promoting 'moral', 'social', 'political' and 'aesthetic' values, and that they have no responsibility for instruction in the remaining types of values listed above. While nations and schools within nations are likely to vary in their perception of responsibility, authorities must choose which values will be chiefly their responsibility and which can and should be left to others.

To some extent how one teaches values depends upon which values are selected as most important. 'Self-oriented' values and 'other-oriented' values probably require different content and approaches. Moreover, instruction in aesthetic values will take a different form from instruction in religious values in most countries. This chapter cannot treat instructional problems that arise across the entire domain of values. Therefore the remainder of the chapter is devoted exclusively to a treatment of moral values, because these present the most complex challenges to social studies teachers and because there is a general belief that schools have some responsibility for their development in students.

Moral Education

A moral act is any corrigible human action that has a significant impact upon the character or well-being of any person or upon any creature capable of feeling pain.[3] To act morally is to be guided by moral norms (principles, rules, standards). Such norms impose moral duties or obligations that are intended to be binding upon people capable of deliberate and reasoned action. A person who consciously refuses to acknowledge such obligations or who acts knowingly in defiance of them is said to act *immorally*. When a person is incapable of guiding his behaviour in ways consistent with moral norms or is unaware of their existence, he is said to be *amoral*.

It is possible to take a moral point of view towards all human actions because the potential exists for every human act to have an impact upon another person. However, people do not regularly consider the moral consequences of the majority of their actions because the impact of their choice on another seems trivial as opposed to significant. The decision whether to purchase a new suit of clothes is rarely seen as a moral issue; it is typically judged to be an economic issue, although not buying the goods may have some impact upon the merchant, and an even smaller impact upon the manufacturer and the labourer who produced it.

Choices judged to be trivial to some may be significant to others. To a vegetarian, the decision to avoid meat may be a moral choice resulting from concern for the rights of animals. Those who eat meat rarely, if ever, think of their food in this way. For them it is mainly an economic decision: can they afford to buy meat or not? Of course, people sometimes claim to be making moral judgements when in fact they are prompted by other considerations. A person refusing to take part in military service may defend his decision with moral arguments, asserting that he is unwilling to accept an obligation to kill another human being. But other reasons — fear, inconvenience to his career, hatred of regimentation — may be the actual reasons he resists military service. Another person, morally opposed to murder, may willingly become a soldier because he believes military service to be a moral obligation, risking his life to protect his countrymen.

Universal Moral Principles versus Specific Virtues

One question that frequently arises in discussions of morality is: are there universal moral principles that guide human conduct everywhere or is morality specific to each culture? In Chapter 1, Wronski referred to a moral principle that has seemingly guided all of the world's major religions. This principle might be stated as follows: act towards other people exactly as you would like them to behave towards you. While this principle is often violated, it appears to enjoy nearly universal appeal.

In recent years various efforts have been made to legislate moral principles to guide the behaviour of people and nations. The 'Universal Declaration of Human Rights' adopted by the United Nations General Assembly in 1948 and the Unesco 'Recommendation concerning Education for International Understanding, Co-operation and Peace and Education relating to Human Rights and Fundamental Freedoms' adopted in 1974 contain statements concerning how people should be treated regardless of race, social class or nationality.

Despite efforts to identify universal moral principles, one is struck by the great diversity of specific moral codes; for example, among some people there are prohibitions about eating any kind of meat; among others the prohibitions are directed against only certain kinds of meat — for example pork; with others, only cannibalism — eating human flesh — is proscribed. Codes of conduct structure relationships between men and women, influence styles of clothing, determine how one can spend time and money, etc. Taken as a whole, human beings have invented an enormous variety of ways to control behaviour through moral norms.

Asian Workship on Moral Education

Some of the wide diversity in moral values is revealed by the following survey. In 1975, fifteen experts from fourteen Asian nations met in a regional workshop on moral education. This workshop, sponsored jointly by the Japanese National Institute for Educational Research and Unesco, reviewed moral education programmes in each of the countries represented and considered ways in which these programmes might be improved. During the course of the workshop the participants were asked to submit a list of moral values deemed important in their own countries. This led to a combined list of 54 values that was later reduced to 44 by eliminating redundancies. Next, the participants were asked to check ten values on the list they felt were 'most representative' of those their country wished most to inculcate through the schools; they were then asked to check the ten they thought were of highest priority from their own professional point of view.

Table 8.1 shows the percentage of votes given to each of the 44 values, divided according to 'national emphasis' and 'professional view'. The highest percentage possible for any particular moral value is 10 per cent (i.e. 15 votes out of a total of 150 votes). The values are listed in alphabetical order, not in order of priority.

To facilitate comparison, the eight values receiving highest priority in each of the columns shown in the table below are displayed in

Table 8.1: Priority of Moral Values

	Values	National Emphasis	Professional View
1.	Adventure	1.3%	0.7%
2.	Bravery, courage	0.7	1.3
3.	Charity, kindness, generosity	4.0	2.7
4.	Co-operation	7.3	4.7
5.	Creativity, innovation	4.7	6.0
6.	Critical thinking	2.7	4.0
7.	Cheerfulness	–	0.7
8.	Courtesy, politeness	2.7	0.7
9.	Cleanliness, orderliness	4.7	0.7
10.	Contentment	–	–
11.	Confidence	–	2.0
12.	Diligence	0.7	1.3
13.	Dignity	1.3	0.7
14.	Firmness, faith	3.3	2.0
15.	Friendliness, hospitability	1.3	2.0
16.	Freedom	3.3	2.7
17.	Gratitude	0.7	–
18.	Humanity	5.3	4.0
19.	Honesty, integrity	5.3	5.3
20.	Humility, modesty	–	0.7
21.	Individuality	1.3	3.3
22.	Justice, fairness	2.0	2.7
23.	Loyalty, patriotism	8.7	5.3
24.	Love for nature, life	1.3	2.7
25.	Love for family	1.3	2.0
26.	Love for school	–	–
27.	Obedience	–	2.0
28.	Open-mindedness	–	1.3
29.	Piety	–	0.7
30.	Peace	1.3	2.0
31.	Punctuality	–	0.7
32.	Perseverance	2.0	1.3
33.	Responsibility	4.7	4.7
34.	Rationality	0.7	1.3
35.	Respect for rules	4.0	2.0
36.	Respect and love for labour	4.0	4.7

Table 8.1: continued

	Values	National Emphasis	Professional View
37.	Sincerity	2.0	2.0
38.	Self-reliance	2.7	1.3
39.	Self-discipline	4.0	5.3
40.	Self-improvement	1.3	2.0
41.	Safety	0.7	0.7
42.	Truth	1.3	2.7
43.	Tolerance, patience	6.7	6.0
44.	Thrift	0.7	1.3

Source: 'Moral Education in Asia', *Research Bulletin of the National Institute for Educational Research*, vol. 14 (1976), p. 47.

Table 8.2: National Emphasis and Professional View on Moral Values

National Emphasis		Professional View	
1. Loyalty, patriotism	8.7%	1. Creativity, innovation	6.0%
2. Co-operation	7.3%	2. Tolerance, patience	6.0%
3. Tolerance, patience	6.7%	3. Honesty, integrity	5.3%
4. Humanity	5.3%	4. Loyalty, patriotism	5.3%
5. Honesty, integrity	5.3%	5. Self-discipline	5.3%
6. Creativity, innovation	4.7%	6. Co-operation	4.7%
7. Cleanliness, orderliness	4.7%	7. Responsibility	4.7%
8. Responsibility	4.7%	8. Respect and love for labour	4.7%

Source: 'Moral Education in Asia', p. 48.

Table 8.2 above. Note the variance between 'national emphasis' and 'professional views'.

Relativity of Values

At the most abstract level, there is something akin to universally accepted moral principles. These relate to the dignity of human life and the requirement that everyone deserves respect. Beneath these abstract moral principles, however, lies a great variety of specific codes of conduct that seek to govern human behaviour. These codes, largely linked to a particular group's culture and experience, may remain stable for many years. On the other hand, anthropological studies of primitive societies and of societies developing in different ways under the impact of industrialisation provide evidence of radically changing values. Margaret Mead found radical shifts in values in family patterns, distribution of power and religion among the Manu people in the Admiralty Islands. In modern India, as a result of the impact of urbanisation and Westernisation, the traditionally regarded lower castes have adopted more and more the values of the higher castes in their family patterns, forms of worship, education and community relations. Srinivasan, the noted Indian sociologist, called this process 'Sanskritization'. Similarly, Max Weber developed the concept of 'Protestant ethic' as a factor in the rise of capitalism in Europe. The Protestant ethic represented a codification of certain personal qualities: strong motivation for achievement, freedom from social preconceptions, self-confidence and farsightedness, that together constitute individual initiative and lead to enterprising conduct. The Protestant ethic identified the good life for the godly; it justified exertion as a means to gain something worth while, assigned human conduct a degree of asceticism and caused people to gain satisfaction from the accumulation of material wealth rather than through its conspicuous consumption.

Values change over time; values also differ between cultures and subcultures. Respect shown by men towards women serves as an illustration. Probably every society accords women respect according to the customs of its own culture. But what constitutes 'respect towards women' varies enormously between countries, between social classes within countries, according to ethnic groups, according to age, etc. What is counted as respect for women in traditional Islamic cultures varies greatly from practices in Western Europe. Indian women are likely to be treated differently according to their caste. And within the United States, 'women's rights' advocates are calling for changes in the legal status of women as well as the informal customs that govern relationships between men and women. The general principle — 'show respect to women' — may be universal, but the manner in which such respect is demonstrated varies greatly.

Moral Autonomy, Moral Dependence and Amorality

A person may appear to be acting morally without actually doing so. Children, for example, seem to be adhering to moral codes when in fact they are behaving prudently. They may not be guided by moral principle at all; rather they are motivated by a desire to win approval or to avoid punishment and shame.

Newborn infants show no evidence of moral values. They acquire or learn them in the process of surviving amid the welter of stimulation into which they are thrown after birth. In time they are able to organise and integrate this 'blooming, buzzing confusion' by taking on a culture that has ready-made solutions. The culture enables individuals to develop their own cognituve maps or conceptions of how the world is built and how they should conduct themselves in it. These conceptions are the values, beliefs, frames of reference, orientations and role perceptions that are needed to survive as a social being.

Since morality must be learned, there is a necessary period of dependency. Moral values are first imposed upon children by parents. They approve of certain forms of behaviour and reward their children for conforming to these standards. At other times, the parents disapprove of aspects of their children's behaviour and punish them for transgressing their rules. The basic teaching scheme consists of all the 'do's' and 'don'ts' with the promise: 'I shall love you (or I shall reward you)' and 'I shall not love you (or I shall punish you).' In time, these enforced rules are 'internalised' in the child through a natural need for love, an aversion to punishment and a desire to model, imitate or identify with parents, teachers and other authorities. The earlier processes are quite unconscious but later children consciously and selectively begin to identify with models that they find in their favourite teachers and other adults. 'The total system of values thus acquired acts as an internal regulator of behaviour, proceeding often quite automatically, aiding the ego in its functions of judging, adapting, mastery, choosing, and in general, controlling the person's impulses.'[4]

Nevertheless, it would be a mistake to look upon the values of an individual as a mere reflection or mirror image of the values of society. To do so one would fall prey to the extreme anthropological fallacy. People build their values and other cognitive maps out of their own personal experiences, though a part of these personal experiences are the values of the society which exist prior to their existence and are communicated to them as members of society. A person's values are rooted in one's personality, as also in the norms of reference groups and of the society to which the individual belongs. People interrelate their values and form value systems that indicate their choices in their affairs. The values and value systems of an individual are unique and characteristic of the person concerned. It is this uniqueness that Allport emphasised when, in his definition of personality, he wrote:

Even the acts and concepts that we apparently 'share' with others are at bottom individual and idiosyncratic. It is true that some acts and concepts are more idiosyncratic than others, but none can be found that lacks the personal flavour.[5]

Many factors guide one's choices. A person may choose on the basis of what is most prudent given the circumstances, or the legal thing to do, or the best economic choice, or the best for one's career. These and other values come into play, but they are not the same as a moral judgement. A moral decision may be congruent with the best legal, prudent and economic decision, or it may violate choices made on other grounds. Peaceful, non-violent civil disobedience such as practised by Mahatma Gandhi and Martin Luther King in the United States was morally correct but imprudent, illegal and expensive. The morally autonomous person may also find it necessary to violate a moral principle in order to behave morally, such as when a person breaks a promise (violation of the principle to keep promises) in order to save a life.

Moral autonomy is not the same as amorality or moral relativism. People who act according to moral principle only when it is to their advantage are not acting morally; they are amoral and are guided solely by self-interest. The morally autonomous individual lives according to moral principles that he is prepared to make universal and that he generalises across situations. He calls forth such principles when the situation seems to warrant a moral choice, and he violates his principles only when a higher moral principle seems at stake.

Moral Development

To be morally autonomous seems to require a level of moral maturity, not unlike intellectual maturity. Lawrence Kohlberg, an American psychologist, has conducted research for more than two decades on the capacity of children for moral reasoning. Like Piaget, Kohlberg believes that the ability of children to reason about moral problems is linked to their cognitive development generally and proceeds in stages. He has identified six stages: at the 'preconventional level' (1) punishment and obedience orientation and (2) the instrumental relativist orientation; at the 'conventional level' (3) the interpersonal sharing orientation and (4) the social maintenance orientation; and at the 'principled level' (5) the social contract, human rights and welfare orientation and (6) the universal ethical principles orientation.

According to Kohlberg, everyone reasons at stage 1 as a child. Most people then move to stage 2, and sometime around age 9 or later move into stage 3. Some people pass into stage 4 in middle or late adolescence; those who reach stage 5 are likely to do so in their late teens or even later in life. Very few people reach stage 6.

Kohlberg believes a person reasons predominately at one stage and uses contiguous stages as a secondary thinking pattern. People move through these stages in an invariant sequence, although many people never reach the highest stages. People articulate moral arguments at their stage of development and at all stages below their own. They can usually understand arguments at one stage higher than the one they occupy.

Kohlberg's research has aroused considerable interest world-wide. While critics have found faults with some of its aspects — for example, researchers have not always been able to replicate the stages and some find cultural bias in the definitions of the particular stages — educators see implications in his research for the goals of school programmes in moral education. Because higher moral stages are presumably better than lower ones and because moral judgement is a necessary, if not sufficient, condition for moral behaviour, advocates of the moral development approach believe that the primary moral education task of schools is to help pupils move to ever higher stages of moral reasoning. By helping students to reason better about moral choices, the schools enable individuals to become morally autonomous.

Apparently two processes combine to produce a moral human being. One is a socialisation process in which an individual learns the particulars of his own culture; the second is developmental in which the individual's capacity for reasoning about moral questions grows apace with his intellectual growth. The schools have a role in facilitating both processes. The schools must contribute to passing on the beliefs and values that rule the culture of which the pupil is a member; they also have a responsibility to assist each child to reach his maximum potential as he develops towards adulthood.

Social Studies Instruction and Moral Education

Moral education is part of the school curriculum of every nation, but it takes many forms. Where there is a dominant religion in the society, moral education may be part of formal religion courses offered by the schools or by religious institutions in co-operation with the schools. In other nations' schools a special, secularised course in moral education is taught. In Japan, moral education is taught one day a week in both elementary schools and lower secondary schools. These courses are

Plate 8: Moral Education in Thailand

This is a moral education class in a secondary school in Thailand, taught by a Buddhist monk. He works closely with another teacher in planning and teaching the course.

taught according to a prescribed syllabus and have no connection with a religious organisation. In still other countries no formal course in moral education is offered and religious instruction is kept separate from the schools. In such situations, moral education is likely to be included as part of other courses – especially the social studies.

As the Asian Workshop on Moral Education noted earlier in this chapter, representatives of each of the fifteen nations described how moral education was included in the curricula of their schools.

While the amount of time devoted formally to moral education varies from country to country, teachers in all nations must cope with problems relating to instructional goals and teaching methods. Whether moral education is presented through a special course or whether it is part of social studies, the task for teachers is everywhere much the same.

Table 8.3: Status of Moral Education in Fifteen Asian Nations

Aspects		AF	BA	BU	IDA	IDN	IR	JA	KO	MA	NE	PA	PH	SI	SL	TH
Is moral education religious or secular?	Entirely based on religion(s)	v														
	Largely based on religion(s)						v								v	
	Based on religion(s) to some extent			v	v	v										v
	Not based on any religion							v	v	v	v	v	v	v		
What is the relationship between moral education and social studies?	Integrated or fused as one subject			v				v	v	v	v			v		v
	Treated as separate subjects with cross-reference	v	v		v	v	v					v	v		v	
	Treated as separate and unrelated subjects															
Is moral education related to other subjects, not including social studies?	Closely related	v	v	v	v	v		v	v	v	v	v	v	v	v	v
	Related somewhat						v									
	Not related at all															
Are other school activities (e.g. assemblies) considered an extension of the classroom teaching of moral education?		v	v	v	v	v	v	v	v	v	v	v	v	v	v	v
Who are responsible for the teaching of moral education?	Specialist teachers (including religion teachers)	v		v	v	v			v	v	v		v	v		v
	Generalist teachers		v	v	v	v		v	v	v	v	v	v	v	v	v
Have teachers been prepared specifically for the teaching of moral education in their pre-service training?		v	v			v		v				v		v	v	v
Do teachers undergo in-service training preparing them to teach moral education?			v	v				v	v		v		v	v	v	v
Is moral education an examination subject?			v	v	v	v	v		v		v	v	v	v	*	v
Duration of first-level education (years)		8	6	4	7	6	5	6	6	6	3	5	6	7	5	7

* Only for Grade V.

Legend: AF – Afghanistan; BA – Bangladesh; BU – Burma; IDA – India; IDN – Indonesia; IR – Iran; JA – Japan; KO – Republic of Korea; MA – Malaysia; NE – Nepal; PA – Pakistan; PH – Philippines; SI – Singapore; SL – Sri Lanka; TH – Thailand

Source: 'Moral Education in Asia', p. 46.

*Teaching Moral Judgements versus Teaching Moral Judgement-making:
the Central Paradox of Moral Education*

The central paradox for moral education instructors is how they can
enable their pupils to acquire deeply held moral principles that will
guide their behaviour without at the same time destroying their capacity
to reason about moral situations. Put in another way, how can teachers
cultivate *habits* of moral behaviour without creating compulsive ideo-
logues who are incapable of acting flexibly and with reason when the
situation demands it?

To think of moral behaviour in terms of habits may be helpful.[6] We
wish children to tell the truth as a matter of habit. Whether to tell the
truth or not is not a question to be decided on the basis of each situation. Telling the truth should become as much a habit, requiring as little
reflection, as walking.

Habits serve us. Because out minds do not have to concentrate on
each separate feature of the physical activity involved in walking, we
can think of other things while we walk. So, too, habits relating to
moral values free the mind to consider other matters as we proceed to
act in terms of our principles. No child should be burdened each day
with conscious moral choice-making on whether to tell the truth.
Ordinarily, telling the truth should be as comfortable and no more
intellectually demanding than walking.

This is not to argue that habits are not challenged or require reflection. When people climb a mountain, manoeuvre across a slippery
surface or walk a tight-rope, they do not walk out of habit alone. All
other thoughts may be purged from their minds as they concentrate on
the simple act of walking. Furthermore, new situations — such as learning to 'walk' on skis or ice skates — require renewed concentration on
balance and mobility. In much the same way, a moral value may be
practised for years as strictly a habit. Suddenly, the individual is confronted with a situation in which a deeply held moral principle is
challenged; it must be thought through. Often this occurs when two or
more deeply held moral principles are in conflict. To obey one principle
forces violation of the other.

Such moral dilemmas, while frequent, do not dominate our lives. In
most situations, acting reflexively on the basis of our habits is all that is
required. But unless children acquire such moral principles early in life,
they are unable to take advantage of what such habits have to offer.
Aristotle said it succinctly:

But the virtues we get by first exercising them, as also happens in the case of the arts as well. For the things we have to learn before we can do them, we learn by doing them, e.g. men become builders by building and lyre players by playing the lyre; so do we become just by doing just acts, temperate by doing temperate acts, brave by doing brave acts . . . It makes no small difference then, whether we form habits of one kind or another from our very youth; it makes a great difference or rather all the difference.[7]

Teachers must also consider the intellectual maturity of students when devising instruction. The reasons they offer to children to justify the moral principles they are promoting must be ones that satisfy children, rather than abstract principles that may be viewed as most important and their ultimate justification to teachers but be beyond the comprehension of youth. For example, teachers should intervene when they find one child or a group of children teasing or ridiculing another child because of some physical handicap or because the child is mentally retarded. Children are unlikely to understand a teacher's appeal to the abstract principle that 'all people deserve respect' but appreciate a reciprocity argument, i.e. 'How would you like it if I were to criticise you because . . .?' By insisting that children do not cruelly tease those with handicaps, teachers enforce the principle of respect for others. This principle can later become internalised to the point that children gain satisfaction when they treat others with kindness and respect.

In general, teachers of young children should seek to cultivate habits of acting on moral principle and seek their justification in terms that can be understood by pupils. Teachers of older youth should concentrate more on encouraging students to be consistent in the application of their principles and to help them reason according to their moral principles in the light of new and confounding situations. The latter process cannot occur if the first is overlooked. Moral reasoning cannot take place in a vacuum; it occurs when deeply held moral principles are in place. Cultivating moral beliefs and helping students to reflect on their beliefs are both the responsibility of the schools.

'Two Birds' – a First-grade Lesson in Moral Education

First-grade teachers have found that lessons that draw upon children's imagination and love of animals can deal with serious issues and influence their beliefs. Plates 9 and 10 were taken during the course of a moral education lesson in a first-grade classroom in Miyazaki, Japan. In a period of 45 minutes the teacher took advantage of a children's game, a fanciful story about two birds and a role-play situation to teach his

Plate 9: First-grade Class in Miyazaki

This photograph shows the beginning of the class prior to the discussion of the two birds.

pupils important lessons about the importance of being sensitive to the feelings of other people and to show them that friendship brings obligations.

The teacher started the lesson by referring to a simple children's game known to all of the pupils. This is a game in which a group of children form a circle around one child who closes his eyes or wears a blindfold, while the others circle around him chanting a tune. When the song ends, the child in the middle of the circle whose eyes are closed is supposed to call out the name of the child facing him. If he is successful, that child enters the circle, the former 'insider' joins the outer circle and the game continues.

In Plate 9 the teacher is discussing this game with the children. Child-like characters have been placed on the chalkboard to depict the game. Note that in the diagram of the game everyone appears to be having a good time except for one child, shown on the right who is standing alone excluded from the game. The teacher asked the pupils how they think that child must feel. The pupils volunteered many ideas

Plate 10: Second Photo of First-grade Class

This photograph shows the conclusion of the class following a discussion of the bird story.

— sad, hurt, disappointed, angry, etc. The teacher summarised this point of the lesson by suggesting that people should do their best to help one another and avoid hurting others.

Then the teacher began to tell a sort of 'Two Birds'. One bird is a beautiful bird who lives in a very nice house. A second bird is a more common-looking bird whose house is very simple. Not aware of the plans of the other, both birds have planned a party on the same day and have invited the same bird-friends to attend their parties. Because it is apparent that it will be impossible to attend both parties, each of the invited birds must decide which invitation to accept. The bird who lives in a nice house lives closer to the other birds and because his family is wealthy there is certain to be very good food and many prizes. The other bird lives much further away; there will be less food and few if any prizes. The teacher asked the class: 'If you were a bird, to which party would you go?' Nearly all of the pupils said they would go to the rich bird's party; about one-sixth of the class elected to go to the party for the poor bird.

The teacher then focused the story on one little bird who had been invited to both parties but could not decide what to do. This bird wanted very much to go to the party offered by the rich bird but feared that no bird would attend the other party, making the poor bird feel very bad. The teacher kept asking the pupils what advice they could give the bird.

Finally, completing the story, the teacher announced that the bird had decided to fly first to the rich bird's house which was close to his house. Then, satisfying himself that all the other birds were attending that party, the bird flew to the poor bird's house, where he proved to be the only guest. The poor bird was very happy to see him, and the host and guest spent a very happy afternoon together. (Plate 10 shows the characters and their relationships from chalkboard depictions.)

When the bird story was completed, the teacher quickly returned to the children's game that had occupied the pupils' attention at the beginning of the lesson. The teacher chose pupils to form a circle in order to play the game in front of the classroom. In order to role-play the initial chalkboard diagram, one child was chosen to stand aside, excluded from the game and asked to show by his facial expression how he felt. Seeing his sadness, the children playing the game expanded their circle and invited him to join them. Of course, this made the pupil very happy.

After role-playing the children's game, the teacher asked the pupils what they would do if they were ever faced with a dilemma of a kind facing the bird with two party invitations. They were also invited to share experiences similar to that of the birds or the excluded child in the game. The teacher, with words of praise and the class through applause, demonstrated their support for morally 'correct' answers and statements. The teacher did not criticise 'anti-social' responses, but clearly did not encourage them.

As the class came to an end, the teacher asked how many children would now prefer to attend a party at the poor bird's house rather than at the rich bird's house. All but two children gave the response the teacher was encouraging — i.e. they would go to the poor bird's house because this bird also needed friends and no other bird might go to the party if they did not. Two children resisted, indicating they still preferred going to the rich bird's house because that party would be the most enjoyable.

This lesson demonstrated effective 'pro-social' moral education in the primary grades. The teacher self-consciously promoted moral values that he — and presumably Japanese society as well — believes Japanese children should acquire. The teacher helped children experience the pleasure of being altruistic as opposed to expedient and selfish. And while the teacher did not force children to come to his conclusions, neither did he leave it so open and neutral that all answers were valued equally. In short, one was rewarded for 'correct answers' and left uncorrected and unpunished for 'wrong' answers. Children seeking the approval of their teachers and peers were surely encouraged to bring their answers into line with the socially approved one.

Moral Education in the Secondary Grade

A programme in moral education that is appropriate for elementary schoolchildren is seldom adequate for older youth. First young children live more protected lives; the range of choices facing them is not so large as they will experience later as older youth and adults. Second, young children strive to satisfy adults whose love and respect they need and desire. Thus, their choices are closely circumscribed by what their parents, grandparents or teachers expect of them; for older youth and adults, peer group influences become more powerful. Third, the capacity of older youth to reflect upon their choices increases with their physical and intellectual maturity. Older youth can imagine a greater number of satisfying, reasonable and defensible decisions in a situation than young children are able to do.

In the lower grades, a legitimate aim of moral education is to develop certain habits with regard to moral principles. These habits are no less important to older youth and adults, but something more is required. In the process of becoming a morally autonomous individual, it is also necessary for individuals to be able to reflect upon the foundations of their moral beliefs and, where the situation demands it, to challenge and amend the foundations. No one should expect a child to think as a moral philosopher; but most adults have the capacity for moral philosophy. The goal of moral autonomy requires that adults be provided with the intellectual skills to act philosophically when the occasion demands it – that is, when acting according to habit is not enough.

What are some of the traits of moral philosophy that should be cultivated among secondary school youth? Undoubtedly there are many, and a full discussion would require more space than this chapter permits but two seem particularly important.

(1) Students should be willing and able to reflect upon their own moral values and to decide in conflict situations which values should be awarded priority given the particular circumstances.

(2) Students should be willing and able to empathise with the moral principles held by others.

Reflection upon One's Own Moral Values. The personal morality of an individual is an awkward bundle of moral principles, some of which are less important than others, some of which are inconsistent — in given circumstances. Individuals often confront situations in which the inconsistencies or levels of priority of their moral principles become apparent. Should a person be willing to kill for his country? Should a person steal food to save a life? Should a person tell a lie to protect a friend? Each of these dilemmas requires choices regarding which value is to be given priority or how the values can be compromised satisfactorily.

A capacity for and a willingness to reflect upon one's moral principles and to act in accordance with such reflection is not the same as the action implied by the term 'situation ethics'. To respond to what seems comfortable and satisfying in a given situation may be merely giving in to what is expedient and prudent. A person who breaks the law because he hopes to profit from it is motivated by fundamentally different principles than one who violates the law publicly and accepts punishment so as to draw attention to the unjust nature of the law. Both have acted illegally; but the latter has behaved morally while the former has behaved amorally or immorally.

In some countries 'moral dilemmas' or 'value conflict situations' are used to force students to reflect on their moral principles, to seek inconsistencies and to establish priorities among them. For instructional purposes a 'moral dilemma' stands for a brief story or anecdote — usually fictional but sometimes based upon real people and events — in which the central characters face a conflict and must decide among two or more moral principles. One such dilemma, used by Kohlberg in his work, concerns a man named Heinz whose wife is dying of cancer and whose life can be saved only through the use of a rare drug, discovered by a local pharmacist. Because the drug is expensive to make and because the pharmacist hopes to become wealthy from his discovery, he charges $ 2,000 for even a small dose, approximately ten times the cost of making it. Heinz, a relatively poor man, tries to borrow the money needed to buy the drug but is able to raise only $ 1,000. Heinz tells the pharmacist that his wife is dying and asks the pharmacist to sell the drug more cheaply or give him more time to pay the balance. The pharmacist refuses, and Heinz is left with his dilemma: should he try to steal the drug in order to save his wife's life?

Kohlberg originally used such dilemmas for purposes of research. How the interviewee defended his choice indicated the stage of moral development he had reached. More recently, Kohlberg and those associated with him have suggested that moral dilemmas can serve instructional purposes as well. They believe that posing such dilemmas in class prepares students to confront similar dilemmas they encounter every day but have no opportunity to analyse or to discuss with others. Perhaps, more importantly, Kohlberg believes that it is through the use of devices such as moral dilemmas that teachers can promote the moral reasoning capacity of youth. The assumption is that requiring students to think about and defend their positions according to moral arguments encourages development and growth in the capacity for moral reasoning.

Ordinarily value analyses in a classroom situation rely primarily upon group discussion techniques: students are encouraged to express their views; the teacher raises questions forcing the students to evaluate their arguments.[8]

In a discussion of values teachers should make certain that students: (1) state their values clearly so that all understand their point of view; (2) define their terms so that students do not embrace different conceptions of the discussion; (3) support their arguments with factual claims and, if the facts are disputed, resolve the disputes if possible; (4) distinguish between definitional statements, factual claims and value claims.

Following a discussion of a 'moral dilemma' or a 'value conflict situation', each student should be able to state (offer a value judgement) what he would do in the situation described and the reason (value principle) he would make that choice. The teacher now has an opportunity to help each student assess the merits of the choice by evaluating the supporting value principle. Four 'tests' are often used.

(a) *New Case Test.* After stating the value principle, the student should apply it to other cases for which it is logically relevant. The value principle may be accepted if further applications appear justified. (For example, in the case of Heinz, should a person steal a drug for a friend or for a stranger who may be dying?)

(b) *Subsumption Test.* This test requires the student to search for a more general principle that is acceptable and the given value principle is seen as a part of the more general principle. (Any action that will save a life is permissible so long as the action does not threaten the life of another.)

(c) *Role Exchange Test*. The student tries to put himself in the role of another person affected by the principle and then considers whether or not he can still accept the principle as it applies to him in his new role. (In the case of Heinz, would the student favour stealing the drug if he were the pharmacist?)

(d) *Universal Consequences Test*. The student should be asked to imagine what the consequences would be if everyone in similar circumstances were to take action in the way he recommends, then decide whether or not he can accept these consequences. (What would happen if every person felt obliged to steal when confronted with the situation facing Heinz? Would the student favour the resulting impact on society?)

Empathise with the Moral Principles Held by Others. Students need the ability and desire to see themselves from a distance; they must understand the cultural basis of their own moral principles and place themselves in the position of others in order to understand why they have reached the decisions they have.

One criticism levelled at those using moral dilemmas in classrooms is that students are rarely asked to confront their own cultural biases. While the moral dilemmas successfully enable students to reflect on their own values, they do not become aware of alternatives based in other cultures, and, equally important, while they may become more enlightened about their own choices, they are poorly prepared to evaluate the moral judgements of those whose culture is different.

The responsibility of social studies to acquaint students with other views regarding moral principles also draws a distinction between what is appropriate and possible with young children as compared to older children. A capacity for empathy — an ability to see the world from another's point of view — is not present in very young children. Indeed, it seems that this capacity does not really become available until around ages 11 or 12. Thereafter, it is a capacity — not a reality. To acquire empathy requires instruction and experience. Instruction directed at children when they are too young may be fruitless; to deny older children such instruction is to diminish their possibility for growth in an important direction.

Thus, moral education at the secondary school level should have at least two major goals: to strengthen student capacity for reasoning about their own moral principles and to enhance their understanding and empathy for moral principles held by others.

'Getting Along in Japanese Society' – a Role-play Activity[9]

Following is a role-play developed by an American professor for use in American schools. The purpose of the exercise is to teach American students something about Japanese values – values that differ in some significant way from those commonly held by American youth. The role-play is reproduced here almost exactly as it was developed for American schools. Thus, it will be necessary to make some adjustments if it is to be used appropriately by teachers in other societies governed by different values. Its inclusion here is justified by the fact that it demonstrates the use of moral dilemmas *and* it provides a device for helping students to think about the moral values held by people in other countries.

Any role-play, simulation or game must inevitably simplify the real world in order to make the exercise feasible. Japanese society is complex like all other societies. Only a few mainstream values can be represented in this exercise. These values are undergoing change, and they are not held with equal strength by all Japanese. Values also vary according to generation, social class and whether people live in large cities or more rural surroundings. Despite these qualifications, this exercise can help students think more deeply about their own moral values while confronting situations that face four hypothetical Japanese citizens.

Procedures. The teacher should begin the activity by announcing that the class will conduct a role-play involving four Japanese people who are facing important decisions. Each student should be asked to imagine that he or she has to make a decision in the situation facing each of the hypothetical Japanese individuals. In so far as possible the students should attempt to put themselves in the place of the person in the story and make the best possible decision they can, given the circumstances.

The teacher should then divide the students into four groups, or as may groups as necessary so that the number of total groups is even (i.e. two, four, six, eight) and that each single group has no less than four and no more than eight students. Groups of this size enable students to conduct a lively discussion while enlisting the participation of everyone.

One half of the groups should be given a copy of 'Rules for Getting Along in Japanese Society' (see page 219) and a copy of 'Situations' (see page 220). The other half should receive the 'Situations' only. The teacher should give somewhat different instructions to the students, depending upon the kind of group to which they have been assigned. The first group should be told to read the 'Rules for Getting Along in Japanese Society' first. After each student has read the 'rules', they should discuss them within their own groups until they fully understand them. Then the students should be given copies of the 'Situations' and asked to decide what they would do if they were faced with the choices indicated in the stories. They should also explain *why* they would decide that way, justifying their decision by reference to the 'Rules for Getting Along in Japanese Society'. After they have made their decisions and decided upon their justifications, they should discuss their choices with other students in their subgroups.

Students in the other groups — that is those who did not receive the 'Rules for Getting Along in Japanese Society' — should be given copies of the 'Situations' and asked to decide what should be done in each case according to what they believe to be best, justifying their answers according to their *own* values. After they have made their individual decisions, they should discuss their choices with others in their subgroup.

After about half an hour, the teacher should bring all the students together. The teacher should write the names of the principal story characters on the chalkboard (Yoshi, Midori, Takashi and Mr Tanabe). Then the teacher should ask individual students what they believe each character should do. The teacher might record student answers on the chalkboard, discriminating the answers according to whether students were part of the group that had been supplied with the 'Rules' or whether they had been in groups without the 'Rules'. As discussion proceeds, it should be clear that while there are differences among decisions by students who were in the same groups, they greatest differences exist among those who came from different groups. And even if their decisions were similar, the justifications for their decisions are likely to be quite different, depending upon whether a student was in the group seeking to behave like a Japanese individual or whether one was trying to respond in terms of his own culture.

At this point the teacher might distribute or read from 'Notes on Situations' that provide information regarding a typical Japanese response to each situation. The discussion could then focus on the moral values that seem to underlie the decision in each situation. The teacher should ask:

(1) what moral values caused people to make their decisions in each situation?
(2) to what extent are the moral principles different, or given different priority, in Japanese culture as compared to our culture?

(3) are there fundamental and universal moral values that underlie both cultures that are expressed differently in the two cultures because of differences in moral codes? What are these universal moral values?

Rules for Getting Along in Japanese Society

1. Japanese find their sense of self within a social group — as a member of a family, a resident of a village, a worker in a company. They view the group as a sort of team, and individual success or failure may be found through the team or group. The individual cannot really win unless the team wins.

    Whereas people in the United States focus on individual success and happiness, Japanese find satisfaction mainly through the achievements of their group. For an American, striking out on one's own while risking loneliness and unpopularity on behalf of a noble cause is a virtue. Japanese believe it is more virtuous to convince the group to recognise the moral demands of life.

2. In Japan individuals experience strong social pressure to conform to traditional values. The young and restless are encouraged to be patient and maintain their ties with family, friends and employers until their views are ultimately accepted.

3. Regardless of one's place in society, each individual is expected to act in accord with accepted modes of behaviour and to meet his obligations to the group, or to the team. So long as a person lives according to the rules, he will be accepted.

4. When a typical Japanese worker accepts employment with a firm, he remains with that firm the rest of his life. The employer accepts responsibility for the employee, and the worker has obligations to the company. Family and social ties are also strong in Japan. Friends are friends for life.

5. If a member of a group makes a mistake, it affects the reputation of the group as a whole. 'Face' is a person's reputation for integrity. When one person 'loses face' by an unacceptable social act, all suffer, especially the leader of the group. Members of a group work together to maintain the group's reputation. When one person is having difficulty, all assume some responsibility for helping solve the problem and containing the damage.

6. The team leader is responsible for the group's behaviour. If an error is made by a member of the group, the leader is accountable; and he is expected to be publicly responsible. Group

members are expected to be loyal to the group and show respect to the leader. Since group members are not easily 'fired', the leader must work hard to make the most of the people in his group.

7. Japanese society is hierarchical and one's position in the hierarchy is determined largely by age and seniority. Promotion and advancement proceed according to age and experience rather than by mere individual achievement. The Japanese seek to discourage competition within a group while maximising the success of the group as a whole. If a person knows that he will belong to the organisation for life and that he will achieve as his group succeeds, it is easier to be patient and await the rewards that are sure to come in time. This rule also serves to strengthen group solidarity, as all succeed as the group succeeds.

8. The best rewards in life are those that come to one as a member of a group or team. Individual success is nice, but if it cannot be shared, it can threaten a person's association with the group. To seek personal reward at the expense of the group is very dangerous. It may brand a person as selfish and ruthlessly ambitious, leading to loss of friends, loneliness and alienation.

9. A Japanese family is not merely the present living members; it includes ancestors and future descendants. Japanese tend to be suspicious of proposals that offer short-term advantages but which appear to mortgage the future. They are equally sceptical of ideas of a single individual that run counter to traditional practices and are untested.

10. Individual interests are subordinate to group or team interest. Personal success is bound up in group or team success. The greatest loss is to become alienated from the group and to pursue one's interest separate from a group.

Situations

1. Yoshi is the only child and the son of a wealthy family that owns a textile plant. Yoshi's wife, whom he loved dearly, died in childbirth just a year ago. He has no desire to remarry; he believes to marry again would be an insult to his wife's memory. However, his parents want him to remarry because they want a grandchild who could inherit the textile plant after Yoshi. Actually, Yoshi doesn't care much for the textile business. He would rather move to Tokyo and become a car dealer. What should Yoshi do?

2. Midori is a 24-year-old single woman employed by a Japanese bank. She has worked for this bank for three years, following her graduation from college. Midori was hired at the same time as nine other people: seven men and two women. They are not only her closest professional colleagues, they are also her best, personal friends. They work together, and they frequently spend holidays and weekends together.

   Midori's supervisors are very pleased with her work and have told her that she is doing better than her friends. In fact she has been offered a promotion in recognition of her achievements. This has not made Midori entirely happy. While she is pleased with this recognition, she is worried about how her promotion might affect relationships with her nine friends. Not only would the promotion result in her becoming the youngest officer in the bank, her rank would be higher than that of her friends. Furthermore, the men expect to build lifetime careers in the bank, while Midori hopes to marry and to have children. She expects to quit her job when her first child is born. What should she do?

3. A seventh-grade teacher named Sato used some very offensive language in his classroom. His students told their shocked parents what he said, and many believe Sato should resign. These parents have brought their complaints to the school principal, Mr Tanabe. What should Mr Tanabe do?

4. Takashi has recently graduated from an agricultural college and returned to the small farming village where he was born. The farmers in this area grow and sell oranges. For years they have moved their oranges to market by handcarts, along steep, narrow dirt roads that cannot be used by cars or trucks. Takashi has estimated that if the farmers were to widen, straighten and pave the road, they could transport more oranges, more quickly, with less damage to the crop. He has calculated that the money borrowed to pave the road could be repaid in ten years by the extra profits that would be made on the increased sale of oranges. However, the farmers like doing things the way they always have in the past. They are especially concerned that improving the road would mean that they must give up some land. What should Takashi do?

Notes on Situations

1. Yoshi would remarry and work in the textile plant. He has obligations to his family to provide descendants, and to maintain the prosperity of the family business. It would be different if he had brothers who could step in and carry on the family business; even then the family might urge him to continue in the business, but if he persisted, they would probably yield so long as his brother were willing to run the company. The family might even provide some money to start his car dealership, if that investment did not threaten the family's long-term prosperity.

2. Midori would likely refuse the promotion, while suggesting that her entire group be consulted about who among them should be advanced first. She would worry that accepting the promotion would cause bad feelings among the group and make it difficult for them to continue as good friends. Without the clear support of her peers, she would be axious about the responsibilities that accompany the new job. Also, she would be afraid that being promoted ahead of male associates might make her seem aggressive and unmarriageable. She would prefer a solution that would not threaten group solidarity.

3. Not only would Mr Tanabe ask the teacher to apologise publicly and resign, but Mr Tanabe would also apologise and possibly resign also because he is responsible for his teachers. He would be expected to assume responsibility for Sato's misbehaviour. His resignation might not be accepted, but it would be expected.

4. Takashi would *not* aggressively advance the idea as *his* own idea. In Japan, impressing the 'bosses' with one's individual talents is less important than knowing how to bring good ideas to the group. Since Takashi is so young, he will have to work through some older man who has more respect and seniority within the village. Moreover, the village elders will have to be convinced that the proposal is in their best interest before the group will accept it. Finally, the plan will require time so that it has the support of everyone. Although it may take several years of patient discussion through proper channels, once the decision is made, all will support it and the farmers will be ready as a group to make necessary sacrifices.

Conclusions

Previous chapters have discussed the importance of social studies instruction for the development of knowledge and skills. Instruction in values is no less important in a sound social studies programme.

Values instruction presents special problems to social studies teachers. Values form the glue that binds a society together. Few people are neutral regarding the values schools should promote. Where people may be willing to leave to professional educators a decision regarding what knowledge and skills should be taught, in most countries the decision about what values to teach is considered too important to leave to professionals acting independently.

There is another issue. In nearly every case, school officials want to prepare students who can 'think for themselves', i.e. who are intellectually autonomous. But they are less comfortable with the thought of moral autonomy. It is less dangerous to challenge a scientific principle or interpretation; challenges to moral principles seem more threatening.

The social studies does not have exclusive authority over the cultivation of values; this responsibility is shared by other aspects of the school and by other institutions in society. Nevertheless, the potential contribution of the social studies teacher is significant and should not be overlooked or avoided.

Notes

1. Philip C. Smith, 'Evaluation and Practical Deliberations in Education', *Educational Theory*, vol. 28, no. 4 (Fall 1978), pp. 279-85.

2. This section on categories of values relies heavily on Nicholas Rescher, *Introduction to Value Theory* (Prentice-Hall, Englewood Cliffs, New Jersey, 1969), pp. 13-19.

3. Philip C. Smith, 'What is Moral Education?' *Viewpoints*, vol. 51, no. 6 (November 1975), p. 19.

4. Karl A. Menninger and Paul W. Pruyser, 'Morals, Values, and Mental Health' in Albert Deutsch and Helen Fishmay (eds.), *The Encyclopedia of Mental Health* (575 Lexington Avenue, New York, 1963).

5. Gordon W. Allport, *Pattern and Growth of Personality* (Holt, Rinehart and Winston, New York, 1961), p. 29.

6. The idea of moral reasoning as habit is developed more fully in Richard S. Peters, 'Reason and Habit: the Paradox of Moral Education' in W.R. Nibbitt (ed.), *Moral Education in a Changing Society* (Faber and Faber, London, 1963), pp. 46-65.

7. Aristotle, *Nichomachian Ethics*, Bk. II, Chapter 3 and 4 as quoted by Peters, 'Reason and Habit'.

8. An excellent source for values analysis discussion techniques and procedures is Lawrence E. Metcalf (ed.), *Values Education: Rationale, Strategies, and Procedures*, 41st Yearbook (National Council for the Social Studies, Washington, DC, 1971).

9. The role-play reproduced here is adapted from one developed by Judith Berling, Professor of Religious Studies, Indiana University, for use at a Conference on Education for Mutual Understanding: Teaching about Japanese-American Relations.

9 MULTI-MEDIA INSTRUCTIONAL MATERIALS AND SOCIAL STUDIES

Ryozo Ito, Yasushi Mizoue, Takaharu Moriwake and Jiro Nagai

Nations differ greatly in the quantity and quality of instructional materials and technology provided to students and teachers. In the richest nations schools have their own libraries; teachers can use such equipment as television, computers, film projectors and slide projectors in their own classrooms; school is available to all students regardless of income; books and supplies are free or inexpensive. In the poorest nations few of these advantages exist. Schools may be overcrowded and there may not be enough space to provide a place for all youth who would like to attend. Often only the most talented or the wealthiest can attend secondary schools and colleges and books and school supplies are in short supply. In any case, many schools lack the electricity to operate mechanical equipment even if money existed to purchase it.

But a school's status in books and equipment is a weak indicator of the quality of its instruction. Teachers who have resources but lack interest may be poor instructors. In contrast, teachers who lack the libraries and equipment available to those in rich nations may provide outstanding instruction because of their own imagination. In the final analysis, what matters most is the knowledge, creativity, energy and devotion of teachers who make the best use of whatever is available.

In most countries, government ministries decide on course syllabuses; either government or private publishers produce the textbooks and other instructional aids. But teachers determine how (or if) these will be used. Ultimately, whether instruction is successful or not depends upon the teacher. This chapter provides suggestions for how teachers can make the most of available materials in whatever circumstances they may find themselves.

General Guidelines for the Use of Multi-media Materials

Social studies can serve many different educational goals. All social studies programmes contribute in some way to helping youth acquire and become committed to their own society and national culture.

Increasingly, educators recognise that national identification and loyalty is not enough. In an increasingly interdependent world, students must also learn about societies other than their own. Social studies goals must include the development of respect for other people and devotion to human rights.

Case Study 1: Teaching about Another Culture[1]

In an effort by two schools in the Philippines to promote international understanding, Japan was chosen as a focal country. Over a period of four months the Philippine pupils studied Japan's geography, history, culture, daily life, government and foreign relations. Teachers prepared special materials and pupils were provided with copies of the teachers' papers.

Pupils worked on individual and group projects for which they did their own research. Most of them prepared scrapbooks, while some brought to school Japanese articles collected from their own houses or from other sources. They wrote, produced and performed dramatic representations of Japanese life. A very popular aspect of the study was an exchange of letters with Japanese schoolchildren. Students saw films and filmstrips as teachers made them aware of Japanese customs and influences which have proved beneficial to the Philippines. The celebrated skills of the Japanese in flower arranging and interior decoration were demonstrated; the tea ceremony and holiday celebrations were described and discussed; and at every stage the importance Japanese people place on their long tradition of education and literacy was emphasised.

The positive changes in pupils' attitudes towards Japan appeared to be real and lasting.

The use of many, high-quality multi-media materials in teaching social studies is important regardless of goals. However, promotion of international education goals for social studies is often given less attention than national education goals. Additionally, the lack of good classroom materials designed to teach international education goals is critical. It seems easier to find materials to promote national goals. Therefore, throughout this chapter we will provide illustrations and case studies that offer suggestions for ways teachers can strengthen their instruction about about people and planetary issues, while recognising that the same principles regarding the use of multi-media materials apply to teaching about one's own society.

*Guideline 1: The More Media Available to a Teacher, the More
Chances Students Have to Fully Comprehend the Subject*

Media offer students enriched opportunities to acquire concepts,
values and skills. While it is possible to teach without textbooks,
pictures, maps, charts and chalkboards, it is easier to teach when
these are available. And while textbooks may be the most powerful
influence on what is taught in a class, even the best textbooks cannot
accomplish all that a teacher might wish. Furthermore, people learn
in various ways. Textbooks are efficient ways to transmit factual
material, but they may prove less powerful in affecting values or
building skills.

All of the senses are involved in learning. Students must see and
hear — even touch, taste and smell. Learning can occur by studying
a picture, listening to a speaker, building a project, visiting a museum
or helping solve a community problem. Each activity offers a different
way to learn. While variety is not itself a virtue, employing a range of
instructional media can arouse interest, instruct, reinforce learning
previously acquired and provide opportunities for students to apply
knowledge and skills.

One authority has grouped instructional media as follows.[2]

(1) *Verbal symbols:* this type of media depends upon carrying its
    message by words. When students are engaged in reading, writ-
    ing, speaking and listening, they are using verbal symbols. Most
    classroom instruction is verbal.

(2) *Visual symbols:* messages conveyed by words can also be trans-
    mitted through tables, charts and graphs. These too depend
    upon reading, but reading of a different type than reading narra-
    tive text.

(3) *Photographs, paintings, radio, recordings:* all of these depend
    upon seeing or hearing. A photograph conveys a perspective of
    reality that may have a greater impact than hundreds of words
    on the same topic. A painting provides the artist's interpretation
    of a person or an event. Radio provides fast reporting of world
    events and transmits the popular culture. Recordings influence
    artistic taste.

(4) *Films and television:* these are planned productions whose
    capacity to provide information and influence attitudes has
    been demonstrated. In the United States, Walter Cronkite, a
    well known news commentator for one of the major television
    networks, was shown by one study to be the 'most trusted person

in the United States'. While no one with similar impact exists for school television, there is no doubt that television and film are powerful classroom media.

(5) *Exhibits:* in the USSR many schools have permanent exhibits that provide information about famous graduates or about events that have deeply affected the school. Frequently such exhibits recall events surrounding World War Two and the devastation the war created in the USSR. Such exhibits provide powerful, continuing instruction for students.

(6) *Field trips:* often the best way to learn about how something is done is to watch it occur in its natural setting. Children who are raised in cities can best understand farms by visiting them; no description of a city could possibly equal the impact that a city visit will have on rural youth. A picture of a factory's assembly line cannot equal the effect of visiting a factory and watching one in operation.

(7) *Demonstrations:* demonstrations and field trips are closely linked. Both depend upon having people show what they can do best. Demonstrations can occur in a classroom, in a school meeting of the entire student body, or in the natural setting away from school.

To find speakers to help in teaching about other nations and cultures is not always easy. Those teachers who work in or near large cities can often find embassies or legations willing to send speakers to the school; if a university is nearby, foreign students may be available as resource persons.

In a British school, much of the success of a programme on the West Indies was due to visits to the school from West Indian people living in the neighbourhood. Talks on food, clothes, customs, art and music led to lively classroom discussion. The pupils were encouraged by what they had learned to attempt performances of calypsos, mimes and puppet plays they composed themselves. The exhibition arranged at the close of the programme was opened for an evening to parents and friends of the children and, on this occasion, a group of West Indians gave a demonstration of music and dance.[3]

(8) *Dramatic participation:* students can also learn through plays, tableaux, pageants and role-play situations. By assuming the role of a character in the dramatisation, students can gain a clearer impression of what another person might feel. Dramatisations can contribute importantly to promoting feelings of empathy towards other people.

Plate 11: Mexican Schoolchildren

Schoolchildren weed the garden of a rural school of Schinton, near San Cristobal de las Cosas. This is one of the 260 youth clubs developed in rural communities by the Chiapas Rural Development Programme (PRODESCH). In these gardens, children grow carrots, radishes, onions and lettuce and have learned how to fertilise their crops.

(9) *Contrived experiences:* teachers and students can create working classroom models that simulate experience outside of the classroom. These simulations can range from establishing small-scale business to simulating international policy-making.

(10)*Direct, purposeful experience:* many nations encourage direct social participation in the school and community. In some nations, China for example, schools actually operate factories or farms in conjunction with the schools. Students spend some time in class, and some working in the school factory or on the farm.[4] In other nations students contribute time to social welfare programmes, participate in election campaigns or help promote activities to improve the community environment. All of these programmes share the goal of linking academic study more closely to the real-life situations that exist outside of the classroom.

Guideline 2: The Media Chosen for Instruction Should be Appropriate to the Stated Objectives. to the Content of the Course, and to the Pupils' Stage of Development

Whether or not media are appropriate depends largely upon how they are used. Excellent media designed for one purpose may prove wholly ineffective when used to achieve another. Dramatisations and role-plays are effective ways to build empathy; they are less efficient in conveying large bodies of facts and generalisations. A powerful film about World War Two might be successful in conveying impressions of the war; it might also foster or maintain feelings of hostility towards people who were former enemies. Photographs can provide fresh insights into a culture; they can also encourage the formation of stereotypes about other people.

Media should be linked to the subject-matter of the course. They must also fit the maturity level of the students. Stories about animals are popular with young children and are often used to teach moral values; they hold less appeal to older youth. Government documents are sometimes appropriate materials to foster enquiry among adolescents; such documents would be beyond the comprehension of very young students. Older students are more capable of relying on verbal symbols; young students need various kinds of concrete objects — pictures, drawings, models — to guide their understanding.

Guideline 3: The Same Media can be Used in Support of Different Teaching Methods

Media do not dictate their use. Only the teacher can decide upon the methods to be employed. For example, a guest speaker can be invited to class to provide current, first-hand information about a topic under study. Or the speaker can be used mainly as an expert witness who responds to students' questions based upon their previous study of the topic. A 16mm. film can be used as a source of evidence; a film may provide conclusions and generalisations. Some teachers occasionally show films without playing the sound track to test their students' knowledge and comprehension of a subject. A lecture can merely provide the questions students need to investigate other sources, or it can provide answers to all of their questions.

The media provide the devices for instruction. The teacher must select the method and strategy.

Guideline 4: Instructional Media are Available from Many Sources. How the Media will be Used is a More Important Factor than their Source

Textbooks are the most common instructional media used in classrooms. Whether textbooks are produced by the government or by publishers, in nearly every nation they must pass through a process of approval before becoming available to students. This process is intended to eliminate errors as well as biased and prejudicial statements. It also ensures that whatever errors or biased statements exist are those that school authorities tolerate or approve. Biased statements are readily apparent when textbooks contain discussions about other nations, especially those that are current or former enemies. Even when textbook authors strive to report objectively the facts of particular international events, they find it difficult to resist assigning the lowest possible motives to the other side and cloaking the actions of their own leaders with lofty goals.

Teachers sometimes find that using multiple texts contributes to a more balanced treatment overall. Even more useful, when possible, is to provide students with excerpts from textbooks in other countries so that they can observe what students in other nations learn about the same events.[5]

While textbooks provide the instructional core, teachers can and should supplement instruction with materials of the types described earlier. The quantity and quality of such materials vary widely from nation to nation. In wealthy nations, schools may face a dilemma unknown to poor nations. Many groups offer free or inexpensive materials for schools to use. Government agencies, corporations, travel agencies, labor unions, foreign embassies and social and professional associations are but a few of the groups producing materials that might be appropriate for a social studies classroom. Such materials can be effective when used thoughtfully. For example, brochures from a multinational corporation may provide accurate, up-to-date information about its operations overseas. However, it may give no description at all — or at best a very distorted picture — about the everyday life of people who live in societies where they have property. Brochures and booklets from travel agencies and embassies are designed to give only the best features about life in other parts of the world. One must look to other sources for accurate information about social problems. (See Appendix A for information about sources.)

Guideline 5: Instructional Media should be Evaluated According to a Set of Criteria in Order to Determine their Impact and Future Use

The following questions might be asked when making judgements about instructional materials:

Is the material consistent with agreed-upon educational goals and instructional objectives?

Did the material contribute to students' cognitive growth and affective development?

Did the material arouse student interest in the topic?

Did it promote the critical thinking and problem-solving abilities of the pupils?

Did the material present varying points of view on issues, especially on controversial questions? Did the treatment seem largely free of error and bias?

Is the material appropriate for the pupils' age?

Is the material accurate, up to date and related to the course content?

Is the material easy to obtain?

Books written about one society for use in another society must be given special scrutiny. Teachers should try to learn whether the authors are qualified to write about the other country. Have they lived there or visited that nation? Has someone from that nation reviewed the work favourably? How are people's values presented? Do the books avoid stereotypes? Are costumes, arts, dances and other elements of the traditional culture portrayed in perspective along with current social and cultural practices? Instruction about other people should not only relay accurate information; it should also encourage appreciation of other cultures.

Various techniques may be used to assess the impact of materials on students. Suggestions for conducting such assessments are presented in Chapter 10.

The following sections are organised around four headings: Reading Materials, Audio-visual Aids, Community Resources and Teacher-developed and Student-developed Materials. Each section provides an explanation of the topic and a few sample lessons to indicate how various resources might be used.

Reading Materials

Social studies is a complex field of study. Its content consists of facts, concepts and generalisations relating to all kinds of social phenomena such as family and community living, activities of great persons and events in the past and present, government institutions and functions and economic systems. Since much of the content of social studies instruction is beyond the direct experience of boys and girls, reading materials carry the principal responsibility for making remote phenomena real and concrete.

Moreover, because social-historical events usually have many causes and can be interpreted from several points of view, it is important that students are exposed to reading materials that present alternative explanations and interpretations. Furthermore, children vary in their capacity to read. Thus materials pitched to different reading levels are needed.

Here are several suggestions for the practical classroom use of reading materials.

(1) Reading materials should be carefully examined with regard to the instructional objectives and to the children's reading level. When using primary source materials, teachers may need to rewrite them in order to match the children's level of reading and understanding.

(2) Usually a textbook is the main reference source for instruction and other reading materials are used to supplement it. But it is

not necessary to think of non-textbook sources as only supplemental. For instance, in teaching world history any printed material that helps students understand the historical event should be used. Practically speaking, in a beginning-level school class engaged in community study and in an upper-level school class focusing on current events, textbooks are useful mainly as secondary sources.

(3) Social studies teachers should also be reading teachers. They can help children learn new words and obtain main ideas from paragraphs. Reading skills taught in other classes can be reinforced as children read social studies books.

Textbooks

Textbooks are the most important source of ideas for teaching social studies; they have a powerful influence upon the social studies throughout the world. Often school courses are built around textbooks: the textbook is selected first; then the course is organised. Textbooks indicate what a teacher must teach and what the children have to learn. Textbooks are designed to be efficient conveyors of information.

Textbooks can be used in different ways. Some teachers begin with chapter one and proceed through the text sequentially, one chapter following another. In this case, the textbook carries the main responsibility for organising instruction. Other teachers use one textbook as a basic guide, selecting chapters from it, while providing other instructional material as well. This approach, avoiding dependence upon a single reference, gives students different points of view and encourages the skill of selecting information from many sources. Still other teachers organise each unit and course themselves. They may use one — or more — textbooks with multiple instructional materials, but they use textbooks as instructional tools, rather than as strait-jackets.

Objectives of Using Social Studies Textbooks. Whatever the values of using more than one textbook, textbooks serve an important purpose for all teachers. They present information in a compact, easy-to-remember form. They present graphic material to help organise data. They provide questions that lead students to reflect on what they have learned. Good textbooks teach students concepts and principles that can be generalised to situations apart from the text. And they focus student investigations and provide new instruction in and reinforcement for study skills.

While textbooks are designed to be used easily by all students,

Plate 12: Japanese Textbooks

Here are some social studies textbooks used in Japan. The three books across
the bottom of the picture are for use in the lower secondary grades (grades 7-9).
All of the others are for the elementary grades.

teachers cannot assume that students will make the best use of their
textbooks without deliberate instruction. Teachers need to point out
how chapters are organised, the use of headings, the purposes of illustrations and what types of answers are expected for end-of-section and
end-of-chapter questions. Students also need assistance in using the
table of contents, index and glossary. (See Chapter 7 for additional
ideas on reading and study skills.)

Supplementary Reading Materials

Despite the importance of textbooks, social studies teachers require
access to many other reading sources. Some of these are described briefly below.

Reference Books. Encyclopaedias, yearbooks, dictionaries, atlases,
manuals and biographies are examples of reference books required by
all social studies teachers. Encyclopaedias should be available in all

school libraries. Even in the elementary school, social studies classes need them. Their value lies in the considerable amount of factual information they provide on many topics. Biographies serve as important sources for teaching history, in particular. Written at a suitable reading level, they can throw light upon the life and society in which the person lived. Yearbooks, atlases and manuals provide up-to-date factual information. Many communities and cities publish pamphlets and handbooks about local history and government. These local publications can enrich community studies.

Source Books. Source books are especially important for history courses because first-hand accounts make past events more real. Source books may be used in at least two ways. Perhaps their most popular use is to supplement and enrich material found in textbooks. But source books may also be used as a lesson's main reading source. In this case, students read a source book in much the same way that they do a textbook. Used in this way source books tend to make students reason inductively rather than deductively.

In order to promote international understanding teachers should also make use of documents available from the United Nations and specialised agencies. For example, a book such as the *Birthright of Man* contains quotations from many cultural traditions and epochs to reveal how human beings everywhere, throughout the ages, have proclaimed human rights.[6] Documents such as the 'Universal Declaration of Human Rights' can be studied to learn what rights nations have agreed to respect; others such as the 'Recommendation Concerning Education for International Understanding, Co-operation and Peace' and 'Education Relating to Human Rights and Fundamental Freedoms' can be examined to find ways in which nations can better exercise the protection of human rights.

Case Study 2: Use of Documents in Japanese Schools
In 1977, a history class of 14-year-old students in a Japanese school studied 'the origin of cultural interchange between Japanese and Americans.' They collected historical documents concerning cultural contacts between Japan and the United States during the earlier period of Japanese modernisation in the nineteenth century. The teacher produced a number of original documents for students' use, translating some of these documents into modern Japanese. The documents included 'The Life of Manjiro', 'Memories of American Hikozo', 'The Navigation Diary of a Japanese Envoy to USA' and

'Seventy-Seven Samurais (Japanese knights) Go to America'. On the basis of the documents, students described the lives and experiences of people who went to the United States in the middle of the nineteenth century.

In an upper level school in Hiroshima, Japan, students used some historical documents relating to the American Revolution in their world history course. The documents included:

(a) Mayflower Compact (1620);
(b) Patrick Henry's address 'Give me liberty, or give me death' (1775);
(c) Thomas Paine's *Common Sense* (1776);
(d) the Declaration of Independence (1776);
(e) Hamilton, Jay and Madison: *The Federalist* (1778).

These documents had been translated and published in Japanese. The teacher selected essential parts of the documents and distributed copies to the students. He placed considerable importance on students' discussions about these documents in order to make their historical understanding vivid and concrete.

Newspapers and Magazines. A special feature of daily newspapers and magazines (weekly or monthly) is that they communicate the latest news and developments to students. Newspapers and magazines are essential resources for supporting current events instruction in the social studies.

Two types of newspapers and magazines are available to social studies teachers: those published primarily for children and those for adults. The former are designed to match children's reading ability. The latter are primarily for adults and can be difficult for beginning students to understand. More advanced students should be able to read newspapers and magazines prepared for adults.

Students should be taught how to read newspapers and magazines productively. Newspapers contain more than news stories. Editorial opinions, feature stories, political cartoons and even advertisements can be used profitably for instruction. For example, advertisements can provide insights into the culture of a people.

Audio-visual Materials

Using audio-visual materials such as pictures, charts, photographs, slides, films, radio, television and specimens can make learning interesting and instruction more effective. Audio-visual aids are used primarily to supplement textbooks and other media. Teachers should examine the merits of each audio-visual aid and select those that will be most effective in view of instructional objectives.

Pictures, Photographs and Illustrations

Pictures, photographs and illustrations are the most widely used visual aids. They can convey meanings more vividly and quickly than words. Carefully selected, they can motivate learners, clarify ideas and summarise instruction. Available from newspapers, magazines, old textbooks, travel agencies, business concerns, government information offices, libraries and commercial publishers and distributors, they can also be drawn or produced by teachers and pupils.

To use these materials most effectively, teachers should:

(1) organise pictures, photographs and illustrations around main ideas connected to instructional objectives, using a few at a time — an entire lesson can be built around the study of a single picture.

(2) teach pupils how to interpret pictures. Pupils can be taught how to 'read' ideas from pictures, photographs and illustrations. (See sample lesson below.)

(3) plan to show pictures, photographs and illustrations so that they can be studied by all students at one time. It is distracting to pass pictures around the classroom while conducting the lesson. Pupils cannot pay attention to the class discussion and study a picture simultaneously. Teachers can use an opaque projector to focus attention on a picture. Pictures can also be displayed on the bulletin board or attached to the chalkboard where pupils can see them.

(4) inform students that pictures, photographs and illustrations are still images selected from a larger scene by an artist or photographer. Pupils should be taught how to identify the creator's bias and allow for it.

Plate 13: Japanese Tourist

Sample Teaching Activity

Following is a photograph that students might be asked to study. Through such study, students can derive greater meaning from photographs. (The example below can help promote feelings of empathy important for building respect for other people.)

Students could be given individual copies of the photograph, or it could be projected on to a screen for the entire class. Then the teacher should ask students: what is going on here? Who are these people? What relationship do they have with each other? What clues are contained in the picture that helped you reach your conclusion?

After students have studied the photograph and answered the above questions, distribute the following line drawing of the photograph. The line drawing draws attention to the photograph's important features. Students may wish to spend additional time expanding on their answers to the questions posed earlier.

After students have studied the photograph and the line drawing, ask them to report their answers to the questions. Their ideas might be noted on the chalkboard.

Figure 9.1: Diagram of Plate 13

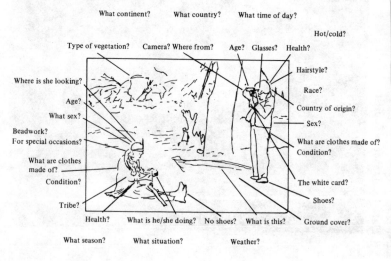

The following information is quoted from the teacher's guide that accompanies the photograph. It may be used to check the student's answers.

Information about the Photographh
   Where? African (costume of left-hand figure). Somewhere not very
      warm (photographer's clothing).
   When? Probably in the middle of the day (there are no distinct sha-
      dows).
   Weather? Overcast (no sharp shadows). Fairly cold (photographer's
      clothing).
   What? It is a photograph of two women. One is sitting on the ground,
      the other is standing taking a photograph.

Sitting figure. An African woman aged 50-60. She has no hair. She is wearning the traditional clothes and ornaments of her tribe. Her clothes are in fairly good condition, probably made of cotton. Her head, neck, wrists and ankles are much decorated with beads and other trinkets. She wears no shoes. She is not looking at the photographer, but concentrating on making a belt. The belt has a diamond pattern and is probably decorated with beads. She seems in good health – she is sitting upright and is able to do intricate work without glasses.

Standing figure. An East Asian woman, probably Japanese or Chinese, aged 40-60, but younger than the African woman. She is well dressed in clean, neatly pressed clothes, probably made of nylon. She has a wrist-watch and a camera, and carries a bag on her right shoulder. The white card may be telling her something about the camera or possibly about the person on the ground. Her hair is styled. She is wearing shoes. She is apparently unaware that her own photograph is being taken. She is wearing glasses.

Other facts. The grass under the tree is very sparse. The object on the ground at the foot of the tree is possibly an old bumper-bar from a car.

Teachers with specialised knowledge may be able to add further information, as follows.

The woman on the ground is a member of the Masai tribe in East Africa. East Africa has a tropical climate, but the photographer's clothes show that it is relatively cold. This suggests that the picture was taken at a fairly high altitude, which points to Kenya. As Japanese are among the main tourists to Kenya, it is probable that the photographer is Japanese. The Masai are not keen to be photographed, and in any case they usually live far from the main roads. Does this offer a clue to the precise location? Under what circumstances would a tourist come across a Masai woman who allowed herself to be photographed?

The background grass is long; this suggests the wet season.

Interpreting the Information. An elderly African woman sits working as she is photographed by a foreigner, possibly a tourist, a middle-aged Japanese woman. The African is wearing tribal dress and ornaments; either she is loyal to her tribal culture, or she has dressed up specially for the photograph. The tourist has not retained the physical aspects of her traditional culture; both her dress and hairstyle are Westernised. The African is probably fairly poor financially, the Japanese relatively well off. The African ignores the photographer, and this suggests that being photographed is, for her, a common experience. The tourist is concentrating on her photograph. Why is she taking it? Is she expecting to produce a tourist snapshot or a record of a human experience?[8]

The teacher might also wish students to speculate about the feelings of the people in the picture. What attitudes might the Japanese woman have towards the African woman? How might the African woman feel being photographed day after day by wealthy tourists? How might a tourist take a picture of someone in another country without offending them or violating their rights?

Chalkboards

The chalkboard is one of the oldest, yet most continuingly useful, instructional aids available to teachers. It can visually clarify many ideas presented during the lesson. Some teachers outline each lesson on the chalkboard to help students see the organisation of ideas. Following are some suggestions for making better use of this tool.

(1) Keep the chalkboard clean, neat and uncluttered.
(2) Adjust room lighting to reduce glare and eyestrain.
(3) Write and print legibly, organising materials in an orderly way.
(4) Write large enough so that all can see.
(5) Avoid crowding. Keep the board work simple and tasteful.
(6) Use underlining, colour and boxes to emphasise key ideas.
(7) Use ruler, compass and stencils to obtain a neat, artistic effect.
(8) Add simple stick figures to illustrate points.
(9) Avoid standing in front of the chalkboard, hiding the materials from the view of some students.

Plate 14: Teacher in the Central African Republic

A teacher-in-training in the Central African Republic oversees a pupil's work in a primary class.

Bulletin Board

Bulletin boards can contribute importantly to social studies instruction when properly utilised. Bulletin board displays can motivate students and interpret, supplement and reinforce instruction. At the beginning of a unit, teachers may wish to display materials that will evoke interest and stimulate questions. During the course of the unit, maps, charts, graphs, cartoons, pictures, posters and other items that contribute to lessons can be posted. At the close of a unit, bulletin boards can display student work, encouraging sharing, discussion and summarisation of learning among students.

Following are some suggestions for using the bulletin board.

(1) Use interesting and captivating captions and materials that are large enough to be seen.
(2) Design the bulletin board, taking balance, order and arrangement of colour into consideration.
(3) Discuss or explain the material on the bulletin board.
(4) Compile a file of materials for bulletin board use. Encourage pupils to post interesting materials on the bulletin board.

Still Projection of Slides, Filmstrips, Transparencies and Opaque Images

Still projection is a method by which visual material — pictures, photographs, graphs, charts, maps and so forth — can be projected on to a screen or similar surface for group viewing. Projected images tend to focus attention more than other methods of visual presentation, because pupil attention is centred on the screen and directed away from other visual stimuli in the classroom. Therefore, still projection provides a convenient and effective means for teachers and pupils to examine together a great variety of visual materials, in both colour and in black and white.

Slides, filmstrips and transparencies are materials whose projected image requires passing a light through them. Opaque projection permits classroom viewing of non-transparent materials from books or other printed sources, as well as of relatively flat objects and specimens. A slide is a relatively small piece of film or other transparent material on which a single pictorial or graphic image has been placed. Mounted slides range in size from 5 X 5 to 8.2 X 10.2 centimetres. A filmstrip is a series of photographic images in fixed sequence on a strip of film, usually 35 mm. Both slides and filmstrips are available commercially. Slides can also be produced easily by a teacher and pupils with a 35 mm camera. The advantage of a filmstrip is that the subject is treated in a logical order. Often the filmstrip is accompanied by an audio tape that provides narration. Therefore the teacher can prepare the lesson with assurance that the pictures will be well organised. The principal disadvantage of a filmstrip is that it is not possible to reorganise the sequence of pictures easily to fit a plan the teacher prefers. Slides are easy to make and can be shown in any order, although they cost more than filmstrips and must be handled carefully to avoid damage.

Transparencies are very large slides, usually 25.4×25.4 centimetres, intended for use with an overhead projector. A teacher can write or draw on transparencies or point out features on graphs, maps or sketches while they are being projected. The effectiveness of transparencies can be enhanced by the use of 'overlays', laying one transparency on top of another. Successive layers of transparencies can show progressive stages of development, sequences, relationships and sectional views. In the social studies classroom, steps in the territorial expansion of a country and the relationships of city location to topography are but two typical examples of how transparency overlays can be used effectively.

Opaque projection is used to show non-transparent materials — pictures, maps, charts and diagrams and pages in books and magazines; illustrations from newspapers; postcards; coins; paper money; stamps; cheques; and documents — on a screen for group observation. A dark room is essential for effective opaque projection. Opaque projections are valuable because a great variety of readily available and cost-free material can be used and illustrative materials can be enlarged to focus attention on significant details in illustrations.[9]

Audio Tapes, Recordings and Radio

Audio tapes, recordings and radio can also contribute to social studies instruction. Dramatisations of historical events appeal to pupils; music correlated with a historical period or a distant part of the world assists in understanding these cultures; excerpts of speeches of famous people, newscasts, reports, debates and other recordings or broadcasts provide important documentary sources for social studies classrooms. Such materials can be purchased from commercial sources or teachers can record their own from radio programmes.

Tape-recordings of interviews with specialists in the community and travel talks by the teacher or other adults are often useful. A classroom visitor's lecture may be recorded for replay and study at a later time. Tape-recordings of class sessions and committee meetings provide records of what occurred for evaluating procedures, techniques and content. Narration or music for filmstrips or slides may be recorded and used as needed. The tape-recorder is a versatile and easy-to-operate device and deserves a place in social studies classrooms.

Films and Television

Films are an effective means of presenting ideas that depend upon action. Events separated from the viewer by time and space can be made to seem immediate and real, as in films showing the great Tokyo earthquake of 1923 or the life of nomads in the desert. Films can sharpen reality by highlighting some things and eliminating others and by pointing up relationships that might otherwise be overlooked. On the screen, the actual size of objects can be enlarged or reduced; time can be speeded up or slowed down. Films can show objects and activities that are better understood when seen at varying rates of size and speed. On the other hand, for this reason, film can leave students with distorted impressions of size, space or time.

Films can provide pupils with a common experience as a basis for discussion and further enquiry. Pupils' attention can be sustained in a dark room with brilliant light coming from the screen. Films are interesting to watch, they hold attention and they may influence attitudes. Social studies teachers should utilise not only instructional films designed for school use, but also documentary, news and commercial dramatic films. Teachers and pupils can also produce their own films with 8 mm. or 16 mm. cinema cameras.

Case Study 3: Use of Film

A unit on the United Nations, taught in a lower secondary school in Japan, depended heavily on the use of 16 mm. films. The unit began by showing two films emphasising the devastating consequences of nuclear war. Discussion followed, emphasising the nature of war, the current political tensions in the world and ways of increasing friendship among nations. The purpose of this portion of the unit was to give students an understanding of existing world tensions and problems and to heighten their interest in peace and specific solutions to differences.

Next, two films on the meaning and structure of the United Nations were shown. The group discussion which followed concentrated on the reasons for the formation of the United Nations and its chief characteristics. Two additional films focused discussion on the effectiveness of the United Nations as a peace-keeping body and linked the work of the organisation to contemporary problems of Japan. Teacher lectures on modern history, covering the period from the League of Nations to the founding of the United Nations, helped set a context for the films.

A final film dealt with the need of individuals for friendship and understanding among human beings. It was selected to add an essential humanistic element to the study.

At the unit's end the various parts of the unit were brought together through further discussions. Students understood better the nature of war and peace, the spirit of the United Nations, its structure and organisation and the contribution the United Nations can make to war prevention.

The following suggestions will help teachers make better use of films.

(1) Select only those films which are pertinent to the instructional objectives; otherwise the film's value is that of entertainment. Preview the film before showing it to the students. Decide when and how to include it in the unit. Is it best at the beginning of a unit to build a common background or to arouse interest? Would it be most useful during the course of the unit to add fresh meaning to the reading materials or to stimulate thought and discussion? Or would it be best at the end of the unit to summarise and reinforce ideas that have been developed?

(2) Before showing the film, introduce it to the pupils and tell them the purpose for seeing it. Discuss questions they should think about as they watch it, what problems or situations to note in the film, and so on. Explain any new words, phrases or major concepts used in the films which are apt to cause difficulty.

(3) After a film has been shown, discuss student responses to the questions provided prior to showing the film. Correct mistaken conclusions and notions, expose points where pupils disagree. Detect and correct size, space and time distortion. It is often useful to show the film a second time as students will have acquired new ways of thinking about it on the basis of class discussion.

Another source of motion pictures is the medium of television. Educational television programmes should contribute directly to attaining instructional objectives. Beyond television programmes designed deliberately for school use, some general television programmes can also be useful for social studies instruction. Documentaries, special reports,

Plate 15: Educational Television in Niger

Schools in Niger have introduced television into their school system on an experimental basis. This photograph shows a classroom using television to supplement other learning activities.

plays, interviews, forums, news reports and other programmes may enrich and extend student learning, especially as regards current events. Special feature programmes on commemorations, campaigns and festivals may help students gain insight into their significance.

Television programmes may be used in the classroom at the same time they are broadcast. Television programmes can also be recorded by video tape-recorder for future use. With a library of video tapes available, teachers can use specific programmes when they best fit instructional needs. On certain occasions, pupils may be encouraged to watch special television programmes in the evening at home with the intention of sharing reactions and impressions with the class on the following day.

The impact of commercial television in some countries on student attitudes can be powerful. Students may acquire distorted views of real life after watching too many adventure shows, crime stories and other sensationalised programmes. Social studies teachers need to teach students how to protect themselves from television as well as how to learn from it.

One problem with using television as an instructional tool is the tendency to use it in place of a teacher. Television is usually a one-way communication device, continuing through the topic whether students have understood the instruction or not. Although educational television may use a televised teacher, the classroom teacher must assume the main responsibility. Only the classroom teacher can select, introduce, follow up, fill in gaps and correct misunderstandings.

Objects and Models

It is often impossible or impractical for pupils to gain first-hand experience with topics under study, but they can have experiences with replicas of them. Objects and models are an important segment of reality. They can help to make the learning situation more real, lifelike and interesting to the pupils. The following objects and models can make social studies instruction about other countries more concrete, authentic and interesting: clothing, ornaments, tools, utensils, dishes, toys, dolls, furniture, products, coins, paper money, manuscripts, documents, diaries, letters, magazines, books, seals, cheques, postage stamps, art objects, sample foods, models of transportation, models of shelter, etc.

Pupils should be permitted to handle and to study the objects closely. If they are fragile, they may be demonstrated before the class. But objects and models represent only a portion of reality. Missing elements must be represented through reading materials, pictures and films. Objects and models can be obtained from public museums, commercial and industrial organisations, or from individuals. Some people may own antiques, old documents or a great-grandfather's diary. Often, those who have travelled abroad have collected materials. Once community members know that their materials can be used effectively in the classroom, they are often willing to share them; and in some instances, they will give them to the school. Pupils themselves may collect and construct objects and models. Such collections may be protected and displayed in a school museum.

Community Resources

Social studies instruction need not be bound by the classroom. Every community, however small, has resources that can strengthen social studies and add to its vitality. People, institutions, organisations, local publications and historical sites are just a few of the local resources that teachers often overlook.

Teachers cannot use community resources effectively until they learn what is available. A teacher should conduct a survey of community resources. In order to keep the information up to date, the survey should be repeated periodically. Pupils might also participate in gathering data. Not only would this help them know their community better, but it could also develop skills of observation, information gathering and content analysis.

Field Trips

Successful field trips require careful planning and co-ordination, full co-operation from parents, faculty and school administrators and meticulous attention to detail prior to and during the trip. When the excursion is over, students should be asked to report, orally or in writing, about some feature of the trip. This helps emphasise the value of the experience and its relevance to the topic under study in the classroom.

Before the field trip, the teacher should meet with the person serving as host at the trip site. This person should be informed about what the students are studying, the kinds of information the trip is expected to reveal and the kind of detail students might find interesting. The host should know what kinds of student questions to expect during the trip and may wish to set aside a particular time for questions and answers.

Students should be prepared through a pre-trip discussion that includes a preview of the physical site, the kinds of information to be sought and information about the trip's host or guide and that person's relationship to the study trip site. This discussion should also emphasise the relationship of the trip to material the class is studying.

Students may be assigned to make special reports on different aspects of the trip. Most worthwhile field trips will have several outstanding features. A trip to a historical site, for example, might be divided into study about the actual event that occurred there, persons involved in the event, the research, work and funds involved in identifying the site as historically significant and several other subjects suggested by the site itself. Some students may be asked to make a detailed map of the trip from the school to the study site. Other students could be assigned to draw illustrations of the actual site or to report on some particular aspect of the visit. By assigning individuals or small groups the responsibility for researching these elements and reporting on their findings after making the trip, the class can receive a far more comprehensive view of the entire study trip.

What kinds of places might students visit? Of course, this depends on the purposes of the lesson and the resources available, but a few examples would include historical sites, farms, factories, local businesses, transportation centres such as bus depots, railroad stations and airports, service organisations and communication centres such as radio and television stations and newspaper offices.

An example of a field trip would be one to a government office. This could be the district office of the national government, the local government agency, a law enforcement agency, a social service agency, a public library or an agricultural assistance agency. The site should be selected according to the subject the class is studying and the available community resources, but an important aspect of the trip should be to illustrate the services available from the government through this particular agency. For example, a trip to a law enforcement agency could answer the question of what to do if someone were to steal something from you. Hosts could explain what services are provided by law enforcement agencies and how one can obtain these services. The agricultural agency might be able to tell citizens why their garden was poor last summer and provide information or materials for improving the crops this year. A trip to the agency site teaches students the physical location of available assistance and the exact procedures they should follow in requesting and receiving assistance. It can also demonstrate the daily operation of the office and the nature of the duties of those who work there. Again, students might be asked to watch for and report on different aspects of the trip, and each student could be asked to prepare a map from his or her home to that particular government agency.

Resource Persons

Local people can be invited to assist instruction by serving as guest speakers, consultants and interviewers. Elderly people enjoy talking to youth about their community's history. Occupational specialists can discuss their work and how students can find a career in their type of work. Public officials can describe community problems and how these problems are being solved.

Plate 16: Tanzanian Craftsman and Pupils

Children frequently learn traditional crafts directly from village craftsmen who pass on their skills. The United Republic of Tanzania is a country that has made student activity in the community a basic aim of education.

Careful planning should precede a resource person's visit so that the time of the visitor, the teacher and the class is not wasted. Before the visit, the teacher needs to explain to the visitor what the class has been studying and how his or her contribution will fit into an ongoing process. The teacher and speaker should agree on the length of the talk and topics it will cover. The speaker should know if students expect to ask questions following the talk. Students also should be prepared for the visitor. They should know the speaker's identity and topic, and should be prepared to ask questions.

Your Community in the World

Typically, teachers consider using community resources to teach students about local customs, traditions and practices. But community study can also be undertaken to promote international education goals and to further understanding and respect for other people.

It is an unusual community that has *no* contact with the outside world. To draw attention to connections between the community and the world system, the teacher and pupils may participate in a wide variety of easily constructed activities.

Most communities produce something that is sold outside the borders of their nation. Students could be asked to trace the movement of local community products to other parts of the world.

In a similar way, students can make lists of all the products they use in a single day. These lists might include food, clothing, buildings, furniture, appliances, cosmetics, books and medicines. Then students can analyse their lists to determine where the products originate. For example, a wooden house might be made with local wood, but the nails, hammers, window glass, doorknobs and other products may have been imported. Or bread that may have been baked locally could use grains unavailable in the local area.

After making these product lists, students should identify the countries of origin on a world map. World areas linked to the local community could be visually connected by pinning lengths of string or brightly coloured yarn from the local community to the trading partners. This would be an effective bulletin board display to remind students of their interdependence with the rest of the world.

Another way to demonstrate local links to other parts of the world is to identify people who have moved to the community from other countries. These people could be invited to speak to the class, to show slides and artifacts of the country they left and describe the adjustments they had to make when moving to their present homes.

Current world events often have much more impact on the local community than students realise. This impact can be shown by asking students to collect newspaper stories for a bulletin board display. After dividing the pupils into several study groups, the teacher can ask one group to find stories about world-wide weather conditions, noting how weather conditions in another part of the world affect the local community. For example, a severe drought in the middle portion of the United States might affect grain supplies and prices in many parts of the world. A typhoon, seriously damaging Japan's rice crops, might increase the demand for available rice and rice products. Other study groups could study world-wide political developments because severe political disruptions in one nation usually affect others shortly. Even stable political systems are subject to changes in public attitudes, interests or policies that have an impact upon international relations. Still other groups could collect newspaper articles about international contacts in such areas as sports, music and tourism. Each week, all newspaper stories and student comments can be mounted in a bulletin board display and discussed for the benefit of the entire class.

Some other topics that highlight the importance of a community's relationship to the rest of the world are the dependence of local employment on world markets, the ethnic backgrounds of students' families and ancestors, and international influences on styles in clothing, music, books, sports, speech, movies and television. Many other topics could be cited, but these should demonstrate that community studies need not serve only parochial educational goals. Community studies can also promote international understanding.

Case Study 4: Use of Community Resources to Study Human Rights
A short, concentrated project in a large, coeducational secondary school in Hiroshima, Japan, was designed to appraise the observance of human rights in Japan. A class of about forty 17-year-old students devoted nearly five weeks to a study that included classroom lectures, field trips in town and to rural districts, and discussions.

Students were able to choose among several courses of study. Each programme included at least one field trip. One group of eight boys and four girls chose a village as the focus of its study. The students lived with farmers' families, two to a household. On the first day, after listening to a talk by the village leader on community history and administration, they were given a general tour of the village, and in the evening they visited families in their homes. The second day was spent working in the fields beside their hosts and in discussion with village youth.

Thirteen boys and fourteen girls chose to visit factories. Their programme included a tour of an automobile factory of 4,000 workers, a visit to a smaller factory of 100 employees and a look at a subcontract workshop with only seven workers. They were also accepted at the local tramway company's workers' union where they learned how a labour union is organised and heard a description of a strike.

On their return to school, each group prepared a report on its experiences, with particular attention to the question of human rights. Each report was presented to the entire class. Their study concluded with a round-table discussion on their findings and the conclusions to be drawn from the experiment.

Teacher- and Student-developed Materials

Some of the best and most successful teaching materials are those developed by the teacher or by the teacher and pupils, working with their own resources. When students participate in creating their own learning materials, they acquire additional skills, interests and enthusiasm in the process. Several suggestions for home-made materials and activities are discussed in this section.

Following a study of other countries and cultures, pupils might want to demonstrate what they have learned by staging a puppet performance. Pupils can make their own puppets, dressing them in costumes representing the countries they have studied. They can write and perform their own puppet play which could contain examples of social activities, songs, dances, family life, religious activities and work from each country.

Puppets may be as simple or as complex as time, materials and pupil skills permit. The easiest puppet to make is a 'shadow puppet'; this involves a cardboard or wooden silhouette held before a bright light so that the puppet's movements are projected as shadows on a screen. These figures, sometimes painted so as to have distinctive features and costumes, are manipulated by a stick held by the puppeteer below the floor level of the puppet stage. A slightly more complex puppet is constructed by making the arms, legs, torso, and head separately and connecting them with brads or pieces of string. Each limb is manipulated by an attached stick which, held below stage level, can be lifted and dropped to make the puppet move.

A different kind of puppet altogether is the finger puppet and its variant, the hand puppet. A finger puppet is merely a piece of cloth or

Plate 17: Pupils and Marionnettes in La Paz

Students in La Paz, Bolivia, learn to manipulate a marionnette. Puppet shows are frequently used by the teaching staff for educational purposes.

Plate 18: Puppet Performance in Mexico

This puppet show is being performed by student teachers from Patzcuaro School of Fundamental Education.

Plate 19: Terrain Model in La Paz

In a mathematics class in La Paz, Bolivia, a terrain model showing Egyptian and pre-Columbian architecture helps students understand abstract geometrical concepts.

paper shaped to fit the human finger and decorated to represent different animal or human characters. Hand puppets may be made from old stockings. By inserting fingers into the stocking's toe and the thumb into the heel, and by holding the fingers to the thumb (the stocking's toe to its heel), the puppeteer can represent the inside of a creature's mouth. Eyes, nose, ears, hair and a tongue can be attached to the figure by embroidery or paint. By opening and closing the 'mouth' and moving the wrist as the long 'neck' of the puppet, the puppet can produce charming effects. The puppeteer sits behind the stage and holds puppetted fingers or hands above the stage floor level for performances.

Teachers or students with greater skills might wish to make marionnettes. Marionnettes are three-dimensional puppets made of wood or papiermâche with jointed limbs manipulated by strings. These strings are attached to a stick held above the puppet. By pulling the nearly invisible strings, the marionnette can be made to move as if free of human control.

A puppet stage can also be simple or complex. A simple stage would be a table top, with puppeteers shielded from the sight of the audience by a cloth draped over the table. An elaborate, decorated stage could be constructed from cardboard or wood and decorated with paint.

Although making elaborate puppets may take considerable time, the same puppets can be used in succeeding years with different pupils. Puppetry is useful in role-play or simulation exercises and is particularly helpful in encouraging very young children to express themselves. Often children who are unable to express ideas, reactions and feelings directly are able to demonstrate their thoughts and feelings through a puppet.

Another activity involves the use of terrain models. These often help pupils visualise a geographic area they are studying. Terrain models can be constructed by filling a wooden or cardboard box with plaster of paris, clay, papiermâche or earth, and then sculpting representations of mountains, streams, plains, forest areas and other geographical features. Terrain models can exhibit changing features of the earth's surface, such as those produced by erosion or volcanic action. A model intended to demonstrate such changes should be made of sand or earth so that students and teachers can manipulate the model's surface. By tilting the terrain and sprinkling it with water, the teacher can show how water pathways form ravines, ditches and eventually canyons.

Conclusion

Social studies can be taught by many methods, using many different materials. Some methods and media seem better suited for teaching particular types of content than others. For example, it is hard to imagine teaching geography without using maps. Geography instruction is also strengthened by using still photography, motion pictures, globes and terrain (or relief) maps. Furthermore, some students will learn more from a dramatisation of a political process or historical event than from a textbook description. These methods help make abstract, symbolic content more immediate and comprehensible for all students. The best teachers will employ as many methods and materials as possible to present their subjects.

Although material resources to support instruction differ greatly from country to country, all teachers have access to some kind of multi-media materials. Teacher-produced and pupil-produced materials, classroom visitors, role-plays or dramatisations, field trips to nearby points of interest and materials available in the community usually cost little or nothing. By creative use of available resources, most teachers can develop instructional programmes to meet their requirements.

Notes

1. *International Understanding at School: an Account of Progress in Unesco's Associated Schools Project* (Unesco, Paris, 1965), pp. 78-80.

2. Edgar Dale, *Audio-Visual Methods of Teaching*, 3rd edn (Dryden Press, New York, 1969).

3. *Education for International Understanding: Examples and Suggestions for Classroom Use* (Unesco, Paris, 1959), p. 53.

4. 'Aspects of Education in China', *Prospects: Quarterly Review of Education*, reprints from vol. V, no. 4 (1975) (Unesco, 1975).

5. For example, see Donald Robinson (ed.), *As Others See Us: International Views of American History* (Houghton Mifflin, Boston, 1969); and Donald Robinson (ed.), *Verdict on America* (Houghton Mifflin, Boston, 1974).

6. Jeanne Hersch (ed.), *Birthright of Man* (Unesco, Paris, 1969).

7. Based upon a photographic packet produced by the Centre for World Development Education, 25 Wilton Road, London SW1V 1JS, United Kingdom. Use of pictures was suggested by an article entitled 'Pictorial Analysis to Understand Development Issues: an Example from the United Kingdom', *Ideas and Action: Action for Development*, vol. 115 (1977/2), pp. 20-2.

8. Ibid., pp. 21-2.

9. *Teaching Guide for Social Studies in Elementary School* (in Japanese) (Ministry of Education, Tokyo, 1961), pp. 71-3.

10 EVALUATION IN SOCIAL STUDIES

P. Olatunde Okunrotifa

Evaluation is the process of collecting and using information to make decisions. Three kinds of decisions in social studies will be addressed in this chapter: evaluation of student achievement, evaluation of student attitudes and evaluation of social studies programmes.

Traditionally, evaluation has meant measuring student achievement, usually at the end of the student's exposure to a course of instruction. Present-day evaluation has become far more embracing, with every component of the learning situation being assessed. This includes details about the learners, particularly their entry behaviour (the amount of knowledge they have, what they can do, etc., at the beginning of a course of study), the teachers and the resources for teaching. As teaching proceeds, it is also evaluated, the success of particular methods judged by how much students have been able to learn and how they react to the subject. Again, at the end of each stage of instruction the learner's achievement and sometimes his or her attitudes are measured. This information enables the teacher to make decisions regarding the appropriateness of the instructional objectives, the content, the teaching methods and the devices used for measuring learning.

Purposes of Evaluation

Educational evaluation can be regarded as important for three different purposes: diagnostic evaluation, formative evaluation and summative evaluation. While one evaluation activity may serve more than one purpose, the practitioner should have a clear understanding of the purpose of any evaluation effort. Figure 10.1 illustrates these three purposes as they relate to both student evaluation and programme evaluation.

Evaluation which takes place prior to beginning a unit of instruction is called 'diagnostic evaluation'. Such pre-instructional evaluation can help teachers obtain information concerning the learner's entry behaviour — the kinds of attitudes, skills and knowledge students already possess that will encourage, limit or prevent teacher and student efforts to achieve desired objectives. One of the advantages of diagnostic evaluation is discovering whether or not students have in their repertoire

Figure 10.1: Questions Illustrative of the Purposes of Educational Evaluation

	Diagnostic Purpose	Formative Purpose	Summative Purpose
Student Evaluation	What missing skills are causing the student's difficulty?	How well is the student progressing toward the stated objectives?	What did the student learn in the course?
Programme Evaluation	What are the causes of the observed problems in the programme?	How well is the programme progressing toward its objectives?	What did the programme accomplish?

the kind of behaviour the teacher wishes to promote. It is conceivable that students may enter the course with far more competence than is assumed for them by the teacher and weeks may be wasted in 'teaching' students what they already know. However, students often know far less than teachers assume they know. They may actually fail to possess the prerequisite ability, knowledge, attitude or skill they need to accomplish the course objectives. In either case, diagnostic evaluation results may suggest modifying original objectives with respect to minimal performance levels and the actual content of the objectives. It may also indicate the need to differentiate instruction among pupils in the classroom.

Diagnostic evaluation can also occur *during* a unit of instruction. The use of diagnostic tools during instruction can help teachers determine the degree to which certain non-instructional factors, such as attitudes towards the teacher, personal habits, relationship with parents or peer rivalry are affecting student progress towards attaining desired objectives. For example, a student may not have a quiet place to study at home and be unable to complete assigned homework. Certain students may come to school without adequate sleep, making it difficult for them to attend to lessons. Fear of failure may cause others not to try at all.

Diagnostic evaluation in this sense should be distinguished from 'formative evaluation' usually conducted during (rather than before or after) a unit of instruction. The purpose of formative evaluation is to help teachers assess students' progress toward attaining desired objectives, to provide teachers and learners with specific feedback regarding students' success in mastering skills or knowledge presented to that point and, if they are not understanding the material, to pinpoint exactly where the students are having problems.

Diagnostic evaluation is most helpful in obtaining insight into general skills, attitudes and characteristics of students, such as how students feel about activities which occur in the classroom. Formative evaluation, on the other hand, is designed specifically for a particular unit of instruction and is intended to locate exactly where in the unit the student is having trouble.

Lastly, evaluation can occur at the end of a unit of instruction in order to determine how much and how well students have learned and to what extent desired objectives have been attained. This kind of evaluation is referred to as 'summative evaluation'. This chapter will provide information about the nature and development of instruments used to conduct diagnostic, formative and summative evaluation in social studies.

Evaluation of Student Achievement

Two major approaches to evaluating student achievement are 'norm-referenced evaluation' and 'criterion-referenced evaluation'. Norm-referenced evaluation rests on judging student achievement by comparing one student's scores to the scores of other students. Interpretation of these comparisons can be based on scores of a large group of students for a standardised test or on scores of a smaller, local group of students for a teacher-made test. The key element is comparing each student's performance to that of other students.

Criterion-referenced evaluation, on the other hand, uses a different comparison. Test items are prepared to measure a student's understanding of a particular objective. A criterion (or standard), which indicates to the teacher that the student has mastered the objective, is chosen. Student scores are then compared to the expected criterion score in order to judge individual achievement. Several objectives can be measured in a single test, although it is desirable to prepare three to ten items for each objective. The main point is to have enough items to give an adequate assessment of each objective and to compare each student result to the predetermined standard for each objective, without reference to how other students are performing.

While these two approaches are different, they are not totally incompatible. Teachers will probably use both approaches from time to time, or even simultaneously, depending on the kind of comparison that is most appropriate for each situation. Therefore, it is important that teachers understand the differences between these approaches and that they use this understanding to make the most appropriate comparisons in judging student achievement.

Having considered the concept and types of evaluation in the fore-going paragraphs, we are ready to study how social studies teachers can develop their own tests and select wisely from among tests prepared by others. Although teachers should design their tests according to the format which is effective for achieving their purposes, there are a number of general principles that should guide all test construction.

Principles of Test Construction

(1)   Test construction must reflect the purpose of the test. Earlier we noted the purposes of diagnostic, formative and summative tests. For a test of students' general achievement in a content area, the questions must be representative of the subject-matter taught and, in the case of norm-referenced tests, should be sufficiently difficult that those who know the subject can be separated from those who do not know it.

(2)   The kind of test item must be determined by the type of beha-viour that the students are expected to demonstrate. If the teacher's interest is in testing students' knowledge of facts, then objective items are more efficient. On the other hand, if the desire is to test students' ability to use their knowledge in a selective and organised way and to present the answer in coherent verbal form, then the essay question is preferable.

(3)   Test items should include a representative sample of the subject-matter content and of the behavioural processes of interest to the examiner.

(4)   Test items must be constructed so that extraneous factors will not prevent the student from correctly answering the questions. Test items should not be linguistically or conceptually ambiguous. Language should be precise and intelligible to the students. An extreme example of an item which violates these two principles would be one written in French for English-speaking fourth-formers (tenth-graders) in Nigeria which, translated, would mean: 'Why do you think that Nigeria is the most important country in Africa?' Apart from the unintelligibility of the language to the students, they can not know what answer is expected

to this question. The meaning of the 'Why' part of the question is unclear.

(5)   Test items which contain internal clues to the correct answers should be avoided. Objective test items are particularly susceptible to violating this principle. In the True-False form of objective items, problem statements that include relative adverbs such as 'sometimes', 'usually' and 'generally' are likely to be true while those that include absolutes like 'never', 'always', 'none' and 'only' are very likely to be false since few things in the world are absolutely true or false while most things are partially true or false.

(6)   The test should be at the proper level of difficulty relative to the students and to the test's purpose. For a norm-referenced achievement test, the level of test difficulty is probably appropriate if the average number of students correctly answering individual items is about 50 per cent, and if the range of scores is between about 20 per cent for some questions to about 80 per cent for other questions. These guide-lines are not appropriate for criterion-referenced evaluation. This approach to evaluation is closely linked to an important educational concept called 'mastery learning' that has had an impact on curriculum development and evaluation in general. Basically, mastery learning advocates assume that the majority of students can learn what is expected of them in school to a level of 'mastery'. This concept challenges the assumption that ability in any group of students is normally distributed in such a way that for any examination student performance should range from very good 'A' to very poor 'E' or 'F'. Mastery learning posits that practically all students can score an 'A'. It bases its contention on research showing that, if a process of forma-tive evaluation and remedial teaching (often simply by peers) is built into the teaching process, and if students are allowed sufficient time, most students can learn everything in the curriculum. If mastery learn-ing becomes generally accepted, then it may have serious implications for testing procedures. The mastery learning procedure lends itself to criterion-referenced evaluation, that is, to comparing students to the subject rather than to other students. The emphasis of norm-referenced test makers on item discrimination and item difficulty are not appropri-ate here. When the objective is to help all students make an 'A', the idea that a good item will discriminate between those who do well on the test and those who do poorly (the index of discrimination) no longer makes sense. In addition, the fact that most items have high

percentages of students securing correct answers (the difficulty index) may no longer be evidence of a bad test. This does not mean that these concepts or indices will become meaningless, but their use will need to be clearly confined to norm-referenced evaluation.

Steps in Test Construction

Test and examination construction requires rigorously planned steps. This is even more true for examinations which influence vital decisions about students' lives and prospects. The following discussions treat major steps in test construction.

Formulation of Objectives. The formulation of social studies objectives is normally the first step in preparing a social studies achievement test. The conscientious social studies teacher will develop a list of objectives before teaching any unit. In recent years, much literature in the field of educational evaluation has been devoted to objectives. Some publications have focused on categories of educational objectives that might have general applicability across all subjects. The major works in this area are those of Benjamin S. Bloom and others who produced the taxonomies of educational objectives in the cognitive, affective and psychomotor domains.[1] Therefore, one way of ensuring adequate coverage is to base the classification of the curriculum objectives on one or the other of these taxonomies.

Some experts have concentrated on the manner in which objectives are stated. Tests can validly measure only observable behaviour; indeed, test items and tasks are merely samples and indicators of desired learner behaviour. To construct effectively test items that fit objectives, therefore, some authorities believe that objectives must be stated in behavioural terms. This has led to a strong movement on behalf of 'behavioural objectives' in curriculum development. Among the chief exponents of behavioural objectives are Tyler, Popham and Mager.[2]

Behavioural objectives have certain characteristics. First, they are stated in specific, measurable and observable terms. Second, the behaviour indicated is that of the student. Furthermore, Mager has identified three essential components of the structure of a behavioural objective. It should contain:

(a) an action verb;
(b) a content reference;
(c) a performance level.

Thus, examples of behavioural objectives include the following.

(a) The student can read extracts from the daily newspaper without making more than one mistake in every twenty words.
(b) The class will answer eight out of ten items correctly on a multiple choice test.
(c) Given two or more different samples of information, students correctly state differences and similarities.
(d) Students apply information in one situation to another, new and different situation.

The behavioural objectives movement has met with very stiff opposition on the grounds that it can only measure trivial education objectives, whereas the more important objectives of education are of a less tangible nature. Another criticism is that behavioural objectives can be so detailed that they become cumbersome, lacking in general applicability and therefore difficult to use. A complete and detailed refutation of these and many other criticisms has been given by Popham. While many educational evaluators settle for their own particular compromise in the debate, some of these criticisms are part of the strong feeling that is sometimes expressed against all measurement, despite the fact that teachers are constantly making evaluative judgements of their students' abilities and performance, whether they do so consciously or not.

Specifying Content to be Covered. After deciding the types and levels of learning to be measured, the teacher's next step in planning a test is to list the general topics or areas studied during the period that the test is to cover. The more the topics into which the subject-matter can be subdivided the better, although this should not be carried to a point of triviality. For example, for a form five (eleventh grade) achievement test in a unit on Nigerian farming and rural land use, the topics may include:

1.1 Basic appraisal of land use
1.2 Methodological problems of discerning land-use patterns
1.3 Farming as decision-making
1.4 The idea of farms as systems
1.5 Nigeria: interplay of physical and economic factors.

No doubt, a few of the topics can be further subdivided into more specific units, for example, the last topic could be divided into changing farming patterns in Nigeria and changes in farming systems and landscape evolution. By studying the syllabuses and all relevant major textbooks, by consulting experienced teachers and experts and even by looking at past tests, new teachers can gain much guidance about topics to be included in a test blueprint.

Preparing the Test Blueprint. With the statement of objectives and the content outline available, the teacher is ready to develop the test plan itself. The example given here is for a paper-and-pencil achievement test. The scope and emphasis of the test is identified in a test blueprint shown in Table 10.1. This two-way table relates the subject-matter content to behavioural processes.

Table 10.1: Test Blueprint for a Social Studies Unit on Farming and Rural Land Use[3]

	Behavioural Objectives					
	Recalls Specific Facts and Terms	Compre-hends (translates and interprets) Data	Applies Concepts and Principles	Identi-fies Main Ideas and Processes	Writes a Well Organ-ised Account	Total (per-centage)
1.1 Basic Appraisal of Land Use	2	4	4	3	2 =	15
1.2 Methodological Problems	2	6	5	4	3 =	20
1.3 Farming as Decision-making	2	6	5	4	3 =	20
1.4 Idea of Farms as Systems	2	6	5	4	3 =	20
1.5 Nigeria: Physical and Economic Factors	2	8	6	5	4 =	25
Total percentage	10	30	25	20	15 =	100

This test blueprint makes use of a technique called 'weighting'. In the classroom, different topics are of differing relative importance to the entire teaching plan, so tests can be 'weighted' by assigning different point values for the corresponding levels of importance. Weights are usually expressed as percentages which must add to 100 per cent. In Table 10.1, for example, the topic 'Basic Appraisal of Land Use' has been assigned a total value of 15 percentage points. In the same way, each of the objectives for the teaching unit should be assigned a relative weight. In Table 10.1 the objective 'Recalls Specific Facts and Terms' is assigned a total value of 10 percentage points to be divided across several topics.

The topics and the behavioural objectives on the two-way table form as many grading categories as the number of *topics* multiplied by the number of *objectives*. The proportion of the test assigned to each grading category is determined by multiplying the percentage assigned to the topic row by the percentage assigned to the objective column. For the first grading category, 'Recall of Specific Facts and Terms about Basic Appraisal of Land Use', the percentage assigned is computed by multiplying the topic weight (15 per cent) by the objective weight (10 per cent). The result is 1.5 per cent, which may be rounded to 2 per cent as long as the percentages of all grading categories add up to 100 per cent. When a test-maker feels that not all topics should be examined under all behavioural objectives, the total of all grading category percentages must still be 100 per cent. In this situation the grading category values, rather than the row and column totals, must be decided in advance and their sums across lines and down the columns then become the individual topics' and individual objectives' totals, respectively.

Considering how much time is available for preparing, presenting and marking the test, and on the kind of test items considered suitable, the test-maker determines how many items will be in the test. The number of items will then be divided across the grading categories of the test blueprint in proportion to the percentage values of the categories. Thus, in a 50-item objective test, only two test items will relate to a grading category of 4 per cent, since 4 per cent of 50 is 2.

There are at least three advantages to using test specifications and blueprints. First, a test written in strict accordance with them is very likely to be an adequate, representative sample of all possible questions that can be drawn on the content area and behavioural objectives concerned. This test will have content validity. Second, it will be possible to draw two independent tests, the items of which are similar in content, objectives, format, number and difficulty levels. Such related tests are known as parallel, equivalent or alternative tests. Third, even if an old test has to be used, it can easily be evaluated in terms of the specifications.

Writing Test Items. The next step in making the test is to write the test items. Classroom teachers who want to construct tests for their pupils need only follow the blueprint and write as many items as are specified. The hints mentioned below will help in the difficult process of writing good test items. The test-maker may need the services of other item writers who are knowledgeable in the specific subject-matter being studied.

Types of Teacher-prepared Tests

Objective Tests. Objective test items can be thought of as either the 'supply' type of item or as the 'selection' type of item. When responding to the 'supply' type of test item, the student must provide the needed words, numbers or symbols to furnish a complete answer. Possible answers to the test items are not listed. When responding to the 'selection' type of test item, the student chooses the correct response from those provided. Examples of this type are the true-false test item, the matching test item and the multiple choice test item.

Supply Test Items. There are two types of supply-type test items: short-answer and completion. They are similar, differing only in the form in which the problem is presented. If presented as a question, it is a short-answer item, whereas if presented as an incomplete statement, it is a completion item. Some examples of these are given below:

> *Short Answer:* What social science examines social institutions and groups in society? _____
>
> *Completion:* Statements indicating relationships between two or more concepts are called _____ .

In constructing this type of test item, it is important to state the test item in such a way that the correct answer is short and specific. There must be only one correct answer and that answer should be a significant word or expression. In completion items, the blank should be placed at the end of the sentence if at all possible.

An important advantage of the supply test item is that the chances of the student's correctly guessing the answer are reduced. However, its usefulness is confined largely to the measurement of specific information. Its most serious limitation is the restricted range of mental processes for which it is suitable.

It is possible to use supply items to test higher levels of knowledge than factual recall, but to do so, one must supply a paragraph or chart which is new to the students and ask questions which would show

Figure 10.2: Age Pyramid

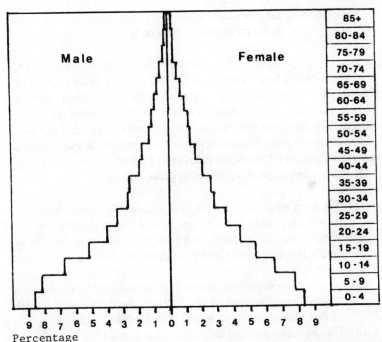

whether students have acquired the desired skills. For example, after studying the concept of an age pyramid, one might wish to test the students' ability to comprehend this new chart.

Short Answer: What percentage of males are between 5 and 9 years of age in Country A? _____

Completion: As people grow older in Country A, the percentage of people in their age group grows _____ .

The True-False Item. This type of item is probably the most familiar of all of the highly objective test items. In spite of its limited usefulness and the actual difficulty of preparation, it is highly popular with many teachers in all subjects.

In this type of item a statement is presented to which the pupil responds by indicating whether it is true or false. There are many variations of this basic pattern:

T   F   If the Cascade Mountains were 800 km. further east, western Oregon would have an increased rainfall.

Yes No   'Good medical care is more important than low taxes.' Is this statement an opinion?

The major advantage of the true-false test item in social studies appears to be that a large sampling of subject-matter can be covered in a relatively short time. Its major limitation is the difficulty of preparing good statements that measure more than the simplest of factual information. As stated before about supply items, in order to test levels of knowledge beyond factual recall, a new paragraph or chart must be provided about which true-false items can be asked.

Here are a few suggestions for writing true-false items.

(1) The item statements should be unequivocally classifiable as true or false, for example the biggest river in Ghana is the Volta.
(2) Avoid grammatical confusions such as double negatives: for example It is *not un*common for new settlements to spring up on new roads.
(3) Avoid statements that are neither completely true nor completely false, for example the Battle of Saratoga and the Battle of Bull Run were fought during the Civil War.
(4) Use the true-false item only if no other type of test item appears appropriate.

Matching Test Items. The matching test item is one in which a student must match up the entries in two lists: an entry list (which corresponds to the question in a multiple-choice item) and a reference list (corresponding to the choices in a multiple-choice item). An example of a typical matching item is the following.

Directions: In the first column are listed studying and learning skills important in the social studies. In the second column are samples of activities demonstrating certain social studies skills. Match the sample activity in the second column with the skill it represents by writing the letter of the best answer in the blank.

_____   (1) locating library   (a) learning to use the telephone
              materials   (b) studying techniques used in
_____   (2) interpreting maps   advertising

		and charts	(c) preparing a timeline of major religious events
___	(3)	detecting propaganda	(d) making a bar graph of oil imports
___	(4)	arranging events chronologically	(e) looking up magazine articles on Unesco
			(f) learning terms related to the United Nations

The matching test item can be useful for measuring the degree to which the student can recall information. On the other hand, it is seldom suitable for measuring the degree to which the student can apply information in a new situation. Some suggestions for writing matching test items are below.

(1) Include more items in the reference list than can be used in the entry list.

(2) Arrange the reference list in systematic order — dates in sequence, names in alphabetical order, etc.

(3) Do not include more than one kind of information in a single matching exercise. For example, do not put names of presidents and inventions in a reference column to be matched with dates.

Multiple-choice Items. This type of item is the most versatile and useful of all objective test items. It can measure in any subject-matter area and at a variety of levels, from mere knowledge of facts to high-level mental processes such as understanding and judgement. It is the test item most commonly used in standardised tests.

A multiple-choice item consists of two parts — a 'stem' and several 'choices'. The stem may be a complete or incomplete statement or a question. The choices usually include one correct answer and three or four incorrect answers, known as 'distractors'.

As stated above, the major advantage of the multiple-choice test item is its wide adaptability to many different types of materials. Its major limitation is the difficulty of preparing good items, particularly writing effective distractors. Here are some suggestions for writing multiple-choice items.

(1) Avoid placing the correct answer too frequently in any one position.

(2) Avoid having similar or related words in both stem and correct

answer. Example: The windvane is an instrument for measuring

A wind direction.
B humidity.
C temperature.
D rainfall.

(3) Avoid making the correct answer consistently longer or shorter than the distractors. Example: The world energy crisis is a result of

A high taxes.
B a demand for fossil fuels which is greater than the supply.
C a shortage of coal.
D strikes.

(4) Avoid using choices that are unrelated to the subject of the item or obviously wrong. Such distractors will be immediately rejected and, hence, are non-functioning. Example: A famous missile launching site is located at

A Pittsburgh.
B Key West.
C Vero Beach.
D Cape Kennedy.

(5) Eliminate from the item any unintended clue to the correct answer. Such clues may arise from grammatical inconsistency. Example: A marriage set up by the personal choice of the couple instead of by parents is called a

A extended marriage.
B arranged marriage.
C love marriage.
D nuclear marriage.

In social studies, the multiple-choice test item is an excellent way to measure different intellectual processes. The following section illustrates some of the mental processes that can be measured by multiple-choice items. The sample items provided are illustrative rather than exhaustive.

Recall

The doctrine that there is a constant tendency for population growth to outstrip the means of subsistence is especially associated with:

A. Adam Smith.
B. T.R. Malthus.
C. J.M. Keynes.
D. A. Marshall.
E. W.H. Beveridge.

Explanation

(1) Which of the following best explains the fertility of the soil in ancient Egypt?

A. rotation of crops
B. annual overflow of the Nile
C. careful cultivation of the soil
D. use of fertilisers
E. type of crops raised

(2) In the twentieth century, the main factor responsible for a significant increase in the world trade in meat is the

A. breeding of new varieties of animals for meat.
B. expansion of grasslands through cultivation of forest land.
C. eradication of pests and diseases.
D. use of cargo-liners with refrigerator facilities.
E. introduction of canning in the meat industry.

Inference

The figures below show the age distribution of the population of the United Kingdom.

	Percentage of total population aged		
	Under 15	15-64	Over 64
1961	23.2	65.0	11.8
1970	24.8	59.6	15.6

The changes between 1961 and 1970 could have been due to a

A. rise in both the birth rate and the death rate.

B.   rise in the birth rate and a fall in the death rate.
C.   rise in the death rate with the birth rate unchanged.
D.   rise in the death rate and a fall in the birth rate.
E.   fall in both the birth rate and the death rate.

Application

Which of the following agents of weathering is most likely to predominate in Timbuktu, Republic of Mali (West Africa)?

A.   seasonal frost
B.   temperature change
C.   recurring rains
D.   plant growth
E.   animal movement

Interpretation

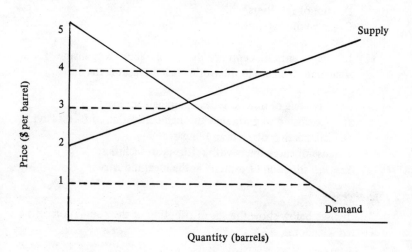

In the above diagram, which is the equilibrium price?

A.   1
B.   2
C.   3
D.   4
E.   5

In the diagram, at which price(s) does supply exceed demand?

    A. 3, 4 and 5
    B. 3 and 4 only
    C. 4 and 5 only
    D. 3 only
    E. 5 only

Essay Test Items. Essay tests are especially valuable when the teacher wishes to assess the ability of students to express their thoughts and ideas in writing. For example, essay items are appropriate for measuring students' capacity to discuss, evaluate, describe, organise, apply and interpret facts. But social studies teachers should also be aware of the limitations of essay tests. A good rule is to avoid using an essay question if a more objective type is equally appropriate. The two most important limitations on essay items are the restriction in the area of content that can be measured and the subjectivity of the scoring. Widespread recognition of these limitations has had much to do with the increased use of objective items. The suggestions below should help overcome some of the limitations of essay questions.

    (1) State questions as specifically as possible so that each pupil will know what response is expected.
    (2) Keep the number of questions and time required to answer them within reasonable limits so that all pupils can respond to all questions. It is recommended that suggested time limits and desired length of answer be given for each question.
    (3) Require all pupils to answer the same question. For example, do not permit pupils to select four questions out of a list of six to answer. This confounds assigning grades because there can be no common base for comparison.

With the guidelines suggested above, essay tests can be used to test various intellectual skills and abilities. It should be pointed out, however, that a single essay question may call for more than one intellectual process. In other words, an essay question may not only call for recall, explanation and application but also for inference. In the few examples provided below, questions are labelled according to what is considered to be the major intellectual skill called for by the question.

Recall

What do the following terms mean?

a. Ghost towns
b. Equilibrium price
c. Indemnity
d. Monsoon
e. Privateer

Synthesis

From your readings about the value conflicts involved in strengthening the powers of the United Nations, describe a plan which would increase the effectiveness of the Security Council in handling threats to world peace.

Explanation

(a) Account for two of the factors which have aided large-scale migration from rural areas to urban areas in any country of your choice.
(b) Explain three problems that may result from this migration.
(c) Discuss three steps which can be taken to solve the problem in the country.

Inference

The following table gives the percentages of population at four groups of ages in Ghana and the United Kingdom.

Age Group (years)	Ghana, 1960 (percentage)	United Kingdom, 1961 (percentage)
0-9	35	15
10-19	18	15
20-59	42	53
Over 60	5	17

Source: *United Nations Demographic Yearbook*, 1964.

Analyse the economic implications of the data above.

Application

Having studied the sociological concept of 'role', describe a situation which illustrates three roles played by a single individual in the course of a day.

Interpretation

Grapes 60	Lemons 15	Olives 25	Oranges 20	Figures in thousand metric tons

Study the table which gives exports from a country in the northern hemisphere.

(a) Draw a diagram to represent this information.
(b) Name and describe the climate indicated by these products, stating reasons for your choice.
(c) Suggest a likely location for the country.

The most difficult aspect of essay testing is not constructing the test item, but scoring students' answers. Here the problem is to objectify the scoring as much as possible. To achieve this purpose, the following guidelines might be useful.

(1) Prepare a scoring key of acceptable responses in advance. List the points to be covered. If appropriate, categorise acceptable responses as essential and desirable.
(2) Decide in advance on the weight (grading percentage) assigned to each question. Inform the pupils of these weightings before they start the test.
(3) Score the test without knowledge of the name of the pupil, if possible. This will minimise the 'halo' effect.
(4) Do not be influenced by handwriting and spelling. These could be evaluated separately, if necessary.
(5) Score the same question for all pupils at one time, that is, score the first question for all before going on to the second question.

Standardised Tests

In addition to teacher-made tests, standardised tests are available in social studies for the evaluation of concepts, information, critical thinking and students' ability to apply understandings and to use work-study skills. A standardised test is a series of questions chosen carefully by a panel of subject experts to measure learning in a particular subject area. Before its release to the educational community, it is administered to appropriate, representative groups in order to establish a basis for the interpretation of scores.

Because the questions (items) included in the final forms of a standardised test have been selected after careful preliminary experimentation, they are usually of high quality and will do a better job of measurement than the items contained in tests prepared by teachers. Because a standardised test has been administered to large representative groups for the purpose of establishing norms, teachers, by comparing the performance of their pupils with the appropriate norms, are able to make an unbiased judgement concerning the relative quality of their students' performances. Evidence from standardised tests may be used to group pupils for instructional purposes according to their levels of ability. Such tests provide valuable initial information for diagnostic purposes. They also help teachers become aware of their instructional weaknesses.

In selecting standardised tests in the social studies, several criteria should be considered in addition to reliability, validity, objectivity, expense and ease of administration. Questions of prime importance are:

Is this test related to the social studies topics being considered?
Does this test cover the key concepts studied by the pupils for whom it is intended?
Is the level of difficulty appropriate for the children?
Is this test the best available for this purpose?
Can the test results be used with information to assess children's progress?
Does this test fit into the total pattern of evaluation?

We recommend that *both* standardised tests and teacher-made tests, as well as any other method of appraisal that yields relevant information, be used when results are designed to:

(a) diagnose individual learning disabilities;
(b) assign students to classrooms or learning groups;
(c) counsel students on educational and vocational choices;
(d) select students for special programmes.

Reporting

After test items have been edited, tried out, assembled into a test, administered and scored, the reporting of the scores may follow. In social studies tests and examinations, this can be considered in two ways.

Criterion-referenced Interpretation. The more common way is to say that the student has 'passed' or 'failed' the test or examination by comparing the student's score with a predetermined criterion (say '50' is the pass mark, when the maximum possible score is 100). This is what is known as criterion-referenced interpretation of test scores. Any score can be identified as the minimum passing standard and any score below that is a failing grade. If a criterion-referenced standard is to be used, then it should be established at the time the test is being constructed and before any answer is scored. Diagnostic tests are usually interpreted with criterion-referenced standards.

Norm-referenced Interpretation. The other way of looking at test scores is to interpret a person's score relative to those of his or her colleagues. Thus, if all of a student's colleagues score very high on a test, say higher than 70 out of a possible 100, then a score of 55 may be considered a failing score. On the other hand, when out of a possible score of 100, the highest score in the class is 30, this would be an excellent score. Of course, a test that is too difficult or too easy for the class will not effectively measure student learning. In a norm-referenced test, some kind of average score in the group is the basis, or standard, for comparison.

The advantage of using the norm model is that the passing score is dependent on the range of scores in the group of examinees. It is useful to follow this technique for most examinations in social studies, since this type of examination may be used without a large body of experience in administering the specific exam.

Evaluation of Student Attitudes

Social studies teachers often include attitudinal goals as part of their instructional programmes. For example, they may wish students to develop more positive attitudes towards co-operation with other nations or towards conservation of natural resources. It is not easy for teachers to evaluate accurately whether or not they have accomplished attitudinal or affective goals. Two general approaches to this problem will be described here briefly: self-reports and observations.

Self-reports of Student Attitudes

While a verbal interview is one method of gathering self-reports about student attitudes, the length of time required for interviews makes this approach inappropriate for many classroom situations. The more commonly used method is the paper-and-pencil questionnaire. Two different types of questionnaire will be described: Likert scales and the semantic differential.

The Likert scale is probably the most familiar technique for assessing attitudes. Under this procedure, statements are listed which reflect both positive and negative attitudes related to an object. Students then mark their level of agreement with each statement using five categories: strongly agree, agree, undecided, disagree and strongly disagree. For scoring purposes, a weight of five (5) is generally given to the most positive response and a weight of one (1) is given to the most negative response. For example, a Likert scale to assess attitudes towards reading a newspaper might look like this:

Directions: Mark an X in the column to show how much you agree with these statements about newspapers.

	Strongly Disagree	Disagree	Un-decided	Agree	Strongly Agree
(1) I enjoy reading international news in the newspaper.					
(2) I enjoy reading national news in the newspaper.					
(3) I enjoy reading local news in the newspaper.					
(4) Reading the newspaper is a waste of time.					
(5) Reading the newspaper will *not* help me in the career I have planned.					

In the first three statements, 'strongly agree' is the most positive towards newspapers and would be scored a '5'. In the last two, 'strongly disagree' is the most positive and would be scored a '5'.

The second questionnaire technique is the semantic differential. With this approach attitudes towards any concept can be evaluated by making six-point scales anchored by adjective opposites. For example, if a teacher has taught a series of lessons about the United Nations and wishes to know what attitude students have developed towards the United Nations, the following scale might serve the purpose:

United Nations

good	____ :	____ :	____ :	____ :	____ :	____ : bad
valuable	____ :	____ :	____ :	____ :	____ :	____ : worthless
effective	____ :	____ :	____ :	____ :	____ :	____ : ineffective
useful	____ :	____ :	____ :	____ :	____ :	____ : useless

Numbers from one to six are assigned to responses, with six being the most positive rating. Then scores from each evaluative scale are added to give a total score. In this example, scores could range from 4 to 24. Several studies have shown that responses to these evaluative adjectives reveal the predominant attitude people hold toward a variety of concepts and subjects.[4]

Observations of Student Attitudes

Classroom teachers frequently observe students on an informal basis to discover their attitudes. Systematic observations of student attitudes are more informative than the usual random observations, but unfortunately systematic observations are time-consuming and often expensive. Nevertheless, structured observations are useful techniques for evaluating attitudes. Three types will be mentioned here: checklists, rating scales and unobtrusive measures. *Checklists* are useful in evaluating the presence or absence of certain attitudes on 'yes or no' scales. *Rating scales* are useful in evaluating the strength of attitudes when wide variation can be expected. *Unobtrusive measures* are non-direct ways of judging attitudes without the physical presence of an observer. An observer's presence or even the knowledge that the teacher is recording an observation can influence students to display attitudes designed to please the observer. The following examples show how these three techniques apply to similar subjects.

Checklists	Yes	No
(1) Does the student respect the family group?	_____	_____
(2) Does the student have a positive attitude about the United Nations?	_____	_____

Rating Scales

(1) To what extent does the student respect the family group?

Not at all   To a great extent

1   2   3   4   5

(2) What is the student's attitude about studying the United Nations?

1   2   3   4   5
Very negative   Very positive

Unobtrusive Measures

(1) How often does the student speak respectfully of family members in conversation?

(2) How many extra books or articles has the student read about the United Nations?

Evaluation of Social Studies Programmes

It should be the goal of social studies educators to develop the best possible educational programme. The evaluation of student progress discussed above is one key element in evaluating the total programme, but other matters should be considered in the broader context of programme evaluation.

The starting-point for discussing programme evaluation is the objectives-based approach.[5] This straightforward approach calls for the statement of objectives for the social studies programme, i.e. 'All students will be able to define the concept of political behaviour' or '80 per cent of the students can describe the causes of World War I'. The programme is then judged on the basis of whether the objectives were reached.

Some difficulties in this approach have led to additional schools of thought about programme evaluation. One problem is that an evaluation of the relative importance of each objective as compared to other possible objectives is not inherent in the objectives-based approach. A second problem is that in order to determine whether or not objectives were reached, teachers are often forced to write concrete, behavioural objectives which are more easily measured, leaving out some important higher level or attitudinal objectives which are not so easily measured.

In response to these problems, various evaluation experts have developed additional approaches. Stufflebeam has proposed the CIPP (*C*ontext, *I*nput, *P*rocess, *P*roduct) approach as a comprehensive method of (1) monitoring the context of any situation to detect problems; (2) evaluating possible inputs to meet the problem; (3) evaluating the procedures of the solution chosen and (4) evaluating the products of the action taken.[6] Stake has proposed the responsive approach in which highly structured measures are rejected in favour of enquiries and interviews which can reveal the full flavour of what happened and what was accomplished in the programme. This approach has been applied to evaluating programmes in the arts.[7] Owens and Wolfe have proposed the jurisprudential approach in which adversaries collect and present arguments for and against the success of the programme.[8] Scriven has proposed the goal-free approach which ignores stated goals and seeks to discover all the effects of the programme, whether intended or unintended.[9]

While these newer approaches may be of interest, the objective-based approach is the easiest to apply to the situation of most teachers, especially in cases where objectives are prescribed by local, regional or national curricula. Therefore, it is recommended as the basic approach in initial attempts to evaluate social studies programmes.

Two important products of a social studies programme are the syllabus and the daily lesson plan. The 'syllabus' is a condensed outline or statement of the main points of a course of study. The 'lesson plan' is a teaching outline of the important points of a single lesson, arranged in the order in which they are to be presented. Standardised instruments for evaluating these aspects of the social studies programme are not widely available. Therefore, teachers should learn how to construct their own evaluation instruments. Some suggestions for doing this are contained in the following sections.

Evaluating Social Studies Syllabuses

In preparing evaluation instruments for a social studies syllabus, it is useful to begin by identifying certain basic issues of syllabuses and questions related to them.

Basic Issues

A. Source:

(i)   Is the syllabus derived from an officially prescribed one?

(ii) Is it derived from a standard text or from a combination of such texts?

(iii) Is it based on the demands of an examination syllabus or is it partly a teaching syllabus?

(iv) To what extent is the syllabus based on an analysis of the learning needs of the students it is meant to serve?

B. Objectives:

(i)   To what extent are the objectives of the social studies syllabus related to national curriculum goals?

(ii) What skills are emphasised in the syllabus?

(iii) What level of competence is demanded of the learners on each social studies skill?

(iv) What type of objectives are stressed — cognitive, affective or both?

C. Depth:

(i)   How detailed is the outline of syllabus content?

(ii) In addition to content, does the social studies syllabus contain statements of objectives and some guidelines on material and methods?

(iii) For what period of instructional time is the syllabus intended — a week, a term, a semester, a school year?

D. Development:

(i)   Was the syllabus developed by a single teacher working entirely alone?

(ii) Was it the result of team work?

(iii) Is the syllabus in the first edition or is it a review of an earlier syllabus?

These questions can form the basis for selecting items to include in questionnaires in order to evaluate social studies syllabuses.

For some topics of the questionnaire, the most appropriate assessment will be through dichotomous items (i.e. 'yes or no' items which indicate the presence or absence of some element). Other topics will require more discriminant items (i.e. items which show in finer detail the range of differences among respondents). Questionnaires with dichtomous items are useful when one needs a general idea of what the syllabus is like and where one wishes to note the presence or absence of various components of a syllabus. A dichotomous-item questionnaire shows the direction of attitude, interest and motivation (that is whether or not these are strong or how positive). Unlike the more discriminant items to be discussed in this chapter, dichotomous-item questionnaires do not show their intensity, i.e. how strong or how positive particular traits are.

The following are sample questions relating to 'source' one of the basic issues considered above. This issue seems appropriate to the dichotomous approach.

Direction: Write an X in the appropriate column.

	Yes	No
(1) Is the syllabus derived from an officially prescribed one?	—	—
(2) Is the syllabus based on a standard textbook?	—	—
(3) Is the syllabus based on a combination of textbooks?	—	—
(4) Is the syllabus based on needs of an external evaluation?	—	—
(5) Is the syllabus based on what learners need to know at their stage of learning?	—	—

The following are examples of more discriminant items based on the questions connected with 'objectives'. In these questions the intensity of opinion is measured at three levels. If more distinctions were preferred, four or five or even more levels of intensity could be devised. In scoring the questionnaire, weight should be assigned to each response level. In these examples, the highest level could be assigned the score '2', the middle one '1' and the lowest '0', indicating the absence of that element.

Direction: Circle the most appropriate answer.

	2	1	0
(1) How closely are the objectives of the social studies syllabus related to national curriculum goals?	closely	not very closely	not at all

(2) To what extent are higher-
   level objectives included?   to a great   somewhat   not at all
                                       extent

(3) To what extent are cognitive
   objectives included?   to a great   somewhat   not at all
                                       extent

(4) To what extent are affective
   objectives included?   to a great   somewhat   not at all
                                       extent

It is important that items of equal importance be given equal weights. If some items are considered more important than others, their weights should be increased to reflect their importance. For example, if some would consider item '1' above to be twice as important as the remaining items, its points should be doubled (i.e. closely = '4', not very closely = '2', not at all = '0').

It is possible to evaluate any single issue or a combination of all basic issues connected with a social studies syllabus. Each basic issue has a number of related questions that can become the source of questions for evaluation instruments. It is also possible to adopt a wide range of procedures for scoring such instruments. There could be a composite score for the entire instrument or different scores for the various sections of the instrument.

Evaluation of Social Studies Lesson Plan

These basic issues and related questions about lesson plans deserve consideration.

Basic Issues	Related Questions
A. The Components of the Plan:	(i) Does the plan contain clear statements of what is to be taught?
	(ii) Does it state clearly the conditions under which it is to be taught?
	(iii) What are the specific objectives of lessons?
B. Outline of Procedure:	(i) Are the various items in the outline arranged in a logical order?
	(ii) Are the procedural steps feasible in view of the peculiar conditions of the school?

(iii) Do the various steps really constitute enabling behaviours that can help both the teacher and the learner realise the stated objectives?

C. Necessary Details: Does the lesson plan contain sufficient details of the following:

(i) how the previous lesson is to be revised;

(ii) questions to be asked of the students;

(iii) exercises and activities to be carried out;

(iv) materials to be used;

(v) the methods of evaluating student progress.

These questions on social studies lesson plans can also provide bases for developing appropriate evaluation instruments. In each case, either dichotomous items or more discriminant ones can be utilised. An alternative, depending upon the purpose of the evaluation, is to combine the two types of items. It is possible to design a separate evaluation instrument for each basic issue or use a single instrument for all of the issues. The single instrument evaluation, however, should be divided into appropriate sections.

Following is an example of a Likert-type instrument for assessing affective traits. It may have five points, such as Strongly Agree, Agree, Uncertain, Disagree and Strongly Disagree. For positive statements these can be scored as '5', '4', '3', '2', '1' and for negative statements the order is usually reversed, because agreeing with a negative statement means a negative attitude. In the example below, the questionnaire items are to assess the extent of detailed information contained in a social studies lesson plan.

The following questionnaire items are merely samples. There is nothing exhaustive about them. Equally, there are no hard and fast rules about the questionnaire format. Just as a Likert-type questionnaire is used for illustration below, the same purpose can be served using a checklist to evaluate the completeness of a lesson plan.

Constructing a checklist for this purpose begins with an analysis of the necessary components of a good lesson plan. The sample checklist presented here is based on the issues and questions about lesson plans already discussed.

Directions: Mark an X in the column which indicates the appropriate rating of the lesson plan on each point. (Likert-type questionnaire.)

	Highly Satis-factory	Satis-factory	Un-decided	Unsatis-factory	Highly Unsatis-factory
(1) Method of revising the previous lesson					
(2) Questions to be asked of learners					
(3) Description of how to treat students' questions					
(4) Activities to be carried out					
(5) Materials to be used					
(6) Explanation of how materials will be used					
(7) Procedures for evaluating student progress					

Directions: Check the blank to indicate the completeness of the lesson plan. (Checklist.)

Does the lesson plan . . .	Yes	No
(1) clearly state what is to be taught?	___	___
(2) clearly state the conditions required for teaching the lesson?	___	___
(3) state specific objectives?	___	___
(4) outline various lesson procedures in a logical order?	___	___
(5) state how the previous lesson is to be revised?	___	___
(6) state questions to be asked of students?	___	___
(7) describe activities to be carried out?	___	___
(8) describe materials to be used?	___	___
(9) describe methods of evaluating student progress?	___	___

Evaluation of Social Studies Lessons

Evaluating the conduct of social studies lessons involves a constellation of steps taken to determine the appropriateness of methods, materials and results achieved. Whether something is appropriate or not depends upon the nature of the subject, lesson objectives, the maturity of the students and other factors. What is appropriate in some circumstances will not be appropriate in others. As already demonstrated in this chapter, a detailed breakdown of such areas of emphasis and their related questions is the first step in constructing an instrument to evaluate a social studies lesson.

Several forms of observation schedules have been developed for the use of classroom observers who wish to make a record of what transpires during a lesson. Most such instruments already in use are based on the Flander's model that calculates the proportion of 'teacher talk' to 'student talk' in a lesson. Several other forms of observation instruments exist; most of these are adaptable to particular subject areas.

Whatever their form, observation schedules have many features in common. First, schedule construction begins with a detailed outline of expected instructional outcomes. This prepares the observer for certain types of teacher and learner behaviour during a lesson. Second, all observation schedules define their categories as clearly as possible. This is to ensure that all users interpret each category in nearly the same way. Third, they all give very clear instructions as to methods of observation and scoring. In most cases the prevalent behaviour during a given period is recorded, usually by means of a tally. Typically, behaviour is sampled according to predetermined 'intervals'. Whatever is taking place during that period of time is recorded. Many such observation moments may be noted on a systematic basis during a single lesson. The length of an 'interval' varies according to the requirements of the observer. However, it is necessary to ensure that the interval is not too long (not longer than half a minute, if possible) so that no valuable piece of information is lost. The scoring, in most cases, involves computing the amount of student participation in a given lesson.

The table below is an example of an observation schedule, based on the Flander's model, that can be used to observe an elementary social studies lesson. There are three broad categories represented in the example: 'teacher talk', 'student talk' and 'break in activity'. Each of the first two categories has several subdivisions. Both desirable and undesirable teacher and learner behaviours are represented, since the objective is to see which of these predominates. The observer may write the tallies next to each subsection or may use a separate score sheet.

A Sample Instrument for Observing an Elementary Social Studies Lesson

A. Teacher activity: (1) presents information;
                        (2) asks questions;

(3) praises or encourages;

(4) accepts and uses student's response;

(5) explains;

(6) rebukes erring student;

(7) directs drill activity;

(8) writes on the blackboard;

(9) reads from a book.

B. Learner activity: (1) listens to teacher;

(2) answers questions;

(3) listens to teacher's explanation;

(4) listens to teacher's reprimand;

(5) takes part in drills;

(6) silence — work-oriented;

(7) listens to reading;

(8) silence — non-work-oriented.

C. Confusion/break in activity.

In developing an observation instrument, the teacher should either show it to other social studies teachers or try it out by observing social studies lessons to see if the categories are exhaustive or superfluous. Second, the evaluator should train a few other observers with whom he or she can jointly observe lessons to determine the degree of inter-observer reliability possible with the instrument. More information about interaction analysis in evaluating instruction is provided below.

The evaluation of social studies instruction is not restricted to the use of systematic observation. Below is a simple, Likert-like question-naire that can be used for evaluating a general social studies lesson (see page 293). This questionnaire, as with all the sample questionnaires in this chapter, is not a final product to be used intact, but is a model to stimulate teachers to develop their own evaluative instruments.

Learner Evaluation of Lessons

The learner, as the major consumer of the product of the teacher's classroom activity, should be considered when evaluating an educa-ational programme. Regular feedback from pupils helps teachers to plan better and teach more effectively.

Learners should evaluate two aspects of a lesson: the 'conduct' of the lesson and the 'impact' of the lesson. The conduct of the lesson includes the teacher (the 'conductor'), the approaches or methods used

Direction: Express your opinion on each of the following aspects of the lesson by writing an X in the appropriate column. (Likert-like questionnaire.)

	Highly Satis- factory	Satis- factory	Un- decided	Unsatis- factory	Highly Unsatis- factory
(1) Quality of audio- visual material					
(2) Method of presentation					
(3) Appropriateness of written exercises					
(4) Teacher's explanation					
(5) Teacher's method of evaluating lesson					
(6) Appropriateness to the intellectual level of students					

for teaching, the time spent on the lesson, the major emphasis of the lesson and the materials used for teaching the lesson. Impact, on the other hand, is measured by how much learners feel they have gained from the lesson. This should include both the cognitive and affective gains.

Several types of instruments can be employed for the purpose of learner evaluation. Every teacher should know how to construct most of them. It may be best to begin with a very simple example such as the one below.

Direction: Underline the word, or group of words which you think should complete each of the following statements about the lesson.

1. The teacher was	friendly/unfriendly.
2. The lesson was	well prepared/poorly prepared.
3. The subject-matter was	not too difficult/too difficult for us.
4. The questions were	well distributed/not well distrib- uted.
5. The teacher's corrections were	harsh/friendly.
6. The lesson was	too short/took just the right amount of time/too long.

7. Skills required by the lesson were	new/ones we have practised before.
8. On the whole the students	learned a lot/learned very little.
9. The lesson moved	too fast/at normal speed/too slow.
10. Materials used for lessons were	very good/not good enough.
11. On the whole, the lesson was	interesting/uninteresting.
12. On the basis of my experience with the lesson I feel like	continuing/not continuing my own study of this subject.

The greatest advantage of this type of instrument is that it is relatively easy to construct, to administer and to score. The teacher can quickly look at the completed questionnaires to see which aspects of the lesson will require improvement in the future. Since the instrument is relatively easy to handle, it can be used with younger pupils. It can also be used profitably in the early stages of teaching children to complete questionnaires.

At a later stage, more complicated questionnaires, like the Likert-type or the semantic differential type, can be used. In constructing Likert-type questionnaires for evaluating social studies lessons, the teacher should follow the same procedure as previously outlined. The teacher or the evaluator should identify the lesson's important components and ask the students to state whether they considered each component to be 'Very Good', 'Good', 'Average', 'Poor' or 'Very Poor'. The questionnaire can be constructed in a wide variety of formats. An example of one format is shown below.

Indicate your judgment of each of the following aspects of the lesson by writing an X in the appropriate column.

	Very Good	Good	Average	Poor	Very Poor
(1) The teacher's instructions					
(2) The teaching aids					
(3) The teacher's explanations					
(4) 'Work-to-do' for students					
(5) Pupil's attention					
(6) The test					
(7) The way the test was corrected					

A semantic differential questionnaire may be used also. It is useful to mix up the order of bipolar adjectives so that children must think as they complete the questionnaire. A sample of the questionnaire is provided below.

Directions: For each of the following pairs of words write an X at the point nearest to the one which best expresses your impression of the lesson.

In my opinion, the lesson on National Coat of Arms was

(1)	well taught	__ __ __ __ __ __	badly taught
(2)	impractical	__ __ __ __ __ __	practical
(3)	uninteresting	__ __ __ __ __ __	interesting
(4)	richly illustrated	__ __ __ __ __ __	poorly illustrated
(5)	useless	__ __ __ __ __ __	useful
(6)	boring	__ __ __ __ __ __	not boring
(7)	very good	__ __ __ __ __ __	very bad
(8)	easy to understand	__ __ __ __ __ __	hard to understand

In addition to using questionnaires, teachers can also use students' free comments. The major advantage of using questionnaires is that they are structured and teachers receive data on topics of greatest interest to them. While it is also useful to give students opportunities to comment freely on issues that concern them, when soliciting free comments from children it is worth while to provide some structure for their comments in order that useful data are provided. This can be done in various ways without destroying opportunities for students to express their own views. It is possible, for example, to give students several broad guidelines within which to structure their responses.

(1) What did you *like best* about the lesson?

_____

_____

_____

(2) What did you *like least* about the lesson?

_____

_____

_____

(3) What major suggestions can you make for the improvement of the lesson?

_____

_____

_____

Conclusion

Social studies instruction is influenced greatly by the evaluation schemes used to measure what students have achieved. A teacher may have selected excellent objectives, have full command of the subject and be an instructional genius, but if he is unable to prepare appropriate tests to measure student outcomes, the students will become frustrated. Tests that fail to measure the stated objectives may prompt students to ignore the objectives and to seek ways to prepare better for the tests. Encouraging students to 'study for the test' is not a bad policy provided that the test allows students to demonstrate effectively what they have been asked to learn.

Notes

1. Some important sources on the taxonomy of education objectives are: B.S. Bloom et al. (eds.), *Taxonomy of Educational Objectives: the Classification of Educational Goals*. Handbook I *Cognitive Domain* (McKay, New York, 1956); D.R. Krathwohl and B.B. Masia, *Taxonomy of Educational Objectives: the Classification of Educational Goals*. Handbook II *Affective Domain* (McKay, New York, 1964).

2. Excellent discussions regarding the use of behavioural objectives can be found in: R.F. Mager, *Preparing Objectives for Programmed Instruction* (Fearon, San Francisco, 1962); W.J. Popham, *Objectives and Instructions*, AERA Monographs in Curriculum Evaluation, No. 1 (Rand McNally, Chicago, 1968); R.W. Tyler, *Basic Principles of Curriculum and Instruction* (University of Chicago Press, Chicago, 1950).

3. Further ideas on the planning and development of geography tests are available in P.O. Okunrotifa, *Evaluation in Geography* (Oxford University Press, Ibadan, 1977).

4. C.E. Osgood, G.J. Suci and P.H. Tannenbaum, *The Measurement of Meaning* (University of Illinois Press, Urbana, Illinois, 1957).

5. Ralph W. Typer, *Basic Principles of Curriculum and Instruction* (University of Chicago Press, Chicago, 1950).

6. Daniel Stufflebeam et al., *Educational Evaluation and Decision-Making* (Peacock Publishers, Itasca, Illinois, 1971).

7. Robert Stake (ed.), *Evaluating the Arts in Education* (Charles E. Merrill Publishing Company, Columbus, Ohio, 1975).

8. Thomas R. Owens, 'Educational Evaluation by Adversary Proceeding' in E.R. House, *School Evaluation: the Politics and Process* (McCutchan Publishing Corporation, Berkeley, 1973).

9. Michael Scriven, 'Goal-Free Evaluation' in E.R. House, *School Evaluation: the Politics and Process* (McCutchan Publishing Corporation, Berkeley, 1973).

10. Some sources for the use of interaction analysis are Edmond J. Amidon and Idin B. Hough, *Interaction Analysis: Theory, Research and Application* (Addison-Wesley, London, 1967); H.H. Anderson, 'The Measurement of Domination and of Socially Integrative Behaviour in Teachers' Contacts with Children', *Children Development*, Vol. 10 (1939), pp. 73-89; Ned A. Flanders, 'Teacher Influence in the Classroom' in Hough (ed.), *Interaction Analysis*, pp. 103-16; Ned A. Flanders, 'Some Relationships among Teacher Influence, Pupil Attitudes and Achievement' in J. Biddle and W.J. AcUena, *Contemporary Research on Teacher Effectiveness* (Holt, Rinehart and Winston, New York).

11 TEACHER EDUCATION IN SOCIAL STUDIES

Jan L. Tucker, with case studies by
James L. Barth and Pacita Andres and
contributions by Chris Adewole,
Leonardo de la Cruz and Robert Farrell

Social studies is mainly a twentieth-century development in education. Indeed, for many nations, social studies as a field of study is barely three decades old. This youthfulness and the parallel recency of teacher education programmes in general require that any description of social studies teacher education on a global basis be tentative and selective, rather than definitive and comprehensive.

This chapter provides a snapshot of social studies teacher education at a specific time in history. Photographs, however, are static, while social studies teacher education is evolving and dynamic. Social studies teacher education is presented here more as a challenge to be met than as a task accomplished.

Social Studies Teacher Education as a Developmental Process

Teacher education programmes in social studies reflect not only the universal aspects of the academic disciplines and the broad-gauged goals of social studies, but also the development needs of particular societies, nations and regions. More than most other subject areas, social studies is shaped by and, in turn, shapes the social, economic and political development of a nation or region. Conceiving social studies teacher education as part of a nation's process of development provides both a way for thinking about the education of social studies teachers across nations and a guideline for each nation in establishing and maintaining teacher training programmes.

This chapter emphasises major issues and trends of teacher education rather than details peculiar to individual nations. Space limitations have ruled out extensive descriptions of specific programmes, except for brief accounts for purposes of illustration. The chapter is intended to be useful for policy-making and programme development at the national or regional levels, leaving to the reader the major responsibility for making applications to situations and circumstances at the local level.

The Vague Nature of Social Studies

Conceiving social studies teacher education as a developmental process is also required by the vague nature of the field itself. The meaning of social studies is still evolving. There are many conceptions of social studies, often standing in competition with one another. Nations differ in the preferred meaning of social studies. Contrast Colombia, for example, with its emphasis on the academic disciplines,[1] especially history and geography, to many African nations where social studies is an integrated subject. Within nations also there are sharp differences of opinion about social studies. In the Philippines, for instance, an important professional issue involves competition between the conceptual approach and the traditional programme based on history. The new approach offers a radical shift from a history-based social studies programme to one that is interdisciplinary, drawing content from history and social sciences. Concepts and generalisations from these disciplines are integrated into topics such as environment, resources, change, social organisation, interdependence and heritage. (See Chapter 3.) These interdisciplinary concepts, generalisations and topics now form the content of many Philippine social studies programmes from grades one to six in the elementary schools, and from first to fourth year at the secondary level. Some historians oppose the conceptual approach, contending it distorts Philippine history.[2]

Lack of an agreed definition for social studies education creates tensions and arguments that divert scarce human and fiscal resources from central developmental tasks and impede the growth of vigorous teacher training programmes.

Teacher Supply and Demand

Another issue is teacher supply and demand. Those nations with a stable rate of population growth that have educational facilities to provide for the great majority of school-age children are experiencing a teacher surplus. For example, in the United States, where total enrolments in elementary and secondary schools increased by 3 per cent between 1965 and 1975, this enrolment will decrease by 8 per cent by 1985. The figures for secondary education are more startling, dropping from a gain of 21 per cent between 1965 and 1975 to a loss of 15 per cent by 1985.[3]

Declining enrolments in elementary and secondary schools have an immediate impact upon teacher training, especially at the pre-service level. Enrolments in social studies pre-service teacher education in the United States declined steadily during the 1970s. In fact, social studies teacher educators tend to view declining enrolment as the primary issue in social studies teacher training.[4] A more fundamental problem, however, is that without young, newly trained teachers the schools will eventually stagnate.

In developing nations, a teacher shortage, rather than a surplus, is often the major issue, especially a shortage of teachers who have received training in recent content and methodology. However, in both teacher-surplus and in teacher-shortage nations, increasing attention is being devoted to in-service teacher training. In the United States and in the nations of the African Social Studies Programme (ASSP), for example, educators recognise that changes must take place within the schools themselves if social studies, as an integrated subject area, is to become effective.

Competition with Other School Subjects

At the elementary school level, in both the Philippines and the United States, social studies must compete for time with the language arts, reading and mathematics curriculum. In the Philippines, for example, school officials have attempted to integrate language arts and social studies in the first and second grades. Social studies educators have vigorously opposed this on grounds that there are distinct social skills that ought to be developed among the young, since this is a stage when they are most susceptible to attitude and value development. The opposing group claims that reading, writing and arithmetic are more important than social studies in the primary grades. They contend that primary school social studies should be merely the content of reading and writing activities. Teacher educators in the United States report a similar problem. Competition among school subjects affects the alloca-tion of resources for teacher training programmes; apparently social studies programmes have not been faring well in the competition.

Low Remuneration of Teachers

Although the social status of elementary and secondary teachers varies from nation to nation, the professional and monetary benefits are generally small when compared to that of other professions. Many teachers hold two jobs in order to have enough income to live at a standard appropriate for a professional career.

In Colombia, a social studies teacher may have two full-time teach-ing positions.[5] Since laws forbidding the hiring of uncertified teachers are not enforced, schools can hire two uncertified teachers for less than it costs to employ one normal school or faculty of education graduate.

Plate 20: Teacher Education Student

The Kingdom of Nepal hopes to provide primary education for all boys and girls by 1980. Shown here is a teacher trainee at the College of Education in Kathmandu, one of an increasing number of people being prepared to teach.

Thus, even upon the completion of a teacher education programme, a graduate cannot be assured of being hired before an uncertified, unqualified competitor.

Such situations practically guarantee that teaching will continue to be a low-status, low-paying profession and a mere stepping stone to something better. This problem undercuts efforts to build strong social studies teacher education programmes. The costs to individuals and to the society are enormous. Only a concerted effort to resolve the economic problems faced by all teachers can end such a situation.

The Importance of Context

Social studies teacher education is often a mixture of the professional and economic problems mentioned above and issues found in a particular nation or region. Context is important. A particular domain, such as in-service education, may have a generally accepted meaning across cultures and nations but have very different origins, purposes and outcomes in specific nations. A teacher education centre, for example, is defined by one set of circumstances in the United Kingdom and by a contrasting context in China. In the former, a teacher education centre is usually a locally based programme where teachers can gain inspiration through learning new content and classroom teaching strategies. In the latter, using the example of the 7 May Cadre Schools created during the Great Proletarian Cultural Revolution, the teacher centre is a place where teachers live for six months or more to develop an entirely new political perspective and world-view. Both can be classified as a 'teacher centre', but the context creates major differences.

Teacher Education as Leadership Training

Given the developmental nature of social studies education, teacher education can be seen as one of leadership training. Teacher educators become change agents and teacher education programmes are instruments of change. Teacher education, therefore, covers all mechanisms, methods and programmes that reach teachers, including the use of media, textbooks, pre-service and in-service programmes and teacher centres. So conceived, teacher education is also responsible for helping develop the political and economic base favourable to social studies in the schools. In this developmental context, the role of social studies teacher educators and teacher education programmes is complex, requiring political and planning skills as well as content knowledge and classroom competence.

Meeting Developmental Needs in Social Studies Teacher Education: Examples from around the World

The case studies and sketches that follow were selected as examples of teacher training programmes in social studies. They were selected because they attempt to deal with certain manifest needs or issues within a nation or region. The major variables included in this framework are indicated in the following questions. How can social studies teacher education respond to: (1) a national mandate to implement social studies in all schools? (2) the need to update the knowledge and skill of classroom teachers who were not previously trained in social studies? (3) the problem of reaching classroom teachers who live in remote areas and are unable to travel to a central location for training? (4) situations in which social studies in the schools is either non-existent or very traditional? (5) the need to provide refresher experiences for experienced social studies teachers who have already received social studies training at the baccalaureate level? (6) the issue of how to prepare traditional social studies teachers who can implement innovative curriculum ideas, such as social participation, reflective enquiry, value analysis and integrated studies about controversial social issues?

The case studies and programme sketches highlight certain variables or a combination of variables. The case of social studies growth and development in Nigeria focuses on teacher training needs created by a government mandate in a nation where social studies as an integrated subject did not exist, where classroom teachers often lacked a baccalaureate degree, and where the universities themselves were unfamiliar with social studies.

The Philippine case describes a national effort to update teacher knowledge and skills through a new delivery system in which many education agencies and institutions at the national, regional and local levels have combined their services in a collaborative programme to facilitate the introduction of new ideas into existing social studies programmes. The Philippine example demonstrates that to meet developmental needs in a nation, maximum impact can be gained through the close co-operation of ministries of education, professional education associations, universities and colleges (including both the education and liberal arts faculties), regional and local education offices and agencies, social studies organisations and consortia, accreditation agencies and assessment boards.

The case of ASSP illustrates how development in separate nations, if undertaken simultaneously and with common objectives, may each be enhanced through an overall, transnational co-ordinating organisation. By pooling experiences and resources, each member nation can benefit.

Social Studies Development in Nigeria[6]

Nigerian national policy on education: Education in Nigeria is no more a private enterprise, but a huge Government venture that has witnessed a progressive evolution of Government's complete and dynamic intervention and active participation. The Federal Government of Nigeria has adopted education as an instrument par excellence for effective national development.[7]

With this statement of policy in 1977 Nigeria made a commitment to education as the vehicle for reaching national goals. National progress is linked with the process of education. Social studies is part of that education for each Nigerian child, by decree of the federal government as contained in the *Policy on Education.* This case study describes how social studies was adopted as part of the school curriculum for all Nigerian children.

The history of social studies in Nigeria is a story of both external and internal forces to Nigeria. In 1967, at a conference held at Queen's College, Oxford, United Kingdom, the notion of social studies as a school subject was proposed for Nigeria and other African nations. This initial meeting led, a year later, to the creation of ASSP. One response to the Oxford conference was a meeting held in Mombasa, Kenya, in 1968 that set forth general objectives which gave support and direction to the growth of social studies in Africa. The following four objectives from the Mombasa conference focus on relevant knowledge, improvement of the human condition and appreciation of diversity and independence. All of these objectives would emerge nine years later as social studies objectives in the Nigerian *National Policy on Education.*

a) to create an awareness and an understanding of the evolving social and physical environment as a whole, its natural, manmade, cultural, and spiritual resources, together with the rational use and conservation of these resources for development;

b) to develop a capacity to learn and acquire skills, including not only the basic skills of listening, speaking, reading and writing, and of calculation, but also the skills of hand, together with the skills of observation, analysis and inference which are essential to the forming of sound judgment;

c) to ensure the acquisition of the relevant knowledge which is an essential prerequisite to personal development as well as to the positive personal contribution to the betterment of mankind;

d) finally it is of the utmost importance to develop a systematic appreciation of the diversity and interdependence of all members of the local community, and of the wider national and international community.[8]

Another force working towards the adoption of social studies, though somewhat earlier than the Oxford conference and the ASSP meeting in Kenya, was the Northern Nigerian Teacher Education Project (NNTEP), part of which focused on the introduction of social studies as a subject field. The Project, lasting from 1964 to 1969, received financial support from private and public foundations in the United States and was co-sponsored by the Northern Nigerian government. Nigerians and Americans from the University of Wisconsin staffed the project with the specific purpose of writing a syllabus and developing teacher education materials that would explain the theory and practice of social studies to co-operating teachers' colleges in Bida, Ilorin, Bauchi, Katsina, Maiduguri and Sokoto.[9] NNTEP was an important factor because the Project, working through the member teachers' colleges and the Institute of Education at Ahmadu Bello University in Zaria, established the concept of social studies at the teacher training level. The objectives, the subject content and the activities of NNTEP provided a guide and a reference for all future national development in social studies.

In 1965 western Nigeria established within Aiyetoro Comprehensive High School a separate social studies demonstration project designed to introduce social studies as a subject field to early post-primary students.[10] The project staff consisted of Nigerians and Americans from the University of Washington. It developed a social studies syllabus and curriculum materials that were appropriate for use in a general education programme. The project at Aiyetoro was yet a third element pressing for the inclusion of social studies as part of the Nigerian school curriculum.

These three forces produced goals (ASSP), materials and syllabus (NNTEP), and project materials (Aiyetoro); they also provided an alternative to Nigeria's traditional separate-subject approach inherited from the British colonial system. Social studies offered a goal of citizenship training through the integration of social science content. The goal of citizenship training was not lost on Nigerians who were in a position to make decisions about the goals of national education. The traditional, separate-subject approach, some educators and political leaders believed, fragmented students' understanding of their place in the social, political and economic development of Nigeria.

The introduction of social studies into the Nigerian school curriculum should be understood as part of a general response to problems of independence and unification. Nigeria became an independent nation in 1960, a Federal Republic in 1963, and, in response to conflicts within the nation, a Federal Military State in 1966, followed a year later by civil war continuing until 1970. Internal conflicts helped to maintain the historic separation dividing religious and tribal groups. The federal government, faced with the task of creating a unified nation, saw social studies as one means for promoting national citizenship. The three groups noted above made it possible to organise a social studies curriculum that would support the notion of nation-building through citizenship education.

In 1969, just before the end of the Civil War, the National Educational Research Council (NERC) sponsored a National Curriculum Conference with the support of the federal government. The Lagos Conference was held with the express purpose of identifying educational goals that would be consistent with national goals. This was a significant conference for social studies because it discussed the idea of a social studies curriculum. The Conference proposed that each state's primary and post-primary educational system should emphasise a relevant education for each individual, provide equal educational opportunity and foster a belief in the worth of each individual through a democratic way of life.[11] The Conference report recommended that social studies be included in the primary and post-primary curriculum of each state.

The Conference defined social studies as a school subject that integrates knowledge about human beings and their relationships. It further defined the goal of social studies as citizenship education with emphasis upon civic responsibility, rational thinking and respect for the opinions of others.[12] In order to satisfy the social studies goal of citizenship education, the Conference recommended the following broad objectives: a social studies programme should help students understand and appreciate democracy, including the duties of a citizen in a democracy; identify how Nigeria became a nation and the need to continue to build that nation; and acquire a sense of social responsibility that recognises one's own worth and the dignity and worth of others.[13] The 1969 Curriculum Conference established broad objectives that articulated the need and appropriate aims for social studies instruction. The task of forming those broad objectives into specific objectives, syllabuses and content was still ahead.

Prior to the 1969 Conference most social studies activity was limited to a small number of teachers' colleges and one comprehensive high school. NNTEP was founded on the belief that the way to introduce social studies was through the training of primary teachers, reasoning that teachers needed to understand the purposes of social studies before a national school syllabus was developed. The next step, as some Nigerian authorities saw it, was to develop a primary social studies syllabus which could be used throughout the nation. In later years this was followed by a syllabus and objectives for secondary schools and for teacher education.

What existed in 1970 were broad general objectives that favoured the introduction of social studies, some experimental syllabuses and materials. While a social studies programme that favoured the integration of the social sciences for the purpose of citizenship was recommended for primary school and the first two years of secondary education, most teachers, with the exception of those who were part of the social studies projects, had been trained in the traditional academic disciplines, such as geography, history and civics, and had received no instruction in social studies theory and practice. As a result they were reluctant to teach social studies, which they did not understand and for which they had no materials.

In 1971 NERC organised a workshop, the 'National Workshop on Primary Education', with the task of developing specific objectives and a national syllabus for use in teaching social studies in primary schools. The Workshop participants drew their general objectives from the National Curriculum Conference and added their own basic objective: namely, social studies should prepare students to be well informed citizens who can contribute to the advancement of their community. To achieve this basic objective they organised the syllabus to include the following: teach respect for law and order, teach the appreciation and necessity of work, teach respect for their own culture and the culture of others and teach about the advantages of co-operation in the community.[14] These objectives were to be met through an 'expanding horizons, spiralling curriculum', starting with the child and his family in the first grade and ending in the sixth grade with people of other lands.[15]

In 1974 NERC sponsored a second Workshop, with the support of the federal government. This Workshop was responsible for developing objectives and a syllabus for teaching post-primary social studies. From this workshop came 'The Grade II Teachers' Syllabus'.[16] That included a spiralling curriculum co-ordinating both primary and post-primary school social studies. The primary school programme essentially followed the syllabus of the 1971 workshop. The post-primary syllabus emphasised the need for students to have compassion for the less fortunate, respect and tolerance for the opinions of others, a willingness to accept change derived from the will of the people, confidence in one's own worth, respect for human dignity, and to be a useful and worthy citizen of Nigeria.[17]

What is significant is the role of NERC in calling the initial, federally supported conference in 1969 and organising the two workshops in 1971 and 1974. The Council, with the consent and encouragement of the federal government, was able to generate the political and intellectual support needed to identify and clarify how social studies could be applied in the Nigerian school system. Without federal encouragement and the Council's support, the introduction and adoption of social studies along guidelines as suggested by the earlier social studies curriculum projects would not have been accepted as easily in Nigerian schools.

In 1973 the federal government organised a seminar of educational experts under the leadership of the National Universities Commission to prepare recommendations on the organisation of the entire educational system. These recommendations were issued in 1977 as the *National Policy on Education* (*NPE*). This was a significant document, clear and concise regarding how the educational system and social studies in particular were to promote a 'dynamic' society. The quotation from *NPE* on page 304 suggests that the federal government intends social studies education to promote 'a sense of unity, patriotism and love of country'.[18] Education is 'the greatest investment that a nation can make for the quick development of its economic, political, sociological, and human resources'.[19] Clearly *NPE* accepted those social studies objectives first advocated in Mombasa, then by the Curriculum Conference in 1969, and finally those refined and applied in the two workshops in 1971 and 1974. In fact, *NPE* extended and clarified the general objectives that were proposed in the earlier projects, conferences and workshops. For example, some of the stated general objectives for primary education became:

(1) the laying of a sound basis for scientific and reflective thinking;
(2) citizenship education as the basis for effective participation in

and contribution to the life of society;

(3) the development in the child of the ability to adapt to his changing environment.

And finally the government prescribed 'the study of social norms and values of the local community and of the country as a whole through civics and social studies'.[20]

For secondary education, *NPE* proposed as policy the following objectives:

(1) raise a generation of people who can think for themselves, respect the views and feelings of others, respect the dignity of labour and appreciate those values specified under our broad national aims, and live as good citizens;

(2) foster Nigerian unity with an emphasis on the common ties that unite us in our diversity.[21]

To achieve these goals

Appropriate measures will be taken to see that training in citizenship goes beyond the usual civics lessons and aims at inculcating, through practical exercises, qualities like public-spiritedness, voluntary service, sense of responsibility, loyalty, sense of fairplay, honesty, respect for opposing opinions and views, self-sacrifice for the good of others.[22]

The following objectives were proposed:

(1) to encourage further the spirit of enquiry and creativity in teachers;

(2) to help teachers to fit into the social life of the community and society at large and to enhance their commitment to national objectives.[23]

What we have seen is the introduction of an idea, social studies as an alternative to the traditional separate social science curriculum. The idea, as it filtered through the different projects, conferences and workshops and commissions, took on a particular Nigerian character. The social studies which had entered the country fifteen years earlier has been revised and shaped to become a Nigerian social studies. It retains the original notion of integrating the social sciences for purposes of citizenship education, but it is now aimed at accomplishing specific national goals.

Although social studies is an integral part of *NPE*, the task remains to train teachers to carry out the prescribed objectives. Steps were taken to train teachers in NNTEP by the Institute of Education at Ahmadu Bello University (ABU) in the early 1970s, and more recently by the Department of Social Studies in the Faculty of Education at ABU. But these were regional efforts that were unable to reach the entire nation. The effort to train teachers in social studies is, according to *NPE*, to be carried out in grade two teachers' colleges, advanced teacher colleges, colleges of education, institutes of education, the national teacher institute and teachers' centres. These institutions are now required to offer primary and post-primary teacher training in social studies throughout the nation.

Among the many and varied efforts to promote social studies are the degree programmes now being offered at some universities and institutes of education. Thirteen universities and 22 advanced teachers' colleges must develop social studies teacher training programmes. Taking leadership among the universities is ABU with its Department of Social Studies. It graduated the first Bachelor of Education degree teachers with majors in social studies in 1977, and by 1979 had graduated over twenty Masters of Education degree social studies teachers and one PhD. The Institute of Education at ABU offers a post-graduate diploma in education and social studies methods courses in its affiliated advanced teachers' colleges. The Institute continues to offer introductory and advanced courses in social studies and sponsors writers' workshops that produce social studies materials.

The significant role that the Institute of Education and the Department of Social Studies at ABU have played in the development of social studies had its origins in NNTEP. Those who were important contributors to the Project in the 1960s continued in the 1970s at ABU to build the necessary support system for social studies. It was important that an institute of higher education identified an interest and took leadership in promoting the theory and practice of social studies. This effort by an institute of higher education is as important as that of the federal government and NERC.

Other universities such as Lagos and Ife have offered an Associate Diploma Course in social studies since 1977. In addition, advanced teachers' colleges in Sokoto, Minna and Akwanga (among others) now offer social studies as a field of study. The institutes of education in the various states and in particular the National Teacher Institute now provide in-service training for primary and post-primary teachers throughout Nigeria.

It would be misleading to claim that social studies is the actual citizenship training now offered in Nigerian schools. The adoption of social studies as a national policy did not automatically convert curricula from traditional separate subjects to social studies in all the nation's schools. In many instances the teachers have not been trained to teach the new subject. Social studies materials are not yet available to many teachers. In the absence of training and materials, teachers continue with the traditional separate courses.[24]

The social studies movement in Nigeria has only begun to gather momentum. The objectives are clear; syllabuses exist; a number of teacher training texts are now available; classroom materials and activities continue to be refined in institute workshops; the number of universities offering degree programmes is increasing; and social studies will be offered regularly in advanced teachers' colleges in the near future. Other organisations and events have contributed to the introduction of social studies. One of these has been the National Association of Social Studies Teachers which, from the early 1970s, has kept alive a sense of social studies identity.

Forces were at work both inside and outside Nigeria to promote the adoption of social studies. It could be that social studies proponents outside Nigeria were accepted because of Nigeria's national crisis in the late 1960s and early 1970s. The appeal of an integrated social studies as an alternative to the traditional, separate-subjects approach came at the right time.

In-service Education in the Philippines[2]

In order to ensure the continuous professional growth of teachers and to meet the changing needs and demands of society, staff development centres in the Philippines have been reorganised and strengthened. These new centres have been designed primarily to upgrade teacher competencies and to serve as dissemination centres for innovations in education.

Staff development centres in the Philippines are classified into four types. They are the National Curriculum Development Centres; the Regional Staff Development Centres; the Development High Schools (DHS); and the Decentralized Learning Resource Centres (DLRC). These constitute the network for teacher training and dissemination at the national, regional and division levels.

In summer 1975, the Social Studies Centre, one of the five National

Curriculum Development Centres under the Ministry of Education and Culture, undertook the training of teams from each of the Regional Staff Development Centres. Each team consisted of a college professor (who was to serve as co-ordinator of the Regional Centre when it became operational), an elementary school teacher, and a secondary school teacher. They attended the following courses: (1) 'Seminar on the Social Sciences', which focused on the disciplines relevant to the concepts found in the social studies curriculum for elementary and secondary schools; (2) 'Instructional Strategies and Procedures in Social Studies' which dealt with the methodology of the 'new' social studies; and (3) 'Educational Psychology' which emphasised the learning theories of Gagne, Piaget and Ausubel. These eight-week courses were taught by the personnel of the National Social Studies Centre. Towards the end of the training, each regional team drew up an action programme which defined their commitments in terms of in-service training for teachers.

At the end of the summer each returned home to manage the Regional Staff Development Centres located in the fourteen regions. These Regional Centres, based at public or private teacher training institutions, work closely with the regional offices of the Ministry of Education and Culture and with the elementary and secondary schools in their respective divisional service areas. Their main responsibility is to conduct summer institutes (elementary schools) for DLRC and DHS teachers. Each sends three classroom teachers from different grade levels to the institute. The programme of training is similar to that offered at the national level.

The 56 DLRCs and the 34 DHSs are located in school divisions. They function as pilot centres for innovations, conducting two- or three-day seminars for teachers in their divisions. The training programme focuses on some aspect of social studies education that teachers have identified as a need and for which the staffs of DLRC and DHS are competent.

The divisional training network has certain unique features, namely: (1) The Administrator's Conference — the principal or the head of the participating school is invited to attend a three-day conference to become acquainted with the new programmes, problems and plans that relate to their respective schools. It is also aimed at obtaining the administrator's commitment to the programme. (2) Incentives for Participants — in addition to being allowed to go on official time to attend these seminars, the training is given consideration for purposes of promotion and for increases in salary. Credits earned in summer institute courses may be counted towards a degree. (3) Incentives for the Institution — books, materials and equipment are provided to participating institutions.

The teacher training linkages maintained at the national, regional and division levels described above have been tested in connection with the Textbook Project. The Textbook Project is one of the basic reforms being implemented under the Ten-year Educational Development Program mandated by Presidential Decree No. 6-A. The project has two essential components: (1) development and distribution of textbooks and teacher's manuals for elementary and secondary schools; and (2) the training and retraining of teachers in the use of the new materials. In a 1977 report prepared by the Educational Development Projects' Implementing Task Force on the effectiveness of the training, the conclusions included: (1) 'Despite the three-stage diffusion of materials, a sufficient amount of information has been absorbed by teachers' and (2) 'extensive practical opportunities are needed during the Level 3 (Division level) program, to enable participating teachers to test their skills in application under the supervision of Level 2 (Regional Level) trainers.'

It would seem, therefore, that recent efforts to strengthen the in-service programme in the Philippines are fruitful and provide valuable insights for further improvement.

The African Social Studies Programme: a Regional Approach

Founded in 1969, ASSP was a direct outgrowth of the same forces described earlier in the Nigerian case study, namely the 1967 meeting in Oxford and the 1968 meeting in Mombasa.

Participants at the Mombasa Conference agreed that while each nation (Botswana, Ethiopia, Ghana, Kenya, Lesotho, Malawi, Nigeria, Sierra Leone, United Republic of Tanzania, Uganda and Zambia) should develop its own social studies programme, an overall co-ordinating organisation was needed to provide mutual assistance for in-country efforts.

ASSP's Co-ordinating Committee consists of one government-appointed representative from each member nation (there are now fourteen members — Liberia, Swaziland and Gambia have joined since 1969). The Co-ordinating Committee is responsible for policy development. In addition, each national representative is responsible for stimulating social studies programme development within his or her nation. The day-to-day operations of the Programme are the responsibility of the Executive Secretary who is in charge of the Centre at Nairobi and all the Programme activities.

ASSP has established the following objectives:

> The primary purpose of the ASSP — African Social Studies Programme and its established Centre — is *to encourage and support in-country efforts* to developing [*sic*] new curricula for Social Studies which will be relevant to the needs and educational goals of member countries. It hopes to achieve this important objective by:
>
> (a) *Collecting and disseminating information* of social studies projects in Africa and elsewhere through reports, newsletters, and original documents.
>
> (b) Assisting member countries to organise workshops, courses, seminars, and conferences for the *exchange of ideas and for the in-service training of teachers* to enable them to adapt the new approach [integrated social studies] to the teaching of Social Studies.
>
> (c) Encouraging the *initiation of research* in Social Studies Teaching and in the development of materials for primary and secondary schools in Africa and to interest and involve professional and University people.[26]

From the viewpoint of ASSP, programmes to prepare social studies teachers at the primary, secondary and tertiary levels of education are needed in all member states. In most parts of the continent, where efforts to introduce an 'integrated approach' to social studies are under way, it has proved difficult to bring the right perspective into classrooms. An integrated approach to social studies has been fully successful only where it has been linked to both in-service and pre-service training of teachers. To ensure a smooth transition from the traditional method, centred around single disciplines, to the integrated approach to learning, it has been necessary to conduct orientation workshops and courses for teachers, school inspectors, curriculum developers and others in the education hierarchy.[27]

ASSP attempts to foster the development of social studies programmes by serving as a clearing-house and facilitator on a transnational, regional basis. It has existed for more than a decade, giving identity and visibility to social studies developments in Africa which, if forced to exist in isolation, would not likely be as fully developed. Collaboration at a transnational level may be time-consuming and appear sometimes to use resources that could otherwise be applied to local efforts. But in the long run, such collaboration can be a useful mechanism for advancing social studies among participating nations.

Two Transnational Developments

The Teacher Centre Movement

Teacher centres have become an international phenomenon. They are generally found in advanced, industrialised nations such as the United Kingdom, the Netherlands, Japan, the United States and the Soviet Union. And, as noted earlier, variations on teacher centres are sometimes found in developing nations, such as China and Cuba.

No universal definition quite covers the variety of teacher centres. Most, however, serve the purpose of providing advanced training on a periodic basis for experienced teachers. Teacher centres are commonly found in nations that have invested a great deal in the development of national curricula and need to disseminate the products to the local schools. One hope for teacher centres is that they can reduce the time it takes to disseminate new knowledge from the point of innovation to each classroom. For example, Americans hope that teacher centres will reduce this time lag from the current ten or more years to two. Also, it is expected that teacher centres will facilitate communication among practitioners about successful classroom practice, giving the centres an opportunity to respond to local community needs. In 1965 each prefectural government in Japan established teacher centres to meet two complementary objectives: (1) the improvement of teacher classroom competence, and (2) the familiarisation of teachers with the National Course of Study. Centres range from small branch operations to those covering an entire prefecture. Staffs are as small as twelve persons and as large as a hundred. Financing comes from four sources: the National Ministry of Education, Prefectural Boards of Education, Municipal Boards of Education or local PTA groups. Teachers are 'expected' to participate, but are not bound legally to do so.[28]

In the United Kingdom, the teacher centres have four purposes. The first is to provide a base for curriculum development and in-service education activities. Major activities include the dissemination, consideration and adaptation of nationally produced materials, the production of curriculum materials reflecting the needs of the local community and the study of such issues as language development and individualisation of instruction. The second purpose is to serve as an information clearing-house for the local area. Third, they provide a wide range of back-up services (loan of materials, repair and maintenance of equipment) to the local schools, and, fourth, they serve as an informal, social meeting place for teachers.[29]

In the United States, teacher centres are encouraged by both the federal and the state governments. The federal government has provided financial support to local school districts for teacher centres. Teacher centres vary according to organisational structures, purposes and activities. A common unifying element is that most of the centres are planned, governed and operated by and for in-service teachers.

The twin purposes of teacher centres are to develop and produce curricula designed to meet the educational needs of the persons in the community, area or state being served and to provide training to improve the skills of teachers to meet better the special educational needs of their pupils. For example, a teacher centre in New York City is producing consumer economics materials for elementary school students. Written in both English and Spanish, they can be used also in bilingual programmes.

A teacher education centre exists in nearly all of the fifty states. In the state of Florida, they are mandated and funded through state legislation. Local school districts in Florida are given a fixed amount per student (currently $5.00) by the state annually to support their centres. Nearby schools and colleges of education receive state funds commensurate with their participation in the centres. Governance of each centre is by a council, typically comprised of twelve classroom teachers, two building principals, two school district administrators, two representatives from the community and one representative from each university serving the centres. Each centre develops its own teacher training plan based upon teacher certification requirements, the assessed needs of the staff and other needs as determined by district and state priorities.

As the demand increases for recurrent training of experienced classroom teachers, it is likely that the teacher centre movement will gain momentum. Because teacher centres often arise from complex consortium arrangements among local education boards, universities and colleges, state or federal offices of education and private agencies, social studies teacher education will need to be reconceived within that developmental framework − reinforcing the thesis that viewing social studies teacher education as a developmental process is useful for economically developed nations as well as economically developing nations.

Field Investigation

Field investigation refers to a professional participant/observer experience for teacher trainees that occurs in a physical location or in a culture that is different from their own. In the Philippines, student teachers are asked to spend eight weeks living and teaching in remote villages. This experience affords the beginning teacher the opportunity to participate fully in the life of the community in a rural area.[30] In Uganda, social studies teachers begin their training by studying the college itself — including its physical location and its governance. Among their activities is the assignment to 'outline the internal problems of the college and to suggest suitable solutions'.[31]

In 1968, Sweden initiated a series of in-service seminars for teachers and teacher trainers under the title 'development education'. Averaging around forty participants, the seminars, generally lasting three to four weeks each, were held in the United Republic of Tanzania, Ethiopia, India, Kenya and various nations in Latin America. Their purpose was to help 'internationalise' Sweden's culture. The seminars were financed by the participants, the Swedish International Development Authority (SIDA) and the National Swedish Board of Education in approximately equal shares. One group arrived in Chile in the midst of demonstrations two months prior to the *coup d'état* of September 1973. Chile was a land in crisis. The Swedish teachers had an intense, emotional experience. For example, during a street demonstration, a member of the group was forced to surrender his film and notes. The experience had various effects on individuals. In a follow-up study, most teachers reported that they had learned a great deal of factual information; some indicated that it was a powerful personal experience as well. Some reported greater consciousness about world events and a greater appreciation for the problems of underdevelopment and for what it means to be materially poor. Much of this new data and these changed beliefs found their way into Swedish classrooms.[32]

Teacher trainees at Shanghai Teachers' University normally spend an average of one month each year on a project that is called a 'new investigation'. Students, working under the supervision of faculty members and non-university technicians, live and work in factories or on rural communes. During this period, the trainees become acquainted with the life of workers and peasants and apply this new knowledge to the development of their teaching skills. The purpose is to provide teacher trainees with an opportunity to live and work with parents and grandparents before becoming teachers of their children and grandchildren.[33]

Throughout the world, there is a growing effort to provide experienced and inexperienced teachers opportunities to incorporate work experience and community life as regular features of their professional preparation.

Summary

Teacher education in social studies, when viewed as a developmental process, serves as a useful starting-point for the design of teacher training programmes and provides the flexibility needed to accommodate the global diversity of national and regional needs.

The unresolved issues that cause social studies to be developmental are: (1) different nations or regions have different reasons for teaching social studies; (2) social studies more than other school subjects influences and is influenced by the social, political and economic values and institutions in the society; (3) social studies has a confusing and sometimes contradictory nature — a problem that exists within nations as well as among nations; (4) separate problems are created by teacher over-supply and under-supply, but there is shared concern about the equality of in-service classroom instruction; (5) social studies competes, usually without success, with reading, writing and arithmetic for a fair share of instruction time; and (6) the low pay and low status of social studies teaching makes it difficult to train and keep good teachers, especially during a period of rising inflation.

Although these problems individually may not be unique to social studies, when taken in the aggregate they present a formidable set of obstacles in the development of adequate teacher training programmes in social studies. Given these complexities, the developers of teacher education programmes should be skilled in the political aspects of programme development as well as technically competent in the subject-matter and teaching strategies. Developers in social studies must be persuasive advocates as well as good scholars and teachers.

Several promising practices were identified to deal with the needs created by these problems. Various agencies related to the training of social studies teachers are working together in the English-speaking, black African nations and the Philippines in collaborative efforts to pool resources and provide better services. Teacher centres have added to the authority of teachers in developing and conducting their own training programmes. Field investigations that require students to spend an extended period — living, working and studying — in a different environment or culture are becoming the norm rather than the exception.

Notes

1. Robert Farrell, unpublished background paper on Colombian social studies, 1979.

2. Leonardo de la Cruz, unpublished background paper on Philippine social studies, 1979.

3. *Statistics of Trends in Education: 1965-66 to 1985-86* (National Center for Education Statistics, US Department of Health, Education and Welfare, US Government Printing Office, Washington, DC, 1977).

4. Jan L. Tucker and William W. Joyce, *Social Studies Teacher Training* (ERIC Clearinghouse on Social Studies/Social Science Education, Boulder, Colorado, 1979).

5. Farrell, unpublished paper cited.

6. This case study was prepared by James Barth.

7. *Federal Republic of Nigeria National Policy on Education* (Federal Ministry of Information Printing Division, Lagos, 1977), p. 1.

8. *Report of a Conference of African Educators, EDC and CREDO on Social Studies* (Mombasa, Kenya, 1968), pp. 7-8.

9. One result of work done by the NNTEP staff is D.L. DuBey, V.O. Onyabe and P.E. Prokupek, *Social Studies Methods for Nigerian Teachers: Inquiry Activities* (Institute of Education, Ahmadu Bello University, Zaria, Nigeria, 1977), pp. ii-iii.

10. *Social Studies for Nigerian Secondary Schools*, Books I & II, Teacher's Edition (Social Studies Department, Comprehensive High School, Aiyetoro, Nigeria, 1968).

11. *Proposals for Curriculum Revision*: a memorandum from the Federal Ministry of Information to the National Curriculum Conference (1969), p. 5.

12. Ibid., p. 4.

13. Ibid., p. 5.

14. *Curriculum Guidelines for Primary School Social Studies Programme* (National Workshop on Primary School Curriculum, Ibadan, Nigeria, 1971), p. 263.

15. D.L. DuBey and J.L. Barth, *Inquiry Methods for Nigerian Social Studies* (Department of Education, Ahmadu Bello University, Zaria, Nigeria, 1977), p. 9.

16. *Grade II Teachers' Syllabus* (Federal Ministry of Education, Lagos, Nigeria, 1974).

17. Ibid., p. 451.

18. *National Policy on Education*, p. 12.

19. Ibid., p. 5.

20. Ibid., p. 7.

21. Ibid., p. 10.

22. Ibid., p. 12.

23. Ibid., p. 25.

24. For a concise statement on 'What are the Major Issues in the Social Studies in Nigeria?' see V.O. Onyabe, 'Social Studies in Nigeria' in H.D. Mehlinger and J.L. Tucker (eds.), *Teaching Social Studies in Other Nations*, Bulletin 60 (National Council for the Social Studies, Washington, DC, 1979), p. 67.

25. This case study was prepared by Pacita Andres.

26. Joseph M.C. Dondo, Abigail Krystall and Dorothy Thomas, 'Report of an Evaluation of the African Social Studies Programme' (mimeo., 1974), p. 10.

27. Chris Adewole, unpublished background paper on ASSP, 1979.

28. Amith P. Buxton, 'Teacher Centers in Japan', *Educational Leadership*, vol. 43, no. 3 (December 1976), pp. 183-9.

29. David Burrell, 'The Teacher Centre: a Critical Analysis', *Educational Leadership*, vol. 33, no. 6 (March 1976), pp. 422-7.

30. de la Cruz, unpublished paper cited.

31. 'Training Syllabus for Social Studies in Uganda' (mimeo., no date).

32. Stig Lindholm, *Seeing for Oneself: a Report on an Experiment in Development Education* (Swedish International Development Authority, Stockholm, 1975).

33. This information is based upon an interview by the author with education faculty and students at Shanghai Teachers' University on 17 October 1978.

APPENDIX A: A GUIDE TO SELECTED RESOURCES FOR TEACHING ABOUT SOCIAL STUDIES

Compiled by Lynn A. Fontana

Introduction

This appendix provides a brief guide to a selected sample of sources of information and knowledge deemed useful for social studies educators. While no single guide can expect to treat the full range of useful organisations and publications, the list that follows can be viewed as a 'starter' list of some of the most important items. The effect of the decision to rely primarily upon English-language sources was to distort the geographical distribution so that most of the organisations and publications are British or American.

The list is organised alphabetically according to the following sections: periodicals, organisations, bibliographies and directories, and statistical data. The guide contains a wide variety of items, ranging from newsletters to subscription journals. Prices (when obtainable) range from free to relatively expensive; pounds are sterling and dollars are US.

Periodicals

Development and Change is a quarterly available only in English. Sponsored by the Institute of the Social Studies, The Hague, Netherlands, the journal covers all aspects of economic and social development processes from a multidisciplinary viewpoint. While its goal is to provide information for graduate students of developing countries, it also serves as a useful reference for classroom teachers who wish to teach about problems in global development.

Address: *Development and Change*
Sage Publications
28 Banner Street   or 275 South Beverly Drive
London EC1 8QU   Beverly Hills, California
United Kingdom   90212, United States
Cost: $ 22.00/year for institutional subscription
$ 14.00/year for individual subscription

Development Forum is a monthly newspaper co-published by the Division of Economics and Social Information (DESI) of the United Nations and United Nations University. It is available in English, French, Spanish, Italian and German and includes articles on topics of global interest such as all aspects of development, environment, population and international trade. The publication provides up-to-date information on programmes and issues related to development in various parts of the world.

Address: *Development Forum*
          CESI; United Nations
          Palais des Nations
          CH-1211 Geneva 10
          Switzerland
Cost: $ 10.00/year

The Futurist is a magazine published six times a year by the World Future Society. The publication treats issues deemed most important to the World Future Society, including communication, technology, world planning, population and human relations. These articles are aimed primarily at forecasting future trends and sharing ideas and speculations on alternative courses of action.

Address: *The Futurist*
          World Future Society
          4916 St Elmo Avenue
          Washington, DC 20014
          United States
Cost: $ 18.00/year

The History Teacher is the quarterly publication of the Society for History Education. The issues contain reports on new educational programmes, history curricula, instructional techniques, methods of evaluating instruction and analyses and interpretations of works of leading historians and history educators. Shorter articles deal with forthcoming workshops and reviews of texts, films and other classroom materials.

Address: *The History Teacher*
          Society for History Education, Inc.
          California State University

Long Beach, California 90840
United States
Cost: $ 10.00/year including membership
         $ 2.40 per issue

Ideas and Action is a bi-monthly publication of the Freedom from
Hunger Campaign/Action for Development of the United Nations Food
and Agriculture Organization (FAO). Available in English, French
and Spanish, it contains articles and information about rural development issues. Particular emphasis is placed on the questions of dependency, self-reliance and effective action, stressing the grass-roots approach
to the solution of local problems of poverty and hunger.

Address: *Ideas and Action*
          Freedom from Hunger Campaign/Action for Development
          Food and Agriculture Organization of the United Nations
          (FAO) 00100 Rome, Italy
Cost: Free

Intercom is the quarterly journal of Global Perspectives in Education,
Inc. (GPE). Its purpose is to explore ways of providing today's students
with more adequate training for life in an age of world-wide interdependence. *Intercom* offers practical classroom suggestions for teachers
and addresses a broader audience of individuals and organisations concerned with the quality of education for tomorrow's world.

Address: *Intercom*
          Global Perspectives in Education, Inc.
          218 East 18th Street
          New York, New York 10003
          United States
Cost: $ 8.00/year

International Journal of Political Education is a quarterly publication
of Vakdidaktiek Maatschappijleer. The journal publishes articles and
comparative studies on socialisation theory and research on the
development of political competencies. It contains reviews of curriculum materials and programmes developed by specialists in many countries. In addition, the journal provides helpful information on conferences, institutions, government decisions and research projects that are
relevant to political education (social studies).

Address: *International Journal of Political Education*
          Elsevier Scientific Publishing Company
          PO Box 211
          Amsterdam, The Netherlands
Cost: Dfl. 55 or $22.50

International Peace Research Newsletter is published by the International Peace Research Association for its members. An English language newsletter, it is published approximately five times each year and contains reports on activities of peace research institutions and peace education groups around the world. It strives to advance interdisciplinary research into the conditions of peace and causes of war, to promote the national and international study of issues related to international peace and to disseminate the results of peace research.

Address: *International Peace Research Newsletter*
          Mr Hylke Tromp, Editor
          Polemological Institute
          University of Groningen, Rijksstraatweg
          76/PO Box 121
          9750 AC Haren (Gr.), The Netherlands
Cost: Swiss Fr. 20.00 or $10.00

International Understanding at School is a bi-annual publication of the Unesco Associated School Project, appearing in English, French and Spanish. The publication provides participating institutions, as well as interested educational bodies and individuals, with updated information on the work of the Associated Schools Project on the subject of education for international co-operation. It reviews and reports on the programmes and processes of schools in the project and reflects on issues pertinent to international education and to the development of continued international understanding.

Address: *International Understanding at School*
          7, Place de Fontenoy
          75700 Paris
          France
Cost: Free

International Social Science Journal is a quarterly publication of Unesco, published in French, English, Spanish and Arabic. The publication includes articles on issues of an international nature from authors around the world, representing various social science disciplines. Particular attention is given to issues such as interdependence, peace and conflict studies, the United Nations, international monetary system, modernisation, technological change, human rights, women, education and the future. It also contains bibliographies, charts and information on international meetings of various organisations.

Address: *International Social Science Journal*
Unesco
7, Place de Fontenoy
Paris 75700
France

In the United States the journal can be ordered from:

UNIPUB
345 Park Avenue Station
New York, New York 10010
United States
Cost: 70ff or $23.00

Journal of Geography is published seven times a year by the National Council for Geographic Education to promote and improve the effectiveness of geographic education from elementary schools through university education. The journal publishes articles on a variety of geographic topics, provides a forum for the discussion of issues and reviews instructional materials.

Address: *Journal of Geography*
Western Illinois University
Macomb, Illinois 61455
United States
Cost: $23.00/year individual membership; institutional subscription is $25.00/year
Single copies can be obtained for $4.00

Journal of Moral Education is published three times annually. The journal, sponsored by the Social Morality Council, may be the only international journal of moral education and development. It publishes articles from throughout the world, including philosophical perspectives on moral education, reports of theoretical and empirical investigation of individuals' moral development and studies of curriculum innovation. Its purpose is to offer a continuing comparative focus on objective teaching methods, materials and curriculum development in moral education in many cultures.

> Address: *Journal of Moral Education*
> NFER Publishing Company, Ltd
> Darville House
> 2 Oxford Road East
> Windsor, Berks. S14 1DF
> United Kingdom
>
> Cost: Annual subscription: £10.00; United States and Canada $24.00
> Single issues: £4.00; United States and Canada $8.00

The New Era is a journal published six times a year by the World Education Fellowship and incorporates the former *World Studies Bulletin* and *Ideas*. It is directed to audiences in some thirty countries and is intended to provide a forum for world-wide discussion of educational ideas and practices among directors of education, inspector heads, teachers, social workers, parents, members of psychology services and teacher educators. Its focus is upon innovations and teaching methods, and it addresses important underlying questions, such as the role of choice and enquiry in the growth and development of children and young people; freedom; personal relationships; authority; and political/economic problems of world society.

> Address: *The New Era*
> 33 Kinnaird Avenue
> London W4 3SH
> United Kingdom
>
> Cost: £5.00/year or dollar equivalent
> 75p an issue

The Nigerian Geographical Journal is a bi-annual publication of the Nigerian Geographical Association. It encourages the study of the geography of Nigeria and other parts of the world and assists in the development and teaching of geography in schools, colleges and other educational institutions.

Address: *The Nigerian Geographical Journal*
           NGA
           Department of Geography
           University of Ibadan
           Ibadan, Nigeria
Cost: $ 3.50

People is a quarterly publication of the International Planned Parent-
hood Federation available in English (ISSN 0301-5645), French
(ISSN 0306-8331), and Spanish (ISSN 0306-8326). It is devoted to
international population problems and developments. Well illustrated,
written in non-technical prose, it is appropriate for use in secondary
schools as well as in colleges and universities. Also available separately
is *Earthwatch*, a regular section of *People* addressed to environmental
issues.

Address: *People*
           International Planned Parenthood Federation
           18-20 Lower Regent Street
           London SW1Y 4PW
           United Kingdom
Cost: *People*: $ 15.00 annual subscription or £5.00
           Earthwatch: 20 copies $ 3.00 or £1.00

Social Education is a monthly publication (October to May) of the
National Council for the Social Studies. The journal provides articles
of interest to elementary, secondary and university social studies
teachers, curriculum developers, supervisors and researchers. Much of
the publication is devoted to methods of improving classroom instruction. Articles reflect an interest in innovative development in social
studies and a concern for issues pertinent to social studies educators at
all levels.

Address: *Social Education*
           National Council for the Social Studies
           3615 Wisconsin Avenue, NW
           Washington, DC 20016
Cost: For members, $ 25.00. A year's comprehensive member-
           ship in NCSS costs $ 35.00 and includes a number of other
           publications and services.

The Social Studies is a bi-monthly publication from Heldref Publications. The journal publishes articles of interest to social studies educators at all levels, pre-school to college. The subject-matter of articles focuses on the social studies, the social sciences and interdisciplinary studies. Articles reflect concern for matters such as the scope and nature of the social studies, curriculum organisation, methods and techniques of teaching, research in social sciences and the enhancement of intercultural understanding.

> Address: *The Social Studies*
> Heldref Publications
> 4000 Albermarle Street, NW
> Washington, DC 20016
> United States
> Cost: $ 17.00/year
> $4.00 a copy

Social Studies Education is available twice a year in February and October from the Social Studies Project. It publishes original contributions to curriculum theory, planning, innovation and practice that are of particular relevance to teachers of the social studies in the West Indies.

> Address: *Social Studies Education*
> Social Studies Project
> School of Education
> UWI, St Augustine
> Trinidad, West Indies
> Cost: $ 5.00/year
> $ 3.00 a single copy

Study of Society is the official journal of the Victorian Advisory Committee on the Teaching of the Social Sciences in Secondary Schools and is sent free of charge to all Australian post-primary schools. Individuals may obtain copies (three issues each year) by joining the Victorian Association of Social Studies Teachers (VASST). *Study of Society* publishes articles and classroom resources regarding all aspects of the social studies in secondary schools. Its purpose is to stimulate and assist secondary school social studies teachers.

> Address: *Study of Society*
> Victorian Association of Social Studies Teachers

PO Box 88
Balaclava, Victoria 3183
Australia

Cost: VASST membership $ 17.50 (includes other VASST pub-
lications)

Teaching Geography is published quarterly from Longman Group Ltd.
It is an international journal designed to serve the needs of geography
teachers in all types of educational institutions. It features discussions
of teaching methods, lessons, syllabuses and units of work within syllabuses; it evaluates the practical usefulness of books and other published
resources; and it promotes exchanges of ideas among university and
school geographers.

Address: *Teaching Geography*
Longman Group Ltd
Periodicals and Directory Division
43/45 Annandale Street
Edinburgh, EH7 4AT
United Kingdom

Cost: £8.00 or $ 19.00, or as part of the membership in the
Geographical Association

Teaching History is a journal published three times a year by the Historical Association. It publishes articles on teaching history from both a
theoretical and practical perspective. Articles reporting research, reviews
of books and programmes related to the teaching of history are also
included.

Address: *Teaching History*
Historical Association
59A Kennington Park Road
London SE11 4JH
United Kingdom

Cost: £3.00 or $ 6.00 annually for non-members

Teaching Politics is the journal of the Politics Association. The publication is aimed at the needs of teachers of politics, government and allied
subjects in secondary and higher education. It provides information
about teaching methods as well as abstracts and reviews of new books
and teaching aids.

Address: *Teaching Politics*
           c/o The Hansard Society
           12 Gower Street
           London WC1E 6DP
           United Kingdom
Cost: Free to members of the Politics Association

Theory and Research in Social Education is the journal of the College and University Faculty Assembly of the National Council for the Social Studies. It is designed to stimulate and communicate systematic research and thinking in social education. It fosters the creation and exchange of ideas and research findings that expand knowledge about purposes, conditions and effects of schooling and about education on society and social relations.

Address: *Theory and Research in Social Education*
           Tom Popkewitz, Editor
           School of Education
           University of Wisconsin
           225 North Mills Street
           Madison, Wisconsin 53706
           United States
Cost: Free to members of the Assembly
           $ 20.00 institutional subscription
           $ 4.00 per copy

The Unesco Courier, a monthly publication (except August and September), is published in sixteen languages: English, French, Spanish, Russian, German, Arabic, Japanese, Italian, Hindu, Tamil, Hebrew, Persian, Dutch, Portuguese, Turkish and Urdu. The journal focuses on issues and problems of a social, economic, political and ecological nature that concern citizens around the world.

Address: *The Unesco Courier*
           7 Place de Fontenoy
           75700 Paris
           France
Cost: 28ff/year

Universal Human Rights is available quarterly and is sponsored by the Division of Behavioral and Social Sciences, University of Maryland.

It explores such problems as human rights and political/economic development; human rights priorities from one country and culture to another; behavioural insights into public opinion; and related efforts to promote human rights. Although it is a scholarly journal aimed at professionals in the field, it can serve as a good resource for social studies teachers who focus on global concerns.

> Address: *Universal Human Rights*
>   Earl M. Coleman Enterprises, Inc.
>   PO Box 143
>   Pine Plains, New York 12567
>   United States
> Cost: $ 39.50 for institutions
> $ 19.50 for individuals

Organisations

The following organisations are examples of those that are helpful to social studies teachers. They are organisations that create, disseminate or catalogue materials related to social studies teaching.

The African Social Studies Programme is a non-profit international organisation promoting social studies curriculum development in African schools. It conducts intra-country and international workshops for African and non-African educators on behalf of an international approach to social studies education in Africa. Utilising locally available material, the organisation also undertakes courses, research, training and technical consultation and assistance to aid African students to gain an understanding of their country's and community's links to the rest of the world.

> Address: The African Social Studies Programme
>   Executive Secretary
>   PO Box 44777
>   Nairobi, Kenya

Canadian Association for Social Studies is the national, professional association of social studies educators and scholars, representing elementary and secondary teachers and teacher educators. It strives to promote the academic and professional growth of its members, acts as a clearing-house for research and new materials and encourages communication and co-ordination concerning social studies and the social sciences.

Address: Canadian Association for Social Studies
PO Box 578
Halifax, Nova Scotia
Canada B3J 2S9

Centre for Applied Research in Education is a public, non-profit organisation that engages in research and training in various educational areas. In the social studies, the Centre has developed the Humanities Curriculum Project (Human Issues Programme) to focus on problems and effects of teaching about race relations. Their research and development efforts have spanned both Europe and the United States. They produce occasional papers.

Address: Center for Applied Research in Education
University of East Anglia
Norwich NR4 7LJ
United Kingdom

Center for Teaching International Relations is a consortium of a number of groups with an interest in global studies. The Center produces and disseminates source materials and teaching materials related to global studies. It also offers in-service teacher education courses on international relations.

Address: Center for Teaching International Relations (CTIR)
University of Denver
Denver, Colorado 80208
United States

Committee on Teaching about Asia is an organisation formed by the merger of committees from the Association for Asian Studies and the Consortium for Asian Studies. The annual dues are $5.00, which includes a subscription to *Focus on Asian Studies* and use of a referral service and the National Asian Studies Network.

Address: Committee on Teaching About Asia
Secretary-Treasurer: R.E. Jorgensen
Director of Dissemination Activities

Division of International Education
US Office of Education
3669 ROB No 3
7th and D Streets, SW
Washington, DC 20202
United States

Educational Resources Center produces materials for the study of
India. These materials include audio-visual and teacher background
materials, student supplementary readings, study units and annotated
bibliographies for all school levels.

Address: Educational Resources Center
PO Box 3554
New Delhi, India 110024

or

Center for International Programs
New York State Education Department
Cultural Education Center
Empire State Plaza
Albany, New York 12230
United States

The Geographical Association is a non-profit organisation that promotes
geographical education at all levels. It provides information and a forum
for the exchange of ideas and holds conferences to assist teachers in
implementing geography in the curriculum. It publishes *Geography* and
Teaching Geography as well as various monographs on special geographic
topics.

Address: The Geographical Association
343 Fulwood Road
Sheffield S10 3BP
United Kingdom

The Global Development Studies Institute is a clearing-house for
materials on global education. It provides detailed curriculum outlines
for the secondary schools and undergraduate courses. In addition,
the institute circulates a newsletter, *Memos*, that annotates materials

relevant to global education from a variety of sources.

> Address: The Global Development Studies Institute
> PO Box 522, 14 Main Street
> Madison, New Jersey 07940
> United States

Institute for World Order is a non-profit educational organisation devoted to building a world order of peace, social justice, economic well-being and ecological balance. It has a broad-based programme of education and policy research and engages a global network of students, educators, scholars, social critics, policy leaders and activists for the purpose of bringing about a more just world order. The Institute publishes a variety of material related to peace education including curriculum and discussion guides, course outlines and annotated resource lists.

> Address: Institute for World Order
> 777 United Nations Plaza
> New York, New York 10017
> United States

The Interorganizational Commission on International Intercultural Education is an informal coalition of individuals representing American professional education associations and private education organisations who seek to promote international/intercultural education in United States elementary and secondary schools. The organisation provides a vehicle for exchanges of ideas on programmes, materials and opportunities for international/intercultural education. It also publishes *The Directory of Resources in Global Education*.

> Address: Overseas Development Council (ICIE)
> 1717 Massachusetts Avenue, NW
> Suite 501
> Washington, DC 20036
> United States

National Council for the Social Studies is a non-profit organisation to promote the teaching of social studies in elementary and secondary schools. Membership in the organisation includes elementary and secondary teachers, university professors and curriculum directors and developers. The organisation sponsors one national and numerous regional meetings to advance discussion and consideration of topics related to social studies education, economics, sociology, political science, history, geography and anthropology. It promotes discussion of these topics through its various publications. The journal, *Social Education*, and newsletter, *The Social Studies Professional*, are included in a regular membership fee of $25.00. Other bulletins and annual publications are included in a comprehensive membership of $35.00.

Address: National Council for the Social Studies
3615 Wisconsin Avenue, NW
Washington, DC 20016
United States

One World Trust is a private, non-profit organisation that encourages and supports the teaching of world studies in secondary schools through curriculum development, evaluation and in-service courses for teachers. Publications of the organisation include *Learning for Change in World Society* (£2.25 plus postage) and *Debate and Decisions: Schools in a World of Change* (£1.50 plus postage). It emphasises issues of world development, human rights, world law order and the environment in their handbooks and journal, *The New Era*.

Address: World Studies Project
c/o One World Trust
24 Palace Chambers, Bridge Street
London SW1
United Kingdom

Politics Association is a non-profit organisation that promotes the teaching of political studies and civic education in a variety of contexts while emphasising the secondary and advanced levels of education. The organisation publishes the bulletin *Grass Roots*, the journal *Teaching Politics* and the work *Political Realities*.

Address: *Politics Association*
16 Gower Street
London WC1E 6DP
United Kingdom

Social Science Education Consortium (SSEC) is an organisation which gathers, selects, analyses and disseminates information pertinent to the improvement of social science education. SSEC has published about eighty items that range from 'how-to-do-it' guides for curriculum planners to materials content and evaluation guides. It also publishes a monthly newsletter and engages in training programmes in social science education. The Consortium is also the site for the Social Studies/Social Science Educational Clearinghouse for the Education Resources Information Center (ERIC). The clearing-house collects and reproduces social studies and social science education materials that are not otherwise avilable in published form.

> Address: Social Science Education Consortium
>   855 Broadway
>   Boulder, Colorado 80302
>   United States

Social Studies Association of Sierra Leone is a non-profit organisation established to promote the teaching of social studies as an integrated subject at the elementary to college levels. Members include teachers, college and university lecturers, curriculum developers and others interested in social studies. The Association sponsors teacher training through conferences focusing on integrated social science subjects including environmental studies and population education. The pro-grammes of the Association and related materials are publicised in *Social Studies News*.

> Address: Social Studies Association of Sierra Leone
>   Institute of Education
>   University of Sierra Leone
>   Private Mail Bag
>   Freetown, Sierra Leone

Social Studies Development Center is an organisation established to provide a continuing base for research, development and diffusion of innovative ideas and practices in social studies. In addition to developing and disseminating curriculum materials in areas of American history and government, world history, global studies and world geography, the Center produces materials for local department chair-persons and supervisors. The Center also distributes a newsletter, *News and Notes*, that serves as a medium for the exchange of ideas and information on trends, ideas. materials and programmes in the social studies.

Address: Social Studies Development Center
513 North Park Avenue
Indiana University
Bloomington, Indiana 47405
United States

UNICEF, the United Nations Children's Fund, founded in 1946, is the only organisation within the United Nations system which is dedicated exclusively to improving the quality of life for underprivileged children. UNICEF co-operates with the governments of over one hundred developing countries to design and extend community-based programmes for children in the interrelated fields of health, nutrition, safer water supply, education and social welfare. In addition, UNICEF provides immediate emergency relief for children and mothers in cases of disaster, natural and man-made alike.

Address: UNICEF Headquarters
United Nations
New York, New York 10017
United States

Vakdidaktiek Maatschappijleer is a university institute that engages in research and training in the area of political education. It also publishes research reports on foreign teaching materials for the social studies and serves as the home office of the *International Journal of Political Education*. For further information write to the address below.

Address: Vakdidaktiek Maatschappijleer
Keizersgracht 73
1015 CE Amsterdam
The Netherlands

Victoria Association of Social Studies Teachers (VASST) is an association that provides support for classroom teachers through in-service training, resource materials, advice and exchanges of ideas. Members are institutions and individuals from public and private elementary and secondary schools and universities. In addition to promoting research and organising conferences, the Association publishes three journals and a newsletter.

> Address: Victoria Association of Social Studies Teachers (VASST)
> 59 Stanley Street
> West Melbourne
> Victoria 3003, Australia

Waikato Social Studies Association promotes the exchange of ideas and information on the teaching of social studies at all curriculum levels. The Association conducts in-service programmes for teachers in primary and secondary schools and develops resource kits for classrooms. The organisation also publishes bulletins, monographs, a newsletter and a bi-annual journal, *Social Studies Observer*. Membership extends throughout New Zealand and overseas.

> Address: Waikato Social Studies Association
> Hamilton Teachers College
> Private Bag
> Hamilton, New Zealand

World Council for Curriculum and Instruction is an international organisation of educators concerned about the promotion of equity, peace and universal human rights. The Council strives to stimulate and facilitate cross-cultural and transnational collaboration on endeavours in the areas of curriculum design, research and evaluation, and theory and practice through conferences and newsletters.

> Address: World Council for Curriculum and Instruction
> Maxine Dunfee, Executive Secretary
> School of Education
> Indiana University
> Bloomington, Indiana 47405
> United States

World Future Studies Federation is an organisation providing a forum for debate in which exchanges, confrontations and stimulation of ideas, visions and plans for the long-term future can take place. It promotes and encourages future studies, interdisciplinary efforts and critical thinking among people throughout the world. The Federation is a non-profit, independent, international association whose members represent some sixty countries from the first, second and third worlds. Among the Federation's activities are organising world conferences, developing courses and publishing a bi-monthly newsletter.

Address: World Future Studies Federation
          Secretariat
          Casella Postale 6203
          Rome Prati, Italy

Bibliographies and Directories

African Geography for Schools: a Handbook for Teachers was prepared for UNESCO by the Commission on the Teaching of Geography of the International Geographical Union and gives suggestions for the development of geography teaching about Africa. It is specifically intended for primary and secondary teachers and teacher training institutions in Africa, but serves as a useful guide for teachers in other countries who wish to teach about Africa.

Address: UNESCO
          7 Place de Fontenoy   or Longmans Group Limited
          Paris 75700   48 Grosvenor Street
          France   London W1
                                   United Kingdom

Checklist of Human Rights Documents, published in co-operation with the Tarlton Law Library, University of Texas, is a monthly bibliography of printed materials focusing on human rights issues.

Address: Earl M. Coleman Enterprises, Inc.
          PO Box 143
          Pine Plains, New York 12567
          United States

The Development Puzzle: a Source Book for Teaching about the Rich World/Poor World, available from the Centre for World Development Education, is a guide to materials and resources for teaching global studies.

Address: Centre for World Development
           128 Buckingham Palace Road
           London SW1
           United Kingdom
Cost: £2.20 (approximately $5.00)

Directory of Resources in Global Education, available from the Overseas Development Council, is a practical guide to information, materials, services and personnel in the field of global education in the United States.

Address: Overseas Development Council
           1717 Massachusetts Avenue, NW
           Suite 501
           Washington, DC 20036
           United States
Cost: $2.50

Directory of Social Studies/Social Science Service Organizations is published jointly by the ERIC Clearinghouse and the Social Science Education Consortium. The directory was compiled by Fran Haley and Regina McCormick and comprehensively describes 111 social studies/ social science organisations. It provides information on type of publications, services and current projects associated with these organisations.

Address: Social Science Education Consortium, Inc.
           855 Broadway
           Boulder, Colorado 80302
           United States
           Order Number: 229-6 (1978)
Cost: $7.95

Educational Documentation and Information is available on a quarterly basis from Unesco. Each publication treats a specific topic and includes selected resources and annotated bibliographies. The topics include developmental education, education for international understanding and population education.

Address: Unesco
           7, Place de Fontenoy
           75700 Paris, France

International Repertory of Institutions for Peace and Conflict Research is available from Unesco. The bibliography identifies institutions engaged in promoting research on problems of peace and provides a list of resources relating to their activities.

    Address: Unesco
               7, Place de Fontenoy
               75700 Paris, France
    Cost: $ 3.20; 90p or 10ff

A Social Studies Professional Library, by John D. Haas, Sydney Meredith and Karen B. Wiley, is available from the Social Science Education Consortium. This work, no. 203 in the SSEC catalogue, is an annotated list of books that could form the core of a social studies professional library.

    Address: Social Science Education Consortium, Inc.
               855 Broadway
               Boulder, Colorado 80302
               United States
    Cost: $ 1.00

Sourcebook for Geography Teaching, prepared for Unesco by the Commission on Teaching Geography of the International Geographical Union, is intended to raise standards of geography teaching and enlarge the contributions of this important subject to better international understanding. Much of the book is devoted to practical suggestions on ways of improving teaching methods and materials necessary for effective teaching of geography. Since its first publication in 1965, the sourcebook has been published in eleven languages.

    Address: Longmans Group Limited
               48 Grosvenor Street
               London, W1
               United Kingdom
    Cost: $ 4.50; 15ff

The Sourcebook for Teaching Geography is presently being revised. For information concerning the revised edition contact:

Unesco
7, Place de Fontenoy
Paris 75700, France

Statistical Data

Social studies educators teaching about various parts of the world require statistical data. For such information it is possible to refer to the publications of the following organisations.

United Nations Publications   United Nations
Room LY2300   or Palais des Nations
New York, New York 10017   C1T 1211 Geneva 10
United States   Switzerland

The following United Nations publications are available in English, French or Spanish:

Commodity Trade Statistics, 1950–. 4 issues a year
Demographic Yearbook, 1948–. Annual
Direction of International Trade, 1949–. Monthly
Economic Survey of Asia and the Far East, 1948–. Annual
Economic Survey of Latin America, 1948–. Annual
Economic Survey of Europe, 1948–. Annual
Monthly Bulletin of Statistics, 1946–
Statistical Yearbook, 1948–. Annual
Summary of Recent Economic Developments in the Middle East, 1951–
World Economic Report, 1948–. Annual
Yearbook of International Trade Statistics, 1950–. Annual

United Nations
Food and Agriculture Organization
(FAO)   UNIPUB
Distribution and Sales Division or 345 Park Avenue Station
Via delle Terme di Caracalla   New York, New York 10010
00100 Rome, Italy   United States

Monthly Bulletin of Statistics
FAO Economic and Social Development Series

FAO Studies in Food and Population
1976 Training for agriculture and rural development
Better Farming Series
FAO Commodity Review and Outlook 1976-77
Rural Home Techniques
Guide to Extension Training
1977 Training for agriculture and rural development
Agricultural Cooperative Marketing (Agriculture Development Paper 53)
Audio-visual aids for cooperative education and training (Agriculture Development Paper 86)
Rural Sociology in Action (Agriculture Development Paper 79)
Training and Extension in the Cooperative Movement (Agriculture Development Paper 74)
Fertilizer Marketing (FAO Marketing Guide 7)
FAO Studies in Agricultural Economics and Statistics 1952-1977 (also FAO Statistics Series 20)
1978 Training for Agriculture and Rural Development
FAO Commodity Review and Outlook 1977-79
FAO Agricultural Commodity Projections 1975-85
FAO Commodity Review and Outlook 1979-80

International Labour Office		ILO Branch Office
Publication Sales Service	or	1750 New York Avenue, NW
CH 1211 Geneva 22		Washington, DC 20006
Switzerland		United States

Yearbook of Labour Statistics, 1979

Organization for Economic Co-operation	
and Development	OECD, Suite 1207
2 rue André-Pascal	1750 Pennsylvania Avenue, NW
75775 Paris, Cedex 16	Washington, DC 20006
France	United States

Labour Force Statistics. Annual
1979 volume: $21.25
Development Cooperation. Annual, each December. Lists aid policies and statistics. 1979 Review; $19.00
OECD *Observer*. 6 issues per year
Articles on OECD activities and recent publications. $9.00 per year

APPENDIX B: INTERNATIONAL MEETING OF EXPERTS ON THE ROLE OF SOCIAL STUDIES IN EDUCATION FOR PEACE AND RESPECT FOR HUMAN RIGHTS

Kellogg Center, Michigan State University, East Lansing, Michigan, USA. 23–29 May 1976

Report

Contents

Introduction

1. A group of 14 experts met at the Kellogg Center, East Lansing, Michigan (USA), from 23 to 29 May 1976, to consider ways of strengthening the contribution of social studies to education for peace and respect for human rights. The meeting was convened by the Director-General in pursuance of resolution 1.26, adopted by the General Conference at its eighteenth session. The experts, who came from 14 member states and participated in a private capacity, are listed in an annex to this document. Also attending were five members of the United States National Commission for Unesco, several observers representing international and national non-governmental organisations and a number of auditors coming from academic communities and teachers' professional associations in the United States, whose names are also given in the annex.

2. The meeting was organised in co-operation with the United States National Commission for Unesco and the National Council for the Social Studies (USA). The local organiser was Dr Stanley P.

Wronski, Professor of Education and Social Science at Michigan State University.

3. Opening the meeting on behalf of the Director-General, Mr Ryon Kwan Kim, of the Section of Education for International Co-operation and Peace, welcomed the participants and observers to the meeting and outlined the background and task of the meeting. First, the speaker defined the term *social studies*, for the purpose of the meeting, as courses of study at primary and secondary school levels presenting components of history, geography, economics and moral and civic education, taught as an integrated discipline or as separate curriculum subjects with an interdisci-plinary emphasis, and said that the deliberations would be more in the nature of an 'expert approach' than an 'official approach'.

4. In outlining the background of the meeting, he said that Unesco's concern and interest in the subject date from the early days of the Organization (i.e. the 1949 Unesco/IBE International Con-ference on Public Education, on the theme of the teaching of geography as a means of developing international understanding, held in Geneva; and the 1950 international seminar on the im-provement of textbooks, particularly history textbooks, convened in Brussels).

5. The launching of Unesco's Associated Schools Project in Educa-tion for International Understanding in 1953 and of Unesco's ten-year Major Project for Mutual Appreciation of Eastern and Western Cultural Values in 1957 gave renewed impetus to the Organization's programme related to the teaching of social studies and the improvement of textbooks from the point of view of their contribution to education for international understanding.

6. Major activities carried out during the 1960s included experi-mental projects for the critical review of secondary school history and geography textbooks, regional seminars and workshops of experts (e.g. a series of eight regional meetings of expert geo-graphers held in Africa, Asia, Oceania and Latin America), and the production of teachers' handbooks and teaching materials (e.g. *Unesco Source Book for Geography Teaching*; *African Geo-graphy for Schools: A Handbook for Teachers*; Monograph on *Teaching Materials on Population, International Understanding and Environmental Education*; *Geografía de América Latina*, etc.).

7. After 1970, Unesco's programme on social studies took on new dimensions consonant with increasing emphasis on teaching

about contemporary world issues based on an interdisciplinary approach in the context of life-long education. New activities encompassed, *inter alia*, an international comparative study of civic education in several member states being carried out in co-operation with the International Social Science Council.

8. As regards the task of the meeting, the speaker first drew the participants' attention to the *Recommendation concerning Education for International Understanding, Co-operation and Peace and Education relating to Human Rights and Fundamental Freedoms*, which was adopted by the General Conference in 1974, and emphasised that it should be referred to throughout the meeting wherever pertinent.

9. He stressed that the meeting should focus its attention on practical and concrete steps to be taken for the strengthening of the role of social studies, since a fair amount of reappraisal of the philosophy and principles underlying international education had been undertaken by a round of high-level expert meetings held in recent years.

10. The speaker stated:

> It is obvious that the series of United Nations conferences on human environment, population, food, the status of women and the law of the sea which have been held in recent years, as well as the Universal Declaration and the Programme of Action on the establishment of a new international economic order adopted by the General Assembly in May 1974, call for serious rethinking and for new strategies on the part of the policy-makers, curriculum planners, teachers and lay people everywhere in the world.

11. Some questions to be asked in this connexion are:

    (a) What are the implications of the new concepts and approaches to social studies for aims concerning cognitive and affective learning and the formation or modification of attitudes in children and young people?
    (b) What are the advantages and problems in adopting an interdisciplinary approach within the spectrum of social studies components?
    (c) How could such an approach be linked to life-long education and the school/community relationship?

(d) What are the problems posed by the inculcation of the fundamentally civic and patriotic ideals encompassed by social studies in many countries, on the one hand, and the need to promote transnational and global perspectives in that subject on the other?

(e) And what of the mass media, and the question of terminology?

12. Mr Kim concluded his talk by inviting the participants' suggestions on some current and proposed programmes such as (a) the regional workshop on the teaching of social studies in Africa (Nairobi, August 1976); (b) sub-regional workshops on the teaching of geography with special reference to the use of modern audio-visual aids in Central America and the Caribbean region (Panama City, August 1976); (c) a regional seminar on the teaching of geography and social studies to be held in Latin America (Mendoza, Argentina, 1977); and (d) the preparation of a source book on the teaching of social studies.

13. Brief addresses of welcome and wishes for the meeting's success were given by several prominent educators, including three members of the United States National Commission for Unesco (Drs Buergenthal, Torney and Wronski) and the representatives of the National Council for the Social Studies (Dr Larkin) and of the Michigan State Department of Education (Mr Canja).

Dr Thomas Buergenthal welcomed the participants on behalf of the United States National Commission for Unesco. He said:

> Let me express the hope that your deliberations will prove productive and that they will help usher in, in all our countries, the long overdue process of effectively relating the social studies to 'education for peace and respect for human rights'.
>
> We live in a world in which neither peace nor respect for human rights is much of a reality and yet both are universally shared aspirations. This is the paradox that confronts 'education for peace and human rights' and presents its greatest challenge. Your agenda for pedagogic action will have to address this issue lest you add more hypocritical verbiage to an already voluminous reservoir of more of the same . . .
>
> The Human Rights Task Force of the United States National Commission for Unesco, which I have the honour to represent here, was established a number of years ago to advise the

National Commission, and through it the Department of State, on all human rights issues falling within Unesco's competence. It is one of the first, if not the first, such body to be established by any National Commission dealing exclusively with the subject of human rights and relevant educational policy. Its creation reflects the United States National Commission's conviction that the honest promotion of universal respect for human rights by all Unesco Member States and by Unesco itself is an indispensable element in any effort that seeks, through education, to promote that type of genuine world peace and international understanding that is worth having and striving for.

Dr Buergenthal then drew attention to the 1974 Unesco Recommendation concerning Education for International Understanding, Co-operation and Peace and Education relating to Human Rights and Fundamental Freedoms. He said:

This international instrument, adopted by the Unesco General Conference, draws on decades of Unesco deliberations and represents an extremely important policy statement bearing directly on the subject of your conference. Moreover, and this is why I put so much emphasis on it, the 1974 Recommendation is unique among international education instruments in proclaiming that education about human rights must be a vital and integral part of international education in every country. The Recommendation, therefore, should serve as a basic background document for your conference.

Ladies and gentlement, let me assure you that the United States National Commission for Unesco has a keen interest in the subject of your deliberations. We are grateful for the opportunity to exchange ideas with you. We fervently hope that by the end of the week we shall have made at least some progress in understanding the role of social studies in education for peace and respect for human rights.

14. All of the speakers affirmed that they strongly supported the Unesco Recommendation on international education. They said that the objectives and principles proclaimed in the Recommendation should form a vital and integral part of social studies education in every nation. It was also mentioned that the United States

National Commission for Unesco had embarked on an effort to promote the implementation of the Recommendation by undertaking the publication of a book on the subject and related activities.

15. Several spoke of the methodology of global education implicit in the spirit of the Recommendation, namely that it should be a comparative cross-cultural study using an integrated multi-disciplinary approach. The hope was also expressed that the meeting would be able to make practical recommendations concerning the implementation of the Recommendation in the field of social studies and moral and civic education.

16. At the opening session, the following officers were elected:

Chairman:	Dr Howard D. Mehlinger (USA)
Vice-Chairmen:	Mr C.A. Adewole (Nigeria)
	Professor Zoya A. Malkova (USSR)
Rapporteur:	Mr Rodney Kuchel (Australia)

17. The basic working paper, 'The Role of Social Studies in the International Education of Children and Young People' by Dr James Becker and Dr Lee Anderson, was distributed to the participants in advance of the meeting. Following the opening session, a background paper entitled 'The Social Studies: their Nature and Potential' was presented to the meeting by its author, Dr Wronski. In addition, a number of position papers prepared by the participants and dealing with the present status and trends in social studies programmes in their respective countries and suggesting action to be taken at national and international levels, were made available for the meeting. Also presented for discussion to the participants in the course of the meeting were written statements by several observers. In connection with the meeting, a display of textbooks and teaching materials from various countries was held. This final report, prepared after the meeting on the basis of main conclusions and suggestions presented by the Rapporteur at the final session, was approved by the Chairman and the Rapporteur on behalf of the participants.

I   General Observations

18. The conviction that social studies has an important role to play
     in promoting education for international co-operation, peace and
     respect for human rights, together with a sense of urgency regard-
     ing needed changes in content and methodology, led to wide-
     ranging discussions. The topics covered during the week-long
     meeting included: problems of definition and objectives in design-
     ing curricula with respect to peace and human rights; the need for
     a new approach to history reflecting more accurately the struggle
     of peoples to achieve or to maintain peace, solidarity and social
     justice; the importance of improving cross-cultural and cross-
     generational communication; the status of teachers as a factor in
     improving international education; and the need for more experi-
     mentation and evaluation in seeking to improve international
     education.

19. Opinions, views and priorities on these topics differed as the
     issues were discussed. The exchange of views and sharing of ideas
     did produce consensus on a number of fundamental points,
     including the following:

   (i)   social studies can and should play a significant role in educa-
          tion for international understanding, peace and respect for
          human rights;
   (ii)   there is a great and immediate need to improve and expand
          social studies education in the primary and secondary school
          and in teacher-training programmes;
   (iii) teachers and other educators responsible for developing
          curricula should be strongly urged to use the Recommenda-
          tion concerning Education for International Understanding,
          Co-operation and Peace and Education relating to Human
          Rights and Fundamental Freedoms, adopted by the General
          Conference at its eighteenth session (Paris, November 1974)*,
          as a framework and basis for developing courses and mater-
          ials in this field. The 'Guiding Principles' (Section III, para-
          graphs 3-6) and 'The Study of the Major Problems of Man-
          kind' (paragraphs 18-19) were especially recommended for
          use in such work;
   (iv)   much of what is taught about peace, human rights and inter-

---

* Hereafter referred to as the 'Recommendation on international education'.

national co-operation in today's schools is remote both from current research and conceptualisations of social scientists and from the realities of a rapidly changing world. It is often outdated, distorted or based on inaccurate information and grossly inadequate in terms of the needs of students and the demands of society;

(v) in order to improve education for peace and respect for human rights, procedures for selecting and training teachers must be given more attention and the status of teachers improved.

20. There was less agreement on such issues as: the extent to which terms like *global perspective, global society* or *global history* are accurate reflections of world conditions or useful ideas for organising materials for the study of peace and human rights; the degree to which an objective study of history or human experience is possible; the necessity, if education for international understanding is to be improved, to change the structure and organisation of schools in the educational systems of various countries; and the need, in teaching for peace and respect for human rights, to integrate materials from the physical and natural sciences with materials and insights from history and the social sciences.

21. Continuity in the discussions was largely achieved by focusing throughout the meeting on selected themes, including:

the relevance of particular concepts, content and methodologies of social studies to education for peace and respect for human rights;

the role of research, innovation and experimentation in the improvement of teaching for peace and respect for human rights; and

specific suggestions regarding practical steps by teachers, specialists and educational authorities in promiting education for peace and human rights.

22. While the group did not produce a single fixed definition of international understanding, there was a strong sentiment that it should be defined in a way consistent with the Recommendation

on international education. Among the elements in such a definition, the following were offered by various experts: the capacity of people to understand the complexity and variety of human relationships affecting cross-cultural and transnational exchanges in social, economic and political affairs; the capacity to view these matters in a world-wide perspective; the ability to see the need to adjust human relations in order to promote peace, respect for human rights and international co-operation. There was also some support for including in the definition the development and enrichment of education for responsible citizenship and effective participation in today's world.

23.   There was general agreement that international education needs to deal with both cognitive and affective areas of learning, and on the importance of helping children and young people to understand that though they live in different communities, with different social systems and ways of life, they must learn to view the achievement of basic human rights, peace and international co-operation as common goals and must recognise interdependence as a reality.

24.   The views expressed in the basic working paper and advanced by some of the participants suggest that the oneness of the modern world deserves special emphasis in education for peace and respect for human rights. In this view, the interpenetration of international and domestic systems, the disappearance of boundaries between domestic and foreign affairs, the rapid expansion of private and non-governmental contacts among nations, the development of interdependent military, economic, political and ecological networks, and the internationalisation of most contemporary social problems including the management of violence, the control of disease, the protection of the environment and the promotion of economic well-being, social justice and human rights — all demonstrate the emergence of a global society and have far-reaching implications for the way children and young people should be taught about the world. For example, they should increasingly be able to see themselves as inhabitants of a single planet, members of a single species, and participants — by virtue of being consumers of the world's products and resources and members of families, other social groups and nations — in a world society. The rights and duties that are inherent in these conditions suggest that education for responsible participation in an interdependent world or global society deserves special attention.

25. Not all of the participants agreed with this view. Some felt that it was more a preview of the future than a description of present-day realities. Further, some felt that by emphasising the unity of mankind and the universal nature of current world problems, the differences, the uniqueness and the intractable character of national and local beliefs and traditions were being overlooked. Some participants also felt that the study of geographic or cultural areas, of foreign policy or relations between nations might be adversely affected by a global approach.

26. A few participants wondered whether such an all-encompassing view might be used to justify the continued dominance of the present holders of economic and political power.

27. There was agreement that increasing interdependence is an important issue, that it is necessary to create a feeling of common concern and solidarity among all peoples regarding the need for efforts to promote peace and respect for human rights, and that terms need to be periodically reviewed in order to ensure that they are not defined in such a way as to perpetuate present inequities in power and wealth.

Concepts and Realities

28. The fact that the concepts and goals associated with education for peace, international co-operation and respect for human rights often seem abstract and far removed from the ordinary concerns of people led the group to suggest that efforts to bring about improvements in this important area of study should, wherever possible, start with the solid realities of everyday life. By beginning with the way international problems are experienced and affect life in one's village and community, the significance of world affairs for the individual will become more apparent. Further, such an approach will make more obvious the opportunities available for people to participate in community activities and events having international dimensions. The result will be to increase the individual's sensitivity to the manner in which his or her actions can effect the lives of individuals in other areas of the world as well as the manner in which actions of people elsewhere affect life in one's own village or community.

29. Awareness of international links can be increased by, for example, drawing attention to the origin of such foods as coffee, tea or chocolate and such products as toys, bicycles or cars; to the different national or ethnic origins of people in the community;

or to world events reported in the mass media which have local significance.

30. Starting with the affairs of local communities was also seen as an appropriate way to facilitate the efforts of teachers to be sensitive to the differences in background and experience of the children they teach. Thus, teachers can help children to acquire a better knowledge and understanding of their own situation and its relationship to that of others and can be more responsive to the needs of and aspirations of their pupils.

31. The relationships between human beings, the natural environment, the man-made environment and cultural patterns are complex and ever-changing, and the way in which social scientists seek to understand and explain these complex relationships also change. It was felt that history and the social sciences provide us with our best access to much of human experience as well as with a variety of ways of studying human affairs. In order to design curricula and materials of high quality in various areas of international education, it was considered that teachers need to be familiar with and capable of using much of the knowledge and many of the tools provided by the social sciences. It was also agreed that opportunities for teachers to keep abreast of the latest developments in these fields of study should be a part of any effort to improve education for international understanding in the schools.

32. A working paper on the role of social studies disciplines and the nature and potential of the social studies in education for peace and respect for human rights contributed greatly to this discussion. 'The Social Studies: their Nature and Potential' offers contrasting definitions and a variety of perspectives regarding the role of the social studies in international education. The definitions in the paper include elements concerning such matters as the needs of the individual and the problems of society.

33. The group shared the author's view that *social studies* refers to 'that part of the school's general education programme which is concerned with the preparation of citizens for participation in a democratic society' and which is related to the social sciences in the following ways: first, the social sciences are 'primary sources of the content of the social studies; the concepts, generalization and methods of inquiry'; second, social studies draw 'data from the social sciences related to societal values, problems, changing conditions' and cultural heritage; and third, in regard to

the psychological foundation of curriculum planning, 'the social studies draw data from the social sciences related to social progress, the human development process and other psycho-methodological aspects of instruction'.

34. As regards the scientific method as it applies to social relations, the paper argues that a key factor is the commitment 'to the value of learning through measured, logical and reflective processes rather than through the intellectual short circuit of "knowing" on the basis of unsupported generalizations'.

35. There was also great interest among the participants in the contribution the various disciplines might make to education for peace and respect for human rights. While it was impossible to devote time to each of the social science disciplines, history, geography and civics or political education did receive special attention.

History

36. Recognising that history has long occupied a special place in the social studies curriculum in many countries and that some kinds of history serve to undermine international understanding, the experts centred discussion on what approaches to the study of history were most desirable and important. There was general agreement that contemporary or recent history and current events needed a greater emphasis. More controversial was the idea of a global approach to history: that is, efforts to view and treat the history of mankind from a global perspective or world-centred frame of reference. This approach contrasts sharply with histories written from the perspective of particular nations, regions or cultures. Some participants felt that such efforts were likely to gloss over the uniqueness of the local and national nature of people's experience and thus present a view of mankind which is invalid.

37. There was more agreement on the proposition that the present international system is a product of the past, is comprehensible in terms of history and is changeable; and that a major contribution of the study of history is that of learning to use primary and secondary sources, the rules of evidence and other skills used by historians. There was vigorous discussion but not consensus on the degree to which historians — or anyone else, for that matter — can be objective, and the extent to which objective laws of social evolution exist.

38.   There was general agreement on the desirability of using comparisons and contrasts regarding historical experience and on the use of historical treatment in dealing with topics such as human rights, economic development and social justice.

Geography

39.   A brief paper, 'New Roles and Potentials for Geography in Social Studies Education for International Understanding, Peace and Human Rights', contributed much to the discussion. It focused on the geographic perspective: (1) the importance of place and the comprehension that a particular place is unique by virtue of its cultural and physical setting; (2) the comprehension that uniqueness can be categorised into a particular class of places with a range of physical and cultural characteristics; (3) the comprehension that places within a particular range collectively result in emerging patterns identifiable as global systems.

40.   These systems require integration of physical, economic, social, cultural and temporal systems. The geographic perspective reveals numerous ways in which all peoples are linked together on planet Earth.

41.   The paper also reports on research by Piaget which reveals that children between the ages of 5 and 14 years spatially move from an egocentric view of their environment to one of sociocentricity. These observations led Piaget to postulate that the developmental notion of country is marked by three stages. During the first stage, nation, state and town represent approximately equal magnitude in the child's reasoning. In the second stage, the child recognises that the state and town are located in the nation, but does not believe they are a part of it. In the third stage, the child makes the correct territorial relationship between nation, state and town.

42.   By replacing unlimited facts with useful concepts and dealing with the question of survival with the global environment in peril, geography can make a major contribution to education for peace, international understanding and respect for human rights. The author notes geography's potential to explain the crucial linking of people to people in the global system.

Moral and Civic Education

43.   The discussions on the role of civics and the relationship of political or civic education to the theme of the conference was

enriched by an oral presentation on 'A Conceptual Framework for Civic Education'. A major purpose of civic education, according to the view expressed, is to prepare citizens to participate in managing community affairs at local, national and international levels, both through governmental and non-governmental channels.

44. In this presentation, the speaker also suggested that the promotion of peace, justice and effective participation were among the more important reasons for providing civic education in schools throughout the world. In regard to content, the speaker gave priority to values such as a broadened sense of community to include local, national and international perspectives; egalitarian approaches emphasising democratic rights and duties, including an emphasis on peaceful negotiation and majority decision-making processes; nationality as a means of improving our understanding of society and our methods of seeking solutions to community problems. Content is the knowledge and insights needed to enable individuals to understand themselves and the social groups they participate in and the analytical and human relations skills needed to understand their society and to participate in it in an effective and responsible manner.

45. Recognising that civic education is only one element in a comprehensive effort to organise the community to deal responsibly with community affairs, the speaker suggested that mobilisation of all major sectors of society is needed if the interests of each and of the community as a whole are to be served. In this regard, he emphasised the need to include in a strategy of civic development concrete proposals for improving inter-group communication, co-operation, conciliation and compromise.

International Education

46. Prior to the meeting, the experts received the main working paper, entitled 'The Role of the Social Studies in the International Education of Children and Young People'. While the working paper (outlined below) was not the topic of discussion for any particular session of the meeting, it did help set the context for the discussions and many of the ideas and suggestions outlined therein were cited by participants. The paper proposes that the social studies should contribute to the global education of students in three major ways:

(a) by developing students' capacity to perceive and understand their involvement in global society and their responsibility towards it;

(b) by developing students' capacity to make judgements and decisions about world affairs which reflect a concern for peace and human rights;

(c) by developing students' capacity to contribute in a positive way to the social life in their own community and to exert an influence on world affairs.

Developing Students' Capacity to Perceive and Understand their Involvement in Global Society

47.   Individuals are involved in global society ecologically, biologically and culturally. Each of us is part of the Earth's biosphere, dependent upon our planet's air, water, land, plant, animal and energy resources, and influenced by the Earth's geography. As members of a single common species of life, we share with all of humanity common physical traits, common needs and common life experiences. Culturally each of us is related to technologies, institutions and processes, languages and beliefs which link us, our communities and our nations to peoples, communities and nations elsewhere in the world. Through these cultural linkages we influence the lives of people elsewhere in the world and they in turn influence ours. These facts suggest three ways in which social studies can help to develop students' capacity to perceive and understand their involvement in global society.

First, by developing students' understanding of themselves as inhabitants of the Earth: this includes providing students with knowledge about (a) ways in which they and other human beings depend on the Earth's biosphere and effect life support systems; (b) the international character of environmental and resource problems; and (c) the ways in which our planet's physical and cultural geography influences human behaviour.

Second, by developing students' understanding of themselves as members of a species of life: including providing students with knowledge about: (a) how they and other human beings are both similar to and different from other animals; (b) the commonalities in the physical traits, in the biological and psychological needs and in the life experiences of all human beings; (c) the nature of culture as a pan-human phenomenon, together with knowledge about geographical variations and historical changes in human culture; and (d) the major events and long-term trends in the universal history of the human species which substantially shape the contemporary human condition.

Third, by developing students' understanding of how they are culturally linked to people living elsewhere in the world: this includes providing students with knowledge about: (a) the technologies, the social institutions and processes, the languages and the beliefs that link them, their communities and their nations to people, communities and nations elsewhere in the world; (b) the ways in which their own lives, their communities and their societies have been influenced and are shaped by these cultural linkages; and (c) the ways in which they and other people in their country affect and influence the lives of people in other societies through these cultural linkages.

Developing Students' Capacity to Make Judgements and Decisions about World Affairs

48. All of us must make judgements and decisions about world affairs. Given the rapid and extensive change characteristic of the modern world, it is impossible to predict the specific kinds of judgement students will have to make as adult citizens, nor can we prescribe what judgements they should make in the future. But social studies can enhance or expand students' *ability* or *capacity* to make 'humane' judgements and 'good' decisions which reflect a concern for peace and human rights. Social studies can contribute to students' judgement and decision-making capabilities in several specific ways.

First, social studies can reduce students' tendencies to perceive and to think of the world egocentrically by developing what Robert Hanvey, in his book *An Attainable Global Perspective*, has called 'perspective consciousness'. This is 'the recognition or awareness on the part of the individual that he or she has a view of the world that is not universally shared, that this view of the world has been and continues to be shaped by influences that often escape conscious detection and that others have views of the world that are profoundly different from one's own'.

Second, social studies can develop students' capacity to process and analyse information about world affairs in a critical spirit, by developing students' skills in comparing, inferring, hypothesising, conceptualising, classifying, imagining and evaluating.

Third, social studies can develop students' ability to think about human activities in a global and systemic way, by developing students' awareness that in an interdependent world many human activities have global consequences; that these consequences have multiple implications for oneself and others and that a given activity is likely to affect the lives of different people in different ways.

Developing Students' Capacity to Exert Influence on World Affairs

49.   In a global age where world-wide interdependence makes itself felt in the daily lives of most human beings, individuals must learn how they might exericse some measure of control and influence over the public affairs of global society, as well as over the public affairs of their local communities and nations. Three ways in which social studies can enhance future citizens' capacity to exert influence in world affairs are:

First, by expanding a student's awareness of the choices confronting individuals, nations and the human species in respect to matters that critically affect their survival and welfare. These choices include those relating to the perpetuation of the war system, to population growth, to inequalities in the distribution of the world's wealth and resources, to the control of technology and to the protection of the earth's biosphere.

Second, by developing a student's knowledge of the ways in which he or she can potentially influence world affairs. This includes knowledge of the actions individuals can take as individuals, as participants in private groups and organisations, in the activities of international agencies and in exercising influence over the foreign policies of their governments.

Third, by promoting the growth of skills and motivations needed to participate in world affairs. This can be done by providing students with opportunities and incentives to become involved in transnational activities and to participate in community affairs and action programmes designed to enhance human welfare and social justice.

II   Primary and Secondary Education

Major Issues and Problems

50. As a preliminary to the consideration of the role of social studies in primary and secondary education, the participants discussed at some length the following selected issues and problems: (a) attitudes; (b) methodology; (c) content and materials; and (d) assessment and evaluation.

(a)   Attitudes

51. Concepts relevant to international peace and respect for human rights need to be taught within a global perspective: this is because of our involvement in global society ecologically, biologically and culturally, referred to earlier. Such concepts can best be developed by beginning with the student's own experiences.

52. Beginning with the young child, the social studies teacher should focus on the development of attitudes and skills which will help the student recognise and respect his own individuality, his strengths and weaknesses and his ability to play a variety of roles in the various groups to which he belongs, sometimes leading and sometimes following but always feeling able to participate. From this level the spiral development of these concepts becomes increasingly complex, following some sort of approximate order: families, communities, nation states, ethnic and cultural groups, the family of mankind. Throughout the introduction and development of these increasingly complex concepts the global perspectives should be developed by using comparative case studies of equivalent situations in other cultures.

53. For example, if we are trying to develop the child's awareness of his participation in his own family, and to understand the relationships, the norms and rituals involved therein, he should also be involved in learning activities which will help him recognise that families in other cultures can be different and yet serve the same basic functions. Always there needs to be an emphasis

on the solidarity of all peoples and respect for diversity and difference.

54.   The participants recognised that a particular value system underlies every educational system and this varies significantly from country to country, but nevertheless there is an urgent need for social studies teachers in all nations to foster the development of values, attitudes and social skills which will lead to a greater understanding of, and empathy with, people of other cultures. It is important to affect values and attitudes consciously in a positive direction regarding international peace and respect for human rights.

55.   It was also recognised that the whole school environment, particularly the social environment, influences the development of attitudes with regard to social participation, co-operation, compromise, group loyalties, tolerance for differences, etc., but that the social studies teacher has a particular role and responsibility in this matter.

56.   In order to develop sound programmes in this important area of social studies education, teachers and others who design programmes need information about student attitudes concerning:

   their own and other nations' peoples;

   the resolution of conflict and war;

   the need for international co-operation and the achievement of a genuine world peace;

   the notion that we have responsibilities for the world environment and for the conditions of people of other nations, with particular regard to the distribution of food and other resources;

   the right of all people to benefit from their rights under the Universal Declaration of Human Rights;

   international organisations — governmental and non-governmental;

   other critical international issues such as hunger, poverty, illiteracy, environmental pollution and destruction.

57. The behaviour of the teacher towards students, other teachers, parents and others in the community may influence the way students view themselves, their families and the community in which they live.

58. Action designed to promote positive attitudes towards peace, justice, human rights and fundamental freedoms should take place at all levels of instruction and should involve a variety of methods and techniques. Such attitudes can be promoted without detracting from the mastery of the more conventional skills and subject-matter, but may require special preparation of teachers who must become acquainted with new, additional materials and new techniques and must learn new roles.

59. Genuine international understanding, co-operation and peace cannot be achieved without respect for human rights, justice and fundamental freedoms. Such attitudes, along with increased knowledge of peoples, nations and international issues and the development of skills needed for responsible participation in an interdependent world, are essential elements in social studies education.

(b)   Methodology

60. Reference has already been made to the need to organise syllabuses around the development of concepts which are appropriate to the goals of global education. The development of these topics will necessitate an interdisciplinary or multidisciplinary approach to the teaching of social studies. The most common contributing disciplines, both in terms of content and methodology, will be sociology, history, geography, politics, anthropology, economics and elements of ethics and civic education.

61. Another aspect of teaching methodology, which has been referred to before but which can be restated because of its fundamental importance, is the need to present all material within an international perspective. A narrow nationalistic approach hinders the process of education for international understanding and peace.

62. The affective learning domain and the development of social skills have been largely neglected in most social studies syllabuses. There is a need to involve students in learning activities which will enable them to participate actively, in a spirit of trust, respect and co-operation, in a variety of social situations both within and without the school (for example, working or playing games with groups whose social or ethnic backgrounds are different from

their own). The student ought not to be a passive absorber of information; rather, he should be involved in active learning together with others in a variety of group situations, discussing, researching, sharing, enquiring and performing socially useful tasks. Participation and involvement are seen not only as desirable classroom strategies but as a necessary outcome of learning.

63.   The use of simulation games and role-playing is often an effective way of getting students to understand and react to situations not actually accessible to them.

64/   A main goal of social studies education is to prepare students to
65.   assume responsibility for their own self-directed behaviour. Each must learn to function individually and as a member of a group pursuing group goals. To be an effective group member requires attitudes favourable to, and skills in, compromise, co-operation, bargaining, negotiation, leadership and decision-making. Students must acquire confidence in themselves and respect for the rights and opinions of others.

66.   These characteristics need to be reflected in the organisation of the school and in the relationships that exist between students and teachers. This implies a change in many schools.

67.   Students need to participate in decision-making about their own learning. A relationship of trust and mutual respect must exist between teachers and students. An authoritarian environment often inhibits the students' ability to develop open and friendly relationships within the classroom.

(c)   Content and Materials

68.   The materials available to students often determine the instructional agenda. Perhaps the main decision regarding what students will learn in a course is made when the teacher or other educational authorities choose the materials to be used.

69.   Instruction is enhanced when a wide range of materials is employed. Whenever possible, the teacher should use films, filmstrips, records, audio tapes, games, simulations and documentary materials in addition to textbooks.

70.   A main problem in many countries is the lack of good instructional materials. In some, for example, teachers are using materials remaining from former colonial periods. In such cases governments should devote resources to developing up-to-date material drawing upon sound scholarship and employing the most advanced

pedagogical techniques. Unesco might also help by developing source books for teachers on some topics.

71. Every country must face the problem of bias and distortion in educational materials. In some cases the distortion results from poor scholarship or careless editing, in others from omission, in still others from political pressures. One way to counteract bias in textbooks is to make a variety of sources available to students and teach them skills in detecting bias. Authors and publishers should also seek to eliminate serious errors and distortions by permitting qualified specialists in other nations to comment on their books.

72. Educational material should draw heavily upon authentic stories and case studies about events close to the students' own experience. Wherever possible cross-cultural case studies should be used to facilitate the growth of a global perspective and a capacity for comparison on the part of the children. Whether the materials are organised around 'problems', subject-matter, disciplines, themes or topics, adequate attention should be devoted to issues relating to human rights and problems of peace, international co-operation, etc.

73. Another problem facing many schools is deciding on criteria to use in selecting instructional materials. Unesco might help by developing a list of criteria for teachers to use in judging whether materials employ a global perspective, advance human rights, etc.

74. One need facing authors and publishers is for reliable data and authentic examples concerning daily life in various nations. Unesco might establish a bank of authentic stories, case studies and pictures to be used by authors.

75. Most of the material provided by the mass media is outside the control of educators. Comic books, television, popular magazines, newspapers and radio all convey messages regarding peace, human rights and international co-operation that affect students' attitudes and knowledge. Educational authorities should seek ways to influence these media in positive directions. In addition, means of helping students learn to use the media for educational purposes should be developed.

(d)   Assessment and Evaluation

76. It is recognised that assessment and evaluation techniques, in most cases, dominate ultimate learning outcomes. Existing assessment techniques largely determine the following:

the content taught;

the teaching methods used;

the nature of the relationship between the student and the teacher;

the students' attitude towards learning and towards himself as a learner.

77. In teaching social studies there is an emphasis on (1) the development of values and attitudes, and (2) the development of enquiry and social skills. Indeed, specific learning objectives must be described in these areas. This being so, the teacher needs to recognise that he or she can make observations about changes in student performance in qualitative terms and that these can be described in narrative. Nevertheless educators need to try to develop instruments that can help measure these changes in attitude and competence at group activities in more objective ways.

78. Students should be involved in evaluating their own performance and that of others; teachers ought not to be the only authority making judgements about student learning.

79. Assessment is essential. It is needed to indicate with some objectivity that learning has taken place. It should not, however, dominate the learning process.

Primary Education

80. These specific comments on primary education fit into the context of the general principles regarding both primary and secondary education.

81. While there is evidence that fundamental attitudes towards race, sex, religion and nationality as well as towards oneself may be shaped in the pre-school years, the period from six to fourteen years of age seems to be of crucial importance in the development of attitudes related to peoples of other cultures and nations.

82. For this reason it is especially important that the primary school environment be one which is conducive to the development of positive attitudes of understanding, respecting and caring about others, particularly those who are seen as different. In some countries, children receive only primary education — if any; thus primary education bears an especially heavy responsibility in this respect.

83. It is also essential that at primary school level children acquire the self-confidence and social skills necessary to participate in a variety

of group activities: it is at this level that the attitudes and skills necessary for co-operation, compromise, respect for harmony, etc., should be developed.

84. The personality of the teacher plays a vital role. The values and attitudes of the teacher, and the way in which they manifest themselves through the teacher's relations with the students and through what he says — particularly with regard to ethnic issues — are very significant in influencing student attitudes.

85. The general principles of effective global education for peace and respect for human rights are again emphasised as being necessary components of primary school social studies teaching:

    (a) the use of an interdisciplinary and conceptual approach in developing syllabuses;

    (b) the use of a variety of carefully selected teaching materials which conform with the spirit of the Unesco Recommendation on international education;

    (c) the need to involve students consciously and deliberately in judgements and the development of positive values with respect to all levels of social relationships;

    (d) the need to emphasise the importance of student activity, participation and involvement in their own school learning and, equally important, in activities outside the school;

    (e) the need for vigorous pursuit of accuracy and objectivity in all aspects of global education;

    (f) the acceptance of international peace, solidarity and respect for human rights as the prime objective of all social studies teaching.

Secondary Education

86. These specific comments regarding secondary education fit within the context of the general principles regarding both primary and secondary education.

87. Education for peace and respect for human rights in the secondary school must build upon what has been achieved in the primary school. As in the primary school, the importance of participatory modes of education is crucial. Within the school there must be opportunity for student dialogue and discussion and for the organisation of various activities which lead to student participation in social processes. Outside the school, there should be opportunities to participate in the life of the community, in

activities such as helping the aged or raising funds for international welfare organisations. The objectives of international education will also be helped by student participation, whether at local, national or international level, in scouting, youth camps, foreign exchange visits or in written correspondence with students from other countries.

88. In the secondary school, the work and activities of the primary school may now be extended to a more sophisticated level. Students will now be older and, in general, better able to deal with the difficult concepts and generalisations involved in education for peace and respect for human rights.

89. While the whole curriculum of the secondary school should contribute to education for peace and respect for human rights, social studies subjects such as history, geography, economics and political science are central to such education. The young should learn about the different social and political systems which operate in the world and about the issues which may lead to world conflict, such as the build-up of weapons by the great powers, the rapid exhaustion of the world's natural resources and the dangers of over population and environmental pollution. There needs to be detailed study of the Universal Declaration of Human Rights and of what this implies, as well as studies of how people have achieved and are achieving their rights and of current situations where people are being deprived of them. History offers the opportunity for specialist work on international situations and human rights, not only concerning such topics as the growth of democracy, the development of trade unions, social reforms, independence movements and the work of international organisations such as the United Nations, but also on contemporary situations in the world in which peace is disrupted or human rights denied. Geography emphasises the global perspective and context in which human affairs take place.

90. Social studies are central to education for peace and respect for human rights because they help to develop the skills and abilities which are needed for understanding and participating in international affairs. Inevitably, in this field of education, political, social and ideological questions have to be considered and differing opinions, prejudices and value judgements weighed. Through social studies students can learn how to deal with data on human affairs (how to recognise bias and omissions, for example) and also develop the ability to understand the situations of others

without necessarily agreeing with them — what is often termed empathy. They can also learn that their aim should be to achieve as objective an understanding as possible of human situations and views.

91. These objectives will be better attained if the methodology of social studies teaching has as its central principle the presentation of a wide range of evidence in a scholarly way so that its sources are clearly apparent and so that students may learn to think and judge for themselves.

III   Teacher Preparation and Training

92. Teacher-training institutions are potentially the greatest source of educational change in an organised, orderly society.

93. The classroom teacher plays the critical role in the educational process. It is therefore essential that teachers of social studies, in particular, should acquire the knowledge and skills needed for effectively fostering international understanding, co-operation and peace and respect for human rights among their pupils.

94. The teacher needs to recognise that teaching methodology embraces not only pedagogical techniques but also pedagogical attitudes, both towards the nature and role of education and towards his or her students.

95. The social environment of the classroom is very important in influencing the development of student attitudes, values and social skills. The trainee teacher needs to develop the ability to create a classroom atmosphere where students can feel free to share, co-operate, compromise and trust and respect each other.

96. The experts of course recognised that, in general, education is directed by national educational policies which are in turn shaped by differing political, economic and social systems and conditions. Under these circumstances, some of the factors hampering the democratisation and modernisation of education conducive to the development of international understanding and respect for human rights might be related to: (a) the difference in social background between teachers and their students (teachers need to be able to empathise with the social conditions and aspirations of their students and set teaching goals according to these needs); (b) the existence of an obsolete educational system reflecting the values and aspirations of a past social order; (c) the particular

purpose which a government might see as a function of its schools, namely to inculcate values and attitudes not always consistent with the Recommendation of international education. It is therefore necessary to provide teacher training which is appropriate to the present educational needs of a country and, at the same time, consistent with a global perspective and the guidelines of the Recommendation.

97.   Teacher-training institutions differ significantly from country to country, but it is possible to formulate some general principles with regard to the training of social studies teachers in all countries so that they in turn can develop within their students the desire to further peace and respect for human rights.

   (a) as has already been noted, the attitudes and personality of the teacher are very important in education for peace and respect for human rights. For this reason, care in the selection of future teachers is essential;

   (b) the status of teachers must be improved to a point where the public respects their skills and purposes — purposes which conform to Unesco guidelines;

   (c) teachers should have experienced more than just 'classroom teaching'. Teacher training should involve future teachers in as wide a range of social and cultural situations as possible. Ideally, they should have the experience of working in a wide variety of jobs with peoples of different cultural and ethnic backgrounds. Trainees should be placed, as far as possible, in the kind of settings in which they will ultimately work. Teacher trainees should also be given, wherever possible, the opportunity to live and study in a foreign culture for at least two months;

   (d) intercultural studies ought to be an integral part of social studies programmes in teacher-training institutions. Such courses should include, for example, study about peoples in other countries through which future teachers can develop an understanding of and empathy with them. Concepts of interrelatedness, interdependence, mutual understanding, peace and respect for human rights need to be fostered. Material which could give rise to misunderstandings or hostility towards other groups or nations should be avoided;

   (e) in teacher training due emphasis should be given to modern foreign languages, recent world history, current social issues and comparative education. The future teacher should also be offered courses which enquire into the ways in which knowledge in the social studies is formed and validated. He should also learn basic methods of instructing his students in analysing and assessing competing claims to soundness, accuracy, veracity, logic, etc., in knowledge;

(f) teacher-training institutions should foster the desire and the skills needed to innovate in the field of global education and should provide trainees with curriculum development skills and commitment to participation in civic action. Teacher training should be carried out within the innovative framework implied by the furtherance of peace and respect for human rights;

(g) there is a need for close co-operation and co-ordination between education departments, curriculum developers and teacher-training institutions throughout the world to develop those materials and methodologies which will most efficiently foster international peace and respect for human rights. This needs to become a common goal for all those involved in education;

(h) objectives need to be prescribed for the cognitive, affective and social skills areas of learning. Too frequently the latter two areas are neglected;

(i) practising teachers need to be involved in realistic in-service programmes which will foster the spirit of the recommendations in this and other Unesco documents and, more particularly, which will give them the skills necessary to implement them;

(j) in-service education and the opportunity for continued involvement in education experimentation are an integral part of the training of any teacher. The objectives of all teacher-training programmes should include the development of attitudes and aptitudes necessary to foster peace, solidarity among peoples and respect for human rights in all teachers.

IV   Research, Innovation and Experimentation

98   Progress in education for peace and respect for human rights is substantially dependent upon advances in basic and applied research, innovative programmes and experimentation.

99.   Six categories of needed research were identified. These categories, together with examples, are:

(a) *Policy-oriented research.* Educational policy-makers must make choices on the basis of existing knowledge. Some of their choices may have an impact on student knowledge and attitudes regarding peace and respect for human rights. For example, some nations establish policies which prevent students of different races, ethnic groups and social classes from attending school together. What is the effect of such school policies on student attitudes towards other people? Is it necessary for students to attend schools that contain people of different races, religions, ethnic groups and social classes in order to build a capacity for empathy towards peoples of other nations?

(b) *Curriculum development and teaching materials.* The process of curriculum development needs to be conducted in a systematic way. Curriculum development teams whose members possess a range of needed skills and experiences should be established to design, develop, test and evaluate instructional materials based upon clearly stated purposes and objectives. All member states face a continuing need to create modern, effective instructional materials for all levels of schooling. The problem is especially acute in less developed nations where the resources to purchase and produce inexpensive instructional materials are least available. As has already been pointed out, such nations are handicapped further in that many of their existing materials are products of a colonial period and are largely irrelevant to the needs of students in developing nations.

(c) *Pedagogical research.* Research on education techniques is required. Success in promoting education for peace and respect for human rights depends upon sound instructional procedures. Research should contribute to finding answers to such questions as: to what degree does role-playing promote empathy? — can simulations and games provide adequate practice and experience in teaching effective participation skills?

(d) *Assessment.* Various kinds of assessment research are needed. One type involves the analysis of existing textbooks, seeking errors, distortions and omissions that may influence students' attitudes towards other people and cultures and human rights. A second type is the assessment of the existing status of student and adult knowledge and beliefs about the world. This will lead to the identification of deficiencies that require remedying. A third type involves the assessment of the impact of schooling on student knowledge, attitudes and skills.

(e) *Research on learning.* Two types of theories compete with one another for explanations of student performance: developmental theories and socialisation theories. The first focuses on organic growth and development as a part of the maturation process. The second relates student knowledge, attitudes and beliefs to student experience. Both theories are significant to instruction for peace and respect for human rights. Each can help teachers respond appropriately to such questions as:

(i) At what age are students able to adopt a global perspective?

(ii) If a teacher seeks to employ children's own experience in their families and communities in order to teach important concepts and generalisations, can their understanding be further enhanced through the use of cross-cultural examples?

(iii) What effect does an authoritarian school atmosphere have on children's capacity to assume responsibility for their own actions?

(iv) At what age are stereotypes formed? How does the study of history, geography and other subjects affect the formation and retention of inappropriate stereotypes?

(f) *Basic research in history and the social sciences.* Many countries lack basic data about their own socio-economic life. Without reliable data about the world, it is difficult to provide valid instruction. Various theories compete with one another for explanations of social phenomena. Further research will be necessary to promote worthwhile social change.

100. A wide range of innovative practices and experimental approaches should be undertaken to improve education for peace and respect for human rights. Some suggestions that deserve special consideration are:

  (a) make greater use of commercial, public and educational television in order to reach a large number of people in a potentially powerful way;

  (b) establish multinational textbook committees whose task is to help eliminate bias in textbooks;

  (c) encourage cross-national testing and use of instructional materials in an effort to help students see the world as others do;

  (d) devise programmes to make students more critical consumers of the mass media, especially their reporting of international news;

  (e) establish teacher exchange programmes for the purpose of extending the transnational perspective of social studies teachers;

  (f) create a test of 'international understanding' that could be used in schools on a cross-national basis;

  (g) produce source books containing basic social indicators about various nations and packets of model lessons drawing upon these data. Both the source books and the model lessons can be used by teachers in social studies courses;

  (h) publish articles about experiments and innovative practices occurring in the member states in the field of social studies as these relate to education for peace and respect for human rights;

  (i) develop 'distance study' courses around topics relating to education for peace and respect for human rights that people who are unable to attend school on a regular basis can enrol in on their own.

101. Various problems affecting research, innovation and experimentation must be overcome if progress is to be made. A few of these problems are:

(a) research results are often poorly disseminated. It is difficult for scholars to learn what other people engaged in similar research have discovered. More effective procedures for disseminating research findings are needed;

(b) current financial investments in educational research, innovation and experimentation fall below the level required for adequate results. Significant progress in education, as in other fields, depends on investments in research and development;

(c) the results of research innovation and experimentation are adopted too slowly. Many factors account for the slow utilisation of research findings. Researchers sometimes work on problems that have few practical applications. Often, important research with practical utility is reported in ways that are obscure to school officials. Frequently, teachers feel alienated from the research activity. One way to overcome this alienation is to include teachers as members of the research team and to seek their advice in defining research problems. Occasionally, researchers withhold their findings until they have received professional credit. Political factors may also interfere with the adoption of innovations;

(d) schools often fail to provide incentives that would encourage teacher experimentation and innovation.

V. Suggestions and Recommendations

Unesco

102. Unesco should:

(a) sponsor regional conferences to consider the outcomes of meetings such as this. The participants in these regional sessions should include educational authorities and technical personnel who are responsible for implementing recommendations or directives in their own countries;

(b) set up innovative projects in various regions of the world to develop materials and methodologies which conform to the spirit of the recommendations made herein;

(c) move ahead rapidly to prepare a source book for the social studies containing information related to teaching about peace, international understanding and human rights.

Included in the publication should be practical information on: values and attitudes, classroom activities, lesson strategies, data on population, industrial production, resources, employment, armaments, etc.; and lists of organisations, agencies and individuals providing services or teaching materials;

(d) assist member states to prepare TV tapes, films, slide tapes or audio tapes which reflect accurately the life and culture of their peoples;

(e) prepare a series of TV tapes, films or audio tapes dealing with the world-wide implications of such issues as poverty, hunger, war, violence and diminishing resources. Short dramatisations are especially needed;

(f) bring together educators from various countries and facilitate communications among educators so that better, more accurate materials in history, geography and other social studies areas may be developed;

(g) call a meeting of experts and take other steps to assist member states in efforts to assess the impact of various media on children's learning about peace, respect for human rights and international co-operation. Such efforts should also provide practical suggestions on how to help children become discriminating users of TV and other media;

(h) encourage ministers of education and national commissioners of education to seek to improve the status of teachers;

(i) assume responsibility for developing and facilitating the use of criteria designed to improve the quality of materials dealing with international understanding and human rights;

(j) encourage the establishment of regional clearing-houses to collect, organise and disseminate research results as well as information about promising practices and materials in the field of teaching about peace, human rights and international co-operation;

(k) provide more support for research in areas of learning and teaching as they relate to peace, human rights and international understanding.

National Commissions for Unesco

103. National Commissions should:

    (a) take the lead in bringing together educational authorities within their respective countries to:

        (i) promote understanding of and develop methods of implementing the Recommendation on international education;

        (ii) review materials widely used in schools in their countries to ascertain the extent to which they promote international understanding, peace and respect for human rights;

        (iii) develop criteria for selecting and using materials designed to promote international understanding, peace and respect for human rights;

    (b) provide incentives and support for teachers who do outstanding work in developing innovative, effective approaches to implementing the Recommendation on international education;

    (c) encourage exchange of teachers and specialists in the field of human rights, peace and international understanding;

    (d) work with the mass media to provide better coverage of the work of Unesco, particularly in the area of international understanding, peace and respect for human rights;

    (e) strengthen further the Associated Schools Project in Education for International Co-operation and Peace.

Education Authorities, Non-governmental Organisations and Teachers

104. As decisions made or not made at this critical moment of history will be crucial to all humanity, and even to the survival of life on this planet, national educational authorities and social studies teachers everywhere are urged to give high priority to initiating and promoting curricula, materials and experiences designed to enable students to become responsible, effective participants in efforts to eradicate conditions which threaten human survival and well-being — inequality, injustice and international relations based on the use of force.

105. The problems and issues listed in paragraph 18 of the Recommendation on international education should be given immediate and urgent attention. They are:

    (a) equality of rights of peoples, and the right of peoples to self-determination;

    (b) the maintenance of peace; different types of war and their causes and effects; disarmament; the inadmissibility of using science and technology for warlike purposes and their use for the purposes of peace and progress; the nature and effect of economic, cultural and political relations between countries and the importance of international law for these relations, particularly for the maintenance of peace;

    (c) action to ensure the exercise and observance of human rights, including those of refugees; racialism and its eradication; the fight against discrimination in its various forms;

    (d) economic growth and social development and their relation to social justice; colonialism and decolonisation; ways and means of assisting developing countries; the struggle against illiteracy; the campaign against disease and famine; the fight for a better quality of life and the highest attainable standard of health; population growth and related questions;

    (e) the use, management and conservation of natural resources; pollution of the environment;

    (f) preservation of the cultural heritage of mankind;

    (g) the role and methods of action of the United Nations system in efforts to solve such problems and possibilities for strengthening and furthering its action.

106. The school should provide a climate conducive to: the growth of understanding and respect for all peoples; a sense of responsibility towards less privileged groups of people; a conviction that equal rights for all are necessary; the acquisition of analytical skills needed for problem-solving and national decision-making; active participation in the affairs of the school and society; and a spirit of co-operation.

107. The quality of the school/community and home/school relationship should be strengthened and efforts made to ensure a positive

relationship in which parents and others in the community will develop a deeper interest in international education through the experience of their children.

108. A spirit of realism should prevail in teaching about peace, international understanding and human rights. The successes and defeats of past efforts to achieve peace and justice should be openly discussed. Factual knowledge and real-life situations should provide the basis for discussion of such topics and issues.

Primary Education

109. Children's attitudes towards learning and towards others are still being formed at this stage of human development. Therefore, it is recommended that schools seek to provide a stimulating environment for healthy social and emotional growth in which children can learn to live harmoniously together and strengthen attitudes of empathy, solidarity and co-operativeness.

110. Every effort should be made to involve the parents in working with the school to achieve the goals and purposes of the Recommendation on international education. The parent is an important authority figure to children at this age.

111. Concrete representation of concepts such as peace, human rights and international co-operation should be made at the child's level of maturity and experience.

112. So far as possible, concepts should be linked to the children's own experience and environment — for example, international trade or interdependence might be demonstrated by having children find products in their homes or communities which came from other countries as well as products which their country exports.

113. Every effort should be made to find suitable stories and materials on the life of children in different countries. It is important not to emphasise the quaint or exotic in studying other cultures.

Secondary Education

114. Emphasis on national civic responsibilities, generally dealt with at this level, should be expanded to include international civic responsibility. The rights and responsibilities that go with participation in an interdependent world need emphasis.

115. Community-oriented programmes and opportunities for student participation in the life of the school and community should be emphasised at this level. Working in factories or fields, providing

service to persons less fortunate, taking an active role in a student council or working with younger children are examples.

116. A wide range of cognitive and affective modes of learning should be employed at this level — skills in participation, creative expression through the arts, learning to learn, making use of large amounts of data from a variety of sources — all can and should be used in seeking to help students develop the capacities needed to be responsible participants in local, national and international affairs.

117. Student exchange programmes should be expanded and improved. Cross-cultural and cross-national experiences are desirable at this age. Experience with such efforts needs to be evaluated and used to improve future efforts in this important area.

Teacher Training

118. In the selection as well as in the preparation of teachers of social studies careful attention should be given to the personality and experience the teacher candidate brings to a training institution. Socially useful work should be an integral part of such preparation, as should cross-cultural experience.

119. Both pre-service and in-service programmes should include study of current world problems and issues such as: depletion of resources, pollution, population growth, continued build-up of destructive weapons, terrorism, poverty and hunger.

120. Special attention should be given to training teachers in the use of materials and methodologies which help students learn to use the media as a source of information and impressions — i.e. information about how news is selected, processed and presented; detecting bias; comparing and contrasting statements of public officials; piecing together fragments of information from different sources to gain insight into what is actually happening; recognising limitations and strengths of various media.

121. Experience in developing and using practical means of evaluating classroom practices should be a part of preparation for teaching; these include self-evaluation, observation by peers, student reactions, before-and-after surveys of attitudes, feelings and information.

122. Improving pre-service and in-service education designed to develop skill in assessing student attitudes, values and knowledge should receive special emphasis. It is essential that teachers be sensitive

to the concerns, learning abilities and disabilities and background of their pupils.

123. The work of the teacher as an innovator and experimenter should be given more emphasis. The teacher's role as a basis for knowledge and as the authority in the classroom is too often emphasised to the neglect of other significant roles such as that of facilitator, resource manager, learner, implementer or innovator.

124. Teacher-training institutions should encourage and assist schools in setting up their own in-service programmes designed to meet the needs of local teachers and to utilise the resources and expertise available in the local community.

Annex: List of Participants and Observers

Experts

KENYA

Mr C.A. Adewole
Executive Secretary
African Social Studies Programme
(ASSP)
PO Box 44777
Nairobi, Kenya

PHILIPPINES

Mr Leonardo D. de la Cruz
Associate Professor and Director,
Undergraduate Studies
College of Education
University of the Philippines System
Quezon City, Philippines

EGYPT

Mr Halim Ibrahim Grais
Social Studies Consultant
Ministry of Education
Home address:
6 Canal Street,
Maadi, Cairo, Egypt

AUSTRALIA

Mr Rodney Kuchel
Faculty Co-ordinator and Teacher of
Upper Secondary Social Studies
State Project Officer for Social
Studies
South Australia
Address: Marion High School
York Avenue
Clovelly Park, 5043
Adelaide, South Australia

FRANCE

M. Serge Lefebvre
Inspecteur départemental de
l'éducation
Directeur de l'Ecole normale
d'instituteurs du Centre de
formation de professeurs de CEG
et du Centre de formation pour
les maîtres de l'enfance inadaptée
Address: Ecole normale
51, rue Charles Dumont
21000 Dijon, France

UNION OF SOVIET SOCIALIST REPUBLICS

Professor Zoya A. Malkova
Deputy Director, Institute of General
Pedagogy
USSR Academy of Pedagogical
Sciences
c/o Commission of the USSR for
Unesco
9 Prospekt Kalinina
Moscow G-19, USSR

UNITED STATES OF AMERICA

Mr Howard D. Mehlinger
Professor of Education and History
Director, Indiana University Social
    Studies Development Center
513 North Park
Bloomington, Indiana 47401, USA

ROMANIA

Mr Emil Paun
Lecturer, Faculty of Philosophy
University of Bucharest
Home address:
    Str. Drumul Tabarei 85
    Bl. TS7, Ap. 26
    Bucharest 7, Romania

COLOMBIA

Mr Alfonso Penaloza Florez
Co-ordinator General del Plan Textos
Instituto Colombiano de Pedagogía
Universidad Pedagógica Nacional
Apartado Aereo 11345
Bogotà, DE, Colombia

JAPAN

Mr Michio Sakurai
Teacher of Social Studies
Senior High School attached to
    Tokyo Gakugei University
315 Higashi Oizumi, Nerima-Ku
Tokyo 177, Japan
Home address:
    2-9-16, Shimorenjaku
    Mitaka City, Tokyo, Japan

IRAN

Mrs Rouhanguiz Sohrab
Directrice générale du Bureau de
    Coordination de Planification
    des Programmes
Ministère de l'Education nationale
Téhéran, Iran

UNITED KINGDOM

Mr David W. Sylvester
Her Majesty's Inspector for History
    and Social Studies
Department of Education and
Science
Elizabeth House, York Road
London SE1 7PH, England
Mailing address:
    85 Cookridge Lane
    Leeds LS16 7NE,
    England

MADAGASCAR

Mr Jean-Marie Tata
Professeur d'histoire et de géographie
Lycée Galliéni
Tananarive
République démocratique de
    Madagascar

SWEDEN

Mr Jan Wester
Primary (senior level) and Upper
    Secondary School
Teacher of Social Studies
Home address:
    Tuvängsvägen 24
    75245 Uppsala, Sweden

Unesco

Mr Ryon Kwan Kim
Programme Specialist
Section of Education for
    International Co-operation and
    Peace
Unesco, Place de Fontenoy
Paris 7e, France

United States National Commission for Unesco

Dr Thomas Buergenthal
(member of the Commission)
Professor of International Law
School of Law
The University of Texas at Austin
2500 Red River
Austin, Texas 78705, USA

Mr Joseph A.A. Graf
(member of the Commission)
4580 Marshall, SE
Kentwood. Michigan 49508, USA

Mr H. Field Haviland
(Vice-Chairman of the Commission)
Professor of International Politics
Fletcher School of International Law
and Diplomacy
Tufts University
Medford, Massachusetts, USA

Mrs Rubie C. Schuster
Project Officer, US National Com-
mission for Unesco (IO/UCS)
Department of State, Suite 500
515 22nd Street, NW
Washington, DC 20520, USA

Ms Judith V. Torney
(member of the Commission)
Associate Professor of Psychology
Department of Psychology
University of Illinois at Chicago
Circle
Box 4348
Chicago, Illinois 60680, USA

Mr Stanley Wronski
(member of the Commission)
Institute for International Studies in
Education
513 Erickson Hall
Michigan State University
East Lansing, Michigan 48824, USA

*National Council for the Social
Studies*

Mr Brian J. Larkin
Executive Director
Suite 406
2030 M Street, NW
Washington, DC 20036, USA

*Michigan State Department of
Education*

Mr Alex Canja
Assistant to the Superintendent
Michigan State Department of
Education
Lansing, Michigan 48933, USA

Observers

Mr Lee F. Anderson
Professor of Political Science and
Education
Northwestern University
Evanston, Illinois 60201, USA

Mr James M. Becker
Director, Mid-America Program for
Global Perspectives in Education
Indiana University
513 North Park Avenue
Bloomington, Indiana 47401, USA

Ms Margaret Carter
Social Studies Co-ordinator
World Council for Curriculum and
Instruction
Ann Arbor Schools
Box 1188
Ann Arbor, Michigan 48106, USA

Mr George E. Lowe
Staff Director
Citizen Education
USOE/HEW
400 6th Street SW
Danahoe Blvd.
Washington, DC 20024, USA

Miss Mary McInnis
Assistant to the US Commissioner
of Education
USOE
400 Maryland Avenue, SW
Washington, DC 20202

Mr Robert Rentschler
World Federation of United Nations
Associations
Office of International Extension
Continuing Education Service
Michigan State University
East Lansing, Michigan 48824, USA

Mr Joseph Stoltman
Chairman, Department of Geography
Western Michigan University
Kalamazoo, Michigan 49008, USA

Auditors

Ms Alice Ahearne
Teacher of French
East Lansing High School
East Lansing, Michigan 48823, USA

Ms Joan Alcorn
Traylor Elementary School
Denver, Colorado 80210, USA

Mr George Barnett
Professor, Philosophy of Education
Michigan State University
East Lansing, Michigan 48824, USA

Mr Eugene Cain
Social Studies Specialist
Michigan Department of Education
Michigan National Tower
Lansing, Michigan 48933, USA

Ms Susan Carpenter
Consultant on Peace Research,
    Education and Development
Center for International Education
Hills Drive
University of Massachusetts
Amherst, Massachusetts 01002, USA

Mr John Chapman
Educational Specialist in Curriculum
American Overseas Schools – Pacific
Michigan State University
East Lansing, Michigan 48824, USA

Ms Elain Hoffman
Teacher
Center for World Studies
Grand Rapids Public Schools
226 Bostwick, NE
Grand Rapids, Michigan 49503, USA

Mr Georges J. Joyaux
Professor, Romance Languages

Michigan State University
526 Wells Hall
East Lansing, Michigan 48824, USA

Mr Adams Koroma
Multi-Cultural Curriculum
    Department
Ann Arbor Public Schools
600 West Jefferson
Ann Arbor, Michigan 48103, USA

Dr Timothy H. Little
Assistant Professor
Elementary and Special Education
Michigan State University
339 Erickson Hall
East Lansing, Michigan 48824, USA

Mr Milan Marich
Associate Professor of Social Studies
University of Michigan 1008 School
    of Education
Ann Arbor, Michigan 48103, USA

Ms Jane L. Mounts
State Social Studies Consultant
Indiana State Department of
    Public Instruction
Division of Curriculum
405 Ballantine Road
Bloomington, Indiana 47401, USA

Mr Robert Novak
College of Education
Michigan State University
East Lansing, Michigan 48824, USA

Ms Barbara Ort
Division of General Education
Michigan Department of Education
Box 420
Lansing, Michigan 48933, USA

Mr William Parrett
Director
Center for World Studies
Grand Rapids Public Schools
226 Bostwick, NE
Grand Rapids, Michigan 49503, USA

Dr Jan L. Tucker
Associate Professor
Florida International University
School of Education
Miami, Florida 33199, USA

Miss Mary Wileden
Assistant
Michigan Department of Education
Box 420
Lansing, Michigan 48933, USA

APPENDIX C: RECOMMENDATION CONCERNING EDUCATION FOR INTERNATIONAL UNDERSTANDING, CO-OPERATION AND PEACE AND EDUCATION RELATING TO HUMAN RIGHTS AND FUNDAMENTAL FREEDOMS

Adopted by the General Conference at its eighteenth session Paris, 19 November 1974

The General Conference of the United Nations Educational, Scientific and Cultural Organization, meeting in Paris from 17 October to 23 November 1974, at its eighteenth session,

Mindful of the responsibility incumbent on States to achieve through education the aims set forth in the Charter of the United Nations, the Constitution of Unesco, the Universal Declaration of Human Rights and the Geneva Conventions for the Protection of Victims of War of 12 August 1949, in order to promote international understanding, co-operation and peace and respect for human rights and fundamental freedoms,

Reaffirming the responsibility which is incumbent on Unesco to encourage and support in Member States any activity designed to ensure the education of all for the advancement of justice, freedom, human rights and peace,

Noting nevertheless that the activity of Unesco and of its Member States sometimes has an impact only on a small minority of the steadily growing numbers of schoolchildren, students, young people and adults continuing their education, and educators, and that the curricula and methods of international education are not always attuned to the needs and aspirations of the participating young people and adults,

Noting moreover that in a number of cases there is still a wide disparity between proclaimed ideals, declared intentions and the actual situation,

Having decided, at its seventeenth session, that this education should be the subject of a recommendation to Member States,

Adopts this nineteenth day of November 1974, the present recommendation.

The General Conference recommends that Member States should apply the following provisions by taking whatever legislative or other steps may be required in conformity with the constitutional practice of each State to give effect within their respective territories to the principles set forth in this recommendation.

The General Conference recommends that Member States bring this recommendation to the attention of the authorities, departments or bodies responsible for school education, higher education and out-of-school education, of the various organizations carrying out educational work among young people and adults such as student and youth movements, associations of pupils' parents, teachers' unions and other interested parties.

The General Conference recommends that Member States submit to it, by dates and in the form to be decided upon by the Conference, reports concerning the action taken by them in pursuance of this recommendation.

I. Significance of terms

1. For the purposes of this recommendation:

(a) The word 'education' implies the entire process of social life by means of which individuals and social groups learn to develop consciously within, and for the benefit of, the national and international communities, the whole of their personal capacities, attitudes, aptitudes and knowledge. This process is not limited to any specific activities.

(b) The terms 'international understanding', 'co-operation' and 'peace' are considered as an indivisible whole based on the principle of friendly relations between peoples and States having different social and political systems and on the respect for human rights and fundamental freedoms. In the text of this recommendation, the different connotations of these terms are sometimes gathered together in a concise expression, 'international education'.

(c) 'Human rights' and 'fundamental freedoms' are those defined in the United Nations Charter, the Universal Declaration of Human Rights and the International Covenants on Economic, Social and Cultural Rights, and on Civil and Political Rights.

II.   Scope

2.   This recommendation applies to all stages and forms of education.

III.   Guiding principles

3.   Education should be infused with the aims and purposes set forth in the Charter of the United Nations, the Constitution of Unesco and the Universal Declaration of Human Rights, particularly Article 26, paragraph 2, of the last-named, which states, 'Education shall be directed to the full development of the human personality and to the strenthening of respect for human rights and fundamental freedoms. It shall promote understanding, tolerance and friendship among all nations, racial or religious groups, and shall further the activities of the United Nations for the maintenance of peace.'

4.   In order to enable every person to contribute actively to the fulfilment of the aims referred to in paragraph 3, and promote international solidarity and co-operation, which are necessary in solving the world problems affecting the individuals' and communities' life and exercise of fundamental rights and freedoms, the following objectives should be regarded as major guiding principles of educational policy.

(a)   an international dimension and a global perspective in education at all levels and in all its forms;

(b)   understanding and respect for all peoples, their cultures, civilizations and ways of life, including domestic ethnic cultures and cultures of other nations;

(c)   awareness of the increasing global interdependence between peoples and nations;

(d)   abilities to communicate with others;

(e)   awareness not only of the rights but also of the duties incumbent upon individuals, social groups and nations towards each other;

(f)   understanding of the necessity for international solidarity and co-operation;

(g)   readiness on the part of the individual to participate in solving the problems of his community, his country and the world at large.

5.   Combining learning, training, information and action, international education should further the appropriate intellectual and

emotional development of the individual. It should develop a sense of social responsibility and of solidarity with less privileged groups and should lead to observance of the principles of equality in everyday conduct. It should also help to develop qualities, aptitudes and abilities which enable the individual to acquire a critical understanding of problems at the national and the international level; to understand and explain facts, opinions and ideas; to work in a group; to accept and participate in free discussions; to observe the elementary rules of procedure applicable to any discussion; and to base value-judgements and decisions on a rational analysis of relevant facts and factors.

6. Education should stress the inadmissibility of recourse to war for purposes of expansion, aggression and domination, or to the use of force and violence for purposes of repression, and should bring every person to understand and assume his or her responsibilities for the maintenance of peace. It should contribute to international understanding and strengthening of world peace and to the activities in the struggle against colonialism and neo-colonialism in all their forms and manifestations, and against all forms and varieties of racialism, fascism, and apartheid as well as other ideologies which breed national and racial hatred and which are contrary to the purposes of this recommendation.

IV. National policy, planning and administration

7. Each Member State should formulate and apply national policies aimed at increasing the efficacy of education in all its forms and strengthening its contribution to international understanding and co-operation, to the maintenance and development of a just peace, to the establishment of social justice, to respect for and application of human rights and fundamental freedoms, and to the eradication of the prejudices, misconceptions, inequalities and all forms of injustice which hinder the achievement of these aims.

8. Member States should in collaboration with the National Commissions take steps to ensure co-operation between ministries and departments and co-ordination of their efforts to plan and carry out concerted programmes of action in international education.

9. Member States should provide, consistent with their constitutional provisions, the financial, administrative, material and moral support necessary to implement this recommendation.

V.   Particular aspects of learning, training and action

Ethical and civic aspects

10. Member States should take appropriate steps to strengthen and develop in the processes of learning and training, attitudes and behaviour based on recognition of the equality and necessary interdependence of nations and peoples.

11. Member States should take steps to ensure that the principles of the Universal Declaration of Human Rights and of the International Convention on the Elimination of All Forms of Racial Discrimination become an integral part of the developing personality of each child, adolescent, young person or adult by applying these principles in the daily conduct of education at each level and in all its forms, thus enabling each individual to contribute personally to the regeneration and extension of education in the direction indicated.

12. Member States should urge educators, in collaboration with pupils, parents, the organizations concerned and the community, to use methods which appeal to the creative imagination of children and adolescents and to their social activities and thereby to prepare them to exercise their rights and freedoms while recognizing and respecting the rights of others and to perform their social duties.

13. Member States should promote, at every stage of education, an active civic training which will enable every person to gain a knowledge of the method of operation and the work of public institutions, whether local, national or international, to become acquainted with the procedures for solving fundamental problems; and to participate in the cultural life of the community and in public affairs. Wherever possible, this participation should increasingly link education and action to solve problems at the local, national and international levels.

14. Education should include critical analysis of the historical and contemporary factors of an economic and political nature underlying the contradictions and tensions between countries, together with study of ways of overcoming these contradictions, which are the real impediments to understanding, true international cooperation and the development of world peace.

15. Education should emphasize the true interests of peoples and their incompatibility with the interests of monopolistic groups holding economic and political power, which practise exploitation and

foment war.

16. Student participation in the organization of studies and of the educational establishment they are attending should itself be considered a factor in civic education and an important element in international education.

Cultural aspects

17. Member States should promote, at various stages and in various types of education, study of different cultures, their reciprocal influences, their perspectives and ways of life, in order to encourage mutual appreciation of the differences between them. Such study should, among other things, give due importance to the teaching of foreign languages, civilizations and cultural heritage as a means of promoting international and inter-cultural understanding.

Study of the major problems of mankind

18. Education should be directed both towards the eradication of conditions which perpetuate and aggravate major problems affecting human survival and well-being — inequality, injustice, international relations based on the use of force — and towards measures of international co-operation likely to help solve them. Education which in this respect must necessarily be of an inter-disciplinary nature should relate to such problems as:

(a) equality of rights of peoples, and the right of peoples to self-determination;

(b) the maintenance of peace; different types of war and their causes and effects; disarmament; the inadmissibility of using science and technology for warlike purposes and their use for the purposes of peace and progress; the nature and effect of economic, cultural and political relations between countries and the importance of international law for these relations, particularly for the maintenance of peace;

(c) action to ensure the exercise and observance of human rights, including those of refugees; racialism and its eradication; the fight against discrimination in its various forms;

(d) economic growth and social development and their relation to social justice; colonialism and decolonization; ways and means of assisting developing countries; the struggle against illiteracy; the campaign against disease and famine; the fight for a better quality of life and the highest attainable standard of health;

population growth and related questions;

(e) the use, management and conservation of natural resources, pollution of the environment;

(f) preservation of the cultural heritage of mankind;

(g) the role and methods of action of the United Nations' system in efforts to solve such problems and possibilities for strengthening and furthering its action.

19. Steps should be taken to develop the study of those sciences and disciplines which are directly related to the exercise of the increasingly varied duties and responsibilities involved in international relations.

Other aspects

20. Member States should encourage educational authorities and educators to give education planned in accordance with this recommendation an interdisciplinary, problem-oriented content adapted to the complexity of the issues involved in the application of human rights and in international co-operation, and in itself illustrating the ideas of reciprocal influence, mutual support and solidarity. Such programmes should be based on adequate research, experimentation and the identification of specific educational objectives.

21. Member States should endeavour to ensure that international educational activity is granted special attention and resources when it is carried out in situations involving particularly delicate or explosive social problems in relations, for example, where there are obvious inequalities in opportunities for access to education.

VI. Action in various sectors of education

22. Increased efforts should be made to develop and infuse an international and inter-cultural dimension at all stages and in all forms of education.

23. Member States should take advantage of the experience of the Associated Schools which carry out, with Unesco's help, programmes of international education. Those concerned with Associated Schools in Member States should strengthen and renew their efforts to extend the programme to other educational institutions and work towards the general application of its

results. In other Member States, similar action should be undertaken as soon as possible. The experience of other educational institutions which have carried out successful programmes of international education should also be studied and disseminated.

24. As pre-school education develops, Member States should encourage in it activities which correspond to the purposes of the recommendation because fundamental attitudes, such as, for example, attitudes on race, are often formed in the pre-school years. In this respect, the attitude of parents should be deemed to be an essential factor for the education of children, and the adult education referred to in paragraph 30 should pay special attention to the preparation of parents for their role in pre-school education. The first school should be designed and organized as a social environment having its own character and value, in which various situations, including games, will enable children to become aware of their rights, to assert themselves freely while accepting their responsibilities, and to improve and extend through direct experience their sense of belonging to larger and larger communities — the family, the school, then the local, national and world communities.

25. Member States should urge the authorities concerned, as well as teachers and students, to re-examine periodically how post-secondary and university education should be improved so that it may contribute more fully to the attainment of the objectives of this recommendation.

26. Higher education should comprise civic training and learning activities for all students that will sharpen their knowledge of the major problems which they should help to solve, provide them with possibilities for direct and continuous action aimed at the solution of those problems, and improve their sense of international co-operation.

27. As post-secondary educational establishments, particularly universities, serve growing numbers of people, they should carry out programmes of international education as part of their broadened function in lifelong education and should in all teaching adopt a global approach. Using all means of communication available to them, they should provide opportunities, facilities for learning and activities adapted to people's real interests, problems and aspirations.

28. In order to develop the study and practice of international co-operation, post-secondary educational establishments should

systematically take advantage of the forms of international action inherent in their role, such as visits from foreign professors and students and professional co-operation between professors and research teams in different countries. In particular, studies and experimental work should be carried out in the linguistic, social, emotional and cultural obstacles, tensions, attitudes and actions which affect both foreign students and host establishments.

29.   Every stage of specialized vocational training should include training to enable students to understand their role and the role of their professions in developing their society, furthering international co-operation, maintaining and developing peace, and to assume their role actively as early as possible.

30.   Whatever the aims and forms of out-of-school education, including adult education, they should be based on the following considerations:

(a)   as far as possible a global approach should be applied in all out-of-school education programmes, which should comprise the appropriate moral, civic, cultural, scientific and technical elements of international education;

(b)   all the parties concerned should combine efforts to adapt and use the mass media of communication, self-education, and interactive learning, and such institutions as museums and public libraries to convey relevant knowledge to the individual, to foster in him or her favourable attitudes and a willingness to take positive action, and to spread knowledge and understanding of the educational campaigns and programmes planned in accordance with the objectives of this recommendation;

(c)   the parties concerned, whether public or private, should endeavour to take advantage of favourable situations and opportunities, such as the social and cultural activities of youth centres and clubs, cultural centres, community centres or trade unions, youth gatherings and festivals, sporting events, contacts with foreign visitors, students or immigrants and exchanges of persons in general.

31.   Steps should be taken to assist the establishment and development of such organizations as student and teacher associations for the United Nations, international relations clubs and Unesco Clubs, which should be associated with the preparation and implementation of co-ordinated programmes of international education.

32. Member States should endeavour to ensure that, at each stage of school and out-of-school education, activities directed towards the objectives of this recommendation be co-ordinated and form a coherent whole within the curricula for the different levels and types of education, learning and training. The principles of co-operation and association which are inherent in this recommendation should be applied in all educational matters.

VII. Teacher preparation

33. Member States should constantly improve the ways and means of preparing and certifying teachers and other educational personnel for their role in pursuing the objectives of this recommendation and should, to this end:

(a) provide teachers with motivations for their subsequent work; commitment to the ethics of human rights and to the aim of changing society, so that human rights are applied in practice; a grasp of the fundamental unity of mankind; ability to instil appreciation of the riches which the diversity of cultures can bestow on every individual, group or nation;

(b) provide basic interdisciplinary knowledge of world problems and the problems of international co-operation, through, among other means, work to solve these problems;

(c) prepare teachers themselves to take an active part in devising programmes of international education and educational equipment and materials, taking into account the aspirations of pupils and working in close collaboration with them;

(d) comprise experiments in the use of active methods of education and training in at least elementary techniques of evaluation, particularly those applicable to the social behaviour and attitudes of children, adolescents and adults;

(e) develop attitudes and skills such as a desire and ability to make educational innovations and to continue his or her training; experience in teamwork and in interdisciplinary studies; knowledge of group dynamics; and the ability to create favourable opportunities and take advantage of them;

(f) include the study of experiments in international education, especially innovative experiments carried out in other countries, and provide those concerned, to the fullest possible extent, with opportunities for making direct contact with foreign teachers.

34.   Member States should provide those concerned with direction, supervision or guidance — for instance, inspectors, educational advisers, principals of teacher-training colleges and organizers of educational activities for young people and adults — with training, information and advice enabling them to help teachers work towards the objectives of this recommendation, taking into account the aspirations of young people with regard to international problems and new educational methods that are likely to improve prospects for fulfilling these aspirations. For these purposes, seminars or refresher courses relating to international and inter-cultural education should be organized to bring together authorities and teachers; other seminars or courses might permit supervisory personnel and teachers to meet with other groups concerned such as parents, students, and teachers' associations. Since there must be a gradual but profound change in the role of education, the results of experiments for the remodelling of structures and hierarchical relations in educational establishments should be reflected in training, information and advice.

35.   Member States should endeavour to ensure that any programme of further training for teachers in service or for personnel responsible for direction includes components of international education and opportunities to compare the results of their experiences in international education.

36.   Member States should encourage and facilitate educational study and refresher courses abroad, particularly by awarding fellowships, and should encourage recognition of such courses as part of the regular process of initial training, appointment, refresher training and promotion of teachers.

37.   Member States should organize or assist bilateral exchanges of teachers at all levels of education.

VIII. Educational equipment and materials

38.   Member States should increase their efforts to facilitate the renewal, production, dissemination and exchange of equipment and materials for international education, giving special consideration to the fact that in many countries pupils and students receive most of their knowledge about international affairs through the mass media outside the school. To meet the needs expressed by those concerned with international education, efforts should be

concentrated on overcoming the lack of teaching aids and on improving their quality. Action should be on the following lines:

(a)   appropriate and constructive use should be made of the entire range of equipment and aids available, from textbooks to television, and of the new educational technology;

(b)   there should be a component of special mass media education in teaching to help the pupils to select and analyse the information conveyed by mass media;

(c)   a global approach, comprising the introduction of international components, serving as a framework for presenting local and national aspects of different subjects and illustrating the scientific and cultural history of mankind, should be employed in textbooks and all other aids to learning, with due regard to the value of the visual arts and music and factors conducive to understanding between different cultures;

(d)   written and audio-visual materials of an interdisciplinary nature illustrating the major problems confronting mankind and showing in each case the need for international co-operation and its practical form should be prepared in the language or languages of instruction of the country with the aid of information supplied by the United Nations, Unesco and other Specialized Agencies.

(e)   documents and other materals illustrating the culture and the way of life of each country, the chief problems with which it is faced, and its participation in activities of world-wide concern should be prepared and communicated to other countries.

39.   Member States should promote appropriate measures to ensure that educational aids, especially textbooks, are free from elements liable to give rise to misunderstanding, mistrust, racialist reactions, contempt or hatred with regard to other groups or peoples. Materials should provide a broad background of knowledge which will help learners to evaluate information and ideas disseminated through the mass media that seem to run counter to the aims of this recommendation.

40.   According to its needs and possibilities, each Member State should establish or help to establish one or more documentation centres offering written and audio-visual material devised according to the objectives of this recommendation and adapted to the different forms and stages of education. These centres should be designed to foster the reform of international education, especially by developing and disseminating innovative ideas and

materials and should also organize and facilitate exchanges of information with other countries.

IX.   Research and experimentation

41.   Member States should stimulate and support research on the foundations, guiding principles, means of implementation and effects of international education and on innovations and experimental activities in this field, such as those taking place in the Associated Schools. This action calls for collaboration by universities, research bodies and centres, teacher-training institutions, adult education training centres and appropriate non-governmental organizations.

42.   Member States should take appropriate steps to ensure that teachers and the various authorities concerned build international education on a sound psychological and sociological basis by applying the results of research carried out in each country on the formation and development of favourable or unfavourable attitudes and behaviour, on attitude change, on the interaction of personality development and education and on the positive or negative effects of educational activity. A substantial part of this research should be devoted to the aspirations of young people concerning international problems and relations.

X.   International co-operation

43.   Member States should consider international co-operation a responsibility in developing international education. In the implementation of this recommendation they should refrain from intervening in matters which are essentially within the domestic jurisdiction of any State in accordance with the United Nations Charter. By their own actions, they should demonstrate that implementing this recommendation is itself an exercise in international understanding and co-operation. They should, for example, organize, or help the appropriate authorities and non-governmental organizations to organize, an increasing number of international meetings and study sessions on international education; strengthen their programmes for the reception of foreign students, research workers, teachers and educators belonging to

workers' associations and adult education associations; promote reciprocal visits by schoolchildren, and student and teacher exchanges; extend and intensify exchanges of information on cultures and ways of life; arrange for the translation or adaptation and dissemination of information and suggestions coming from other countries.

44. Member States should encourage the co-operation between their Associated Schools and those of other countries with the help of Unesco in order to promote mutual benefits by expanding their experiences in a wider international perspective.

45. Member States should encourage wider exchanges of textbooks, especially history and geography textbooks, and should, where appropriate, take measures, by concluding, if possible, bilateral and multilateral agreements, for the reciprocal study and revision of textbooks and other educational materials in order to ensure that they are accurate, balanced, up to date and unprejudiced and will enhance mutual knowledge and understanding between different peoples.

CONTRIBUTORS

Stanley P. Wronski holds a joint appointment as Professor in the College of Education and the College of Social Science at Michigan State University.

Denis Lawton is Professor of Education and Deputy Director of the University of London Institute of Education. Until recently he served as the Head of the Curriculum Studies Department.

Talabi Aisie Lucan is National Curriculum Coordinator and Head of the National Curriculum Center, Institute of Education, at the University of Sierra Leone.

Zoya A. Malkova is Director of the Institute of General Pedagogics, Academy of Pedagogical Sciences, Moscow.

David Dufty is Senior Lecturer in the Department of Education at the University of Sydney. John Cleverley, also a member of the faculty of the University of Sydney, serves as a consultant to the Ministry of Education in Papua New Guinea.

Howard D. Mehlinger holds a joint appointment as Professor in the School of Education and the Department of History at Indiana University. He is also Dean of the School of Education at Indiana University.

Alan Backler is a geographer and a Project Director in the Social Studies Development Center at Indiana University. Sae-gu Chung, a member of the Korean Educational Development Institute in Seoul, is a specialist in inquiry teaching-learning. Raji Jaiman, a former social studies teacher in India, is pursuing advanced graduate study in the United States. John J. Patrick is Professor of Education at Indiana University and a Project Director in the Indiana University Social Studies Development Center.

H.C. Ganguli is Senior Professor of Psychology in the Department of Psychology at the University of Delhi. G.P. Mehrota is a Reader of Education at the University of Delhi.

Jiro Nagai is Professor of Education at Hiroshima University. Ryozo Ito, Yasushi Mizoue and Takaharu Moriwake are all Associate Professors in the Division of Social Studies Education, Department of Education, Hiroshima University.

P. Olatunde Okunrotifa is Professor and Head of the Department of Teacher Education at the University of Ibadan in Nigeria.

Jan L. Tucker is Professor of Education at Florida International University. Chris A. Adewole is Executive Secretary of the African Social Studies Programme which is based in Nairobi, Kenya. Pacita Andres is a member of the Curriculum Development Center in the Philippines. James L. Barth is Professor of Education at Purdue University. Leonardo de la Cruz is Professor of Education at the University of the Philippines. He is currently on leave to serve as a Unesco Regional Advisor for Population Education in Asia. Robert Farrell is a Professor of Education at Florida International University.

Lynn A. Fontana, a former secondary school teacher, has recently completed a doctoral degree in social studies education at Indiana University and is employed by the Close Up Foundation.

INDEX

academic disciplies 21, 40-55; education for peace and 355; in the integrated model 65-6; social studies in 21-2; subject matter of 24-5; *see also specific disciplines*
achievement, student: evaluation of 263-81; non-instructional factors in 262
acting 158
adaptation 70
adolescent pupils 99
affective dimension 33-4, 346, 380; international education and 352, 363-4
Africa 299
African Geography for Schools . . . 339
African Social Studies Programme 300, 303-4, 313-14, 331
age pyramid test (case study) 271
Allport, G.W. 203-4
amorality 198, 204
ancient civilisations (case study) 179-80
anthropology 18, 42-6
area studies 54
Aristotle 208-9
arms race 87-8
Asian Workshop on Moral Education 199, 206-7
assessment *see* evaluation
atlases 236
attainment *see* achievement, student
attitudes 346, 261-3; classroom 182; evaluation of 281-4; global perspective and 361, 366-7; measurement of change in 366; observation of 283-4; teacher 369; *see also* values
audio tapes 245-6
audio-visual materials 238-50, 397
Australia: Asian Social Studies course 104-5; curriculum in 25, 118-24
Ausubel, D. 139-40

Bach, G.L. 49
beliefs *see* values
bias 231, 238, 365, 397

bibliographical sources 321-31, 339-42
biographies 236
Bloom, B.S. 103, 266
booklets 232
books 255; *see also* textbooks
Boulding, Kenneth 68
Brezhnev, Leonid 87, 99
brochures 232
Brown, G. 104
Bruner, J. 45, 156
Buergenthal, T. 347-8
Bulgaria 84, 85, 86, 91
bulletin board 244, 253

Canadian Association for Social Studies 331-2
case-studies 365
Center for Teaching International Relations 332
Central African Republic 243
Centre for Applied Research in Education 332
chalkboards 242
change 43, 70
Checklist of Human Rights Documents 339
child-centered education 36
children, moral values of 202-4
China 29-30, 302, 317
cholera deaths (case study) 171-5
citizen education 21, 25-6, 365-7; for global understanding 26-7; in Nigeria 305-6, 310, 311
civic action projects 185-6
civic activity 379, 390; skills 160, 182-9
civics 18, 24-5; in the curriculum 47; *see also* political studies
classroom conditions 182, 369, 379
classroom trips 94, 98-9
clearing houses 379
cognitive development 62; international education and 352; moral development and 204
cognitive processes 32-3, 346, 380
collaboration, transnational 314, 371
collectors' days 94
Colombia 299, teachers in 300